Management Accounting for Profit Control

McGRAW-HILL ACCOUNTING SERIES
NORTON M. BEDFORD, *Consulting Editor*

Blocker and Weltmer—Cost Accounting
Easton and Newton—Accounting and Analysis of Financial Data
Foulke—Practical Financial Statement Analysis
Henrici—Standard Costs for Manufacturing
Jencks—Auditing Principles
Johnson—Accounting Systems in Modern Business
Keller—Management Accounting for Profit Control
MacFarland, Ayars, and Stone—Accounting Fundamentals
Smith and Ashburne—Financial and Administrative Accounting
Walker and Davies—Industrial Internal Auditing

Dean F. H. Elwell of the University of Wisconsin was Consulting Editor of the McGraw-Hill Accounting Series from its inception until his retirement in 1955.

Management Accounting for Profit Control

I. Wayne Keller, D.C.S., C.P.A.

CONTROLLER, ARMSTRONG CORK COMPANY

McGRAW-HILL BOOK COMPANY, INC.

New York · Toronto · London · 1957

MANAGEMENT ACCOUNTING FOR PROFIT CONTROL

Library of Congress Catalog Card Number 56–9630

VI

33454

THE MAPLE PRESS COMPANY, YORK, PA.

Preface

The objective of management in an economy of free competitive enterprise should be to earn the maximum profit consistent with the long-range stability and growth of the company and the current economic and social conditions of the nation. This is the optimum profit. It may not be the maximum profit which could be realized in some years. The optimum-profit objective must be determined for each year, not only for a company but also for its product lines, plants, and divisions.

It is the function of the managerial accountant to aid management in setting optimum-profit objectives and in developing plans to meet the objectives, to provide control reports to guide management decisions, and to analyze and interpret performance to indicate where and what corrective action is necessary if the objectives are not being met. Standard costs and budgetary planning and control procedures are the tools of the managerial accountant, and coordinated periodic and special reports are his communication system.

The purpose of this book is to present an interrelated system of accounting, controlling, and reporting for industrial and commercial enterprises. Greater emphasis is placed upon the requirements of management for control information, and the accountant's function as a member of the management team, than upon technical cost accounting and budgetary planning and control procedures. General and corporate accounting procedures are included only to the extent that they are related to the management accounting functions.

The presentation is directed both to students and to accountants of industrial and commercial companies. From the author's experience in hiring and training college graduates for management accounting positions it appears that few comprehend the interrelationship of the several phases of accounting and controllership. They have had courses in accounting principles, cost accounting, and budgeting, but they look upon these as separate functions rather than as units of an integrated system. They are proficient in their technical knowledge but deficient in their understanding of its application for management purposes. It is also the author's experience in contacts with practicing accountants that many have failed to realize the importance of planning and control in business or have failed to convince management of its value, particularly in the medium- and small-sized companies. This book is intended to complement the student's accounting and management courses and show how they are related. It is also intended to show the opportunities for the managerial accountant to contribute to, and participate in, the profitable operation of his company.

In order to present an integrated system of cost accounting, budgeting, and reporting, most of the illustrations are based on a hypothetical company manufacturing fiberboard. Alternative procedures are held to a minimum so as not to obscure the primary objective of showing how all phases of accounting are interrelated in their use for management. Frequent reference is made to the necessity for adaptation to the needs of a specific company. The training and experience of the accountant will indicate the areas where he must make such adaptations. The data in one illustration do not, in most instances, carry over and relate to those in another. Neither are they intended to indicate income and cost levels or operating ratios of the fiberboard industry or any other industry. They are intended only to show the relationship of procedures and reports in one area to those of other areas.

The author wishes to express his appreciation to the National Association of Cost Accountants for their permission to include portions of his articles which they had published. He is also indebted to the members of his staff for the helpful suggestions which they have made, and to Stella W. Musser for her assistance in preparing the manuscript.

I. WAYNE KELLER

Contents

vii

Contents

CHAPTER 1

Organization for
Management Accounting

If an enterprise is to earn the optimum profit, its managers must know the effects on income, costs, and assets of possible courses of action, of the plan of operation selected for a given period, and of the actual operations for the period in comparison with the plan. These requirements are existent in all enterprises from the smallest to the largest. They are met through the application of cost accounting, especially standard cost accounting, and budgetary-control processes, which are the tools of management accounting. Techniques, procedures, and the form and content of reports will vary with the type and size of the enterprise, but the basic principles of management accounting can and should be applied in every company as an essential tool of management.

Effect of Size and Type of Business

The need for management accounting increases in direct ratio to the number of operating units and management personnel in the business. A comparison may be made with human transportation. A man walking usually uses no control devices. He knows the route he wants to follow, and his senses are all the aids he requires to reach his objective. He may carry a pedometer if he wishes to record the distance he covers, and in unmarked territory he will use a compass to set his course. However, as soon as he uses an automobile, so as to cover the same or greater distances with less effort and more speed, he needs instruments. His senses are not sufficiently accurate to gauge his speed to keep within established limits, and they are of no value in keeping him informed of the amount of gas in the tank, the maintenance of satisfactory oil pressure, and the rate of charge or discharge of the battery. Without instruments (control data for management), he can be certain that these were satisfactory

1

only when the trip has been completed without mishap. Even then he does not know what will fail on the next trip. Only when the car ceases to operate does he know that he is in trouble. If he chooses to fly, he encounters a more complex situation requiring more skill in operating techniques and more instruments to keep him informed of actual conditions and approaching difficulties. The larger and faster the plane, the greater the need for more and better instruments. A point is reached in size when it no longer is possible for one man to operate the plane. A crew is needed, and each man of the crew must have specialized instruments to aid him in doing his share of the work effectively and safely, and a communications system is required to coordinate the functions of the crew.

A one-man business has little or no need for control data, for the operator-producer-distributor knows what he has done and what he is doing. He is less certain of what he plans to do and usually does not evaluate the probable consequences of his plans. His tendency is to rely on his business sense and hope that the majority of his decisions will pay off. However, with a bit of simple management accounting which he can do himself, he can check his opinions and substantially increase the possibilities of avoiding disaster. For example, the application in a simple way of the techniques of the cash budget would prove helpful if a large order is received which will be produced over a relatively long period, with collection delayed until completion and delivery. The probable necessity of bank loans would be anticipated as to time and amount by a simple cash budget, and this information would prove useful and probably facilitate the securing of the loans.

Moving to the other extreme, the multiplant company is like the multiengine plane. Every member of the crew must know what is happening in the mechanisms for which he is responsible and must have every possible indication of what may happen. In addition, these data must be transmitted to the captain and other crew members, and their probable effects upon the other parts of the plane must be evaluated. Just as a drop in pressure in one oil line will reduce the total power of a plane, a failure to attain planned labor efficiency in one operation will reduce the profit potential of a company. All deviations from established plans must be evaluated and communicated to the persons having responsibility, so that decisions can be made as to when and how to correct or compensate for the failure in order to reach the planned objective with maximum safety and minimum delay. In business this process of establishing, recording, evaluating, and communicating history and plans is management accounting.

Just as the types of controls and instruments are different on a bomber from those on a passenger plane and also vary according to the make of the plane, so will management accounting techniques vary by type of business and between businesses of the same type. In manufacturing enterprises, with both production and distribution functions, management accounting will be more extensive and complex than in merchandising or financial enterprises. However, it is needed and used in all kinds of business: manufacturing, mining, farming, merchandising, financial, etc. Different purposes require different procedures and different applications of the same basic procedures. The purposes to be served for reasons of business policy will determine the methods.

Emphasis on Profit and Loss Statement

Emphasis on the management phases of the accounting process is consistent with, and essential to, the trend to the profit and loss statement as the most significant of the financial statements, with coincident deemphasis of the importance of the balance sheet and statement of surplus. The demonstrated ability of a business to earn a satisfactory profit in accordance with predetermined plans and to develop reasonable plans for a continuation and improvement of the profit level can only result in satisfactory ratios on the balance sheet and assure the availability of funds for future growth and development. Thus management accounting includes the planning, or budgeting, function as well as the current and historical, or accounting, function. This does not mean that all phases of management accounting are to be recorded in the books of account. Day-to-day control information, special cost studies, and all phases of budgeting are related to, or based upon, information recorded in the books but are not recorded as accounting transactions.

Responsibility of Chief Accounting Officer

All phases of management accounting are conducted most efficiently if they are under the responsibility of the chief accounting officer. He may have the title of controller, treasurer, secretary, chief accountant, works accountant or accountant. The significant factors are the duties and responsibilities of the job and not the title. This concentration of responsibility under the chief accounting officer is desirable for reasons of consistency, efficiency, and independence. Management accounting information must be consistent with the information recorded in the books, if it is to be reliable and is to be accepted throughout the organization. When various phases of the work are conducted under separate responsibilities, the tendency is toward duplication of effort and inefficiency. To the fullest extent possible, the original records which give rise to the accounting entries should also provide the information for control. Independence is also vital to effective management accounting. The engineer who develops a new machine to increase efficiency may find it difficult to be completely objective in his evaluation of the results the machine is supposed to, or did, achieve. The head of a budget department not under the responsibility of the chief accounting officer may present reports which do not reflect the facts, either because he does not have them or because he chooses to modify them to bring them into agreement with his budgeting methods and procedures. The chief accounting officer would have no psychological or procedural reasons for these attitudes and with his professional attitude of independence will call the plays as he sees them.

Organization of the Accounting Department

Just as the accounting and budgeting methods and procedures are adapted to meet the needs of the specific enterprise, so too is the organization structure of the accounting department. The size of the department and the division of responsibility vary directly with the size and complexity of the enterprise. In the smallest units a clerk or several

EXHIBIT 1-1
ACCOUNTING ORGANIZATION—SMALL COMPANY

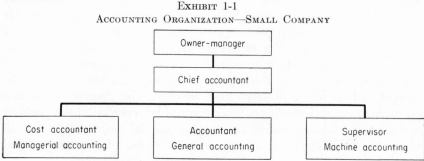

clerks may process the original records, while the accounting function is handled by a public accountant. Because the manager of such a business, like a man walking, rarely needs control data, he gets his management accounting service from his public accountant or through infrequent assistance from a professional management consultant. A larger business may have a chief accountant with the functions divided as to control and corporate accounting, each headed by a competent individual (Exhibit 1-1). In this organization the cost and budget functions are conducted by the cost accountant and the general books, customers' ledgers, accounts payable, and payroll work by the accountant. If the enterprise is large enough to use machine accounting, this function may be set up as a separate unit servicing the other two.

In the largest enterprises two types of organization may be used: The responsibilities may be divided (1) according to accounting function (cost accounting, budgeting, etc.) or, (2) to the extent possible, according to divisions or factories.

Exhibit 1-2 is a typical organization chart for an accounting department set up according to accounting functions. In this type of organiza-

EXHIBIT 1-2
ACCOUNTING ORGANIZATION BY ACCOUNTING FUNCTIONS

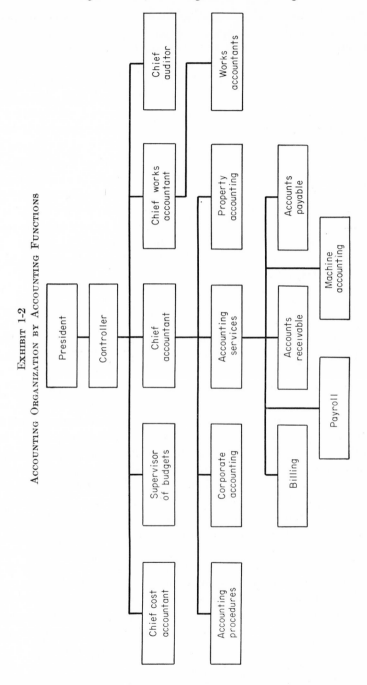

tion structure there is a cost section under a chief cost accountant, a budget section under a supervisor of budgets, the general accounting and accounting services under a chief accountant, and the internal auditing section under a chief auditor. If it is a single-factory company, each of these has line responsibility for his functions in the factory. In the multiplant company this may also be true, or their line responsibility may be limited to the work performed in the central office with functional responsibility for the work of their functions performed in the factories. In this latter, line responsibility for factory budgeting and accounting may be placed under a chief works accountant, as is done in the organization shown in Exhibit 1-2. The principal advantage of dividing responsibilities according to accounting functions is that each section head specializes in one phase of the work. He is able to adapt new ideas developed in one unit of the business to other units through his specialized knowledge of his function in each unit.

In contrast with the organization by accounting functions is the organization according to units of the company. Exhibit 1-3 shows a typical organization chart for this type. Here there is a division controller for each division of the business. Each has under his line responsibility the management accounting functions performed in the central office and is functionally responsible for the accounting and budgeting in the factories identified with the division. Since it is not practicable to separate all accounting by divisions and since it is frequently more economical to perform some functions on a consolidated basis, the positions of chief accountant and chief auditor are retained with the same responsibilities that they would have in an organization by accounting function. The principal advantage of organization by division is that each division controller can concentrate on specific problems of one division and can more easily adapt methods and procedures to the peculiar requirements of his division. This is particularly important when the nature of the business of the several divisions is quite different, as in an electrical products company which may have industrial equipment, appliance, motor, and parts divisions. Each has different manufacturing and distribution methods, and each requires specialized cost accounting and budgeting procedures. A secondary advantage of organizing the accounting department by company divisions is the development of well-rounded personnel. Personnel do not specialize on one phase of accounting and thus become better trained and qualified to fill top positions in which a working knowledge of all the accounting functions is necessary.

Centralization or Decentralization

The extent of accounting centralization or decentralization in multiunit companies is not dependent upon the type of organization structure

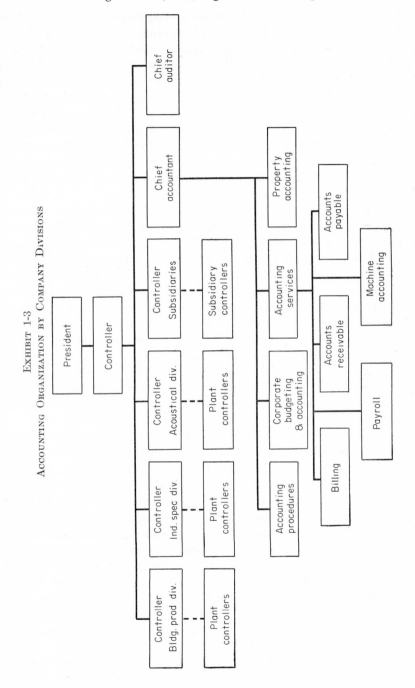

EXHIBIT 1-3
ACCOUNTING ORGANIZATION BY COMPANY DIVISIONS

of the accounting department—by accounting functions or by divisions. It is determined by considerations of effectiveness and cost of the accounting process. For most effective management accounting it is essential that the maximum decentralization consistent with a reasonable cost for processing the data be achieved. With the emphasis of management accounting on the current and future income and costs of the business, rather than on the historical, the time of the availability of the data is of prime importance. Effectiveness is lost if it is necessary to send original records to the central office for processing and interpretation. By the time the results are returned to the operating units, conditions have changed, and the reports are of no more interest to the operating management than last week's newspapers.

Costs can and must be controlled at the levels where the responsibility for incurring them is placed. For direct material and labor and for most items of factory expense this is in the factory. To accomplish this control each factory must have its own inventory and usage reports; prepare, compute, and distribute the earnings of the workers paid on an hourly or incentive basis; process vendors' invoices for the materials and services which it purchases; calculate the unit cost of production and, where standards and budgets are in use, make the comparisons of the actual costs with the allowances. Where machine accounting service is available in the central office but is not practical in each factory because of the limited volume of data to be processed, the accounting functions may be carried to the point necessary for control in the plant and the data then submitted to the central office for final processing and consolidation.

There are a number of methods which can be used to submit information to the central office for consolidation for top-level internal reporting and for the preparation of financial statements. Control information can be summarized from the original records in the factories and the records themselves sent to the central office for processing. This procedure may prove to be the most economical where centralized machine accounting is available. In other instances the summaries prepared in the factory may be carried to the point where summary journal entries are prepared for the central office. When this is done, all of the supporting detail remains at the factories, and the central office is dependent upon the factories for interpretation and explanation of their operating results. When decentralization is carried to the point of having each factory do its own billing and pay its own vendors invoices and payroll, it is desirable to carry a full set of books at the factory. These tie into the general books through intracompany control accounts, and financial statements are submitted to the central office for consolidation for corporate reporting purposes. Within individual companies different plants may report their figures to the central office in different ways determined by the mailing time, ability of a factory to support a machine accounting unit, variations in sales and production organization structure, and similar considerations.

Qualifications of Personnel

The ultimate effectiveness of the management accounting process will depend upon the personnel selected to operate it and not upon the type of the organization structure nor the extent of centralization or decentralization. There is no one adjective which can be used with "accountant" to express all the attributes which the personnel who administer and conduct the accounting processes of a business enterprise should possess. Certainly they must be more than accountants. If they have as their prime objective the maintenance of a system of accounts which will record properly the transactions of the enterprise and permit the preparation of financial statements which present fairly the financial position of the company and the results of its operations in conformity with generally accepted accounting principles, they will fall far short of achieving management accounting. Their prime objective must be the development, presentation, and interpretation of information which will implement management decisions and guide its action, so that the profits, which are a reflection of the results of this action, are as satisfactory as they possibly can be. Under certain conditions the objective may have to be even broader than this; it may have to include the stimulation of management action. This emphasis on the management point of view does not mean that accounting principles are to be compromised to the will of management. Such action would undermine all of the management accounting work, for it would remove the drive for results to the extent that failure to achieve results would be hidden in incomplete or misleading statements. Adherence to accepted principles is vital, but the management accounting process must supplement the financial accounting process with vast amounts of operating data which may or may not be completely reconcilable with the books of account.

To achieve the objective of management accounting the personnel of the accounting department must (1) have an interest in, and knowledge of, all phases of the management and staff functions of the enterprise, (2) believe implicitly in a "profit and loss" economic system, (3) rate above average as persons, (4) recognize the need for constant revision and improvement in the management accounting process, and (5) be skilled in the art and science of accounting.

The managerial accountant does not live a cloistered business life surrounded by his books and reports and securing his knowledge of his company from the paper work which crosses his desk. Even if he has theoretical training or even actual experience in all phases of business operation, an obvious impossibility, he has to maintain close contact with all other staffs and operating units in order to know the specific application of the theories and techniques in the operation of his company. Lacking such personal knowledge, he must make frequent contacts to acquire as much of it as possible and to keep in touch with developments and plans before they are reflected in the accounts. Income accounting and sales analysis cannot be effective if the accountant does not know the methods of distribution, classes of customers, end use of the products, geographical distribution, price structure, competitive situation, and advertising media of his company. This knowledge he acquires through discussion with the sales and advertising managers and through attendance at meetings of the sales organization. In the production area a knowledge of raw materials and their sources, methods of production, production equipment, flow of products through work centers, requirements of service operations, labor relations, etc., is requried, and again it is secured through observations in the plant, discussion with production personnel, and attendance at meetings of the production organization. Also, the management accounting function must be coordinated with the work of the other staff departments—industrial engineering, engineering, purchasing, traffic, research, and general administration. This calls for more contacts and meetings. In all these contacts the objective is to gain knowledge to be used to form and adapt the management accounting function to help each area to do its job more effectively. After this is done and useful data are compiled, they must be presented and interpreted. This again requires personal contacts for maximum effectiveness.

The extent of these contacts will vary with the degree of responsibility of each position in the accounting department. The chief accounting officer will participate in all top-level meetings, while a cost-control clerk may have his contacts limited to the foreman of a single production operation. Whatever the extent of the contacts, the objective is the same: to gain knowledge, to secure the point of view and need for management data of the head of the function or area, and to present and interpret the data.

In implementing the management function through accounting the accountant must believe implicitly in a "profit and loss" economic system. His constant goal must be the guidance of management to an optimum profit. At times this may be a higher profit level than the management feels is justified or attainable and at other times a lower level. At all times the cost level over which this profit is realized must be a minimum consistent with the quality of products or services represented as being offered to the customers of the company. With this goal for the guidance of management, the accountant will serve as a balance wheel as he makes his contacts throughout the organization.

There is no room in this concept for the idea that the inefficient shall be subsidized nor that any group shall profit to the detriment or disadvantage of another. Profits realized as a result of either of these circumstances are not optimum profits in that they cannot be expected to continue indefinitely. The working of the basic laws of economics, social forces, and the ingenuity of competitors will soon destroy such profits.

In making his contacts and exerting his influence for optimum profits the managerial accountant must rate above average as a person. He must possess in large measure the ability to communicate, do creative thinking, organize and work with people, be diplomatic, be intellectually honest, persevere in driving toward his objectives, and maintain a sense of humor. A serious deficiency in any of these qualities will tend to make his work ineffective and limit the degree of success and the position in his company which he attains.

Then too, he must recognize a need for constant adaptation of the management accounting process to changing conditions and for improving it. Nothing is more fluid than modern business. Economic conditions change, product lines change, production processes change, markets and customer preferences change, and management personnel changes. Then, too, the specific enterprise grows and expands or, occasionally, contracts. Every one of these changes requires modification and adaptation of the accounting and related records and reports. Beyond this is the need for constant improvement. This stems from two sources: (1) development of the management skills of the organization and (2) developments in the field of management accounting. In a business where there has been little need for, or reliance on, operating data, the initial management accounting can be very simple, as simple as the pedometer and compass used by a man when walking. As management skill in the application of these fundamental data to the operation of the business increases, or the size of the business increases, the need for, and effective use of, further information becomes apparent and must be met. The accountant should sense this need and develop the data rather than have a request for it come from management, for usually they sense a need for more information but do not know what they want or the form in which they want it. At the same time the accountant must not develop a system which is beyond the needs of management or their ability to use it. All the controls of a multiengine plane are needed to fly it safely and effectively, but they would certainly confuse and interfere with the operation of an automobile. Making improvements suggested by developments in the general field of accounting, as disclosed in association meetings and publications, would be governed by the same considerations of the needs of the specific organization. There is no universal applicability of any management accounting technique.

Finally, the managerial accountant must be proficient in all branches of accountancy, and have a professional attitude in his work. While substantial portions of the control phases of his work are not strictly a part of the accounting process and are not reflected in the books of account, they influence the results which are so reflected. Therefore it is necessary to know the effect of actions and decisions in every area of the company on profit or loss and on assets, liabilities, or equity. At no time may procedures be followed which are not in conformity with accepted accounting practice. The professional attitude of independence, while having a somewhat different implication when applied to the accountant in business than when applied to the public accountant, is essential for effective management accounting. It is necessary that plans be evaluated and results reported with complete impartiality and objectivity. Principles must be followed not only because statements will be published but more importantly because management must have the true facts and all the facts if they are to make intelligent, informed decisions. The entire organization for management accounting must be directed toward this objective.

REVIEW QUESTIONS

1. Define management accounting.
2. Why is the emphasis of management accounting on the operating statement rather than on the balance sheet?
3. What effect does the size of a company have on the organization structure of its accounting department?
4. What differences would be found between the accounting system of a manufacturer and that of a wholesale distributor?
5. Who should have the responsibility for administering the cost accounting program? The budgetary planning and control program? Why?
6. Is better control effected through centralization or decentralization of the management accounting functions? Explain.
7. What is the most important qualification of a managerial accountant?
8. Define optimum profit.
9. In adapting a management accounting system for use in a specific company, what factors must be considered?
10. Discuss the importance of objectivity and independence in management accounting.

PROBLEM

A dairy company has plants in four cities within a radius of 100 miles. Three plants, A, B, and C, receive raw milk, pasteurize and bottle it, and distribute it in their territories. Milk receipts in excess of their requirements are pasteurized and transferred in bulk to the fourth plant, D. Plant D also receives raw milk, processes it, and delivers to customers in its territory. In addition it manufactures ice cream and powdered milk. Ice cream is sold in each of the four territories with all deliveries made from plant D. Powdered milk is sold in bulk to a few large accounts.

The president is the chief executive officer. There is a sales manager for fluid milk and another for ice cream. The president handles the sale of powdered milk. There is a general production manager, and each plant has a manager who reports to him. The general offices are located at plant D, and all management functions except those of the plant managers are centralized.

Customers' accounts for fluid milk are paid at the respective plant; for ice cream and powdered milk, at the general offices. Vendors' invoices are received and approved at each plant and forwarded to the general office for payment. Quantities and butterfat content of raw milk are recorded at the plants and forwarded to the general office for computation and payment to suppliers. Time records are sent to the general office where hourly and salary payrolls are prepared.

Size of the company is indicated by the following:

	Employees	Annual sales
Plant A...............	100	$ 500,000
Plant B...............	150	700,000
Plant C...............	225	1,500,000
Plant D...............	480	
Ice cream............	———	3,000,000
Fluid milk............	———	700,000
Powdered milk.........	———	250,000
General office...........	50	

The company uses standard costs and has a complete program of budgetary control.

Chart and describe the accounting organization you would recommend.

CHAPTER 2

Cost Accounting

Management accounting for profit control includes income accounting, cost accounting, and budgetary planning and control. Of these processes cost accounting is the keystone. Costs must be less than income if a profit is to be realized. Therefore, sales prices must be established through a markup on costs which will produce the desired profit, or if competition sets the prices, costs must be controlled and held below these prices. In either event cost planning is essential. Actual costs must be determined and compared with those planned to guide management toward their profit objective. To meet these requirements costs must be determined not only in total but also by areas of management responsibility and by products.

Cost determination and control do not necessarily involve accounting. It is possible to perform these functions without recording the costs in the books of account. In fact, costs will not always be in agreement with the accounts. Different costs are required for different management purposes. Since the accounts can reflect only costs which are acceptable for financial statement preparation, any costs for other purposes will be complementary to the books of account. However, the best practice is to record the costs used for financial statement preparation and establish the relationship of all other costs to these. This provides a factual base which lends credence and acceptability to the complementary cost data.

Field of Cost Accounting

Practice which has evolved over a period of many years has broadened the scope of cost accounting from the basic function of recording costs in the accounts. Today cost accounting may be defined as the planning, determination, recording, analysis, and interpretation of the costs of producing and distributing products.

Emphasis has shifted from the accounting functions to the management uses of costs. There are thousands of cost accountants who never make a journal entry or post a ledger. But they must know the relationship of the data which they use to the ledger accounts and the effect of transactions and decisions on the balance sheet and statement of profit and loss. Otherwise they cannot provide proper guidance to management.

Costs must be planned and determined by areas of management responsibility and by product lines. Profit control is, in large measure, cost control. Each member of the management team from the chief executive to the foreman is constantly making decisions which affect costs and has responsibility for certain costs. The cost accountant assists in planning the costs to be incurred under the responsibility of each manager, compiles the actual costs, compares them with those planned, and analyzes and interprets them as to their effects on profit. While the incurrence of costs is by areas of responsibility, they can be recovered only through the sale of products or services. Therefore, they must be related to the units produced and sold to provide a measurement of the profit contribution of each product, both as planned and as realized. Again, analysis and interpretation is a fundamental part of the process.

Cost Elements

Costs arise from cash expenditures, accruals, usage of items from inventory, and the amortization of capital expenditures over the life of an asset. A cash payment to a carpenter for repairing a broken door is a cost. Coal used from a storage pile becomes a cost when the coal is used. An accrual for a property tax gives rise to a cost. The annual depreciation of a machine is a cost.

For accounting purposes costs are grouped under three categories referred to as "cost elements." These are direct material, direct labor, and expense.

Direct material is a cost which arises from the usage of material which becomes a component part of the product produced and can be measured in relation to the units produced. Lumber for the bases of mousetraps would be direct material. Ink used for stamping the manufacturer's name on the base would not be direct material, since it may be impossible and would certainly be impracticable to measure the usage in relation to the units of production.

Direct labor is a cost which arises from the payment of wages based on time or production and which changes the form or location of a product and can be measured in relation to the units produced. The labor for sawing lumber into blocks for mousetrap bases would be direct labor. The janitor who cleans the sawdust and shavings from the floor would not be direct labor. He does no work on the product, and his time bears no direct relationship to the number of units produced.

Expense includes all costs which are not direct material or direct labor. Expense is further classified as to factory or manufacturing expense, distribution expense, and administrative expense. Each of these three expense groups may be broken into subgroups according to the practice of a particular company; for example, distribution expense may be separated into selling expense, sample expense, and advertising expense.

Practice is not uniform as to the classification of costs between direct material and expense or direct labor and expense. In many companies practicality rather than adherence to generally accepted accounting definitions determines how an item is classified as to cost element.

Expense is also referred to as "burden" or as "overhead." These latter designations are widely used but have a connotation of excessiveness or undesirability. Expense is essential to the operation of a business and should not be designated by a term which invites criticism and unwarranted pressure for its elimination.

Cost per Unit

Great emphasis has been placed upon the determination of the cost per unit of product. In fact some writers have defined cost accounting as the determination of the cost per unit of product made or sold. This is an important phase of cost accounting, but it does not begin to cover the scope of costing for management purposes.

Unit costs are required for pricing purposes, valuation of inventories, and determination of cost of goods sold. They are also used to provide comparisons of costs of different periods. When they are predetermined, they are related to activity to provide a dollar total to be compared with the actual dollars incurred.

The unit cost of a product or function is determined by dividing the dollars of incurred cost by units of activity. The total dollars of direct material used in manufacturing mousetraps divided by the number of traps produced would give the unit direct material cost of a trap. If the direct materials were recorded separately for bases, springs, and bait plates, each would be divided by the respective units produced to arrive at its unit cost. These unit costs would then be added to arrive at the unit direct-material cost per trap.

Costs may be accumulated for a given lot of a product and the unit cost determined on the basis of the number in the lot. This is referred to as job-order costing. Or, costs may be determined for each step in the production process and divided by the units produced in the respective step or process. This is referred to as process costing. Under process costing the unit cost of each process may be combined to arrive at the total unit cost of the finished product.

Cost by Responsibility

For management accounting the determination of the costs incurred under the responsibility of each manager is of equal importance with the determination of unit costs. It is necessary to know what costs were incurred and to compare these with costs of other periods or with planned costs to know if they are being controlled. A knowledge of cost levels and trends is essential for effective management.

Areas of management responsibility should be established according to the production sequence and the distribution and administrative functions. In a mousetrap factory one foreman may be responsible for making wooden bases, another for making the metal parts, and another for assembling the bases and metal parts into finished traps. Here there would be three distinct areas of responsibility, and the costs incurred in each would be recorded for it separately from all other costs. The costs of each foreman would then be measured, analyzed, and interpreted to aid him in controlling them and to inform his superiors of the extent to which control was being effected. For control purposes actual unit costs are not essential. Total actual costs by elements can be measured against planned unit costs extended by units of activity.

Cost of Products

Sales prices are set for each product and income is realized from the sale of products. Therefore, to provide management information on the contribution of different products to profit, cost must also be accumulated by products.

Under job-order costing this is automatic. Each job or lot is of a specific product, so that the job costs can be summarized by products for comparison with sales income of the products.

Under process costing it is necessary to identify costs by products where more than one product is produced in an operation. If the trap company made mousetraps and rattraps and bases for both were formed in the same operation, costs would be so identified. The total cost of each kind of trap would then be the sum of the costs incurred for it in each operation. Costs are not always identifiable by products in the earlier stages of production. Where this is true, the total cost of the operation is assigned to products on the basis of the usage of the partially processed material at the first point at which it can be identified as to product.

Inventories

It is a principle of accounting that appropriate costs be matched against revenues. Cost accounting procedures provide for this through the inventory accounts. Until a cost can appropriately be matched against revenue, it is carried in an inventory account. Inventories are recorded under at least three accounts: (1) raw material and supplies (2) work in process and (3) finished stock. These three major classifications may be broken into subclassifications as required by specific companies. This may be done through separate general-ledger accounts or in the subsidiary inventory ledgers. However, it is common practice to carry separate ledger accounts for raw materials and for supplies.

The methods of valuing the inventories are discussed in subsequent chapters.

RAW MATERIAL

The raw-material inventory includes those materials which will be classified as direct material when they are used. An expenditure for wire which will be used to make mousetrap springs cannot appropriately be matched against revenues at the time the purchase is made. Accordingly, the value of the wire is carried in the Raw Material Inventory account until it enters into the production process.

Freight on raw materials is customarily added to the purchase price and carried in the Raw Material Inventory account as part of the value of the raw material. Freight paid to bring raw material to the factory cannot appropriately be matched against revenue at the time it is paid. However, when freight costs are low in relation to the value of the raw material, they may be charged as expense when they are incurred and ignored in the raw-material inventory values.

Where the labor and expense costs of unloading and storing raw material are significant, they may be added to the raw-material inventory value. This is usually accomplished by adding an estimated cost per unit of raw material to the purchase price plus freight-in. Again, this is done because the costs of unloading and storage cannot appropriately be matched against revenues of the period in which these costs are incurred.

SUPPLIES

Supplies inventories include items such as fuel, lubricating oil, sandpaper, paper towels, maintenance materials, and stationery. These are materials which are charged to expense accounts when they are used rather than to the direct-material element of cost.

Freight on supplies, and unloading and storage costs, may be added to the inventory value of the items, as for raw material. It is more common practice to charge these costs to expense as they are incurred. This is done because of the relatively low cost per unit of supplies and the amount of clerical effort required to carry them in the inventory value of the many supply items.

WORK IN PROCESS

The work-in-process inventory includes all items which have started through the production processes but have not been completed. As raw materials are used, their value is transferred from the raw-material inventory into the work-in-process inventory. The fact that they have entered into the production process does not mean that their cost can appropriately be matched against revenues. The time when they will be sold as components of the finished product may be months or even years away. It is true that some items may be components of finished products which are sold in the same month or year in which the raw materials are used. However, this is not known when the raw materials are used. Simplicity of record keeping makes it more expedient to carry all raw-material values into the work-in-process inventory when they are used.

Direct labor is also added to the work-in-process inventory. As with raw material usage, direct labor costs cannot appropriately be matched against revenues of the period when the labor is expanded upon the product. They must be carried forward in inventory values until it is sold.

Expenses incurred in the factory are also added to work-in-process inventory values. The reasons are the same as those slated for direct labor.

FINISHED STOCK

When the production of a product has been completed, its value (total direct material, direct labor, and factory expense) is transferred from the work-in-process inventory to the finished-stock inventory. It is carried in this account until the product is shipped to the customer. At that time it is removed from the inventory account and charged to the cost of goods sold. Then it can appropriately be matched against revenues, for the shipment has given rise to revenue from the sale of the product.

Practice varies with respect to the treatment of the costs of warehousing the finished product. Some companies add them to finished-stock inventory values, and others charge them directly to cost of goods sold.

Any crating or other package material used at time of shipment, and the labor and expense of shipping, are customarily charged directly to the cost of goods sold.

Cost Planning and Control

It is obvious that while costs incurred in the factory are appropriately matched against revenues only when the product is sold, such matching does not provide for cost planning and control. Costs are incurred when raw material and supplies are purchased, when time is expended by workers, and when charges are made to capital-asset and deferred-expense accounts which will be charged to current-expense accounts of future periods. Costs must be planned before they are incurred and be controlled while they are being incurred. The planning and control functions are the more important and interesting phases of cost accounting. They are a vital function of management accounting, as discussed in subsequent chapters.

REVIEW QUESTIONS

1. Describe the scope of cost accounting.
2. What are the elements of cost? Define each.
3. What are the management uses of unit costs?
4. What is meant by the determination of costs by areas of responsibility?
5. Why should costs be determined for each product?
6. How are costs of products determined under job-order costing? Under process costing?
7. What is meant by the accounting principle that appropriate costs be matched against revenues?
8. What is the function of inventories in cost accounting?
9. What are the three costs which may be included in raw-material inventory values?
10. What costs are included in work-in-process inventory values?
11. Describe several costs which may or may not be included in finished-stock inventory values.
12. What is the relationship of cost accounting to management accounting for profit control?

CHAPTER 3

The Chart of Accounts

The skeleton of any accounting system is the chart of accounts. It may exist without being formalized as such, and the accountants of many small companies may state that they have no chart of accounts. In these instances the accounts carried on the general ledger and the areas, jobs, or products for which costs are compiled do in effect constitute a chart of accounts. If no effort has been directed toward its formal development, it is more likely to be either sketchy and inadequate or cumbersome and excessively detailed. In either event the accounting process will function less effectively than it would if it were based on a well-coordinated system.

Coordination of Accounting and Control Information

The initial step in preparing for management accounting is to set up a system of account classification which will provide both for the general or corporate accounts, and the supporting detail of operating information. These two phases of the accounting process must be integrated for maximum effectiveness. This does not mean that all of the control detail will be recorded in the general books. It does mean that a substantial portion of the data accumulated for control purposes can be summarized and carried forward as the accounting transactions are recorded. For example, direct labor costs would not be recorded on the general ledger by operations or jobs. This detail information would be carried in the subsidiary records, and the totals of these would be the amounts posted to the ledger accounts. Likewise the distribution of vendors' invoices to inventory accounts and expense records in detail for control data would be posted to these ledger accounts in total. In the small company this can be accomplished through adding machine tapes of the original records or through columnar journals and registers. In the larger companies this method becomes too cumbersome and expensive, and some type of machine summary is usually employed. Irrespective of the method used, the important point is that actual management accounting data and the general-ledger accounts have their origin in the same original records, and these should be developed so as to be in agreement and provide the maximum dual use of the records for greatest economy.

Of equal importance with the attainment of efficiency and economy in the accounting process is the assurance of uniformity and consistency. This can be achieved only if like transactions are always recorded in the same accounts. Without a chart of accounts this may not occur with transactions which are infrequent but none the less very important, even in a very small enterprise. In the larger enterprises, with many operations and a number of plants, uniformity of interpretation and classification of the transactions becomes more of a problem. Here the chart of accounts becomes indispensable.

Definitions

Unfortunately accounting terminology is not standardized, and this is particularly true of management accounting terminology. For this reason the following definitions are given for this book.

ADMINISTRATIVE EXPENSE · All operating costs which are neither factory costs nor distribution costs.

AREA OF RESPONSIBILITY · A unit of a business under a supervisor; a plant, an operation in a plant, a district sales office, etc.

CLASSIFICATIONS · The finest detail of income or cost used in an area of responsibility.

CONTROL ACCOUNT · A general-ledger account supported by a subsidiary ledger or records.

CONTROL DATA · The detailed information required by any level of management.

DEPARTMENT · An area of responsibility, or point of control of costs, for more than one operation.

DIRECT EXPENSE · Expense which varies in ratio to activity and can be applied directly to products.

DISTRIBUTION EXPENSE · All costs of marketing a product, including sales effort, sales management, order processing, delivery, advertising, promotion, and samples.

FACTORY · A manufacturing plant.

FACTORY COSTS · All costs incurred in manufacturing products.

INCOME · The money value received or accrued from the sale of products and services and from miscellaneous sources such as royalties, rents, interest, and dividends.

INDIRECT EXPENSE · Expense which does not vary in ratio to activity and must be assigned or allocated to operations, or within an operation to products.

OPERATION · A portion of a factory under one supervisor and performing one function or several closely related functions in the production of products or in servicing other operations.

PERIOD EXPENSE · Expense which does not vary in ratio to activity and is charged to profit and loss of each period.

PLANT · A factory—sometimes a company will have two or more completely unrelated production units in one building or group of buildings (an electrical company manufacturing light bulbs and motors) and designate each unit as a plant.

SECTION · A subdivision of a department or an operation.

SOURCES · Major components of expense.

WORK CENTER · An operation.

Building the Chart of Accounts

The chart of accounts is simply a listing of the accounts to be reflected on the general ledger and of the supporting detail which is required for control purposes with brief but complete descriptions of each account and subclassification. The first step in setting up a formal chart of accounts is to make a detailed review of all the accounting transactions of a past period of sufficient length to include nearly all types of entries. As each is encountered, it should be examined as to the accounts affected and in the light of the extent of control detail desired. From this a determination is made of the accounts required. An expedient method of doing this is to write each account name on a small piece of paper, as its necessity is established, with the traditional T under the title. These are then placed on a bulletin board with thumbtacks and string used to join the two sides of the transaction. Payment of vendors' invoices would be indicated by a line from the credit side of the Cash in Banks T to the debit side of the Accounts Payable T. When all transactions have been set up in this manner, the board will appear as an almost unintelligible maze. However, as transactions are traced, the various lines will be found to merge in many instances and with some rearrangement of the relative positions of the accounts will present a concise picture of the flow of transactions. From this a listing of the accounts can be made and, if desired, a flow chart drawn to provide a permanent graphic record of the flow of transactions.

For management accounting more detail is needed than is provided by the balance sheet and revenue and expense accounts of the general ledger. For economy it is essential that this detail be developed simulta-

neously with the accumulation and summarization of the data which will
be reflected in the general accounts. Therefore this information should
be provided for through an extension of the chart of accounts and not as
an independent process.

The first step is to provide for the accumulation of control data by
areas of responsibility. If these areas are not defined, an organization job
must be done on the entire management structure—sales, production, and
administration. This is a management, not an accounting, function. But
unless the management takes this step and makes a definite assignment
of responsibilities, the management accounting process will be ineffective and for the most part a waste of money.

With the areas of responsibility established, the next step is to determine the income realized and costs incurred by each area. The process of
doing this is similar to that used for the general-ledger accounts, the
examination of historical records. Since the charting of the accounting
transactions has already been done, both the debit and credit sides of the
transaction are not needed for setting up the control records. Thus a
listing of items under each responsibility is adequate.

Basic Data Required for Management

The control data should include the following:

1. Income
   a. Responsibility under which it is realized
   b. Areas from which it is realized
   c. Detail of products or services sold
   d. Customer classification
2. Cost
   a. Elements of cost
   b. Responsibility under which each cost is incurred
   c. Area or unit of the business
   d. Detail as to components of cost elements, frequently referred to as
      "classifications"

These requirements are discussed briefly in the paragraphs following,
in order to provide background for the illustrative charts of accounts.
They are elaborated upon in subsequent chapters.

In a small company the detail on sales income may be very limited. If
a single product or service is sold in a limited geographical area, the
general-ledger accounts may provide all the information which is needed.
In the largest companies the sales income detail is voluminous. All
degrees of variation in the amount of information on sales income which
is compiled will occur between these two extremes, depending upon the

size of business, the composition of its product line, and the desires of management.

In large companies with a number of plants and products the responsibility for sales may be placed according to manufacturing plants. In this case a sales manager carries on the distribution function for each plant. Sales are recorded as to point of manufacture of the product. The total sales of all plants are consolidated for recording in the general ledger if centralized accounts are maintained. If each plant maintains a subsidiary ledger, the entry in it would be for the total sales of the plant. If sales responsibility is not placed by plants, the recording would be by sales divisions or departments of a division. The accounting entries would be made on the same basis as when sales responsibility follows plant lines, in total with centralized accounting and by divisions with separate division ledgers. The sales account or accounts in the ledgers would be supported by subsidiary records showing sales by product lines.

Under each sales responsibility there should be further detail as to the geographical area in which the sales were made. This may be established according to sales territories as established for district offices or may be accumulated by states, by counties, or by trading areas. In each of these geographical areas sales should be detailed by classes of customers. The records should be maintained in a manner which will permit ready summary of company totals by areas, by product lines, or by classes of customers.

Cost detail is needed in all companies regardless of size. The basic pattern for accumulating these data will tend to be the same in every company. Differences will be in extent and amount of detail rather than kind. Individual records for each plant of multiplant companies are desirable, even when the accounting work is centralized.

The first breakdown of costs is by cost elements: direct material, direct labor, and expense. Expense may be further broken down into kinds of expense as, for example, direct manufacturing expense, indirect manufacturing expense, experimental expense, distribution expense, and administrative expense, referred to as "expense-control accounts." Accounts are usually carried in the general ledger for the cost elements in order to provide a permanent record for financial reports and tax returns. The extent to which the elements maintain their identity through work-in-process and finished-stock inventories into the Cost of Sales account will be determined by the cost accounting system in use.

In some cases the expense accounts are carried on the general books as to expense sources—Salaries, Indirect Labor, Supplies, Depreciation, etc. This usually is not practical because of the excessive number of accounts. The more common practice is to carry only the expense-control accounts in the general ledger and to maintain a subsidiary ledger in which the expense sources are recorded for each control account. Some expense sources as recorded in the subsidiary ledger would be:

Salaries	Stationery
Commissions	Travel
Indirect Labor	Postage
Supplies	Rent
Sacks and Containers	Depreciation
Maintenance Material	Taxes
Maintenance Labor	Insurance

Responsibility for costs usually extends very far down in the organization. Thus certain costs will be incurred under the responsibility of the foreman of an operation, the manager of a district office or warehouse, the supervisor of a section of a staff department, etc. Other costs will be charged to these operations for purposes of total cost determination, even though the responsibility for control of the costs rests in some other area. Control of direct labor in an operation is the responsibility of the foreman of the operation. The cost of maintenance work done under the responsibility of a central maintenance department is not under the control of the foreman but is charged to the operation. Rent of a district office is determined by lease agreements made by the real estate department but is charged to the district office. Therefore the management accounting detail should provide for reporting both by responsibility and by area to be charged. This may be accomplished through a dual posting of charges, by responsibility, and by area to be charged. Or, the detail may be maintained only by cost responsibility and then be distributed to the cost-determination areas as a total. This latter method has the disadvantage of taking into the cost-determination area a sum of costs with no details as to their composition or where they originated, which raises frequent questions as to the total costs of an operation.

The final breakdown of costs is into components of the elements. Material usage in a foundry may be detailed as to pig iron and scrap. In an ice-cream plant it may be detailed as to cream, whole milk, condensed milk, sugar, and fruits and flavors. Direct labor in the bottling plant of a brewery may be detailed as to bottling, capping, pasteurizing, and inspecting. Sources of expense also require classification detail for control. In a machine shop supplies may be classified as to wiping rags and cutting oil, and indirect labor as to machine setup, material transfer, janitor, watchmen, etc. Classifications of expense components are usually recorded and summarized in the areas where the costs are incurred and are not carried beyond that point for control or accounting purposes.

Use of Codes

The recording and analysis of accounting transactions is usually expedited by the use of codes. Each account has a code designation, as does each detail breakdown under the account. Substantial amounts of time are saved by using the code instead of writing a description of the account and its related income or cost detail. This is especially true in the original records, where the code or portion of the code can be pre-printed on the forms used. This latter step also reduces the possibility of error.

Coding systems may be alphabetical, numerical, or a combination of the two. With the increased use of machine accounting the tendency is toward the use of numerical codes because of the ease with which they can be transferred to punched cards and because certain mechanical accounting equipment does not carry alphabetical characters. The numerical code is also more flexible than the alphabetical or combination and thus requires less frequent revision. In setting up a coding system it is desirable to provide for more expansion than can possibly be vis-ualized at the time. If this is done, the code need not be revised for many years, a desirable feature because the information of prior years need not be recoded and can be interpreted without reference to one or more obsolete codes.

The following is an illustrative coding system of a relatively small single-plant dairy company. The code consists of seven digits grouped three, two and two.

ACCOUNT	RESPONSIBILITY	CLASSIFICATION
000	00	00

The first three digits designate the accounts carried on the general ledger. For assets and liabilities only these three digits are used. For revenue and expense the responsibility and classification digits are added to provide control data. Three expense-control accounts (300, 400, and 500) are carried on the general ledger, and a subsidiary expense ledger is maintained in which expenses are recorded by sources and responsi-bility. To provide for this the two zeros of the expense accounts are re-placed by the expense-source codes. (Salesmen's Salaries would be coded 401.) The fourth and fifth digits designate responsibility which is identi-cal with operations. The sixth and seventh digits indicate the classifica-tion of income or cost. It is to be noted that certain codes which ordinarily would be used have been omitted in the illustration, particularly in the expense classifications.

BALANCE SHEET

Assets		*Liabilities*	
Code	*Account*	*Code*	*Account*
011	Cash in Bank	061	Accounts Payable
012	Cash Imprest Funds	062	Accrued Taxes
021	Accounts Receivable	071	Funded Debt
031	Raw Material	082	Reserve for Depreciation—
032	Work in Process		Buildings
033	Supplies	083	Reserve for Depreciation—
037	Prepaid Expense		Machinery
041	Land	084	Reserve for Depreciation—
042	Buildings		Furniture and Fixtures
043	Machinery	085	Reserve for Depreciation—
044	Furniture and Fixtures		Delivery Equipment
045	Delivery Equipment	086	Reserve for Depreciation—
046	Ice-cream Cabinets		Ice-cream Cabinets
051	Good Will	091	Capital Stock
		092	Paid-in Surplus
		095	Earned Surplus

Revenue and Expense

Code	*Account*
101	Gross Sales
105	Sales Returns and Allowances
201	Raw Material
202	Direct Labor
300	Factory Expense
400	Distribution Expense
500	Administrative Expense
601	Miscellaneous Income
605	Miscellaneous Expense
701	Reserve for Contingencies
801	State Taxes on Income
802	Federal Taxes on Income

EXPENSE SOURCES

Code	Description	Code	Description
01	Salaries	41	Stationery
02	Indirect Labor	42	Postage
03	Overtime and Shift Differential	43	Telephone and Telegraph
		45	Travel
05	Vacation Pay	51	Rent
10	Supplies	61	Depreciation—Buildings
11	Bottles and Cases	62	Depreciation—Machinery
12	Cans	63	Depreciation—Furniture and Fixtures
20	Maintenance Material		
21	Maintenance Labor	64	Depreciation—Delivery Equipment
22	Maintenance by Outside Firms		
		71	Property Taxes
31	Fuel	72	Salary and Wage Taxes
32	Electricity	81	Insurance
33	Water	91	Miscellaneous

Operations

01	Milk Sales Department	34	Cold Rooms
05	Ice-cream Sales Department	41	Ice-cream Mixing
10	General Office	42	Ice-cream Freezing
20	General Plant	43	Ice-cream Packaging
21	Boiler Room	44	Ice-cream Specialties
22	Refrigeration	45	Hardening Rooms
31	Milk Receiving	51	Milk Delivery
32	Pasteurizing	55	Ice-cream Delivery
33	Bottling	66	Service Department

Cost Classification

01	Watchmen	24	Delivery Equipment
02	Janitors	25	Cabinets
03	Firemen	31	Coal
04	Inspectors	32	Oil
05	Cold-room Attendants	51	Milk
11	Cleaning Supplies	52	Cream
12	Brushes and Brooms	53	Sugar
21	Buildings	54	Fruit and Flavors
22	Machinery	55	Specialty Materials
23	Furniture and Fixtures	56	Package Materials

Income Classification

81	Bottled Milk	92	Packaged Ice Cream
82	Bulk Milk	93	Ice-cream Specialties
91	Bulk Ice Cream	94	Supplies and Equipment

Illustrative applications of the codes follow:

	Account	Responsibility	Classification
Sale of bottled milk....................	101	01	81
Return of packaged ice cream...........	105	05	92
Sugar used in ice-cream making..........	201	41	53
Direct-labor pasteurizing................	202	32	00
Brushes for the bottling operation........	310	33	12
Maintenance labor on ice-cream packaging machine.........................	321	43	22
Coal for boilers........................	331	21	31
Salaries of milk salesmen................	401	01	00
Travel of president.....................	545	10	00

Many illustrations in this text are based on a hypothetical fiberboard company with a number of plants, sales divisions, and subsidiaries. It is assumed that this company uses a 16-digit code. In this code the designations are as follows:

CORPORATION AND PLANT OR DIVISION	ACCOUNT CONTROL SOURCE	DEPARTMENT	OPERATION	CLASSIFICATION
000	00000	00	000	000

In this code responsibility is designated as "department" and the work center as "operation." Portions of this code follow to illustrate the account and control designations:

CORPORATION AND PLANT OR DIVISION

110   General Office
121   Harrisburg Plant
122   Atlanta Plant
123   Richmond Plant
124   Mobile Plant
150   Building Products Division
    151   New York District Office
    152   Chicago District Office
    153   Los Angeles District Office
    155   Birmingham District Office

160 Industrial Specialties Division
  161 New York District Office
  162 Chicago District Office
  163 Los Angeles District Office
  164 Houston District Office
  165 Birmingham District Office
170 Acoustical Division
  171 New York District Office
  172 Chicago District Office
  173 Los Angeles District Office
  176 Kansas City District Office
210 Western Distributors, Inc.
310 Ecco International, Inc.

ACCOUNTS
Assets

01101	Cash—Current	02105	Deferred Variances
01104	Cash—Payroll Deposit Account	02201	General Stores
		02202	Coal
01201	Accounts Receivable—Trade	02500	Intercompany Accounts
		03101	Land
01202	Notes Receivable—Trade	03201	Buildings
01301	Sundry Accounts Receivable	03203	Machinery
		04100	Capital Stock—Domestic Subsidiaries
02101	Materials in Transit		
02102	Raw Materials	04200	Other Investments
02103	Work in Process	04600	Other Noncurrent Assets
02113	Chest Stock	05104	Deferred Expense—Insurance
02123	Jobs in Process		
02104	Finished Stock	05105	Deferred Expense—Rent

Revenue and Expense

10101	Sales Trade—Domestic	12116	Variance—Scrap
10102	Sales Trade—Foreign	12117	Deferred Variances
10201	Sales Returns	13100	Incurred Factory Expense
10401	Quantity Discounts		
11101	Standard Cost of Goods Sold—Domestic	13400	Applied Factory Expense
		14100	Selling Expense
12101	Variance—Material Purchasing	15100	Administrative Expense
		16000	Miscellaneous Income and Expense
12106	Variance—Direct Labor		
12109	Variance—Material Usage		

EXPENSE SOURCES USED WITH EXPENSE ACCOUNTS

02	Salaries	33	Postage
03	Indirect Labor	34	Telephone and Telegraph
04	Vacation Pay	35	Publications
07	Pensions	36	Consulting Services
09	Supplies	37	Donations
13	Maintenance Material	38	Association Dues
14	Maintenance Labor	41	Employee Benefit Programs
15	Maintenance Services	42	Taxes—Payroll
21	Fuel	51	Rent
22	Water	52	Depreciation
23	Electricity (Purchased)	53	Taxes—General
31	Stationery	54	Insurance
32	Travel		

DEPARTMENTS

02	Machine Shop	35	Warehouse
19	Yard	36	Shipping
22	Power	40	Advertising
30	Material Preparation		

OPERATIONS

001	Plant—General	332	Drying
040	Plant—Controller	333	Dry Saws
102	Machine Shop	420	Preparation
150	Stores	421	Fabrication
158	Boiler Room	422	Finishing
220	Wood Grinders	522	Shipping
331	Forming	601	Advertising—General

COST CLASSIFICATIONS

001	Make-up Pay	101	Machinery Repair
003	Bailing Scrap Paper	201	Loose Equipment and Tools
011	Cleaning Drums	301	Building Repairs
040	Inspectors	604	Magazine Space

COMMODITY CLASSIFICATIONS (USED FOR DIRECT MATERIAL AND LABOR)

521	Standard Roof Insulation	523	Industrial Stock
522	Acoustical Stock	576	Cut Specialties

SALES COMMODITY CODES

(Sales commodity codes are used as the ninth to sixteenth digits. Major commodity groups appear in the "department" position, specific products in the "operation" position, and customer classification in the "classification" position.)

MAJOR COMMODITIES

02   Roof Insulation   14   Industrial Products
                    21   Acoustical Material

SPECIFIC PRODUCTS

521   Standard Roof Insulation   576   Cut Specialties

CUSTOMER CLASSIFICATION

109   Roofing Contractors   112   Mail-order Houses

Illustrative applications of the codes follow:

Sale of standard roof insulation to roofing contractors in
    the Birmingham territory...................... 155—10101—02—521—109
Actual direct labor—forming blanks for cut parts in the
    Atlanta plant.................................... 122—12106—00—331—576
Maintenance labor on grinders in the Atlanta plant..... 122—13114—02—220—101

Machine Accounting

Thus far emphasis has been placed on the use of a numerical system of codes for purposes of uniformity and economy. Of greater importance is that the use of codes is necessary if machine accounting is used. A small company would not have a sufficient volume of transactions to do all the accounting on machines. Frequently a start is made with sales analysis, and this is followed by the payroll distribution. Large companies with many transactions find it economical to use one of the several methods of machine accounting for recording and summarizing all transactions. In their installations one of the punched-card methods is usually used. The original records may be prepared on the cards to be punched or prepared on report forms and cards punched from these, or the punched cards may be prepared from tapes secured from the recently developed "common-language machines." With the original information including general journal entries transferred to punched cards, the process becomes one of mechanical summarization until the account balances are secured for the balance sheet, the operating statement, and either a posting summary for the general ledger or even the ledger itself.

The advantages of machine accounting are flexibility, speed, and economy. There is almost no limit to the combinations of information which may be secured. For example, if each sales invoice is coded and the data transferred to a punched card, the same cards will provide total company sales, sales of each division, sales by district offices, sales by product lines, and sales by classes of customers, simply by sorting according to the information desired. If total sales of each product line are desired, the sort would be of all sales cards. If sales of each district office by product lines are desired, the sort would first be by district offices and then by product lines within each office. Direct labor can be determined by product lines, by operations, by product lines in each operation, etc. All this work can be done more rapidly by machine than by hand sorting and totaling with calculating machines. This reduces the lag between the close of each period and the time the control reports and financial statements are available.

Because no enterprise is static, the chart of accounts must be under constant review and adaptation to changing conditions. Responsibility must be assigned to someone to initiate changes and to approve changes requested by others. This may be one of the duties of one person on the accounting staff of a small company. Large companies have several persons assigned to this work, as is indicated by the organization chart shown in Exhibit 1-3. On this organization chart this group is designated as the "Accounting Procedures" section.

REVIEW QUESTIONS

1. Why should the accounting functions and the control functions be coordinated?
2. How does a chart of accounts aid in coordinating accounting and control?
3. What is the purpose of numerical or alphabetical coding of accounting and control data?
4. In addition to the data required for accounting entries, what information should be provided by the original records of income and costs?
5. Define source, department, operation, and classification as used in this text.
6. What are the advantages and disadvantages of mechanical processing of accounting and control data?
7. How would the chart of accounts of a manufacturing company differ from that of a bank?
8. How would the chart of a single-plant company manufacturing one product differ from that of a company having several plants and manufacturing many products?
9. How would you develop a chart of accounts for a manufacturing company which had not been using a coding system?
10. How frequently should the basic coding system of a company be revised?

PROBLEM

A plastics manufacturer makes electrical items such as switches, plugs, and outlets; makes caps for bottles; and does custom molding for other manufacturers. There is a sales manager for each of these three major sales classifications. There are three plants, located in Kalamazoo, Camden, and Los Angeles, each producing all the items. Each plant has a manager reporting to a general production manager.

The production operations in each plant are preforming, flat-bed molding, rotary molding, injection molding, inspection, finishing, and cap lining. Service operations are plant administration, maintenance, mold and tool making, steam generation and distribution, and electric generation and distribution.

General offices are located at Camden, and district sales offices are located at New York, Louisville, Chicago, Los Angeles, and Pittsburgh.

Prepare a chart of accounts, with codes, for the company. General-ledger accounts need not be shown, but four digits should be allowed in the code for these. Include several illustrative codes for departments, operations, and classifications not mentioned specifically above but needed to record management accounting data.

CHAPTER 4

Accounting for Material

The accounting for direct material begins with the issuance of the purchase requisition and ends only when the finished product has been shipped to the customer. In the course of this cycle the other two elements of cost, labor and expense, become part of material cost to the extent that they are applied to production and included in inventory values. Therefore the span of accounting for direct material in effect covers the entire production cycle. While value is increased as each production operation is completed, the basic records and procedures of material accounting are applicable until the finished product is shipped.

Indirect (expense) materials, which are charged to inventory accounts as purchased, can be accounted for by the same procedures used for direct materials up to the point of requisition of the indirect materials from inventory. At that point they are charged to an expense account, and the accounting procedures for expense become applicable. Accounting procedures for indirect materials and services charged directly to expense accounts and for capital expenditures parallel those for direct material up to the payment of the invoice.

Purchase Requisition

The first record in the materials accounting sequence is the purchase requisition. This is used to request the purchasing agent to order a material or service. It is important that the individuals authorized to issue purchase requisitions be limited to such personnel as foremen, storekeepers, and production, sales, and staff dpeartment heads. Frequently a limit is placed on the total value of goods or services which the purchasing agent may proceed to order on the basis of a purchase requisition without securing approval of designated executives such as the controller, treasurer, or vice-president. This limitation of authority to issue a requisition and procedure for top-management approval is not needless red tape, for the purchase requisition originates a substantial percentage of the total costs of a company. The charging of this cost to operations will be delayed for some time if the purchase requisition is issued for material for inventory, but ultimately the cost must be absorbed, and control can only be effected before cost is incurred.

Purchase requisitions may be dispensed with in those instances where agreements are made with a supplier to meet specified requirements over a period of time. Such agreements are blanket purchase requisitions. For example, if an agreement is made with an outside firm to wash the office windows at stated intervals during the next 12 months, a purchase requisition would not be issued each time the windows are washed or a payment is to be made.

Exhibit 4-1
Purchase Requisition

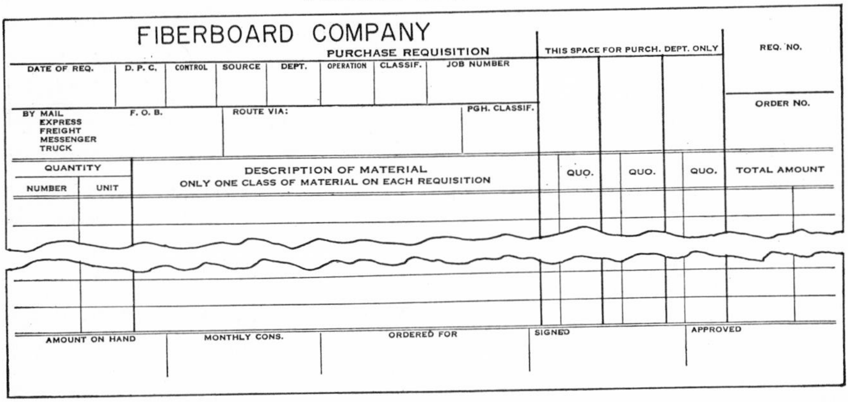
FIBERBOARD COMPANY
PURCHASE REQUISITION
DATE OF REQ. | D. P. C. | CONTROL | SOURCE | DEPT. | OPERATION | CLASSIF. | JOB NUMBER
THIS SPACE FOR PURCH. DEPT. ONLY
REQ. NO.
ORDER NO.
BY MAIL
EXPRESS
FREIGHT
MESSENGER
TRUCK
F. O. B. | ROUTE VIA: | PGH. CLASSIF.
QUANTITY: NUMBER | UNIT
DESCRIPTION OF MATERIAL
ONLY ONE CLASS OF MATERIAL ON EACH REQUISITION
QUO. | QUO. | QUO. | TOTAL AMOUNT
AMOUNT ON HAND | MONTHLY CONS. | ORDERED FOR | SIGNED | APPROVED

A typical purchase requisition is shown as Exhibit 4-1. It is designed for use for either materials or services. At the top of the form provision is made for inserting the 16-digit code of the fiberboard company listed in Chapter 3. This code is placed on the requisition by the person originating it and determines the account to be charged when the material or service is received and the invoice is entered for payment. It is important that the originator insert the code, for in this manner he controls the charges to accounts for which he has responsibility. In many companies a copy of the requisition is sent to the accounting department for checking of the propriety of the code. The originator also inserts the quantity to be ordered, the description of the material, the amount on hand, the monthly consumption, and any special notation as to the purpose for which the material is ordered. A copy may also be sent to the traffic department for shipping instructions, or these may be inserted by the purchasing department. Provision is made for the purchasing agent to record three price quotations. After these are received and entered, he inserts the dollar amount of the order and notes the vendor with whom the order is to be placed.

Purchase Orders

A purchase order (Exhibit 4-2) is prepared from the purchase requisition, with sufficient copies to meet the requirements of the company

Exhibit 4-2
Purchase Order

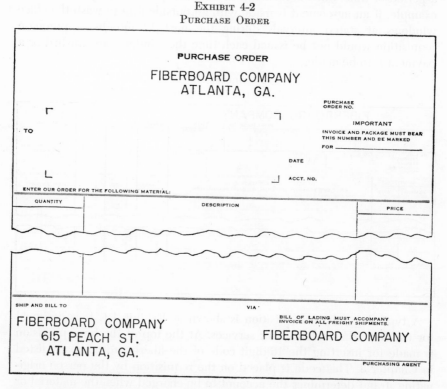

organization structure. Usually at least four are prepared, the original for the vendor and copies for the purchasing department files, the accounts payable department, and the receiving department. The copy for the latter department may have the quantity ordered blocked out so that the count of material at receiving will not be influenced by the quantities shown on the purchase order.

The purchase order is a vital document in the materials accounting process, for when it is accepted by the vendor, it becomes a contract. As such it has established a commitment for the acquisition of materials at a stated price. As a contract it must be complete and specific. Therefore, following the listing of items ordered would be stated the required delivery date, packing and shipping instructions, billing instructions, and terms of payment. It is customery to include clauses and conditions as to warranty, patent infringement, contractor's liability when services are to be performed, etc. Such clauses may be inserted as required or be printed on the face or back of the order with a definite and well-marked statement that they are a part of the contract.

Receiving Reports

When material is received, the quantity is determined by counting, weighing, or other measurement by the receiving department. This is

EXHIBIT 4-3
RECEIVING REPORT

RECEIVING RECORD						No. 1 ACCOUNTS PAYABLE COPY			
ORDERED FROM						DATE		ENT. NO.	
RECEIVED FROM						ORD. NO.		REQ. NO.	
SHIPPING POINT						CODE			
						PROJECT		WEIGHT	
						CHG. PREPAID		COLLECT	
						VIA			
						BOXES	CRT'NS	CRATES	PKGS.	BAGS	BBLS.	DRUMS
						CAR			
						SEAL			
						CHECKED BY		DATE POST.	
						REC'D BY		DATE	

done to assure that payment is made only for goods actually received. It also provides the quantities to be entered on the inventory records. Any error in count will result in inventory differences and distort subsequent inventory and cost-control processes.

The receiving department prepares receiving reports, either on a special form (Exhibit 4-3) or on a receiving copy or copies of the purchase order. Copies of the receiving reports are distributed to other departments requiring the information for subsequent records. A typical distribution of copies would be to accounts payable, inventory control, storeroom, cost accounting, and purchasing. If the materials are to be tested, a copy of the receiving report is sent to the laboratory with a sample of the material. Approval of the laboratory is then reported to the accounts payable department and the storeroom prior to payment of the invoice or usage of the material. For raw material the accounting-department copy of the receiving report provides the quantities to be posted to the detailed inventory records (Exhibit 4-6).

Payment of Invoices

Vendors' invoices are sent to the accounts payable department. Here they are matched with the receiving reports, purchase orders, and laboratory-test reports. Quantities, prices, discounts, transportation charges, and the net amount of the invoice are verified. Any discrepancies are referred to the purchasing department for approval or correction.

EXHIBIT 4-4

ACCOUNTS PAYABLE VOUCHER

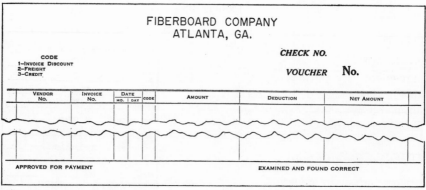

Many companies require vendors' invoices to be submitted in duplicate or triplicate, so that copies may be sent to the departments requiring information as to quantities, prices, and total amounts, such as the accounting department for the actual costs to be recorded on the detailed inventory ledger cards. Other companies maintain an invoice register in which approved invoices are recorded for control, and the original is then routed through the other departments requiring information from it. Still others prepare a summary of the data for the other departments and retain the invoice in the accounts payable department.

Approved vendors' invoices are filed by vendor, by date of payment. On that date a voucher is prepared (Exhibit 4-4), on which are listed the invoices of the vendor covered by the voucher. If credits are due from the vendor, these are also listed on the voucher. The check is drawn for the net amount indicated by the voucher. A combination check and voucher form is used frequently. The upper portion is the check, and the lower portion, perforated for separation, is the voucher listing the items covered. The check and original voucher are sent to the vendor, and the voucher copy, with a copy of the check appearing on it, is filed with the invoices by vendor. A third copy may be filed by voucher number. For cross reference invoices are numbered and recorded in an invoice register showing the invoice number, vendor, and voucher number. The recording in the invoice register may be done when the invoices are received or after they are attached to the voucher for payment.

Internal Control

The purchasing, receiving, and payment procedures for goods and services are a vital part of the system of internal control. The authorization of persons who may issue purchase requisitions and the limitation of the authority of the purchasing department to placing purchase orders only on properly approved requisitions prevents the indiscriminate ordering of goods and services. The matching of purchase orders, receiving records, and vendors' invoices assures that payments are not made for goods and services not received and that the terms of the invoice are in agreement with those specified in the purchase order. This entire process aids in the control of costs, for any payment for goods and services must ultimately be reflected in the accounts as a cost of the current period or of a future period.

Distribution of Charges

Distribution to inventory, expense, and capital accounts of charges originating from vendors' invoices may be accomplished in many ways. In smaller companies a voucher register may be used, with a voucher prepared for each invoice. Approved invoices are entered in the register and distribution to accounts made in columns established for repetitive charges and a miscellaneous column for less frequent charges. If a voucher is not prepared for each invoice, the distribution may be made in the invoice register as each invoice is recorded. Another method is to have perforated sections on the lower portion of the voucher. Separate account charges are recorded on each of these, and they are then separated, sorted, and totaled by account. Entries are then made in the general journal for the total for each account and subsidiary records posted from the detail sections.

When machine accounting is used the distribution is made by preparing a card for each charge on each invoice and mechanically sorting and summarizing these. After charges originating on vendors' invoices are recorded, it may be necessary to make changes because of transfer of materials to departments other than those for which they are ordered, errors made in coding the charges, etc. This may be accomplished through credit requisitions (Exhibit 4-5). These are summarized for each accounting period as to debits and credits for journalizing and posting to the respective accounts. These credit requisitions are approved by both the department charged and the department credited, so that each will have knowledge of the effect on their inventories or costs.

This procedure for accounting for expenditures, from the initiation of the purchase requisition to the distribution of the charges from vendors' invoices, is applicable to all expenditures—for raw material, supplies, services, direct-expense items, and capital items. From this point forward

EXHIBIT 4-5
CREDIT REQUISITION

CREDIT REQUISITION .... 19.......
(Date)

ORDER OR PROJECT NO. ....   ORDER OR PROJECT NO. ....

CREDIT CODE						CHARGE CODE					
C.P.D.	Control	Source	Dept.	Oper.	Class.	C.P.D.	Control	Source	Dept.	Oper.	Class.

Signed.. Signed..

Dept.. Dept..

DESCRIPTION	QUANTITY	PRICE	VALUE

this chapter will cover procedures applicable only to materials charged to inventory accounts as purchased.

Inventory Records

Inventories are usually classified as raw materials, work in process, finished stock, or supplies. In any one company additional classifications may be used either as accounts on the general ledger or in subsidiary records. For example, the supplies inventory may be broken down into general stores, one-purpose repair parts, stationery, and fuel.

Supplies other than fuel are usually kept in one or more storerooms with perpetual inventory records for each item maintained on cards (Exhibit 4-6). Items are issued from the storerooms only upon submission of authorized requisitions. These show the accounting code to be charged and a description of the material. The storekeeper inserts the value of the item on the requisitions, and they are summarized as to charges to the respective accounts and credited to the supplies inventory.

Exhibit 4-7 is a typical requisition for supplies, in this instance a tabulating card on which the data can be punched for machine accounting. Fuel usage is determined by recording weights or gallons moving to the boilers or by disappearance, that is, quantity on opening inventory plus

Exhibit 4-6
Perpetual Inventory Card

PERPETUAL INVENTORY

Plant ____________ Location ____________

								Account	Max.	Min.
Received				Issued				Inventory		
Date	P.O. No.	Quantity	Cost	Date	Req. No.	Quantity	Cost	Quantity	Value

Exhibit 4-7
Stores Requisition

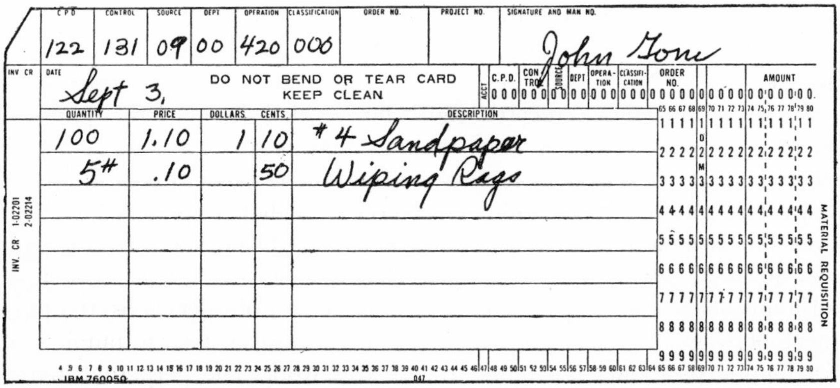

purchases minus closing inventory. The latter requires a physical inventory at the close of each accounting period. The perpetual inventory records for supplies usually show the value of the items also, to facilitate the costing of requisitions. The bases of valuation are discussed later in this chapter.

Accounting for supplies is frequently simplified by charging those items to expense as purchased which have a low unit value and are carried in small quantities. When this is done, the stores records show quantities only. Such items customarily used for maintenance purposes are charged as expense of the maintenance department and other items as expense of the department initiating the purchase requisition or customarily using them if purchase requisitions are issued by the storeskeeper on the basis of his indicated minimum inventories. This simplified procedure may be carried one step further by inserting a divider in the stock bin or drawer to separate the minimum stock and issuing a purchase requisition for the item when this minimum is reached. When this procedure is followed, it is not necessary to carry perpetual inventory cards for items expensed as purchased.

Perpetual records are also maintained for raw materials and finished stock. Because of the frequent movement of these items and the many variations in methods of valuing them, the perpetual records usually do not show values. Otherwise they are identical with those used for supplies inventories.

Work in process which is actually moving through the productive operations does not lend itself to perpetual inventory techniques, since movement is frequent and fairly rapid. In these instances inventories are secured through physical count at the close of each accounting period. The forms used for recording the count may be filed as the supporting records for the ledger control account, or they may be transferred to summary listings. When material is partially processed and then held for further processing, either in a storeroom or in production operations, perpetual records are desirable.

PHYSICAL COUNTS

Perpetual inventory records must be verified by periodic physical counts. This may be done on a rotating basis with some items counted each day or week, or a complete count may be made at the end of a year. The rotating verification is preferable in that it spreads the work over the year and usually the physical count can be made by foremen and clerks as part of their regular work schedule. In contrast, a count of all items at one time usually requires a shutdown of operations, the payment of wages for inventory taking, and the use of a large number of production personnel not familiar with this work. The perpetual inventory cards should be marked as to the date of physical count and adjusted for any differences. The quantity differences should be valued according to the basis of inventory valuation and the adjustment made to the control accounts on the general ledger. The amount of the adjustment is debited or credited to an account Difference, Perpetual and Physical Inventory, with the contra debit or credit to the inventory account, and is reflected in profit and loss in the period in which the count is made. Thus the results of rotating checks are reflected from month to month rather than at the close of the accounting period.

Valuation of Inventories

One of the most important aspects of accounting for materials is the valuation of the inventories. The general principles applicable to the valuation of inventories of mercantile and manufacturing enterprises are stated in *Accounting Research Bulletin* 29, issued by the Committee on Accounting Procedure, American Institute of Accountants. Any basis of valuation which is not inconsistent with the statements of this bulletin is considered to be in conformity with generally accepted accounting practice.

While the prime consideration in the valuation of inventories is cost, there are a number of acceptable methods of determining the cost of inventories at the close of any accounting period. The most commonly used methods are first-in first-out (fifo), average, and last-in first-out (lifo). The selection of the method for determining cost for inventory valuation is important, for it has a direct bearing on the cost of goods sold and consequently on profit. When a method is selected, it must be used consistently and cannot be changed from year to year in order to secure the most favorable cost of sales for each year. Therefore the method must be selected in the light of the probable effects on the cost of goods sold over a period of years. The effect of the three methods can best be appraised by following a series of transactions with all data identical except for the method of determining cost for the valuation of the closing inventory.

The basic data and calculations are presented in Exhibit 4-8 where cost for the closing inventory is determined under the fifo method. With an opening inventory of 10,000 units at $2.10, the first 1,000 units sold are charged to cost of goods sold at this opening inventory rate. The October 18 shipment of 4,000 units is costed on the basis of the first receipts of the year: January 9, 1,000 at $2.21; January 27, 1,000 at $2.31; and February 16, 2,000 at $2.41. The 1,000 each shipped on November 12 and December 10 are costed on the basis of the 2,000 received on March 3. Therefore the cost of the 13,000 on inventory December 31 is composed of the receipts of March 29, October 4 and 23, November 24, and December 31, and the value is the sum of the costs of these receipts.

Exhibit 4-9 uses the same basic data as Exhibit 4-8, but with cost determined on an average basis. Here each purchase is added to inventory and an average rate determined. Shipments are charged into cost of sales at this average until another lot is received, when a new average unit inventory cost is calculated. In actual practice it is customary to summarize shipments for a month, credit these to inventory at the average cost rate as of the first of the month, and then add to the remainder the summarized receipts of the month and calculate a new average rate at which shipments of the next month are costed. This latter procedure has the advantage of simplicity and results in substantially the same inventory value as when a new average is determined when each individual lot is received.

EXHIBIT 4-8
FIFO INVENTORY VALUATION

Date	Receipts			Shipments			Inventory		
	Quantity	Cost	Value	Quantity	Cost	Value	Quantity	Cost	Value
Jan. 1.......							10,000	$2.10	$21,000
9.......	1,000	$2.21	$ 2,210				11,000	——	23,210
12......				2,000	$2.10	$ 4,200	9,000	——	19,010
27......	1,000	2.31	2,310				10,000	——	21,320
Feb. 10......				4,000	2.10	8,400	6,000	——	12,920
16......	2,000	2.41	4,820				8,000	——	17,740
Mar. 3.......	2,000	2.40	4,800				10,000	——	22,540
17......				4,000	2.10	8,400	6,000	——	14,140
29......	4,000	2.29	9,160				10,000	——	23,300
Oct. 4.......	2,000	2.14	4,280				12,000	——	27,580
18......				4,000	*	9,340	8,000	——	18,240
23......	2,000	2.04	4,080				10,000	——	22,320
Nov. 12......				1,000	2.40	2,400	9,000	——	19,920
24......	3,000	2.00	6,000				12,000	——	25,920
Dec. 10......				1,000	2.40	2,400	11,000	——	23,520
31......	2,000	2.02	4,040				13,000	——	27,560
Total.......	19,000	$2.195	$41,700	16,000	——	$35,140		——	

*		
1,000	2.21	2,210
1,000	2.31	2,310
2,000	2.41	4,820
4,000	——	9,340

Both the fifo and average cost methods permit the costing of sales each month and carrying forward a known inventory cost rate. In contrast, under the lifo method the cost of goods sold and the closing inventory value can be determined only after the final lot of the year has been received. The reason for this is that withdrawals are costed on the basis of the inverse sequence of receipts; i.e., the last in is the first out. The calculation of cost of goods sold and cost for inventory valuation under a "straight" lifo method is shown at the top of Exhibit 4-10. Since calculations can only be made at the close of the year, the receipts are added to the opening inventory to arrive at the total inventory to account for. From this is deducted the closing inventory. Since the last in is the first out, the shipments of 16,000 are assumed to have been made up of the receipts of December 31, November 24, October 23, October 4, March 29, March 3, and 1,000 of the receipts of February 16.

There are two variations of the lifo method which are permissible for inventory valuation for Federal income tax computation and therefore are commonly used. Under the straight lifo method as presented here the costs of additions to inventory in any year are the costs of the first

EXHIBIT 4-9
AVERAGE COST INVENTORY VALUATION

Date	Receipts			Shipments			Inventory		
	Quantity	Cost	Value	Quantity	Cost	Value	Quantity	Cost	Value
Jan. 1.......							10,000	$2.10	$21,000
9.......	1,000	$2.21	$ 2,210				11,000	2.11	23,210
12.......				2,000	$2.11	$ 4,220	9,000	2.11	18,990
27.......	1,000	2.31	2,310				10,000	2.13	21,300
Feb. 10.......				4,000	2.13	8,520	6,000	2.13	12,780
16.......	2,000	2.41	4,820				8,000	2.20	17,600
Mar. 3.......	2,000	2.40	4,800				10,000	2.24	22,400
17.......				4,000	2.24	8,960	6,000	2.24	13,440
29.......	4,000	2.29	9,160				10,000	2.26	22,600
Oct. 4.......	2,000	2.14	4,280				12,000	2.24	26,880
18.......				4,000	2.24	8,960	8,000	2.24	17,920
23.......	2,000	2.04	4,080				10,000	2.20	22,000
Nov. 12.......				1,000	2.20	2,200	9,000	2.20	19,800
24.......	3,000	2.00	6,000				12,000	2.15	25,800
Dec. 10.......				1,000	2.15	2,150	11,000	2.15	23,650
31.......	2,000	2.02	4,040				13,000	2.13	27,690
Total.......	19,000		$41,700	16,000		$35,010			

equivalent quantity of purchases of the year. Under the first variation the cost of the additions is taken at the average cost rate of the year. Under the second variation the costs of the additions in any year are the costs of the last equivalent quantity of purchases in the year. These are illustrated in the second and third portions of Exhibit 4-10.

Under the lifo method, regardless of the method used for costing additions to inventory in any one year, the years are on a straight lifo basis as to additions and reductions. Thus, the cost used for valuation the first year the lifo method is used is the cost used for that quantity in every year so long as the quantity at the close of any year is not less than the original quantity. Cost of additions in a year as determined by the method selected (fifo, average, or lifo for the year) also is used year after year so long as that quantity plus the original quantity remains on inventory. Reductions in inventory result in the elimination of the additions of the most recent year and from there on back into the original quantity if the inventory drops that far. Exhibit 4-11 shows closing inventories for 6 years. As quantities on hand at the close of the year in-

EXHIBIT 4-10
LIFO COST INVENTORY VALUATION

	Quantity		Cost		Value
Straight lifo:					
Inventory Jan. 1	——	10,000	$2.10	——	$21,000
Receipts	——	19,000	——	——	41,700
Total	——	29,000	——	——	62,700
Inventory Dec. 31	——	13,000			
Jan. 1 Inventory	10,000	——	2.10	$21,000	
Receipts: Jan. 9	1,000	——	2.21	2,210	
Jan. 27	1,000	——	2.31	2,310	
Feb. 16	1,000	——	2.41	2,410	
Total	13,000	——	——	——	27,930
Shipments	——	16,000	——	——	$34,770
Additions at average cost:					
Inventory Jan. 1	——	10,000	2.10	——	$21,000
Receipts	——	19,000	2.195	——	41,700
Total	——	29,000	——	——	62,700
Inventory Dec. 31	——	13,000	——		
Jan. 1 Inventory	10,000	——	2.10	21,000	
Added Inventory	3,000	——	2.195	6,585	
Total	13,000	——	——	——	27,585
Shipments	——	16,000	——	——	$35,115
Additions at fifo cost:					
Inventory Jan. 1	——	10,000	2.10	——	$21,000
Receipts	——	19,000	——	——	41,700
Total	——	29,000	——	——	62,700
Inventory Dec. 31	——	13,000			
Jan. 1 Inventory	10,000	——	2.10	21,000	
Receipts: Dec. 31	2,000	——	2.02	4,040	
Nov. 24	1,000	——	2.00	2,000	
Total	13,000	——	——	——	27,040
Shipments	——	16,000	——	——	$35,660

creased in the first and second years, they were costed at the applicable rate for the respective year. In the third year the reduction in quantities removed the additions of the second year and 1,000 of those of the first year. In the fourth year quantities increased, and the increase was costed on the basis of costs of that year. In the fifth year a substantial reduction in quantities took out the fourth and first years' additions and

1,000 of the original quantity. Lifo costs of these passed out of the picture with this reduction, and in the sixth year the increase over the fifth year was costed on the basis of acquisitions in the sixth year.

The method of determining lifo valuation discussed here is known as the "unit method." Valuations are based on specific unit costs. Recent

EXHIBIT 4-11
LIFO INVENTORY—6 YEARS

	Quantity	Rate	Value
Opening inventory at cost—first year................	10,000	$2.10	$21,000
Closing inventory:			
First year—opening inventory....................	10,000	2.10	21,000
first year's additions..................	3,000	2.31	6,930
Total...........................	13,000	——	$27,930
Second year—first year's opening inventory.........	10,000	2.10	$21,000
first year's additions................	3,000	2.31	6,930
second year's additions..............	2,000	2.20	4,400
Total...........................	15,000	——	$32,330
Third year—first year's opening inventory..........	10,000	2.10	$21,000
first year's additions................	2,000	2.31	4,620
Total...........................	12,000	——	$25,620
Fourth year—first year's opening inventory.........	10,000	2.10	$21,000
first year's additions................	2,000	2.31	4,620
fourth year's additions..............	1,000	2.50	2,500
Total...........................	13,000	——	$28,120
Fifth year—remainder of first year's opening inventory.............................	9,000	2.10	$18,900
Sixth year—remainder of first year's opening inventory.............................	9,000	2.10	$18,900
sixth year's additions................	1,000	2.60	2,600
Total...........................	10,000	——	$21,500

developments in lifo accounting have brought the "dollar basis" into use. Instead of using specific unit costs, the total dollar value of inventories is used and index factors applied to adjust cost to lifo. The effect on cost of sales is the same as that of the unit method, the charging of the last costs to cost of sales. This method is used primarily by department stores but is also being adopted by some manufacturing companies.

Cost need not be determined on the same basis for all inventories. It is not infrequent in a company to determine cost by different methods for different classes of inventory or even for different items in a class. Fifo cost is used more widely than any other. However, supplies are frequently valued on average cost. This simplifies the work of the stores-keeper in that he does not have to match withdrawals with each lot purchased. Another frequent practice is to determine cost for major raw materials on a lifo basis and for all other materials on a fifo basis.

When the current replacement cost of material on inventory at the close of a year is less than the cost at which it is valued or if the goods cannot be used or sold at a value equivalent to their cost on inventory less estimated cost of disposal, the inventory value is reduced to market. Thus the acceptable basis of inventory valuation is the "lower of cost or market." Adjustments to market are reflected at the close of the accounting period when they are known. They may be estimated for interim accounting and reports, but such estimates must be corrected to reflect true market conditions at the close of the year. To the extent that inventory values must be reduced from cost to market, profits are reduced. So, here too inventory valuation is an important factor in profit determination and control.

Application of Inventory Costs

Perpetual inventory records (Exhibit 4-6) should be maintained for all raw materials if maximum control is to be achieved. Some raw materials can be carried in central storerooms. However, when the material is bulky, this is impractical, and storage is in areas adjacent to the production operation in which they are used. Charges to Work in Process are determined by requisitions from central stores or by usage reported by operators or clerks in the production operations (Exhibits 7-7 and 13-1).

If fifo or average costs are used for valuation purposes, the detail records should show unit cost and dollar value. This provides for continuous valuation for checking with the general-ledger control accounts. If lifo costs are used, an estimated or standard value is used during the year, with adjustments made to the lifo value at the close of the year. The requisitions or usage reports for direct materials are priced at the applicable unit rates determined on the basis selected for interim inventory valuation. These are summarized and charged to Work in Process:

Dr.   Work in Process
Cr.   Raw Material

When job costs are compiled, the summary is made by jobs, and the charges to each job are posted to the job cost cards. With a process cost system the summary is by production operations using the material. The total posted to jobs or the total charged to all operations will agree with the amounts recorded on the general ledger. The cost of raw material used divided by the units produced provides the unit direct-material cost.

Inventory Obsolescence

Obsolescence of inventories should be determined on the basis of changes in materials specifications or lack of movement from inventory.

EXHIBIT 4-12
REQUEST FOR INVENTORY REVALUATION

FIBERBOARD COMPANY

Request for Inventory Revaluation Because of Obsolescence

Copy No. 2

CLASSIFICATION:

Raw Material ☐   Date_____
Shipping and Packing Supplies ☐
Goods-in-Process ☐   Plant_____ Request No._____
Finished Stock ☐
General Use Stores ☐   Approval for the following obsolescence is requested:
One-Purpose Stores ☐

Comodity No.	Quantity	Unit	Description	Present Value	Markdown	New Value	Recommended Disposition
TOTALS							

Discussion and Explanation of this Request:

APPROVALS:

Plant Manager

Prod. Management

Division Mgr.

Prod. Plan. Dept.

Final

Frequent reviews should be made of all inventories, and when obsolescence is indicated, a request for revaluation (Exhibit 4-12) should be prepared for approval by management. The difference between original and obsolete value should be recorded by a charge to an operating account, Inventory Obsolescence, and a credit to Inventory. If the material is scrapped, this will be for the full inventory value of the material. If it is anticipated that the material can be sold at reduced value or used in areas where it will be worth less than its value, the entry would be only for the amount of write-down. Some companies carry a salvage inventory and transfer to it materials which may be sold or used at reduced values. Where this is done the entry would be:

Dr.   Salvage Inventory
Dr.   Inventory Obsolescence
     Cr.   Raw Material or Supplies

When repair parts for specific machines are carried in the supplies inventory, it may be desirable to anticipate the obsolescence which will occur if the machine is scrapped or sold before the parts are used. This is accomplished by arbitrarily setting a percentage by which the value will be reduced for each year for which there was no movement of the part from inventory or by relating the annual write-down to the expected life of the machine. Such parts carried in the supplies inventory would be gears, bearings, etc., which have a cost which is low in relation to the value of the machine. Major spare parts for a machine would be capitalized and depreciated along with the machine and not carried in the supplies inventory.

REVIEW QUESTIONS

1. Why is the purchase requisition important in the control of material costs?
2. What internal uses are made of the copies of the purchase order?
3. How do receiving reports assist in protecting company assets?
4. What factors must be considered before an invoice is approved for payment?
5. What is the purpose of the distribution to accounts of charges originating from vendors' invoices?
6. What differences are there between the accounting procedures for purchases of raw materials and for purchases of machinery?
7. Why are raw materials and supplies carried in separate inventory accounts?
8. What are perpetual inventories?
9. How frequently and by what methods should perpetual inventories be verified?
10. How does the valuation of inventories affect profit?
11. Describe the fifo method of inventory valuation.
12. Describe the lifo method of inventory valuation.
13. What are the advantages and disadvantages of the lifo method of inventory valuation?
14. What is meant by the unit method of lifo valuation? The dollar basis?
15. What are the causes of inventory obsolescence?

PROBLEMS

1. A mousetrap manufacturing company uses lumber, wire, and brass plate in its product. The summary of vendors' invoices for goods and services for a

month is shown below. All the goods and services were received, and the invoices are in order for payment.

Lumber......................	$5,183
Wire........................	1,968
Brass plate.................	779
Window washing.............	97
Coal........................	1,310
New automobile.............	2,000
Desk........................	100
Machinery repair............	420
Nuts and bolts..............	46

Inventory accounts are Supplies, Raw Material, Work in Process, and Finished Stock.

Prepare a summary journal entry distributing the charges to the proper accounts.

2. Inventory of a given raw material at cost, not in excess of market, at January 1 was 20,000 units and $30,000.

During the year purchases were as follows:

Jan. 14.....................	2,000	$ 3,100
Mar. 19....................	3,000	4,800
Apr. through Sept...........	100,000	155,000
Nov. 2.....................	2,000	3,260
Dec. 7.....................	2,000	3,300

Usage during the year was 107,000 units.

a. Determine the December 31 inventory quantity and value on the fifo method.

b. Assuming the company adopted the lifo method of inventory valuation for the year, what would the value of the closing inventory have been on the straight lifo basis?

CHAPTER 5

Accounting for Labor

Labor costs may be defined as the payments to workers which are based on the hours worked or the quantities of material produced. These costs are referred to as "wages," in contrast with "salaries," which are based upon a rate per week or month and are less directly related to hours worked or production. The accounting for labor costs begins with the hiring of the employee and extends through the distribution of his gross earnings to jobs, products, and work centers. It includes the accounting for deductions required by law or by agreements with employees; for supplementary costs such as overtime premium, shift differential, vacation pay, group insurance, and retirement plans; and for substantiation of compliance with Federal and state laws governing hours of work and earnings per hour.

Employment Records

Since the first step in wage payment is to ascertain that payments are made only to bona fide employees, the employment record is a part of the payroll process. For adequate internal control the employment function should be separate from that of the supervision of the employee. This is accomplished by having a central employment office for the plant, or in smaller plants having the plant manager or other executive do the hiring. The person who does the hiring issues written authorizations to place the employees on the payroll. These, after being approved as required by plant policy, are sent to the paymaster or payroll department and become the authorization for payment of wages when time or production are reported for the employee. They are supplemented by U.S. Treasury Department Form W-4, which establishes the withholding exemptions for Federal income tax. The employment-record form is designed not only for use when an employee is hired but also for authorizing subsequent changes in rates, jobs, etc., and also for termination of employment. The file of initial and subsequent forms for each employee

54

is an integral part of his employment record, with the latest one determining his payroll status.

The employment card is frequently supplemented by a more detailed personnel record providing information as to skills and prior experience of the employee and for a record of his history while employed by the company. In a large company or plant it is desirable to have these supplementary records on cards which can be "key-sorted," or have the

EXHIBIT 5-1

TIME RECORD

Division _____				TIME RECORD													
Dept. _____		CODE:															
Section _____		I ILLNESS								H HOLIDAY							
D.O. or Plant _____		ID ILLNESS DISABILITY BENEFITS PAYABLE (Issue 1693)								V VACATION							
		A ABSENCE (Other reason) PAID								VH Extra Day Off Due to							
Approval: _____		AN ABSENCE (Other reason) NOT PAID (Issue 1693)								Holiday During Vacation							
Approval: _____		TB ABSENCE (For Time-Off) SUBJECT TO MAKE UP								S SCHEDULED DAY OFF							

For complete description of codes refer to Company Policy.

THE UNDERSIGNED AGREES THAT THE REGULAR SALARY RECEIVED IS COMPENSATION FOR UP TO EIGHT HOURS A DAY OR FORTY HOURS A WORK WEEK AND THE RESPECTIVE HOURS OF WORK HERE STATED ARE CORRECT. NAME	WEEK ENDING:										THESE COLUMNS FOR HOME OFFICE USE						
	MON.	TUE.	WED.	THU.	FRI.	SAT.	SUN.	WEEK TOTAL	✓	STAN. TOTAL HRS./WK.	DAILY O.T.	SAT.	SUN.	HOL.	TOTAL O.T. HRS.	LESS T.B OR S.H#S.	TOTAL HOURS TO PAY
Emp. Sig.																	
Emp. Sig.																	
Emp. Sig.																	
Emp. Sig.																	
Emp. Sig.																	
Emp. Sig.																	
Emp. Sig.																	

Remarks or Explanation Pertaining to Schedule of Working or Overtime.

1. Standard Total Hours Per Week for each employee is the total number of hours the employee regularly works each week (i.e., total weekly hours not including overtime hours).

Note: Standard Total Hours Per Week: Enter only for those employees who worked daily or weekly overtime.

2. If overtime compensation is requested for more than one employee on this form, show Standard Total Hours Per Week for each employee concerned.

information transferred in code to punched cards to expedite the selection of employees for jobs requiring their special skills or for transfer and promotion.

Time-worked Records

It is customary for employees paid on the basis of hours worked or units produced to record their hours worked by ringing in and out on a time-clock card. However, in some plants the hours worked are recorded on time sheets (Exhibit 5-1) by the foreman or a clerk, and this is signed by the employee to indicate his acceptance of its accuracy. The time-clock cards or time sheets may be for a week or for a day depending upon the requirements of the plant. When clock cards are used, the hours worked may also be posted to a permanent record (Exhibit 5-2) to provide information for the foreman as to shifts worked, daily and weekly overtime worked, and conformance with Federal and state legislation regarding premium hours of overtime.

Computation of Gross Wages

The method of determining gross wages, the cost system used, the products, and the production processes all have an important bearing

EXHIBIT 5-2
HOURS-OF-WORK RECORD

HOURS OF WORK RECORD

CLOCK No.

YEAR _____   NAME

WEEK ENDING	CLOCK RINGS							DAILY HOURS							HOURS WORKED	DAILY HRS. PER WEEK	7TH DAY AND HOLIDAYS	WALSH HEALY	WEEKLY	TOTAL HRS. WORKED TO DATE	AVE. HRS. PER WEEK	WEEKS WORKED
	S	M	T	W	T	F	S	S	M	T	W	T	F	S			PREMIUM OVERTIME HRS.						
Jan. 2																						
Jan. 9																						
Jan. 16																						
Jan. 23																						
Jan. 30																						
Feb. 6																						
May 29																						
June 5																						
June 12																						
June 19																						
June 26																						

Form 4111.

THIS RECORD IS PERMANENT — FILE IN PERSONNEL FOLDER AFTER COMPLETION

upon the forms used and procedures for calculating employees' gross wages. There are three basic methods of determining employee earnings:

1. A stated rate per hour worked
2. A stated rate per unit of production
3. Incentive plans under which increments are added to earnings at hourly rates as the quantity or quality of production exceeds standard levels

HOURLY RATES

If the employee is paid a stated rate per hour, his gross wages can be computed on the clock card or time sheet by extending the hours worked by his hourly rate. Premiums paid for overtime work can also be calculated on these records. However, because gross wages must be distributed to operations, to job orders, and sometimes to products, it is more frequent practice to make the calculations on other forms which provide for both calculation and distribution. The hours recorded on these are always checked against those recorded on the attendance records to assure that the hours paid are in agreement with the recorded hours worked.

When a job-order cost system is used, the employees may be required to ring in and out on a record card at the start and finish of each job. Production is then recorded on these cards, rates per hour are applied, and wages computed for each job. Such cards then serve both for wage

EXHIBIT 5-3
TIME CARD

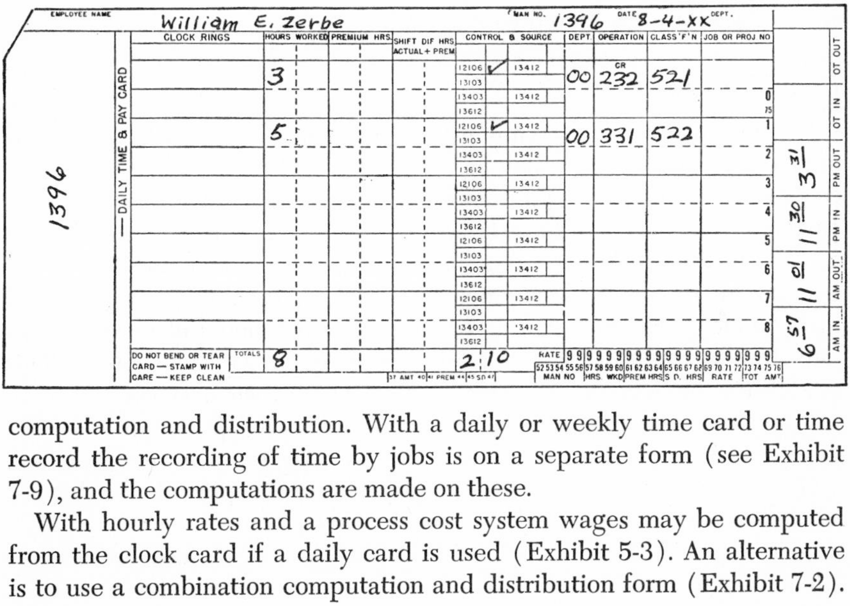
EMPLOYEE NAME William E. Zerbe MAN NO. 1396 DATE 8-4-XX DEPT.
CLOCK RINGS | HOURS WORKED | PREMIUM HRS. | SHIFT DIF HRS ACTUAL + PREM | CONTROL & SOURCE | DEPT | OPERATION | CLASS'F'N | JOB OR PROJ NO
3 | 12106 | 13412 | 00 | 232 | 521
5 | 12106 | 13412 | 00 | 331 | 522
DAILY TIME & PAY CARD
1396
AM IN 6 57 | AM OUT 11 01 | PM IN 11 30 | PM OUT 3 31 | OT IN | OT OUT
DO NOT BEND OR TEAR CARD — STAMP WITH CARE — KEEP CLEAN | TOTALS 8 | 2.10
RATE | MAN NO | HRS. WKD | PREM HRS | S. D. HRS | RATE | TOT. AMT.

computation and distribution. With a daily or weekly time card or time record the recording of time by jobs is on a separate form (see Exhibit 7-9), and the computations are made on these.

With hourly rates and a process cost system wages may be computed from the clock card if a daily card is used (Exhibit 5-3). An alternative is to use a combination computation and distribution form (Exhibit 7-2).

PIECE RATES

When wages are paid at a rate per unit of production, the forms and procedures of calculation can be the same as for rates per hour, with units produced rather than hours worked determining the amounts earned. It is not uncommon to guarantee a minimum rate per hour. If this is done, the wages based on production must be summarized and a rate per hour determined for the period for which a minimum hourly rate is guaranteed—a day, a week, or other pay period. If wages on a production basis average less than the guaranteed minimum per hour, "make-up" pay must be added to bring hourly wages up to the minimum. Exhibit 5-4 illustrates the computation of gross wages for piecework with a guaranteed average hourly rate per day of $2.00. Make-up pay may be classified either as direct or indirect labor, depending upon company policy.

INCENTIVE PLANS

There are innumerable incentive plans and modifications of plans, but in all of them the calculation of wages is too complex to be made on the time card or other hours of work record. Exhibit 5-5 is an example of the computation of gross wages under an incentive plan, with a process cost system in use. In this illustration the incentive pay is based on the production of a crew of workers rather than of an individual. Incentive is paid on measured work, and space is provided on the form for two different charges for unmeasured work.

Premium Pay

Payment of overtime premium for hours worked in excess of a stated number per day or week may be required by law or by agreements with employees. When such premium is paid and an incentive plan for wage payment is in effect, the overtime premium pay is usually based on the actual rate per hour earned rather than on the base hourly rate. For example, in Exhibit 5-5, the employees worked 10 hours and are entitled to overtime premium (time and half time) on 2 hours of work. Therefore straight-time earnings including bonus are shown as a subtotal. This establishes the average rates per hour on which their overtime premium will be based. An extra half-hour rate on 2 hours is 1 premium hour, and this is shown in the hours column for computing the overtime premium.

Overtime premium cannot be assumed to be applicable to the last job performed in any one day or week. That job may or may not have been the specific cause of the overtime work. Therefore overtime premium is generally considered to be an expense item to be applied as such along with all other expense items to all products or jobs worked on in the operation where it was incurred.

An additional increment per hour is usually paid for hours worked on other than the day shift. The rate may be different for the second than for the third shift. With a day shift from 7 A.M. to 3 P.M. a differential may be paid for the 3 P.M. to 11 P.M. shift and a higher differential for the 11 P.M. to 7 A.M. shift. Usually the shift differential is a flat rate per straight-time hour worked on the shift, without regard to incentive earnings. In Exhibit 5-5 the employees worked on the 3-to-11 shift with a shift differential of $0.05 per hour, and it is assumed that this rate does not change because of the 2 hours of overtime which they worked. Shift differential is an expense item irrespective of the specific labor charges.

EXHIBIT 5-4

LABOR REPORT—PIECEWORK

FORM 4056

Plant *Atlanta*   CPD *122*

LABOR REPORT

Date *Oct 3, 19—*

Clock No.	Name	DIRECT LABOR 12106								Control				INDIRECT LABOR			
		Dept.	Opr.	Class	P or D	Quantity	Rate	Hrs.	Amt.	Source	Dept.	Opera.	Class	Dr, *Wr or Project No.	Rate	Hrs.	Amt.
7416	Kenneth More	00	422	522	P	13100	.001	7	13 10	131 14	06	422	000	1986	2.00	1	2 00
										131 03	00	422	001				90
1492	Elmer Black	00	422	522	P	17000	.001	8	17 00								
1493	Richard Almy	60	422	523	D	1540	.01	8	15 40	131 03	00	422	001				60
1496	Geo May	00	422	523	P	1600	.01	8	16 00								
1499	Wm Thomas	00	422	523	P	650	.01	3	6 50	131 14	00	422	000	1986	2.00	5	10 00
	Totals								67 90								13 50

Foreman *E. Rich*

EXHIBIT 5-5

LABOR REPORT—INCENTIVE

Operation 422   FINISHING   Shift 11-7 (3-11)   Date Oct. 3, 19

Performance index:
$$\frac{\text{STD MAN MIN}}{\text{ACT MAN MIN}} = 120$$

% Bonus:
$$\frac{P.I.-70}{2} = 25$$

Element	Production units	S.M.M./Unit 800	Std man min
MACHINE SET UP	2	2.	160
SANDING 12 X 12	428.5 M SQ.FT.	6.9	986
CUTTING 12 X 12	90 "	5.2	621
CUTTING 24 X 24	70 "	8.3	364
BEVELING 12 X 12	90 "	8.6	747
BEVELING 24 X 24	70 "	9.6	602
DRILLING 12 X 12	80 "	8.2	768
DRILLING 24 X 24		1.9	
PAINTING 12 X 12	80 "	1.7	152
PAINTING 24 X 24			
SUB-TOTAL			4,400

ADD ALLOWABLE DELAY: ELAPSED MIN. 20 X MEN 9 X .70   135

TOTAL STD. MAN MIN   4,535

ACTUAL MAN MIN   MEASURED MAN HRS   63 X 60   3,780

Clock No.	HRS	RATE	ST. TIME	BONUS	TOTAL	JOB OR CLASS	HRS	RATE	AMT.	JOB OR CLASS	HRS	RATE	AMT	Sub-total	OT premium HRS	RATE	AMT.	Shift diff HRS	RATE	AMT.	Total earnings
			12106 (Measured work)	Earnings				13103 Unmeasured work													
576	7	2.40	16.80	4.20	21.00	101	3	2.20	6.60					27.60	1	2.76	2.76	10	.05	.50	30.86
577	7	2.00	14.00	3.50	17.50	101	3	2.00	6.00					23.50	1	2.35	2.35	10	.05	.50	26.35
596	7	2.00	14.00	3.50	17.50	101	3	2.00	6.00					23.50	1	2.35	2.35	10	.05	.50	26.35
614	7	1.80	12.60	3.15	15.75	101	3	1.80	5.40					21.15	1	2.12	2.12	10	.05	.50	23.77
615	7	2.00	14.00	3.50	17.50	101	3	2.00	6.00					23.50	1	2.35	2.35	10	.05	.50	26.35
690	7	2.00	14.00	3.50	17.50	101	3	2.00	6.00					23.50	1	2.35	2.35	10	.05	.50	26.35
693	7	2.00	14.00	3.50	17.50	101	3	2.00	6.00					23.50	1	2.35	2.35	10	.05	.50	26.35
710	7	2.00	14.00	3.50	17.50	101	3	2.00	6.00					23.50	1	2.35	2.35	10	.05	.50	26.35
712	7	1.80	12.60	3.15	15.75	101	3	1.80	5.40					21.15	1	2.12	2.12	10	.05	.50	23.77
TOTAL 63			126.00	31.50	157.50		27		53.40					210.90			21.10			4.50	236.50

Clerk Sinclair

Foreman W. Borden

W – Hours worked   P – Overtime premium hours

The jobs or products worked on during a shift which requires a differential cannot be assumed to be the cause for working that shift. Therefore shift differential costs are included with expense just as are overtime premium costs.

Internal Control

The payroll procedures outlined in the preceding sections are designed to provide internal control over wage payments. For proper control it is first necessary to establish that wages are paid only to employees who are on the payroll and are not absent. A very common fraud is the padding of payrolls. Fictitious names are added to the payroll. Time or production are then reported for these names. When the payroll checks are drawn, they are extracted by the person or persons who padded the payroll and retained by them. Another method is to report time or production for employees who are absent for a full pay period.

Such frauds are prevented by a division of responsibilities and of clerical functions so as to require collusion. An example is the division of the employment and supervisory responsibilities. Another would be having one clerk compute the earnings and another prepare the checks and distribute them to the workers.

When employees are paid piece rates or incentives, they may attempt to report more production than they actually had. Here the production used for payroll purposes should be checked against that used in the cost accounting and cost-control records. Significant deviations between quantities shown on the perpetual inventories and those determined by physical counts should be investigated. The difference may be caused by reporting excessive production.

Distribution of Gross Earnings

Gross earnings as calculated on the time records, individual or crew production reports, or other forms are the costs charged to the respective accounts, i.e., direct labor to jobs or operations and to products, and indirect labor to operations and classifications. The method of making the distribution to these accounts will depend upon the number of employees and the number of charges for each employee or crew for each day. If the number of charges per day is not great, a hand distribution is the more economical. As the number increases a point is reached at which mechanical distribution is the better method. The labor report illustrated for the job-order cost system (Exhibit 7-9) was designed for manual distribution. This is accomplished by separation of the lower portion of the form, each portion containing a charge to a separate job or account, sorting these by jobs and accounts and making the postings from them. If earnings are calculated weekly instead of daily, the distribution methods are identical, but the frequency of distribution is reduced accordingly. It is important that the labor distribution be balanced with the total gross wages after each distribution is made. Errors are detected and corrected before the peak of work at the closing for the month. With manual distribution, adding-machine tapes are prepared for gross wages from the earnings-computation forms and of the postings to jobs or accounts, and the totals must be in agreement. With machine accounting, cumulative totals are carried of gross wages and charges to accounts and provide an automatic verification.

The accounting entries for gross labor costs are made from the distribution summaries. The entry is:

Dr. Work in Process (direct labor)
Dr. Expense (indirect labor, maintenance labor, etc.)
Dr. Fixed Assets (labor expended in construction of plant and equipment)
   Cr. Gross Payroll Accrued

With a daily calculation and distribution of earnings the total of the days of the month is the amount of the entry. When the calculation and distribution is made weekly, a separate calculation must be made for any portion of a week falling at the beginning or the end of a month if the books are to be closed monthly or if monthly variance and budget reports are desired. Thus for any one month there may be six periods to consider: the part of a week at the beginning of the month, the four full weeks of the month, and the part of a week at the end of a month.

Payroll Register and Deductions

The summarization of gross earnings by employee for each pay period is the first step in the preparation of the payroll register. Legal and agreed-upon deductions are then computed to arrive at the net amount to be paid to the employee. Income tax withheld and employee social-security taxes are based on the gross earnings. Certain retirement insurance plans and other employee benefit programs may include voluntary employee contributions based on his gross earnings. Other deductions such as the employee's share of hospitalization insurance cost are usually stated amounts per month, as are authorized deductions for government bonds, building and loan shares, savings funds, etc. With the number of deductions found in the average company it is customary to schedule those other than withheld income tax and social-security tax for different pay periods in the month, so as to equalize in so far as possible the impact on net earnings. This injects a schedule problem into the deduction procedure and requires the correlation of the specified deductions with the gross earnings of the proper pay period.

The payroll register is a listing of employees, by clock number and name, which shows the gross earnings, the deductions, the net pay and the check numbers where payment is made by check.

As with the labor distribution, the calculation of the amount of the deductions and the calculation of net pay may be done manually or mechanically. The volume of work and the time in which it must be completed will determine the most economical method to be used. If the work is done manually, the deductions are calculated and posted to the payroll register and deducted from gross earnings on it. If punched cards are used, the deductions are computed mechanically, they are collated with the gross earnings cards, and the payroll register showing gross earnings, deductions, and net earnings is prepared by the machine in one operation. The cards containing this summary information may also be used for preparing the pay checks by machine. The totals of the payroll register provide the amounts for the entries to the several accounts:

> Dr.   Gross Payroll Paid
>   Cr.   Cash (net earnings)
>   Cr.   Federal Income Tax Withheld
>   Cr.   FICA Tax Withheld
>   Cr.   Due Employees for Purchase of
>   U.S. Savings Bonds
>   Cr.   Employee Retirement Contribution
>   Cr.   Etc.

When this entry is made, the net balance of the Gross Payroll Paid and Gross Payroll Accrued accounts is the liability for unpaid wages. It is desirable to debit a separate account, Gross Payroll Paid, rather than Gross Payroll Accrued. By so doing the accrued account reflects total wage costs for the period, and the paid account reflects actual payments. These totals provide information for tax returns, other external and internal reports, and historical records.

Subsidiary deductions records are maintained for each employee for each class of deduction. These are used for the preparations of tax returns, issuance of bonds, payments to the employees' accounts in building and loan associations and banks, credits to retirement funds, etc. It is desirable to maintain separate control accounts on the general ledger for each of these, so as to record the company liability as long as the funds are in its custody. For example, deductions for bonds are credited to an account Due Employees for Purchase of U.S. Savings Bonds. When the bonds are issued, a check is drawn paying for them, and the entry is made debiting the liability account and crediting Cash.

Supplementary Costs of Labor

In addition to the accounting for gross earnings and deductions, the handling of the so-called "fringe benefits," or supplementary costs of labor, is also a part of the labor accounting process. The nature of these varies from company to company. Those most frequently encountered are vacation pay, nonworked-holiday pay, retirement, and group insurance. These costs are generally treated as expense and charged to separate source accounts by operations in the subsidiary expense ledgers. The amount charged to each operation is based on the total direct and indirect labor cost of the operation. Under this procedure they become a part of the total expense of each operation, and further accounting for them follows the accounting procedure for all expense. Sometimes these costs are related to the distribution of gross payroll and distributed to the same cost accounts (jobs, operations, products, indirect labor classifications, etc.) as the gross earnings. This has the disadvantage of requiring additional effort with no significant effect upon the unit costs of individual jobs or operations. Substantial accuracy is achieved through their treatment as expense.

Since vacation pay and nonworked-holiday costs are not incurred in ratio to the labor cost of a month and tend to bulk heavily in certain months of the year, special accounting treatment is desirable. The objective of this is to charge into costs of each month approximately one-twelfth of the annual cost of these items. This is accomplished through the use of equalizing accounts. An estimate of the amount for the year is made at the beginning of the year and adjusted from month to month for indicated significant changes in the estimate. Each month an entry is made for an amount determined by dividing the current estimate for the year minus the amount already taken up as cost by the number of months remaining in the year. For example, vacation-pay cost for the year of $48,000 was estimated at the beginning of the year. Four thousand dollars was charged to operations in both January and February. Then, because of a change in wage rates, it was indicated that the year's cost would be $52,400. This left $44,400 to be absorbed in the remaining 10 months. The monthly charge for those months was $4,400. The entry for such costs, which are equalized, is:

> Dr. Expense
>   Cr. Vacation and Holiday Pay Equalization

When vacation pay or holiday pay is determined, it is recorded by the following entry:

> Dr. Vacation and Holiday Pay Equalization
>   Cr. Gross Payroll Accrued

Payments are recorded as follows:

> Dr.   Gross Payroll Paid
>   Cr.   Cash (Net Vacation or Holiday Pay)
>   Cr.   Federal Income Tax Withheld
>   Cr.   Social Security Tax Withheld

Another accepted accounting procedure for vacation pay is to accrue it currently on the basis of the gross payroll of the period. If the average vacation period is 2 weeks, an amount equal to 2% of the gross payroll is accrued at the time gross payroll is recorded. The entry is:

> Dr.   Vacation Pay Expense
>   Cr.   Accrued Vacation Pay

When payments are made the entry is:

> Dr.   Accrued Vacation Pay
>   Cr.   Cash, etc.

Any difference between amounts accrued and amounts paid is reflected as adjustments to expense and to the accrual account at the close of the accounting period.

Costs of fringe benefits which tend to vary from month to month in ratio to the wage cost of the month are charged to costs as determined and recorded. Employer costs of a retirement plan based on employee earnings would be an example of these. They are recorded by the following entry:

> Dr.   Expense
>   Cr.   Employer Retirement Contributions

The procedures discussed for accounting for labor costs may be followed for the most part for salary costs, i.e., payments to employees at stated amounts per week or per month. Variations in procedure are indicated by the two basic differences between labor costs and salary costs: (1) the base gross earnings are known and need not be computed in relation to hours worked or production and (2) all charges are to expense accounts.

Direct Labor Costs

The portion of the gross payroll accrued which is direct labor provides that element of the cost of production. Under a job-order cost system it is related to the production on the job order to arrive at the unit direct labor cost of the job. Under a process cost system it is recorded by operations and product lines within each operation. The production units of the operation and of products are then related to these direct labor costs. These procedures are discussed in detail in subsequent chapters.

REVIEW QUESTIONS

1. Do employment records have any function in the control of labor costs? Explain.
2. What are the two major purposes of records of time worked?
3. How may employee earnings be determined?
4. What is premium pay? Is it classified as labor or expense? Why?
5. What accounts are debited when Gross Payroll Accrued is credited?
6. In addition to the accounting entries, what further steps are required for control purposes in accounting for gross wages?
7. What are the advantages of a daily computation and distribution of gross wages?
8. How do deductions from gross wages affect the costs of production?
9. What is the function of the payroll register?
10. What are supplementary costs of labor?
11. What purpose is served by equalizing certain supplementary costs of labor?
12. What are the basic differences in computing and accounting for salaries as compared with wages?

PROBLEMS

1. A factory has 10 workers. Their clock numbers, hours of work for a week, and guaranteed minimum hourly rates are listed in Table P5-1.

TABLE P5-1

Clock no.	Hours	Rate
1	40	$2.00
2	40	2.20
3	48	2.00
4	40	2.10
5	40	2.40
6	40	2.00
7	40	1.80
8	40	2.00
9	40	2.00
10	40	2.00

Time and half is paid for all hours over 40 per week.

Number 5 is the maintenance man and number 7 is the janitor. All the others are working directly on production.

Numbers 1, 6, and 8 are on piecework at a rate of $0.002 per piece. For the week their production reports show: number 1—40,000, number 6—50,000, and number 8—30,000.

Numbers 9 and 10 are on incentive and earn a bonus of 10% of their base pay for the week.

a. Compute the gross wages for each employee.

b. Prepare a journal entry distributing the gross wages to direct labor and factory expense.

2. A company is negotiating a new labor contract. The present contract provides for 40 hours of vacation pay per year after completion of 1 year of service and 80 hours after completion of 5 years of service. It also provides for six paid holidays per year. There is a retirement plan under which the employer contributes an amount equivalent to 4% of all payments to employees into a trusteed retirement fund. Employer wage taxes are 2% of all payments to employees. Group insurance and hospitalization are provided by the employer, and the cost is based on the number of employees on the payroll.

For the past year, under the expiring contract, the following costs were incurred:

Gross earnings..........................	1,060,000 hr @ $2.40		$2,544,000.00
Vacation pay—516 employees.............	38,600 hr @	2.40	92,640.00
Holiday pay............................	24,960 hr @	2.40	59,904.00
Retirement.............................			107,861.76
Employer wage taxes.....................			53,930.88
Group insurance........................			50,410.00
Hospitalization.........................			20,820.00

The company proposes a $0.10-per-hour increase.

The union requests an $0.08-per-hour increase, 80 hours of vacation pay per year after 1 year of service, and 120 hours after 5 years, and a seventh paid holiday.

What are the added costs of the company proposal and of the union request, based on the year just completed? Assume no change in employer wage tax rates.

CHAPTER 6

Accounting for
Actual Factory Expense

In the preceding chapters accounting procedures for material and labor were discussed. In each of these there were many phases which were applicable to both direct material and labor and expense material and labor. The reason for this was that up to some point, which varies for material and labor and even for items of each of these, no distinction need be made for accounting. However, beyond that point expense material and labor become a part of, and flow into, the procedures for expense.

Definition of Factory Expense

Direct material becomes a component part of the finished product *and* can be measured in relation to the units of production. Direct labor is expended directly on the product in the course of its fabrication or movement *and* can be measured in relation to the units of production. Therefore the unit costs of direct material and direct labor of a given product are constant, assuming effective cost control and no change in price or wage levels. In contrast indirect (i.e., expense) material and labor bear no direct relationship to the product, either physically or in cost per unit. They have the characteristics of expense and must ultimately be accounted for as expense. In addition to indirect material and labor there are many other items of cost in the factory which are neither labor nor material and therefore are included in the factory expense element. Since direct material and direct labor can be defined, the definition of the third element of factory cost, factory expense, must be one of exclusion. Factory expense is the total of all costs in the manufacturing plant which cannot be classified as direct material or direct labor. The dividing line between direct material and expense material and between direct labor and expense labor is not sharp. In any plant there are material and labor items which could be classified either as direct or as expense. Under these conditions effectiveness of control and economy of accounting determine how they should be classified.

Factory Expense Sources

The charts of accounts illustrated in Chapter 3 show typical segregations of factory expense into sources. The original records which provide the accounting entries for expense are indicated by the expense source. Many of these have already been covered in the accounting procedures for material and labor. For the expense sources listed in Chapter 3 the following are examples of the points of origin:

02 Salaries—salary roll
03 Indirect Labor—payroll
04 Vacation Pay and Awards—payroll
07 Pensions—pension roll
09 Supplies ⎱ *a.* Voucher register for items charged to ex-
11 Sacks and Containers ⎰   pense as purchased, or
13 Maintenance Material ⎰ *b.* Stores requisitions summary for materials withdrawn from stores
14 Maintenance Labor—payroll
15 Maintenance Services—voucher register
21 Fuel—general journal based on the summary of reported usage
22 Water—voucher register
23 Electricity—voucher register (if purchased)
31 Stationery—(same as supplies)
32 Travel—general journal based on the summary of expense reports
33 Postage
    a. Voucher register
    b. General journal based on distribution of metered charges or stamp usage
34 Telephone and Telegraph ⎱
35 Publications ⎰
36 Consulting Services ⎰ Voucher register
37 Donations ⎰
38 Association Dues ⎰
41 Employee Benefit Programs
    a. Salary roll and payroll, or
    b. General journal based on total wage and salary payments
51 Rent—lease register or general journal
52 Depreciation—plant and equipment ledger or general journal
53 Taxes
    a. Voucher register, or
    b. Tax register if applied equally over months of the year
54 Insurance—insurance register

Subsidiary Expense Ledgers

All entries for factory expense must carry a complete code to provide for recording by general-ledger control account and in the subsidiary expense ledger by source, responsibility for expense, operation charged, and classification for detailed control. For example, for the fiberboard-company chart of accounts illustrated in Chapter 3 maintenance material for machinery repairs in the finishing operation of the Mobile plant, made by the machine shop, would be coded:

PLANT	CONTROL	SOURCE	DEPARTMENT	OPERATION	CLASSIFICATION
124	131	13	02	422	101

The subsidiary expense ledger has a separate page for each operation, which shows the expense by source (Exhibit 6-1). The classification detail may be recorded in the subsidiary ledger if a limited number of classifications are used. More often this detail is posted only to auxiliary control records along with the indication of the responsibility for the expense if that is other than the operation to which it is charged. If machine accounting is not used, the subsidiary ledgers are set up to provide for posting from the original records. When this is done, the sources are shown as headings of columns and postings are made daily with reference in the left-hand column as to the date of entry and original record from which it originated (Exhibit 6-1). With machine accounting all charges are summarized by operation and source and a single posting made to the subsidiary ledger, or the ledger itself is prepared by the machine.

Distribution of Service Operations

After expenses are recorded by operations, the total expenses of each service operation are distributed to the production operations which it serves. Service operations are those which perform any function not directly related to the products manufactured. Typical service operations are general plant, steam plant, electric generation and distribution, maintenance department, and materials transfer. The general plant operation would include general supervision and clerical services, staff departments, travel, stationery, telephone, and the other expenses which are applicable to the entire plant. It would not include general administrative expenses of the company which are not related to the manufacturing functions. For example, in a small single-plant company the president may also be the plant manager. Some portion, or possibly all, of his salary would be charged as administrative expense and not as general plant expense.

EXHIBIT 6-1

FACTORY EXPENSE LEDGER

MONTH OF AUGUST, 19—

Operation 331 Forming

Date	Reference	13102 Salaries	13103 Ind. labor	13109 Supplies	13113 Maint. mat'l.	13114 Maint. labor	13131 Stationery	13152 Depreciation	13142 13153 Taxes	13154 Insurance	Other	Total
1	Voucher 8-007			15.80								15.80
4	Voucher 8-042				29.76							29.76
6	Req. summary			96.07	53.40		10.50					159.97
6	Payroll		3,200.80			1,406.35						4,607.15
9	Voucher 8-117						125.00					125.00
13	Payroll		4,162.10			143.75						4,305.85
13	Req. summary			140.00	1,483.10							1,623.10
15	Salary roll	4,200.00										4,200.00
17	Voucher 8-143				46.90							46.90
20	Payroll		3,818.20			76.90						3,895.10
24	Voucher 8-169						15.00					15.00
27	Payroll		3,300.50			60.10						3,360.60
27	Req. summary			37.00			5.00					42.00
31	Salary roll	4,250.00										4,250.00
31	Accrued wages		1,653.09			40.11						1,693.20
31	Gen. journal							4,175.00			13132 Travel 96.60	4,271.60
31	Req. summary				18.60							18.60
31	Voucher 8-120			40.00								40.00
31	Tax register								(G) 1,400.00			1,400.00
31	Insurance register									1,500.00		1,500.00
31	Labor summary								(P) 597.58		13104 Vac. Pay 428.57	1,026.15
31	General journal										13141 Emp. Benefits 1,792.73	1,792.73
	Total	8,450.00	16,134.69	328.87	1,631.76	1,727.21	155.50	4,175.00	1,997.58	1,500.00	2,317.90	38,418.51
	Share:											
	Maint. dept.											1,554.49
	Steam dept.											16,360.90
	Electric dept.											18,540.10
	General plant											10,403.00
	Total											85,277.00
	Machine-hours											530
	Rate per hour											160.90

Also, there may be service operations which apply only to certain related productive operations. In a fiberboard plant there may be a general foreman for all primary operations—grinding, pulping, forming, etc. The salary of this general foreman and his clerks and other staff, and other related expenses, would be recorded in a service operation designated Primary Operations—General. The total cost of this operation would then be distributed to the productive operations under his general supervision.

Service-operation expenses are distributed to productive operations on the basis of service rendered. For some services the basis is apparent. For others a basis or bases must be developed which provides for a reasonable distribution. Since some service operations render service to other service operations, the problem of where to start the distribution is encountered. One procedure is to start with the operation which draws the least service from others and distribute it, disregarding the services which it uses. Then the one which draws the least on the remaining ones is distributed, and so on, until all distributions have been made. An alternate procedure is to estimate the cost of services of other operations and add these estimates to the specific expenses of each service operation. From this total the estimated amount taken to other service operations is deducted and the remainder distributed to the productive operations.

Typical Bases of Distribution

In a typical plant, because the amounts of electricity and steam used by the maintenance department are not significant, the expense of this latter department is distributed first. For this distribution the hours or dollars of maintenance labor expended in other operations are used. Dollars may be the better base, because the skilled and therefore higher-paid mechanics are the ones who use the more expensive machines and tools in their work. The steam-plant expense is distributed next. Here the basis is pounds of steam used. It is usually not practical to have meters for each, or even for any, operation. Instead the engineers calculate steam requirements per operating hour of each operation. The hours operated times this rate provides a reasonable basis for distribution, and differences between the calculated usage and the total pounds generated should not be major. If steam is used to generate electricity, it should be metered to provide an accurate cost of electricity. The remainder of the steam-plant costs would then be distributed to other operations. Costs of electricity and the transformer and distribution facilities are distributed on kilowatts used. Here again usage may have to be calculated. The rated horsepower of motors, watts of lighting, etc., can be used to determine kilowatts per operating hour to be used for the distribution. Weight or value of raw material used would be one basis for distributing the expense of the materials transfer department.

Expenses of service operations related to a specific group of productive operations are also distributed to those productive operations. Here again, the basis of distribution must be one which is representative of the demands of each productive operation. If supervision, timekeeping, and labor-cost control are the major functions of such a service operation, it could be distributed on labor hours or dollars. If direct material, labor, and expense are all significant, the sum of these for each of the productive operations would be used as a basis of distribution.

Typical Distribution Bases for General Plant Expense

The selection of a basis for general plant expense presents a more difficult problem. Because the total of general plant expense is usually significant and because it is composed of so many different kinds of expenses which do not apply uniformly to all productive operations, it should be segregated into groups of expenses before distribution. For this reason it is desirable to set up a number of operations for recording general plant expense in the subsidiary ledger. These would be determined by the different methods of production in the productive operations. A highly mechanized operation with relatively low labor costs would be charged with substantially less general plant expense related to personnel than would an operation which was largely handwork. It is important that bases of distribution be selected which are relative to the demands of the productive operations for each type of service included in the general plant expense. Typical operations and logical bases of distribution are:

General plant administration:

This would include all salaries and other expenses not charged to other general plant operations. It would be distributed on the total of the direct raw-material usage, direct labor incurred, and specific expense of each productive operation.

General plant personnel:

This would include the expenses of employment, labor relations, employee recreation, payroll, gate guards, and industrial engineering. It would be distributed on the total direct and indirect labor hours.

General plant purchasing:

This would include the expense of the purchasing department and be distributed on total value of raw material and stores used in each productive operation.

General plant inventory control:

This would include the expense of the production control and scheduling department, of the inventory-records clerks, etc. It would be distributed on the basis of the value of inventories in each operation.

General plant space charges:

This would include building depreciation and maintenance not charged directly to other operations, watchmen, janitors, grounds upkeep, etc. It would be distributed on square feet of floor space occupied by productive operations.

Distribution of General Plant Expense to Products

Where costs are determined by product lines, the general plant expense may not be distributed to productive operations. Instead it may be distributed directly to product lines. This is done on the theory that bases of distribution to productive operations are selected more or less arbitrarily. Since this is true, it is considered to be just as satisfactory to select arbitrary bases for distribution directly to product lines.

When this is done, the distribution base most frequently used is estimated application of effort. Such estimates are made at the beginning of each year and used for that year unless a major change occurs, in which event an adjustment to the distribution ratios is made. Because effort by product lines varies for different groups in the general plant administrative functions, it is desirable to carry different operations, as indicated for distribution to productive operations. Separate estimates are then made of the percentage of effort expended by each group on each product line, and these are used to distribute the actual expense of each month.

Applying Actual Expense to Job Orders

When the expenses of the service operations have been distributed to productive operations, they are added to the expenses specific to these to secure the total expense cost of each operation. This sum, when divided by the production units of the operation for the period, results in the actual expense rate for the operation. The production units may be expressed in physical units, such as pounds or square yards, direct labor hours, direct-labor dollars, machine hours, prime cost (direct material and labor), or some other unit which measures fairly the activity of the productive operation.

When general plant expense has been distributed to product lines, instead of to productive operations, rates are determined for these expenses per unit of finished product. In doing this the dollars of expense assigned to a product for all general plant groups are totaled, and one rate per unit of product is calculated.

The actual expense rates are used for applying factory expense to job orders under job-order cost systems, if estimated rates have not been used during the month. An entry is then made debiting Work in Process and crediting Applied Expense for the total expense applied to the job orders. If no errors have been made in posting, the applied and actual expense will be substantially in agreement. Some slight difference may occur because the rates are, for practical reasons, not carried to sufficient decimal places to result in absolute accuracy. Such slight differences may be ignored from month to month and charged against profit and loss at the end of each year. If estimated rates were used for applying expense to job orders, the difference between the applied and actual expense may be charged to profit and loss of the period or at the end of the year, or the estimated rates may be corrected to actual by the application of adjusting rates as either debits or credits to bring the applied estimated expense to actual.

It should be noted that any expense in a productive operation which is specific to a given order is charged to that order as a direct expense. It is therefore excluded from the total expense of the operation when rates are calculated. This is accomplished by posting the total of these direct charges as a credit on the subsidiary expense ledger for the operation. The total of these credits agrees with the total direct expense posted to job cost cards and is recorded as a debit to Work in Process and a credit to Applied Expense.

Application of Actual Expense under Process Costs

Under a process cost system the total specific and allocated expense of each productive operation is charged to Work in Process and credited to Applied Expense. It is added to the direct material and labor cost of the operation to arrive at the in-process inventory value of material moving on for further processing and finally, in combination with all operations, is part of the sum transferred from In-process Inventory to Finished-stock Inventory for finished production.

When production cost summaries are prepared on the basis of product lines, the operational expense rates are applied to the activity units reported for each product. This expense plus the direct material and labor provides the total actual product cost. As when expense is applied to job orders, there may be a slight difference between the total applied expense and actual expense because of not carrying rates to enough decimal places. These differences may be ignored during the year and, to the extent that they do not cancel out in a year, cleared into profit and loss at the end of the year.

When separate product rates are used for general plant expense, they are applied to the finished production units in the cost ledgers. The entry is a debit to Work in Process and a credit to Applied Expense. This expense is then added to all other costs of the product to arrive at the value to be debited to Finished Stock and credited to Work in Process.

Multiple Expense Rates

For some productive operations it may be desirable to have two or more expense rates in order to arrive at more nearly accurate product costs. For example, in fabricating special parts from fiberboard blanks there may be no constant relationship of labor costs to machine time. Some may require relatively high man-hours and low machine-hours and vice versa. Where such conditions exist, an expense rate may be determined per labor hour for those expenses which relate to labor—supervision, employee benefits, payroll taxes, etc. Another rate would be determined for those expenses which relate to machinery—maintenance, depreciation, property taxes, insurance, etc.

There can be no stated rule as to when more than one expense rate should be used for an operation. Only judgment based on an intimate knowledge of products and production processes will determine when more than one rate is needed to secure reasonable product costs. When they are used, it is necessary to establish comparable activity units by products on which to apply the rates. The accounting entries are the same as when a single rate is used for an operation.

REVIEW QUESTIONS

1. Define factory expense.
2. In what original records does factory expense originate?
3. What is the purpose of subsidiary expense ledgers?
4. What are service operations?
5. What is the basic rule for the distribution of expenses of service operations to productive operations?
6. Should expenses of all service operations be distributed to productive operations?
7. What is meant by the application of expense?
8. Why is it advantageous to use estimated expense rates under a job-order cost system?
9. What disposition is made of the difference between the balance of the Expense Incurred account and that of the Applied Expense account at the end of a month? At the end of a year?
10. When should multiple expense rates be used?

PROBLEM

The factory expense ledger for a plastics molding company is shown in Table P6a.

Time and production data for the month are shown in Table P6b.

TABLE P6a
FACTORY EXPENSE LEDGER

Source	General Plant	Hydraulic Power	Machine Shop	Preforming	Molding	Inspecting and Finishing	Packing and Shipping
Salaries...............	$ 5,000		$ 1,000	$ 800	$ 1,600	$ 800	$ 600
Indirect labor...........	2,700	$ 800	3,100	200	3,800	1,700	900
Supplies...............	800	100	1,900	100	1,000	400	200
Maintenance material.....	2,000	50	1,100	500	2,100		
Maintenance labor........	2,000	100	800	200	4,600		100
Maintenance services......	2,480	50	100		300		20
Fuel...................	1,400		100				
Water.................	200						
Electricity.............	500	500	700	700	1,800	100	50
Stationery.............	200		80		110	72	70
Travel................	240						
Postage...............	300						
Telephone and telegraph...	160						
Employee benefit programs	900	80	900	240	1,200	360	80
Employer wage taxes......	200	20	170	60	300	90	20
Property taxes...........	1,400	200	620	300	800	100	100
Insurance..............	700	100	310	200	500	50	50
Depreciation...........	2,800	300	820	600	1,590	150	110
Total.................	$23,980	$2,300	$11,700	$3,900	$19,700	$3,822	$2,300

TABLE P6b

Operation	Direct labor hours	Direct labor dollars	Machine-hours	Production
Preforming.....................	800	$1,600	800	1,800,000
Molding........................	2,400	5,760	3,600	1,800,000
Inspecting and finishing..........	1,200	2,160		1,650,000
Packing and shipping............	600	1,200		1,500,000

During the month the machine shop charged $4,700 of labor to making tools and dies, which were capitalized.

General plant expense is distributed to productive operations on total direct and indirect labor dollars incurred in each operation.

The engineers have determined that 10% of the hydraulic power is required for the preforming machines and 90% for the molding machines.

Make the necessary distributions of service operations, and determine appropriate expense rates for the productive operations.

CHAPTER 7

Cost Accounting
Procedure for Actual Costs

There are two basic cost accounting systems: (1) process costing and (2) job-order costing. Reference has already been made to these in preceding chapters. It is the purpose of either system to provide for the accumulation of costs, record them in the books of account, and apply them to inventories and cost of goods sold.

This chapter summarizes and illustrates the cost accounting procedures for actual costs under both systems. The procedures are illustrative rather than definitive. Adaptations and modifications of the systems as presented would be necessary to meet the requirements of specific plants.

PROCESS COSTS

Where Process Costs Are Used

The process cost accounting system is the best costing procedure when production is for stock from which deliveries may be made to any customer. When production is to customer specification but the volume of goods produced under any one specification is large, it may also be desirable to use process costing. Whenever there is a problem of keeping portions of one order from being mixed with portions of another for the same product, the process system should be used. Process cost systems are usually found in such industries as cigarette, cigar, cement, hosiery, textile, dairy, floor covering, paper, fiberboard, structural glass, glass containers, insulating material, wire and cable, electrical equipment and appliances, chemical and oil refining.

The distinguishing feature of the process cost system is the accumulation of costs by operations. With the proper organization structure in the production department this means that they are also accumulated by responsibility. This has an obvious advantage in measuring performance under each responsibility.

The process cost system can be used where more than one product is processed in an operation. This is done by assigning a product designation to all direct-material and direct-labor charges. Costs are accumulated by products in each operation, and production is reported by products. Since all products passing through each operation utilize common equipment, expense is charged to products on the basis of their relative usage of the facilities. Such charges may be made as a percentage of direct labor, a rate per machine-hour, a rate per unit of product, or other basis which provides a fair and accurate cost. Total cost elements by product divided by production units of the product provides unit cost.

Procedures for a Process Cost System

A plant producing fiberboard insulation and building materials from ground wood will be used to illustrate the process cost system. Wood is ground and refined into pulp. This is formed into board, similarly to the processes for making paper. At the end of the forming machine there is a saw (wet saw) which cuts the continuous wet sheet into large boards. These boards pass through a dryer to remove moisture and are sawed to smaller sizes as they leave the dryer. This may be the finished size (roof insulation), or the cut boards (acoustical stock, industrial stock, etc.) may be further processed by cutting to still smaller sizes, beveling, painting, drilling, etc. The illustration will be limited to the cost accounting up to the sawing of the boards to size as they leave the dryer.

The ground wood is suspended in water and held in stock chests for use by the board-forming operation. As stock is drawn from the chests, other raw materials are added before it flows on to the forming machine. Since the consistency of the stock (ratio of wood fiber to total fiber and water) is known, usage of fiber is computed from the amount of stock drawn from the chests for a given run of a product. This batch report is shown as Exhibit 7-1. Other raw materials are weighed as they are added to the stock and the usage reported on appropriate forms.

Because the direct labor force at the board-forming machine works as a crew, the direct labor reports (Exhibit 7-2) are by crew rather than a separate report for each man. Individual earnings are summarized by man for payroll purposes, and the summaries for cost purposes are made from the totals for the crew.

Expense is relative to the hours the forming machine operates. Therefore the batch report (Exhibit 7-1) also shows the machine-hours. After total expense of the operation is determined for the month, a rate per hour is calculated. This rate is then applied to the hours reported for each product to arrive at the total expense dollars assigned to each product.

There is no direct-material or direct labor cost in drying. Dryer hours are equivalent to forming-machine hours, because the speed of material passing through the dryers is determined by the speed at which the boards can be formed. Assignment of dryer expense to products is on the same basis as that of the forming machine—total dryer expense divided by total hours to derive a rate to be applied to the dryer hours reported for each product.

EXHIBIT 7-1
MATERIAL USAGE AND PRODUCTION REPORT

WET END BATCH REPORT

Batch No. *8140* Freeness *50 %* Date *aug. 8*

Specification No. *6* Dept. *Board Mill* Shift No. *2*

Boards to Dryer	Total	Boards Checked Out of Dryer	Width	Length	Thickness
(10) THH THH THH					
THH IIII	*240*	*240*	*12'3"*	*16'4"*	*1"*

Time
Start *1:30 P.M.*
Stop *4:30 P.M.*

Shift Foreman *alden* Wet Saw Operator *Smith*

Made for *Roof Insulation to be cut 3-48" × 8-24"*

Production is reported at the dry saws (Exhibit 7-3). If the product does not require further fabrication after being sawed to size as it comes from the dryer, it is packaged at the sawing operation. Packing-material usage reports carry the product designation. Direct labor reports at the sawing operation are by crews, similar to those for board forming. Crew size varies with the type and size of boards being produced. Expense is relative to machine-hours, which are the same as forming and drying hours, since there is no break in production from forming machine to dry saws. The total actual expense of the sawing operation is assigned to products on this basis.

Unit cost is determined in a cost summary book (Exhibit 7-4). Here credit is given for the scrap, which can be reused in the stock, at an estimated value approximately equivalent to the cost of the wood fiber

EXHIBIT 7-2

DAILY TIME AND DISTRIBUTION SHEET

DAILY TIME AND DISTRIBUTION SHEET

DATE Aug 8 19—

1ST SHIFT
2ND SHIFT
3RD SHIFT

CLOCK NO.	NAME AND JOB	SHIFT	Rate	OP 331 62522		OP 331 62522		Shift Diff	REMARKS	TOTAL HOURS	TOTAL AMOUNT
110	Machine Tender McClure	2	2 10	5	10 50	3	6 30	80		8	17 60
174	Pulp Operator Bolden	2	1 90	5	9 50	3	5 70	80		8	16 00
963	Pulp Helper Jones	2	1 60	5	8 00	3	4 80	80		8	13 60
910	Pulp Helper 1st	2	1 60	5	8 00	3	4 80	80		8	13 60
212	Caring Up	2	1 60	5	8 00	3	4 80	80		6	13 60
188	Clean Up Willschen	2	1 60	5	8 00	3	4 80	80		6	13 60
318	Wet Lap Smith	2	1 80	5	9 00	3	5 40	80		6	15 20
TOTAL HOURS				35		21				56	
TOTAL DOLLARS					61 00		36 60	5 60			103 20

it contains. The totals of the cost summary book provide the bases for cost accounting entries. A flow chart of these is shown in Exhibit 7-5. The flow of cost of wood grinding is shown on this chart to indicate the cost of chest stock, but the accounting entries for this are not described below. Note that two work-in-process accounts are carried, Chest Stock

Exhibit 7-3

PRODUCTION REPORT, PROCESS COSTS

	PRODUCT AND SIZE		PRODUCT AND SIZE		PRODUCT AND SIZE		PRODUCT AND SIZE	
	\multicolumn{8}{c	}{DRY SAW PRODUCTION}
	\multicolumn{8}{c	}{FIRST SHIFT DATE *Aug 7, 19--*}
BATCH NUMBER	Good	Cull	Good	Cull	Good	Cull	Good	Cull
TOTALS								
	\multicolumn{8}{c	}{SECOND SHIFT}
BATCH NUMBER	*Acoustical Stock 49×49×¾*		*Roof Insulation 24×48×1*					
	Good	Cull	Good	Cull	Good	Cull	Good	Cull
8139	11000	490						
8140			5600	160				
TOTALS	11000	490	5600	160				
	\multicolumn{8}{c	}{THIRD SHIFT}
BATCH NUMBER	Good	Cull	Good	Cull	Good	Cull	Good	Cull

and Work in Process, the former being a subdivision of work in process used to segregate and control inventory.

Accounting Entries

The accounting entries for a process cost system may be made from summaries of the cost elements or from summaries of costs as accumulated by products. Under either method debits are made to the Work in Process account for the three cost elements as incurred in all operations up to, and sometimes including, finished-stock warehousing. Direct material, direct labor, and expense of the Shipping Operation are debited either to Finished Stock or directly to Cost of Goods Sold. If the charge is to Finished Stock, this account would be credited, and Cost of Goods sold would be debited for the total factory cost of the product when it is shipped to customers. If the debit for shipping costs is made directly to Cost of Goods Sold, the credits to Finished Stock and the debits to Cost

EXHIBIT 7-4
FINAL COST SUMMARY

August, 19—

ROOF INSULATION   24 by 48 by ¾   #521

Description	Unit	Quantity	Actual rate	Total cost
Material—Chest stock.........	100 lb	124,900	$ 2.00	$2,498.00
Margose...........	lb	31	1.10	34.10
Rekol..............	lb	22	2.30	50.60
Kraft paper.........	lb	120	0.20	24.00
Tape..............	Roll	156	0.09	14.04
Cull credit 8/7..............	Boards	160	0.01	(1.60)
8/9..............	Boards	200	0.01	(2.00)
Labor—Forming 8/7...........	———	———	———	36.60
Dry saw 8/7...........	———	———	———	19.50
Forming 8/7...........	———	———	———	47.10
Dry saw 8/9...........	———	———	———	42.16
Expense—Forming 8/7.........	hr	3		
ˮ 8/9.........	hr	4		
		7	160.90	1,126.30
Dryer..............	hr	7	63.00	441.00
Dry saw...........	hr	7	10.30	72.10
Total....................	M sq ft	104,000	$ 42.33	$4,401.90
Production 8/7..........	Boards	5,600		
8/9..........	Boards	7,400		
Total....................	———	13,000		

of Goods Sold would be for the value of the product as carried in finished-stock inventory.

When entries are made from summaries by cost elements, all requisitions or usage reports for direct material are totaled and one entry made:

> Dr. Work in Process
> Cr.   Raw Material

Direct labor is summarized from the payroll distribution and recorded as:

> Dr. Work in Process
> Cr.   Gross Payroll Accrued

or, as in Exhibit 7-5, is first debited to Direct Labor and then credited
to this account and charged to Work in Process. This provides a ready
reference in the accounts as to the amount of direct labor incurred.
Expense Materials have been debited to Factory Expense and credited to
appropriate accounts and Indirect Labor debited to Expense and credited to Gross Payroll Accrued in the accounting for expense. Other expense sources have also been debited as costs arose from the other journals and subsidiary records. Thus, the Factory Expense account has a

EXHIBIT 7-5
FLOW CHART OF ACCOUNTING TRANSACTIONS, PROCESS COST SYSTEM

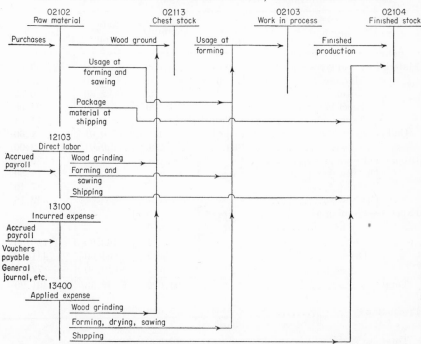

debit balance which is the actual expense of the period. It is customary
not to credit this account for the expense included in the cost of products
at either actual or estimated rates. Instead, a separate account is used
for Applied Expense, and the entry is:

Dr.   Work in Process
Cr.   Applied Expense

When costs are accumulated by products in cost summary books (Exhibit 7-4), separate entries are sometimes recorded for each product, or
the cost elements recorded for each product may be summarized and

entered in total for all products. Where special work in process accounts are used for partially processed material, as for chest stock in the illustration, these accounts are credited for the value of the material used.

JOB-ORDER COSTS

Where Job-order Costs Are Used

The job-order cost system is the best costing procedure when production is to customer specification with infrequent repeat orders. It is the only cost system adaptable to the construction industry. In manufacturing it is used by machine shops, industrial specialty manufacturers, printers, etc.

For effective and accurate cost determination by job orders it is essential that a specific lot, or order, of material can be identified in, and followed through, each step of the production process. If this cannot be done and different lots become intermingled, cost information will be more misleading than helpful.

Some industries or companies which do not manufacture to customer specifications use the job-order cost system for the reason that they produce their product in lots. That is, they start a given quantity through the production process each day or each week and accumulate costs for each lot. In such companies the cost system is actually being adapted to the production-scheduling method. This is not a valid reason for its use. There are no identifying features in the products themselves which result in a natural separation of orders. As a result workers will frequently place items of two or more lots in one pile or container. When this happens, production is reported for a job-order which was not charged with the material and labor costs incurred prior to intermingling, and conversely costs appear on orders for which no production is reported. This results in inaccurate costs, and control is lost. True, this can be held to a minimum, but it requires very close supervision and very detailed records, both of which add unnecessary costs.

Frequently a business starts as a specialty manufacturer producing materials to customer specification and rightly adopts the job-order cost system. In the course of its growth and market development its products find acceptance by a few customers or even one customer whose business takes the full production capacity. This is a signal for a reexamination of the cost system, for production may actually have changed from a job-order to a process basis. If this has occurred, a change should be made away from the job-order cost system.

Some factories have a combination of production for stock (process basis) and production for specific orders. In these instances the process

Exhibit 7-6
Job Cost Sheet

JOB COST SHEET							No. *595/4*	
Customer		*Frigibox, Inc.*						
Order received *9/11__*			To be completed *10/20/__*		Commodity code		*576*	
Quantity on order *30,000*			Material *#143*			Print No.	*763-14-091*	
Blank size		*48"x 96" (Cut two parts per blank)*						
Item		*Bottom insulating panel*						
Description		*44"x 36" Notched and drilled per print*						

Material			Production							
Date	Amount		Date	Scrap	Good	Rate	Per	DR. FINISHED STOCK	
9/6	*10,086*	*40*	*9/10*	*300*	*10,200*	*280.00*	*M*	*2856*	*00*
			10/14	*1000*	*20,000*			*5758*	*96*
9/7	*(1799*	*34)*							
	8287	*06*							
				1300	*30,200*			*8614*	*96*

Other charges			Cost summary		
Date	Reference	Amount			
9/4	*Voucher 9-076*	*170*	*80*	Material	*8287*	*06*
				Labor	*64*	*60*
				Applied expense	*92*	*50*
				Other charges	*170*	*80*
				Total	*8614*	*96*
				Cost per *1000*	*285*	*26*

(Front)

cost system is used for some products or work centers and the job-order cost system for others. For example, a fiberboard company manufacturing special cut parts for refrigerator insulation may use a process cost system for the manufacture of the board from which the parts will be cut and a job-order cost system for the fabrication of the parts cut to customer order.

In companies which use the process cost system exclusively for production costs it is common practice to use job orders to identify certain nonproduction expenditures such as major maintenance or construction

EXHIBIT 7-6 (CONTINUED)

		Direct labor				Applied expense		
						No. *59514*		
Operation	Date	Clock No.	Production	Amount		Rate	Amount	
420	*9/6*	*1118*	*15,754*	*11*	*00*	*110%*	*12*	*10*
421	*9/7*	*1473*	*10,500*	*8*	*40*	*150%*	*12*	*60*
	10/9	*1510*	*21,000*	*16*	*80*		*25*	*20*
				25	*20*		*37*	*80*
422	*9/10*	*2308*	*10,500*	*9*	*10*	*150%*	*13*	*65*
	10/12	*2308*	*21,000*	*19*	*30*		*28*	*95*
				28	*40*		*42*	*60*
	Total			*64*	*60*		*92*	*50*

(Back)

work. The job costs in these cases simply provide subsidiary detail not readily determinable from the process cost records.

Job-order Numbers

Under a job-order cost system the distinguishing feature of the original cost records is that material requisitions, labor tickets, and vouchers' payable to the extent possible carry the job number to which the cost will be charged. This job number is in addition to the codes established in the chart of accounts. Thus, in the fiberboard manufacturing company, portions of whose chart of accounts are listed in Chapter 3, the coding of actual direct labor for manufacturing refrigerator insulation and using job-order costs would be:

PLANT	ACCOUNT	DEPARTMENT	OPERATION	CLASSIFICATION	JOB
122	12106	00	421	576	58514
ATLANTA	DIRECT LABOR	NOT REQUIRED	FABRICATION	CUT SPECIALTIES	

Procedures for a Job-order Cost System

The heart of the job-order cost system is the job cost sheet (Exhibit 7-6). Where only job-order costs are used, the file of cost sheets for jobs

EXHIBIT 7-7
MATERIAL REQUISITION

MATERIAL REQUISITION or RETURN					
Date _9/6_		Operation _420_		Comm. No. _576_	
Description & size	Pieces	Sq. ft.	Rate	Value	
Issued: #143 1" Homo. 4'x8'	15,760	504,320	.02	$10,086.40	
Total issued					
Returns & credits:					
Total returns & credits					
Foreman *John Jone*			Storekeeper *a. L. Bus*		

in process is the subsidiary ledger providing the detail supporting the Work in Process account of the general ledger. Where both job-order and process costs are used, it is customary to carry two general-ledger accounts for work in process—Standard Products in Process and Job Orders in Process. In this instance the latter is supported by the job-order cost sheets. In both instances the data on the cost sheets for completed orders provide the information for credits to Work in Process and charges to Finished Stock for material produced on job orders. The illustration is a cost sheet for the production of a specially cut fiberboard part for refrigerator insulation.

A combined material-requisition and material-returns form is shown in Exhibits 7-7 and 7-8. In the first illustration it is used as a material requisition for blanks to be fabricated. Quantities required are inserted by the foreman, who signs the requisition and sends it to the processed-material stores. A storeskeeper issues the stock and signs the requisition to indicate his approval of the quantities issued. Area of the board is then calculated, priced, and extended, and the value posted to the job cost sheet. In Exhibit 7-8 the form is used for the return of materials to stores, in this instance unused blanks and usable trim. The foreman issues the return form, inserts quantities, and sends it to stores with the mate-

EXHIBIT 7-8
MATERIAL RETURN

MATERIAL REQUISITION or RETURN					
Date 9/7/ Operation 420			Comm No 576		
Description & size	Pieces	Sq ft	Rate	Value	
Issued					
Total issued					
Returns & credits.					
#143 1" Homo. 4'x8'	6	192	.02	3.84	
#143 1" Homo. 48"x 23"	15,750	119,700	.015	1795.50	
				1799.34	
Foreman John Jone			Storekeeper S. Buss		

rial. A storeskeeper signs it, indicating the receipt of those quantities. Then follows the determination of the value of the return, which is posted to the cost sheet as a credit. When raw materials are used, they are requisitioned from raw-material inventory and the charges posted to each cost sheet, following the procedure illustrated for Processed Material—Blanks.

Direct labor is recorded on forms which provide for the computation of the daily earnings of each worker and for the direct labor charges to each job. In Exhibit 7-9 direct labor is recorded on a combination summary and job-ticket form. The first recording is to the individual job tickets comprising the lower portion of the form. These in turn are summarized on the upper portion, and the form is separated. The upper portion is used for payroll and accounting purposes, and the job tickets are sorted by jobs and the charges posted to the cost sheet.

EXHIBIT 7-9

DIRECT LABOR REPORT, JOB-ORDER SYSTEM

Form 57 12-44   **DIRECT LABOR**

DATE 9/7/			NAME *Amos Miller*					CLOCK NO. 1473	
C.P.D.	CONTROL	SOURCE	DEPT.	OPR.	COMM.	HOURS		AMOUNT	
120	121	06	60	421	576	5		10	30
					577	3		6	00
					TOTAL	8		16	30

FACT. ORDER NO. 59514		COMM. NO. 576		OPERATION 421		MINOR OPER. —		CLOCK NO. 1473	
GRADE 143-1" H		TIME START 7:00		TIME STOP 11.00		HOURS 4		MINUTES —	
QUANTITY		HOURS	RATE.	RATE UNIT		VALUE			
PIECES	POUNDS					DOLLARS	CENTS		
10,500		4	.80	1000		8.	40		

FACT. ORDER NO. 6301		COMM. NO. 576		OPERATION 421		MINOR OPER. 2		CLOCK NO. 1473	
GRADE 146-½"		TIME START 11.30		TIME STOP 12:30		HOURS 1		MINUTES —	
QUANTITY		HOURS	RATE	RATE UNIT		VALUE			
PIECES	POUNDS					DOLLARS	CENTS		
2000		1	.95	1000		1	90		

FACT. ORDER NO. 6306		COMM. NO. 577		OPERATION 422		MINOR OPER. —		CLOCK NO. 1473	
GRADE 146-½		TIME START 12:30		TIME STOP 3:30		HOURS 3		MINUTES —	
QUANTITY		HOURS	RATE	RATE UNIT		VALUE			
PIECES	POUNDS					DOLLARS	CENTS		
8100		3	2.00			6	00		

FACT. ORDER NO.		COMM. NO.		OPERATION		MINOR OPER.		CLOCK NO.	
GRADE OR COMP.		TIME START		TIME STOP		HOURS		MINUTES	
QUANTITY		HOURS	RATE	RATE UNIT		VALUE			
PIECES	POUNDS					DOLLARS	CENTS		

FACT. ORDER NO.		COMM. NO.		OPERATION		MINOR OPER.		CLOCK NO.	
GRADE OR COMP.		TIME START		TIME STOP		HOURS		MINUTES	
QUANTITY		HOURS	RATE	RATE UNIT		VALUE			
PIECES	POUNDS					DOLLARS	CENTS		

In Exhibit 7-6 expense is applied to each job as percentages of the direct labor of each operation. Other bases of application could be used. These expense rates are based on estimated total labor and total expense of each operation for the year. Thus actual expense rates do not have to be determined before expense is applied to the cost sheets. Any differ-

EXHIBIT 7-10
PRODUCTION REPORT, JOB-ORDER COSTS

FORM C-63

Commodity_____ *840*

Factory Order No.____ *59514*

Grade ____ *#143 1" Homo*

Customer____ *Frigibox Inc.*

Part No. Size____ *44" X 36"*

	Date	Quantity	Op.
Production—Good	9/10	10,200	37
Scrap		300	37
Transferred to			
Stocked			
Shipped	9/10	10,000	

Production Completed	Not Completed ✓
To be sent to Office for all material sent to Stock, Inspection or Packing.	**N⁰** 9

ence between actual and applied expense is charged or credited to current profit or loss.

If purchases are made for a specific job order, such as a special material, or special tools or jigs, the job-order number is indicated on the purchase requisition. When the invoice is received, it is charged directly to the job indicated by this job-order number.

Quantities of finished production are secured when material is inspected or packed for shipment. Exhibit 7-10 is a typical production report prepared at the inspection operation. It shows the good production, the scrap, and the disposition of the good production as to transfer to another operation, stock, or shipment.

Accounting Entries

The accounting entries for a job-order cost system are the same as for a process cost system. The work-in-process account is frequently designated Jobs in Process. Exhibit 7-11 is a flow chart of the accounting entries for a job-order cost system. It indicates the entries when a process

Exhibit 7-11
FLOW CHART OF ACCOUNTING TRANSACTIONS, JOB-ORDER COST SYSTEM

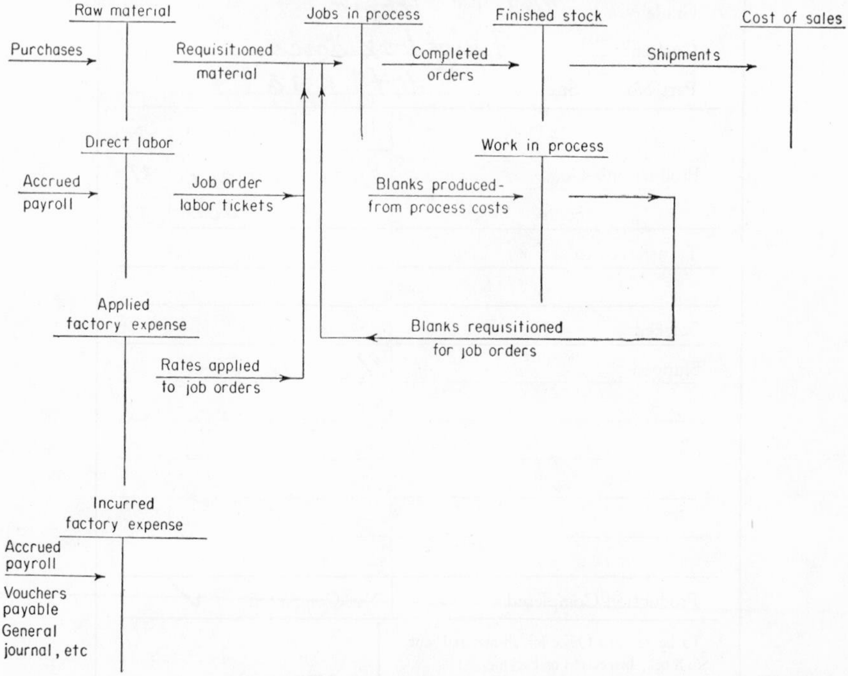

cost system is used to make material subsequently used on job orders. If only a job-order system is used, the account Work in Process and the entries related to it would be eliminated. Net material charges to job orders are debited to Jobs in Process and credited either to Raw Material or Work-in-Process Inventory from summaries of the requisitions. Direct labor is summarized from the upper portion of the labor reports, charged to Jobs in Process, and credited to the Direct Labor account. Expense is applied to jobs at estimated rates and is summarized from the cost sheets, charged to Jobs in Process, and credited to Applied Factory Expense. The difference between applied and incurred expense indicates the degree to which estimated expense rates are high or low. This provides the data for adjusting the estimated rates when the difference is significant.

If the order is completed, the actual cost per unit is determined and the cost transferred from Jobs in Process to Finished Stock. A journal entry may be made for each completion or a summary prepared and a single entry made at the close of each month. If production on an order is not completed and the production report indicates that material has been shipped, Jobs in Process is credited and Finished Stock charged at an estimated unit cost. This estimated cost is adjusted to actual when production of the final portion of the order is reported. Quantities scrapped are shown on the production reports to permit a reconciliation of reported production by work centers with finished-goods production. However, no accounting entries are made for this scrap, since total unit cost is determined on the basis of good production.

REVIEW QUESTIONS

1. In what types of businesses are process cost accounting systems used?
2. What is the unit for which costs are determined under a process cost accounting system?
3. Why must costs be identified with products under a process cost system?
4. How are costs of succeeding operations affected by costs of prior operations?
5. What reports and original records are required for a process cost system?
6. How are costs summarized?
7. When would incurred costs be debited to Work in Process? To Finished Stock?
8. What are the major differences between process and job-order cost accounting systems?
9. What is the primary factor which determines whether or not a job-order cost system can be used?
10. Under what conditions would both process costs and job-order costs be used in the same plant?
11. How does the job-order number relate to the codes in the chart of accounts?
12. Is there any difference between the original records for a process system and those for a job-order system?
13. On what bases should expenses be applied to job orders?
14. When sales are made of part of a job-order lot before all production is completed, how is the cost of goods sold determined?

PROBLEMS

1. The mousetrap company produces a single line of traps. The bases are wood, and the mechanism is a metal spring and a two-piece metal release

which also holds the bait. Lumber is sawed to size for the bases. Wire is formed into springs. Releases are punched from brass plate. Punching time is the same for both parts. Bases, springs, and the two parts of the release are assembled into finished traps, which are packed at the assembly operation in boxes holding 1 dozen traps and placed in the finished-stock warehouse. These boxes are packed in larger cartons at the time of shipment.

On January 1 the in-process and finished-stock inventories were:

Cut bases.............	10,000 @ 0.012	$ 120.00
Springs...............	12,000 @ 0.007	84.00
Release A.............	8,000 @ 0.004	32.00
Release B.............	11,000 @ 0.008	88.00
Finished traps.........	63,000 @ 0.048	3,024.00

For the month of January factory costs were as follows:

Material:

Lumber used..................	$1,310
Wire used....................	236
Brass plate used—A...........	284
Brass plate used—B...........	675
Boxes used...................	1,050
Cartons used.................	439

Labor:

Base cutting..................	$374
Spring forming................	240
Release forming...............	273
Assembly.....................	717
Shipping.....................	270

Expense:

Base cutting..................	$266
Spring forming................	256
Release forming...............	546
Assembly.....................	375
Shipping.....................	83

January production was:

Cut bases..................	128,000
Springs....................	124,000
Release A..................	138,000
Release B..................	135,000
Traps assembled............	126,000
Traps shipped..............	132,000

Calculate the cost of production in each operation, the cost of goods sold, and the closing inventory quantities and values. Prepare summary journal entries for charges to Work in Process, Finished Stock, and Cost of Goods Sold. Post the opening inventory values and January transactions to T accounts for

Work in Process and Finished Stock. Check and prove the closing inventory balances of the T accounts.

2. A small manufacturer of molded plastic products uses a job-order cost system. The productive operations are preforming, molding, inspecting and finishing, and packing and shipping.

There are no jobs in process at the beginning of the year.

Actual costs for the month of January are shown in table P7-2a.

TABLE P7-2a
JANUARY COSTS
Raw Material

	Preforming	Packing and shipping
Job no. 1...........	$ 987	$38
Job no. 2...........	416	11
Job no. 3...........	1,410	63
Job no. 4...........	1,118	

Direct Labor

	Preforming	Molding	Inspecting and finishing	Packing and shipping
Job no. 1.........	$50	$294	$ 118	$ 70
Job no. 2.........	28	110	30	30
Job no. 3.........	92	620	1,210	110
Job no. 4.........	76	418	96	

Factory Expense

Preforming.....................	$ 150
Molding......................	2,220
Inspecting and finishing..........	1,400
Packing and shipping............	225

Factory expense is applied to job orders at estimated rates as percentages of direct labor, as follows:

Per cent

Preforming......................	50
Molding........................	150
Inspecting and finishing...........	100
Packing and shipping.............	50

There is no count of production at preforming, and all preformed material is molded immediately. Contracts with customers permit variations in the quantity shipped of plus or minus 5% of the quantity ordered. For January, data on orders, production, and shipments are shown in table P7-2b.

TABLE P7-2*b*
JANUARY UNITS

Order No.	Ordered	Molded	Inspected and finished		Packed	Shipped
			Good	Scrap		
1	10,000	11,000	9,900	1,100	9,900	9,900
2	5,000	5,400	5,100	300	5,100	5,100
3	40,000	42,000	40,880	1,120	10,000	10,000
4	25,000	26,000	25,100	900		

It was estimated that the unit cost of order number 3 would be $0.16.

a. Determine the cost of goods sold for the month of January.

b. Determine the January 31 inventory value.

c. Determine the over or under applied factory expense for January.

CHAPTER 8

Standards and
Standard Costs

A standard, as used in management account-
ing, is a predetermined cost. *The primary purpose of standards is to
measure costs and provide information for the control of costs.* When
used for this purpose standards may be expressed in units (e.g., pieces
per man-hour) or in unit values (e.g., direct labor cost per unit). A
secondary use of standards is for standard cost accounting. For this
purpose they must be expressed in money values. Usually, in building
standard costs, standard units are determined first, and then these are
priced at the appropriate rates for material and labor. Therefore the
standard units are customarily referred to simply as "standards" or
"physical standards," and after these are evaluated, they are referred to
as "standard costs."

DIFFERENCE BETWEEN "STANDARDS" AND "STANDARD COST"

The term "standard cost" is customarily used in the broadest sense to
include standard direct material, standard direct labor, and standard
factory expense, or total standard factory costs. But for control purposes
the terms "standards" or "standard cost" are applied to the measurement
and control of the costs of direct material, direct labor, and scrap. Expense is controlled through expense "budgets" rather than expense
"standards." The technique for developing standards for material, labor,
and scrap is different in many respects from that for developing expense
budgets and standard expense rates. Therefore factory expense budgets
and expense standards will be covered in other chapters.

Many companies, particularly the smaller ones, which use standards
for cost control do not record the standard costs on the books. Neither do
they develop total unit standard costs—material, labor, and expense—for

97

all operations. They set standards only for significant costs in certain areas where close control is considered to be necessary. These standards may be in units rather than dollars and the comparison made with actual units. For example, a standard may be set for inspecting fiberboard acoustical tile at 1.2 labor hours per 1,000 square feet. Actual hours of inspection labor are then compared with the standard hours, 1.2 times the square feet inspected. This comparison will tell the foreman how well he is controlling his inspection labor costs, even though he receives no reports expressed in dollars and cents.

STANDARDS REQUIRE PLACEMENT OF RESPONSIBILITY

The use of standards presupposes the clear placement of responsibility for cost control by operations. Unless this is done, there will be no possibility of initiating corrective action if standards are not met. Therefore the first step in installing standards is to designate operations in the plant. An operation is a function or group of closely related functions within a plant under the responsibility of a supervisor, usually with the title of foreman. It may be physically located in a defined area, as would be the board-forming operation in a fiberboard plant. Or, its activities may extend over the entire plant as in the case of a materials-transfer department. Standards are established for the materials used and for each function of direct labor in each operation. In addition specifications of production are set which state just what is to be done in each operation and the sequence of the operations.

METHODS OF SETTING STANDARDS

Standards should be based on a scientific study of the quantities of material and units of labor which should be used to produce the product, that is, they should be engineered standards. The setting of standards is the responsibility of the technical staffs of a plant, such as industrial engineers, design engineers, and chemists. After the standard is set tentatively by the technicians, it must be reviewed with, and approved by, the foreman in whose operation it will be applied. Unless the foreman agrees that a standard is fair, his reaction to variances will be defensive rather than corrective. After the standards are set, they may be submitted to the accountants for valuation and conversion into standard costs.

In smaller plants, which do not have technical personnel to set standards, past experience modified by the judgment of the foreman and other management and staff personnel may be used. In such cases the setting of standards usually is primarily the responsibility of the accountants. Sometimes the accountants' development of standard *costs* is short-cut by setting them on the basis of past actual costs rather than establishing physical standards and then evaluating them. This has the disadvantage of not providing control standards in units and also of making it impossible to segregate the effects of cost rates and efficiency on costs.

TYPES OF STANDARDS

Two types of standards have been found acceptable for cost-control purposes: (1) the attainable standard and (2) the perfection standard. The former can be used for cost control and for the development of standard costs. The latter is used only for cost control and may supplement the use of attainable standards. The basic consideration in selecting either or both types is how well they will serve the purposes of cost control.

Attainable Standards

The attainable standard may be defined as that cost which should be attained under efficient operation of existing facilities using specified materials. The attainable standard does not cover inefficiencies which are expected during the period because of such factors as inefficient utilization of labor due to low or unbalanced volume, inadequate labor supply, inadequate supplies of standard raw materials, rearrangement of facilities, construction work, major maintenance programs, and others of a similar character. This means that the standards reflect the cost level expected for efficient operation in the period to which they apply. This type is used in most plants, because within its scope all the requirements of effective management can be met. The standards are set at the beginning of an accounting period, usually a year, and used to measure performance throughout the period.

However, some plants change standards less frequently than each accounting period, with some using the same standards for as long as 10 years. These, sometimes referred to as "basic standards," are not revised unless major changes are made in production facilities or product specifications. They are attainable and usually, with improvements in methods, should be exceeded after they are in use for some time. The major objection to this type of standard is that a variance is usually expected, and, for control purposes, variances must be measured against the expected variance rather than the actual cost against the attainable standard cost.

Still other plants change their standards during an accounting period for all changes in production or product specifications. This constant use of current standards provides an excellent measurement of production efficiency but makes it difficult to compare operations at various times during the period. Also, cost reductions effected during the period are immediately canceled out in the reports by the change in standards. This tends to dampen the enthusiasm of the organization, because they do not have the results of their efforts reflected during the remainder of the period as gains against the standards.

The disadvantages of basic and current attainable standards become more pronounced when they are converted into standard costs. For, in addition to the problems resulting from changes in specifications, there are also the problems resulting from changes in wage rates and material prices.

DIRECT-MATERIAL STANDARDS

Attainable direct-material standards are based on the kind and quantity of material which should be used to produce a finished product of specified quality. For a manufacturing process starting with basic raw materials the first step is for the chemists to establish specifications for the raw materials to be used. They then set the standard formulas showing the quantities of each raw material to be used in a standard lot or batch. Allowance is made for normal losses in initial processing, and, considering this, the yield in quantity of finished or semifinished product is determined. Formulation specifications include the standard procedure for processing as to sequence of processes and time in the various processes. The chemists also set the physical specifications as to density, consistency, tensile strength, etc., of the product to be derived from the formula. These data are recorded in a permanent record (Exhibit 8-1), which also shows the required approvals of the standards.

With these specifications established still other standards must be determined before a standard material cost can be calculated by the accountant. While the chemists specified the quantity of material to be weighed or measured into the batch, allowances for shrinkage due to spilling, adherence to containers, evaporation, etc., must also be set, so that the quantity going into the batch can be converted into equivalent units purchased. For example, a formula may call for 980 pounds of a certain liquid. This is the quantity measured into the formula. However the industrial engineers, production-control department, or other staff having the responsibility determine that of every 100 pounds purchased 2 pounds will unavoidably be lost through absorption by filters and spillage. This means that 1,000 pounds of liquid must be purchased for every 980 pounds actually measured into the formula. Other losses may occur in the operation or in subsequent operations which were not covered in the chemists' specifications. The standard allowance for these is set just as is the allowance for shrinkage of raw material. These data are recorded on the same type of records, and the entire file becomes the supporting data for the accountants' cost calculation.

Raw-material unit price standards are usually set by the purchasing department. In some companies these standards are approved by an economist or other person outside the purchasing department who is familiar with market prices. The prices are set at the average expected for the period during which the standards will be used. Files of the rates are maintained in the purchasing and accounting departments.

EXHIBIT 8-1
MATERIAL SPECIFICATION FOR STANDARD COST

MATERIAL SPECIFICATION FOR STANDARD COST

Operation No. 331
Index No. 42
Plant Atlanta
Date Issued Dec. 3, 1957
Date Effective Jan 1, 1958

Product Wall Boards - 1/24 x 48" x 1"

Cost Class:—Formula ☒ Process Loss ☐ Weight Per Unit ☐ Defect Loss ☐ Scrap Loss ☐ ☐

1000 Square Feet

Chart Stock	750 lb.
Margose	3 lb.
Rekol	2 lb.
Alpod	1 lb.
# 3 Paint	2 gal.

APPROVALS

	________	________ DATE
SUPERVISING CHEMIST	________	________ DATE
PLANT CONTROLLER	________	________ DATE
CHIEF INDUSTRIAL ENGINEER	________	________ DATE
GENERAL FOREMAN	________	________ DATE
SUPERINTENDENT	________	________ DATE
MANAGER	________	________ DATE
MANAGER, QUALITY CONTROL	________	________ DATE

From these data as to standard quantities and prices the accountant builds the standard cost of direct material.

If the product is one which is assembled from purchased parts or fabricated from processed materials such as steel plate, rods, or shapes, the specifications would be set by design engineers instead of chemists. However the procedure for building a standard cost would parallel that described for a product manufactured from basic raw materials.

DIRECT LABOR STANDARDS, PIECEWORK RATES

The methods used to develop direct labor standards will be dependent upon the methods used to calculate employee earnings. If wage payments are based on straight piecework rates, these rates become the direct labor standard costs, and unit standards are not required. It is expected that the workers will earn enough on the basis of the piecework rates to meet guaranteed minimum earnings per hour. Make-up pay, that is, amounts required to bring average hourly earnings up to the guaranteed minimum, would be paid only to the most inefficient workers. Provision for this is not built into the standard costs, since it is a cost which should not be incurred under efficient operation. Sometimes when wage increases are granted the piecework rates are not revised. Instead a flat amount per hour worked is added to the piece-rate earnings.

When this is done it is necessary to add an increment to the piece rates to provide for the added rate per hour in the standard costs. Such addition is made on the basis of the time studies on which the piece rates were set. If the piece rate for a given item is $0.15 and that is based on a standard of $1/10$ hour per piece, an added hourly increment of $0.12 would result in a standard cost of $0.15 plus $1/10$ of $0.12 or $.162 per piece.

DIRECT LABOR STANDARDS, INCENTIVE PLANS

When wage payments are based on incentive plans other than piecework rates, the expected incentive earnings must be calculated to arrive at the attainable standard cost. While there are many variations in these incentive plans, all provide for an increase in the effective hourly rate of the employee after a selected level of production efficiency is attained. Standard man-minutes or -hours for performing each operation are set by time and motion study engineers. From these a level is selected at which incentive earnings start. This level may be used as the basis for calculating standard time allowances for comparison with actual time for control purposes, or the efficiency level expected to be attained may be selected for this purpose. The latter is used for the standard costs, and this standard time unit is extended at the effective hourly rate at this level of efficiency to arrive at the standard unit cost. Under a plan where earnings above a selected efficiency level are shared 50-50 by the employer and employee the determination of the standard cost would be as shown in Table 8-1.

TABLE 8-1

Base for incentives—20 man-minutes per piece
Expected efficiency level—15 man-minutes per piece
Base hourly rate—$2.40 or $0.04 per minute

$$\text{Standard cost} = \$0.04 \left(20 - \frac{20 - 15}{2} \right) = \$0.70$$

DIRECT LABOR STANDARDS, HOURLY RATES

When wages are paid on a straight rate-per-hour basis, standard production per hour is set on the basis of time and motion studies, or on the basis of past experience. The standard minutes or hours set by such study make allowance for all factors which normally influence the degree of efficiency attained, so that they reflect the normal performance of the average worker. In small plants where technical staffs are not available, the accountant may set the time standards on past experience modified by the judgment of the foremen as to expected changes. These standards, scientific or based on experience, are evaluated at the labor rates in effect for the respective operations to establish standard labor costs.

INDIVIDUAL AND CREW STANDARDS

In setting labor standards it is desirable to provide for the measurement of individual performance wherever possible. This permits detailed analysis of performance within operations when standards are not met. However, many operations require a crew of men working as a group with the performance of each limited by the least efficient member of the crew or by the speed of the machine they are operating. In these instances a standard is set for the specified crew. Various skills and wage rates may be included in the crew. The rate applied to the standard hours to determine standard costs is a composite for the crew. In a fiberboard mill the crew of the forming machine would include the following crew and hourly rates: one machine tender at $2.10, one pulp operator at $1.90, one wet-saw operator at $1.80, and three helpers at $1.60, resulting in a composite rate of $10.60 per hour. With the operation paced by the speed of the machine and a standard of 0.45 hours per 1,000 square feet, including allowance for delays, the standard direct labor cost is $4.77 per 1,000 square feet.

STANDARDS FOR QUALITY INCENTIVES

In addition to incentives based on quantity of production an additional bonus is paid in some plants based on the quality of the production. This is particularly true in industries where the product cannot be inspected at each operation. In the manufacture of certain products many defects cannot be detected before the final inspection of the goods. These may have been caused in any stage of the production cycle. For example, fiberboard acoustical stock which is produced in large sheets to be cut, drilled, beveled, and painted as acoustical tile would not be inspected at the dry saw. Each run would be numbered and recorded with the clock numbers of the men on the crew which produced it. When the inspectors inspect the finished tile, they would classify defects as to the board-forming or finishing operations. Bonuses would then be paid to the members of the board-forming crew if the percentage of defects chargeable to them was less than the incentive standard. In this case the standard labor cost of board forming would include the quality bonus expected to be paid on that operation.

Direct labor standards are recorded on suitable forms for each operation. These provide for approval of the respective foremen, and copies are kept on file in the production and accounting departments.

SCRAP STANDARDS

While the raw material standards reflect the yields in the operations in which the materials are used, losses occur in subsequent operations, and final inspection may result in rejects or seconds. Standards are set for such losses wherever they normally occur. These are set by the engineering or production-control department on the basis of measured allowances or experience. For example, where rolls of cloth must be joined together, it may be determined that 1 yard will be lost in making the splice, and this will be set as the standard. In addition there will be unavoidable breaks in the material as it is running over the machines. There is no basis for measuring how many of these there should be nor how much material will be lost at each break. The standard for such items can be set only on average past experience. When scrap occurs after the first operation, the labor and expense of prior operations is lost in addition to the material loss. Therefore, standard scrap allowances must include provision for the total cost of scrap.

TESTING THE STANDARDS

Frequently attainable standards are tested by the accounting department before they are used. As the standard data sheets are received from the respective staffs, they are applied to production of a selected past period, usually a representative month. The resulting allowances are compared with the actuals of the period. A deviation of plus or minus 2% or 3% is considered reasonable. Larger deviations must be explained by contemplated changes in methods or abnormal conditions in the period selected for the test.

The attainable material and labor standard costs have many uses in addition to that of cost control. These will be discussed in subsequent chapters.

Perfection Standards

The perfection standard is the cost which should result from perfect operation within existing product specifications and with existing equipment. It is based on the assumption that materials are always within specification limits, there is no shrinkage or spillage, scrap is at an absolute minimum, equipment is always in top-notch condition, and each operator performs his job in the best prescribed manner. The combination of all these conditions will result in a minimum cost level. From practical experience it is evident that perfect operation can never be attained. However, it is a goal toward which all operating and staff personnel should strive, if a plant is to maintain its competitive position at a satisfactory profit level.

Perfection standards may supplement attainable standards for the purpose of effecting sharper control of certain costs or may be the only standards used. They are expressed in appropriate physical units such as man-hours, square feet, pounds, gallons, etc. Being expressed in units they simplify and expedite the application to production and comparison with actuals. A perfection standard is not set for every component of cost. The need for control and the value of a perfection standard to implement control are determined prior to any decision to build the standards for any segment or cost component of an operation.

METHODS OF SETTING PERFECTION STANDARDS

Since the standards represent perfect performance, they cannot be set on average past experience. Instead, one of the following methods, in order of preference, is usually used:

1. *Theoretical mathematical calculations*

This represents the best basis for a perfection standard, since the calculations cannot be affected in any way by unusually good or poor operation in the past. They will represent the best and most economical practice. Data to make the necessary calculation are usually available from material specifications, machine or equipment designers, the job engineer, or from actual timed observation of the man, machine, or equipment.

2. *Supervised tests*

The second method for setting a standard, which also eliminates the variables of past performance, is the supervised test. In this method someone familiar with the operation involved, and with the ability to judge the approach to perfect operating conditions, observes the operation and uses the observed data as perfect operation. The observer may be a group made up of plant staff and line personnel. This method is used in many plants today in establishing machine capacity for incentive purposes and represents the maximum-quality output for a given piece of equipment.

3. Statistical analysis

Statistical determination of the tenth percentile or the ninetieth percentile of a series of results of past performance is useful in setting a standard where the best performance ever attained should represent perfect operation. In this case instead of selecting the best performance as the actual standard, the best 10% of the results are arbitrarily discarded as being the result of probable laboratory, measuring, or accounting errors. For example, it has been necessary to determine a standard yield:

a. After all results which were outside of manufacturing standard limits were eliminated, the remaining results were tabulated statistically (Table 8-2) to show their frequency and range of distribution, and the cumulative frequency was calculated.

TABLE 8-2

Range of yields	Occurrence	Cumulative total
60.0–60.9	2	2
61.0–61.9	2	4
62.0–62.9	3	7
63.0–63.9	3	10
64.0–64.9	4	14
65.0–65.9	5	19
66.0–66.9	7	26
67.0–67.9	8	34
68.0–68.9	9	43
69.0–69.9	8	51
70.0–70.9	8	59
71.0–71.9	5	64
72.0–72.9	4	68
73.0–73.9	3	71
74.0–74.9	2	73
75.0–75.9	2	75

b. Since the total number of occurrences equals 75, then 90% of 75 equals the case which occurs at the 67.5 point in the scale of cumulative totals.

c. By inspection this case is found in the 72.0 to 72.9 cell. This cell contains four cases, and its range is 0.9.

d. Therefore the determination of the ninetieth percentile can be formulated as follows:

$$72.0 + \left(\frac{67.5 - 64}{4} \times 0.9 \right) = 72.7875$$

e. In this case the standard yield is 72.7875%.

COMPARISON WITH ATTAINABLE STANDARDS

Comparison of certain allowances in attainable standards and perfection standards is made in Table 8-3 and indicates the significant differences between the two.

TABLE 8-3
Labor Allowances

Item	Attainable standards	Perfection standards
1. Mechanical down time...	Allowed on past performance	Not allowed
2. Operating down time.....	Allowed on past performance	Not allowed
3. Scrap production........	Adjusted past performance	Minimum process losses only
4. Crew balance............	Adjusted past performance	Not allowed
5. Substandard raw materials.................	Past performance	Top-quality level
6. Setup or change-overs....	Average of past performance	Scheduled setup only or once per order

Material Allowances

1. Spillage, shrinkage, etc...	Past performance	Not allowed
2. Process losses..........	Past performance	Minimum only
3. Defective production.....	Adjusted past performance	Not allowed
4. Substandard raw materials	Adjusted past performance	Not allowed

MATERIAL STANDARDS

The perfection standard for material is the cost of material used directly in the manufacture of commodities, measured in units such as square feet, gallons, pounds, etc., necessary to produce a specified unit of production when following the best known method of operation. The task of building the standard consists of an analysis of the data furnished in the standard material specification, and an analysis of the process loss points to determine whether they are consistent with the best operating conditions. Generally, these losses are divided as follows:

1. Measurable losses controllable by good operating technique
2. Measurable losses not controllable by the operator, such as trim losses which can be approximated but not controlled and are characteristic of the product
3. Unknown losses, which include all material variations (losses and gains) which show up through balancing inventories, receipts, etc., and cannot be definitely accounted for. These are controllable in that they

should not occur if inventories, usage, and transfers are measured accurately. Each loss is checked to determine whether or not it is consistent with the best method of operation, and an allowance is included in the perfection standard only for the absolute minimum of measurable losses.

LABOR STANDARDS

The development of perfection standards for labor does not follow necessarily the cost accounting classification of costs. Both direct and indirect labor functions may be combined in order to arrive at a minimum labor cost for an operation. For example, time study may indicate that a working leader of a crew (direct labor) is actually working 40% of the time and the machine setter (indirect labor) is actually working 60% of the time. Four other members, either direct or indirect labor, are each working 100% of the time. The perfection standard would allow five men, even though job classification and cost classification lines are crossed. Labor relations and other considerations may make it impossible to combine the work of the leader and the machine setter. But the objective is perfection, not practicality.

The perfection standard for labor is the cost, measured in man- or machine-hours, necessary to produce a specified unit of production when following the best known method of operation. The task of building the standard consists of (1) analyzing the work done in the operation or department and (2) recording the necessary work under three classifications:

1. Direct work—work that varies directly as the amount of production varies.

2. Indirect work—work that varies with the unit operated such as start-up or shutdown.

3. General work—work that must be done regardless of production, such as cleaning aisles, rest rooms, etc. This is usually a function of time. By totaling the three classifications of work for an operation, a perfection standard for labor is developed for a particular product run or operation.

APPROVAL OF STANDARDS

It is important that the detail work sheets used in developing perfection standards be retained during the period the standards are in use. They are used for relatively long periods, and frequent reference to them is necessary in analyzing actual performance and interpreting variations. The standards themselves are recorded on appropriate forms and are approved by the appropriate members of the organization, just as are the attainable standards.

REVIEW QUESTIONS

1. What is the difference between standards and standard costs?
2. Is it possible to have a standard cost accounting system if standards are not set?
3. How does the use of standards relate to the organization structure of a plant?
4. Who should set the standards? Who should approve them?
5. Define an attainable standard.
6. What types of attainable standards may be used?
7. What effect does the method of determining employee earnings have on direct labor standards? On direct labor standard costs?
8. Should all labor incentives be based on the quantity produced?
9. Why should there be any standard allowance for scrap?
10. Define a perfection standard.
11. How are perfection standards set?
12. What are the major differences between attainable and perfection standards?
13. Why are accounting classifications of costs ignored in using perfection standards for labor?
14. What management purposes are served by standards and standard costs?
15. How frequently should standards be changed? What are the advantages and disadvantages of changes?

PROBLEMS

1. A plastics molding company makes brown and white furniture rests. Operations are molding, inspecting, packing, and shipping.

The standard cost of brown phenolic molding powder is $0.343 per pound and of white urea molding powder is $0.49 per pound. Controlled tests indicate that the reported weight of powder used at the molding operation is 2% less than the weight purchased. Specifications at molding are for the usage of 0.48 ounces of powder per furniture rest.

Operators of the molding presses are paid incentives. Inspectors and packers are paid piecework rates, and shippers are paid hourly rates. Labor costs are the same for brown and for white rests.

The base hourly rate for molding-press operators is $2.10. The base for incentive pay is 10 man-minutes per 100, and the expected efficiency level is 8 man-minutes per 100. Gains from production above the incentive base are split 60% to the worker and 40% to the company.

Inspectors and packers are paid $0.15 per 100 rests. The hourly rate in the shipping operation is $1.80, and the industrial engineers have set a shipping standard of 3 man-minutes per 100 rests.

a. Calculate the standard material cost per 100 pieces for both brown and white rests.

b. Calculate the standard labor cost per 100 rests.

2. In setting a perfection standard for labor in an operation by supervised tests it is determined that on the average the personnel are actually working in each hour as follows:

	Minutes
1 Leader...................,.........	37
4 Machine operators...........	41 each
2 Helpers....................	23 each
1 Machine tender.............	27
1 Materials mover............	40
1 Lubricator.................	46

The maximum output attainable from the single machine of the operation is 12,000 units per hour.

In a given 8-hour day, with a full crew working, 85,000 units were produced. There was no machine setup or job change.

What percentage of perfection was achieved?

(Note that the failure to achieve perfection is caused by a combination of crew unbalance and of production at less than machine capacity.)

CHAPTER 9

Absorption Costing

The cost systems of most companies provide for the inclusion of all factory expense in inventory values at either actual or standard rates. This procedure is known as "absorption costing." Under it the accounting for actual factory expense follows that discussed in Chapter 6. All expenses of service operations are allocated to productive operations, and the total of the incurred and allocated expense of each productive operation is related to the units produced, or other measure of activity, to determine an expense rate for each operation.

These actual expense rates are used for applying expense to job orders under a job-order cost system. If a process cost system is used, the actual expense of each operation is added to its material usage and direct labor to arrive at the total cost carried forward to the next operation in the production sequence or to finished-stock inventory values. If several products pass through the same productive operation, the expense rates are used to apply expense by product lines to secure total factory cost of each product.

Predetermined Rates Desirable

Some factory expenses do not change with, or in direct ratio to, changes in production volume, e.g., depreciation, property taxes, and insurance. Because they do not, actual factory expense rates will increase when volume declines and will decrease when volume increases. Also, actual expense cannot be applied until the subsidiary expense ledger work is completed, and this delays the closing work and the preparation of periodic cost reports. For these reasons predetermined expense rates are frequently used, even if the rest of the cost system is on an actual cost basis. Under a standard cost system these predetermined rates are called "standard expense rates," and this designation is used in the remainder of this chapter.

111

Selecting an Expense Absorption Level

The first step in building standard expense rates is to establish a level of activity at which the total factory expense will be absorbed, that is, applied to production. Under an actual cost system this is the estimated production level for the period. Under a standard cost system it is a "normal" volume. This volume may be based on the average sales over a period of years which includes maximum and minimum levels or on a percentage of production capacity. In either case it should be stated in terms of finished units of products. Setting the normal volume on the basis of average sales is the better procedure, for it can thus be used for other management accounting purposes, as discussed in later chapters.

Normal volumes based on average sales are determined for each major product group in the line, not as a composite for the entire plant or company. The average should include a forward look as well as historical experience. This is particularly important if a product is reflecting a definite increasing or decreasing volume trend. The normal volume based on sales must give consideration to production capacity. It cannot be in excess of the capacity of any one production operation. Neither should it require capacity operation over a year or period of years. Seasonal sales patterns make it impossible to achieve capacity production throughout the year in some industries. Depressed years for an industry or for the entire economy make it impossible to achieve capacity production year after year in any plant or industry. Thus, the acceptable ratio of normal sales volume to productive capacity will vary by type of industry. For products having a relatively stable sales level it may be as high as 85%. For products with marked seasonal or cyclical variations a ratio of 60% may be high enough. The perfect normal volume is one at which total expense is exactly absorbed over a period of years with underabsorption in some and overabsorption in others.

There are instances where average sales do not provide an acceptable expense absorption volume. If a new plant has been built, especially for making a new product, average market potential may be unknown. If a product reflects a down trend which indicates that plant capacity will never be utilized, an absorption volume based on sales may, when related to fixed expenses of the plant, result in standard expense rates which would be so high that they could not be used for inventory valuation nor for pricing the finished product. This is a signal that new products must be added, and realistic expense rates must be developed which will provide a sound pricing base for these new products. Therefore, if normal sales volume is substantially below production capacity or is indeterminable, the expense absorption volume should be based on a reasonable percentage of capacity. In practice, this percentage usually falls in the 70 to 80 range.

Also, when a normal volume based on sales indicates capacity operation for a period of years, it should not be considered to be acceptable. Such a condition is a signal that additional capacity will soon be required. When that capacity is added, the total of at least some expense sources will be increased, e.g., depreciation, maintenance, insurance, and taxes. If the normal volume based on sales potential was correct before adding the capacity, it will probably be correct after adding the capacity. It was determined on the ability to sell, not to produce. With no change in normal volume, and the added costs resulting from the added capacity, expense rates will increase. This will create problems in inventory valuation and cost determination for pricing. This may be avoided by using a percentage of capacity when normal volume based on sales indicates capacity operation. This percentage will be determined by the historical record of the ratio of sales to capacity. Thus, when the capacity is increased and the new and higher costs are related to the normal sales volume, there will be little or no change in expense rates.

Activity by Operations at Normal Volume

After normal volumes are established in terms of finished units by product lines, they must be converted into units of production in each productive operation. Exhibit 9-1 illustrates this calculation for a fiberboard plant producing wallboard, roof insulation, and acoustical tile. Conversion is made in reverse order of the flow of production. No consideration is given to in-process inventories in this calculation. It is assumed that everything sold at normal volume is processed in entirety in the year. Where scrap, trim, or other process losses occur, the production of the succeeding operation must be increased by the standard allowances for these to arrive at the gross production of an operation, for its capacity is stated in terms of the total units it processes irrespective of whether they are good or bad. The production of one of the earlier operations may determine that of all others which precede it. In the illustration the gross production of the dry saws must be dried and formed and wood must be ground for this quantity of board. Therefore production of drying, forming, and grinding are all computed on the basis of the gross production going to the dry saws.

After production in units is determined for each productive operation, the units are converted into the units used in the expense budget for establishing budget allowances, where these are other than product units. For example, the finishing operation in Exhibit 9-1 shows an activity of 30 million square feet of acoustical tile. The activity base for

EXHIBIT 9-1
NORMAL VOLUME BY OPERATION

		Normal volume					
	Unit	½-in. Wallboard	¾-in. Roof insulation	¾-in. Acoustical tile	Total	Per cent of capacity	Capacity
Sales............................	M sq ft	30,400	11,100	28,500	70,000		
Operation:							
522 Shipping..................	M sq ft	30,400	11,100	28,500	70,000		
521 Warehousing.............	M sq ft	30,400	11,100	28,500	70,000	70	100,000
422 Finishing —Finished production...	M sq ft			28,500			
—Scrap 5% of gross production...							
Gross production...	M sq ft			30,000	30,000	60	50,000
420 Preparation—Finished production...	M sq ft	30,400	11,100		41,500		
—Scrap 2% of gross production...							
Gross production...	M sq ft	31,020	11,327		42,347	84.7	50,000
333 Dry saws —Finished production...	M sq ft	31,020	11,327	30,000	72,347		
—Trim 2% of gross production...							
Gross production...	M sq ft	31,653	11,558	30,612	73,823	73.8	100,000
332 Drying —Hours per 1,000 sq ft...		0.068	0.068	0.091			
—Production...	hr	2,152	786	2,786	5,724	79.5	7,200
331 Forming —(Same as dryer).......							
—Production........	hr	2,152	786	2,786	5,724	79.5	7,200
220 Grinding —Lb wood pulp per 1,000 sq ft...		750	1,100	1,125			
—Production..................	M lb	23,740	12,714	34,438	70,892	70.9	100,000

budget allowance in this operation is standard direct labor hours. Several sizes and types of tile are produced, each of which has a different standard labor hour rate per 1,000 square feet. Therefore the finished-operation production is broken down into the normal mixture of sizes and types. The footage of each of these is extended at its labor-hour rate to establish standard direct labor hours at normal volume for the operation.

After the activities of the productive operations are determined, a calculation is made of their requirements from service operations at normal volume. The total requirements of the productive operation thus establish the normal volumes of the service operations.

Normal Expense Rates

Normal expense rates are usually based on the expense budget developed for the control of expense (Chapter 15). A budget which can be adjusted to any level of production activity is referred to as a flexible budget. In these budgets the expenses which do not vary directly with changes in volume are budgeted separately as fixed expense. Those which vary with volume are budgeted at rates per unit of production. With a flexible budget the dollars of expense for each operation at normal volume are determined by taking the budgeted fixed expense for that level of production, plus the budgeted variable expense rates times the normal activity units.

If expense budgets are not built, the expense at normal volume must be estimated. Such estimates are based on prior experience for comparable volumes, adjusted for changes in cost levels such as wage increases.

Expenses of the service operations are allocated to the productive operations on the basis of service rendered as discussed previously in Chapter 6, "Accounting for Actual Factory Expense." The total of the specific and allocated expenses of each production operation at expense absorption volume is the amount related to activity units to establish standard expense rates. The activity unit selected should be one which provides a fair application of expense to products. Wherever machine time is the dominant factor in the production of an operation, as with the board-forming machine in the fiberboard plant, a rate per machine-hour is best. Where labor is dominant, as in an inspection operation, a rate per standard labor hour or dollar is best. In some operations two expense rates may be required, one on machine-hours for the expense related to the machines and the other on labor for the expense related to labor. This is necessary if both machine and labor expenses are significant and there are changes in the number or skills of the men on a machine crew as different products are processed.

It is desirable that the activity units used in the flexible budget for expense control (Chapter 15) be the same as those used for applying factory expense to production. This eliminates an extra calculation before expense rates are determined. For example, if the activity basis in the flexible budget is standard machine-hours, the number of hours at expense absorption volume divided into the dollars of standard expense at that volume equals the standard expense rate per machine-hour. If different activity bases are used for the flexible budget and for standard expense, a conversion must be made. For example, if budget activity is expressed in standard direct labor hours and a standard expense rate is desired as a percentage of standard direct labor cost, the standard labor hours must be converted into standard labor dollars before the standard expense rate is calculated. The reasons for not using the flexible budget activity bases for expense rates would be (1) that they do not provide a fair application of expense to production but do provide the best basis for flexible budget allowances or (2) that the use of some other base would be more expedient when used in conjunction with the rates for other cost elements.

Calculating Absorbed Expense

The amount of expense absorbed into inventory values is determined by applying the normal expense rates to production quantities. There are two methods of doing this. The first is most generally used where a complete standard cost system is employed. It consists of converting the expense rate into a rate per unit of product. Continuing with the finishing operation of the fiberboard plant, normal volume was first calculated in square feet and then converted to standard direct labor hours, the activity base for the flexible budget. Relating the budgeted expenses to the labor hours at normal volume provided the expense dollars at normal volume. Since labor rates do not change when different types of tile are produced, the variation in labor cost is due entirely to the amount of time required to finish each type. Therefore expense at normal volume can be related to direct labor cost at normal volume to arrive at expense as a percentage of direct labor. This percentage applied to the standard labor cost of an item will provide the standard expense as a rate per unit of product. These are then used to compute the absorbed expense by extending production units at standard expense rates per unit of product (Exhibit 12-5). This conversion to rates per unit of product is made on the work sheets used to build product standard factory costs.

However, it is not essential that this be done in order to absorb expense into inventory values. An alternate procedure, which will result in absorbing the same dollars of expense, is to calculate the standard activity units (machine-hours, labor hours, etc.) required for the actual units produced and then apply the standard operational rates to these. This results in one calculation for each operation to determine absorbed expense but requires a number of calculations to determine the standard activity units. If it is desired to know absorbed expense by product lines, the first and more generally used procedure is necessary. Otherwise the one is selected which requires the least effort.

After the amount of absorbed expense is determined it is recorded as follows:

> Dr. Work in Process
> Cr. Absorbed Factory Expense

Variance Due to Volume

For purposes of determining the effect of production volume on profit and loss, the standard fixed and standard variable expense rates are frequently computed and applied separately. Then a comparison of the fixed expense absorbed with the dollars of standard fixed expense will show the over- or underabsorption due to the level of production volume. With fixed expense in an operation of $12,000 per month and an expense absorption level of 100 standard machine-hours per month the standard fixed expense rate is $120 per hour. With actual activity, based on units of product produced, of 90 machine-hours the underabsorption, or volume variance loss, would be:

$$\$12,000 - (90 \times \$120) = \$1,200$$
or
$$(100 - 90) \times \$120 = \$1,200$$

It is to be noted that such variances are the result of the level of production volume, not sales volume. For example, if production is above normal volume because inventory is being increased and sales are below normal volume, there will be a volume variance gain in the plant, even though the sales volume would indicate a volume variance loss.

In companies determining costs and profit and loss by product lines, separate volume variances are computed for each product in each operation. Fixed expenses are allocated to product lines on the basis of relative volume at expense absorption volume. This is done on the premise that the operation is staffed and equipped to meet the normal volume demands of each product and therefore each product should carry a normal share of the fixed expense. In any one month this procedure may result in volume variance gains on one product and losses on another in the same operation. This is justifiable, since a product which is at or above expense absorption volume should not be penalized by volume variance losses of another which is below. Exhibit 9-2 illustrates a calculation of volume variances by product lines.

EXHIBIT 9-2

CALCULATION OF VOLUME VARIANCE BY PRODUCT LINES
FORMING OPERATION

	Standard per month		February actual		
	Machine-hours at normal volume	Fixed expense	Standard machine-hours	Fixed absorbed	Volume variance
Wallboard.......	132	$ 9,240	110	$ 7,700	$(1,540)*
Roof insulation...	106	7,420	94	6,580	(840)
Acoustical tile....	179	12,530	200	14,000	1,470
	417	$29,190	404	$28,280	$(910)

* Parentheses denote underabsorption.

EXHIBIT 9-3

RECONCILIATION OF BUDGET AND VOLUME VARIANCES
WITH OVER- OR UNDERABSORBED EXPENSE

Expense budget:

Fixed................ $29,190 per month

Variable............ $ 90 per standard machine-hour

Activity basis—standard machine-hours

Expense standard:

Normal volume of 417 machine-hours per month

Fixed expense rate........... $ 70

Variable expense rate........   90

Total expense rate.......... $160

Month of February:

Activity 404 standard machine-hours

Actual expense................................ $65,252

Absorbed expense 404 × $160.................   64,640

Unabsorbed expense.......................... $ (612)

Budget allowance—Fixed...................... $29,190

Variable 404 × $90.........   36,360

Total.................... $65,550

Actual expense..............................   65,252

Spending gain............................... $ 298

Fixed absorbed 404 × $70..................... $28,280

Standard and budgeted fixed...................   29,190

Volume loss................................. $ (910)

Volume loss ($910) − spending gain $298 = ($612) unabsorbed

Since the standard variable expense rates were based on the variable allowances in the flexible budget, the variable standard expense absorbed and the budget allowance for variable expense in any period will be the same. Therefore there can be no variance in variable expense resulting from the level at which expense is absorbed.

Analysis of Expense Variances

The difference between total actual factory expense and total absorbed factory expense for a plant or for an operation within a plant is due to two factors: (1) control—spending more than allowed in the budget and (2) production volume—level of production relative to expense absorption volume. Therefore the variance of actual expense from the budgeted expense, plus the volume variance, equals the difference between the actual factory expense and the absorbed factory expense. This is illustrated in Exhibit 9-3. This analysis is used to explain deviations from budgeted profit by areas of responsibility for the deviations and for other reports to management which will be discussed in other chapters.

REVIEW QUESTIONS

1. What is meant by the "absorption" of factory expense?
2. Discuss the relative advantages of actual and predetermined expense rates.
3. What level of activity should be used in determining factory expense rates?
4. Define normal volume.
5. Under what conditions would it be undesirable to use average sales as the expense absorption volume?
6. Why are expense absorption volumes determined for each productive operation?
7. How are the dollars of expense at expense absorption volume determined for each productive operation?
8. When should more than one expense rate be determined for an operation?
9. What are the advantages of using the same activity units for expense rates and for variable expense allowances in flexible budgets?
10. What are the two methods which may be used to calculate absorbed expense?
11. When are expense variances experienced which are due to production volume?
12. Explain the conditions under which one product would show a volume variance gain in an operation and another product show a volume variance loss in the same operation.

PROBLEM

A company has built a new plant with a practical capacity of 1,200,000 units per year, at three shifts, 5 days per week. Sales budgeted for the first year of operation are 400,000 units, and estimated sales are 700,000 in the second year, 800,000 in the third year, 800,000 in the fourth year, and 900,000 in the fifth year. There are no major seasonal fluctuations in the industry, and production facilities are balanced so that the entire plant can be considered as a unit. It is decided to absorb expense at 70% of practical capacity. Fixed expenses are budgeted at $500,000 for one-shift operation for the first year and are estimated to be $756,000 per year for three-shift operation in subsequent years. Variable expenses are budgeted at $0.25 per unit of production.

1. Does the selected expense absorption volume appear to be satisfactory?

2. Calculate the normal factory expense rate per unit of production at expense absorption volume.

3. In January of the second year 60,000 units are produced. With fixed expense of $756,000 per year, what was the January volume variance?

CHAPTER 10

Direct Costing

In recent years there has been a definite trend in cost accounting procedure toward the exclusion of some or all fixed factory expenses from inventory values. This procedure is generally referred to as "direct costing." Under it the factory cost applied to production for valuing work-in-process and finished-stock inventories includes direct material, direct labor, and variable expense. The fixed expenses are charged directly against profit or loss of the period in which they are incurred. Actually, this is not a new procedure. It was referred to in at least two of the early articles on cost accounting, one published in 1898 and the other in 1902. Also, some few companies have always excluded certain factory expenses from inventory values.

Absorption Costing Generally Accepted Practice

In the development of cost accounting techniques since the turn of the century, the trend has been toward the allocation of all service-department costs to productive operations, and the use of these specific and allocated operation expenses to determine expense rates. As a result, such rates include both fixed and variable components of factory expense. The application of these rates to job orders or products (absorption costing) at either actual or standard, and their use for inventory valuation, became general practice. This is recognized in Statement 3 of Accounting Research Bulletin 29—*Inventory Pricing*, issued by the Committee on Accounting Procedure, American Institute of Accountants, in July, 1947. This says: "The primary basis of accounting for inventories is cost, which has been defined generally as the price paid or consideration given to acquire an asset. As applied to inventories, cost means in principle the sum of the applicable expenditures and charges directly or indirectly incurred in bringing an article to its existing condition and location." Since fixed factory expense is indirectly incurred, and sometimes directly incurred, in the manufacture of an article, many accountants take the position that it must be included in costs used for inventory valuation.

However, this interpretation is not universal, and the discussion in the Institute bulletin, which follows the statement, does appear to permit certain exclusions. One sentence of this states: "It should also be recognized that the exclusion of *all* overheads from inventory costs does not constitute an accepted accounting procedure." The proponents of direct costing argue that the exclusion of fixed costs from inventory values is permissible since "all overheads" are not excluded.

Renewed Interest in Direct Costing

The first of the recent articles on direct costing appeared in the late 1930s, before Bulletin 29 was issued. These writings presented the procedure as one which would improve internal reporting and facilitate the analysis and interpretation of operating results. The idea did not find ready acceptance by companies which were using absorption costing methods. Over the next 10 years few companies made the change, and the position of absorption costing was strengthened by the issuance of Bulletin 29. Then in the early 1950s business began to experience the prewar seasonal and cyclical fluctuations. These resulted in overabsorption and underabsorption of fixed expense in different periods, which affected reported profits of the periods. This renewed the interest in direct costing, and it was discussed extensively in programs and publications of accounting and management associations. As a result of this impetus, it is currently being adopted by many companies.

Advantages of Direct Costing

The advantages of direct costing are:

1. Profits of a period are not affected by changes in the absorption of fixed expense resulting from building or reducing inventory.

2. Fixed factory expense is emphasized by appearing on all internal reports.

3. Marginal balance (the difference between net sales income and direct costs) of different product groups can be appraised relatively without distortion by allocations of fixed expense or amounts of fixed expense absorbed.

4. The effects of increases or decreases in volume in either existing or new products can be determined easily by calculating the increase or decrease in marginal balance.

5. The effects on profits of changes in sales price and changes in costs other than fixed expense can be computed simply by calculating the effect on the marginal balance.

Comparative Effects on Profit and Loss

The comparative effects of absorption costing and direct costing on net profit are shown in Exhibit 10-1. This illustration assumes that actual

EXHIBIT 10-1
COMPARISON OF EFFECTS ON NET PROFIT OF
ABSORPTION COSTING AND DIRECT COSTING

Basic Data

Per unit

Standard cost—Direct material.........	$0.60
Direct labor.............	0.40
Variable expense.........	0.15
Fixed expense...........	0.35
Total.................	$1.50

[Fixed expense of $420,000 per year divided by 1,200,000 units at expense absorption (standard) volume equals $0.35 per unit.]

Sales price......... $2.00 per unit

	First quarter	Second quarter	Third quarter	Fourth quarter	Year
Units produced....................	300,000	280,000	300,000	350,000	1,230,000
Units sold........................	300,000	300,000	280,000	300,000	1,180,000

Absorption Costing

	First quarter	Second quarter	Third quarter	Fourth quarter	Year
Sales..............................	$600,000	$600,000	$560,000	$600,000	$2,360,000
Standard factory cost...............	450,000	450,000	420,000	450,000	1,770,000
Variances—Price...................	6,000	6,000	6,000	7,000	25,000
Efficiency...............	(9,000)	(9,000)	(9,000)	(10,500)	(37,500)
Volume.................	——	7,000	——	(17,500)	(10,500)
Adjusted factory cost...............	$447,000	$454,000	$417,000	$429,000	$1,747,000
Gross profit.....................	153,000	146,000	143,000	171,000	613,000
Selling expense.....................	60,000	60,000	60,000	60,000	240,000
Administrative expense..............	30,000	30,000	30,000	30,000	120,000
Net profit.......................	$ 63,000	$ 56,000	$ 53,000	$ 81,000	$ 253,000

Direct Costing

	First quarter	Second quarter	Third quarter	Fourth quarter	Year
Sales..............................	$600,000	$600,000	$560,000	$600,000	$2,360,000
Standard variable factory cost........	345,000	345,000	322,000	345,000	1,357,000
Variances—Price...................	6,000	6,000	6,000	7,000	25,000
Efficiency...............	(9,000)	(9,000)	(9,000)	(10,500)	(37,500)
Adjusted variable factory cost........	$342,000	$342,000	$319,000	$341,500	$1,344,500
Contribution to fixed expense and profit	258,000	258,000	241,000	258,500	1,015,500
Fixed factory expense...............	105,000	105,000	105,000	105,000	420,000
Selling expense.....................	60,000	60,000	60,000	60,000	240,000
Administrative expense.............	30,000	30,000	30,000	30,000	120,000
Net profit.......................	$ 63,000	$ 63,000	$ 46,000	$ 63,500	$ 235,500

* Parentheses denote gains.

fixed expenses are the same as the amounts budgeted, so that the comparison will not be distorted by changes in fixed expense. It also assumes production of one product. The absorption-costing figures of the illustration are developed under the procedures customarily used for standard expense rates. The direct-costing figures reflect the same sales and production conditions as the absorption-costing ones, except that fixed expense of each period is charged against profit and loss of the period.

In the first quarter, with both sales and production levels at expense absorption volume, profits were the same under both methods. In the second quarter, sales continued at this level but production dropped below it, the excess of sales over production coming from inventory on hand at the beginning of the year. Production below expense absorption volume reduced profits under absorption costing by $7,000 (20,000 units at $0.35). It is difficult to present a clear explanation of this in analyzing operating results for management, because they expect the same sales volume, with no change in costs or sales prices, to produce the same profit. Under direct costing, profits do change in direct ratio to sales volume.

In the third quarter, sales declined and production volume increased in comparison with the second quarter. Under both costing methods profits were lower than in the preceding quarter. This lower profit was due entirely to lower sales volume. However, under absorption costing the decline in profit from the first to the second quarter was explained as being due to a decline in production volume. On this basis, management would expect an increase in profit in the third quarter when production volume increased. Instead they are shown a further decline in profit. This was due to the fact that the favorable effect of more production was not great enough to offset the adverse effect of lower sales. Such an explanation is quite involved and tends to reduce confidence in profit analysis. Under direct costing, the explanation of the drop in profit from the second to the third quarter is very simple. Sales were 20,000 units lower. Each unit of sales contributed $0.85 to fixed expense and profit, and the decline in profit was $17,000—20,000 × ($2.00 — $1.15). Profits are earned when the goods are sold, not when they are produced, and the change in profit is in direct ratio to the change in sales volume.

In the fourth quarter, production volume was 50,000 units above expense absorption level and also above sales volume. This higher production volume caused greater price and efficiency variances. Under absorption costing it also resulted in an overabsorption of fixed expense of $17,500, with an equal effect on profit. Under direct costing, except for the effect of higher price and efficiency variances, the profit of the fourth quarter is the same as that of the first and second quarters when the same number of units were sold.

Fixed Expense Charged to Operations in Proper Year

Profit for the year was also $17,500 higher under absorption costing than under direct costing. This represents fixed expense applied to inventory in excess of the amount incurred. This overabsorbed fixed expense included in the value of the increased inventory is carried forward into the next year. If inventory is reduced in that year, operations will be charged with all the fixed expense of that year plus the fixed expense included in the inventory value of goods on hand at the beginning of the year which are sold during the year. This means that operations of that year must support more than a year's fixed expense and are proportionately less profitable. The opposite is true when inventory is increased.

Fixed Expense Highlighted

Absorption costing obscures the total dollars of fixed expense in internal reports; direct costing highlights it. The profit and loss report for a product or a plant which shows one figure for Cost of Goods Sold (either standard or actual), and variances from standards if standard costs are used, does not inform management of the amount of fixed expense which must be recovered in each period. Neither does the "volume variance" give any indication of this. The plant budgets do show the fixed expense for the plant and each operation, but they do not show it by product lines. Sales managers, particularly, should know what the fixed expense is on each of their product lines. If this information is compiled for them as a special report, it is not correlated with the income and other costs, and may be forgotten after several months. With fixed factory expense shown on each internal profit and loss report, this does not happen. Experience has shown that when general and sales managers were first given reports prepared on the direct-costing basis, they were amazed at the amount of fixed factory expense and its effect on profit. In many instances steps were taken to effect reductions and secure closer control of operating schedules to achieve greater production with no increase in fixed expense.

Direct Costing Facilitates Special Studies

Most special studies of the relative profitability of products, territories, etc., of the effect of changes in volume, and of changes in sales prices and variable costs should not include fixed factory expenses. These are not involved in the management decisions in the areas mentioned. To the extent that they are allocated, they tend to distort rather than add to the studies. If fixed expense rates are used in these special studies, consideration must be given to changes in profit resulting from changes in the amount of fixed expense absorbed, or to the changes in the rates due to changes in the factors on which they are based.

Therefore, in making special studies the expenses or expense rates must be analyzed and the fixed portion excluded and treated separately if absorption costing is used. Under direct costing this step is not required. Time is saved, and the possibility of error is reduced. Also, the studies will be prepared on the same basis as the operating reports and thus be more easily understood by management.

It must be recognized, however, that there are times when fixed expenses must be considered in reaching a decision. Since all direct-cost operating reports show these expenses, they are readily available when required.

Problem of Determining Fixed Expense

Direct costing is not without its problems. The first of these is the determination of the fixed expense. If flexible budgets are not in use, the fixed expense must be calculated. If they are, in changing from absorption to direct costing it is usually desirable to reexamine both the variable and fixed expense. It may be that steps in fixed expense which occur as activity expands to 6- or 7-day operation, or for other reasons, are provided for in the flexible-budget variable rate. Conversely, items may be included as variable which are actually fixed. These conditions should not be found where the flexible budgets are subjected to frequent review and are built in sufficient detail to reveal such inaccuracies. However, it should not be assumed that they do not exist. The fixed character of all expense items should be tested. If units of production times a standard or budgeted rate per unit does not result in a fair allowance for the item, it is a fixed expense for direct-costing purposes.

Sometimes the fixed portion of the factory expense is approximated for direct-costing purposes without making a detailed study of the variability of each item of expense. This is done by plotting actual expense at a number of activity levels on a scatter chart. On this the vertical axis indicates dollars of expense and the horizontal axis activity. A line is drawn through the average position of the points to the vertical axis. The point at which it touches this indicates the approximate dollars of fixed expense.

Problem of Allocating Fixed Expense to Product Lines

A second problem is the allocation of fixed expense to product lines, if profit or loss is desired by product lines. Under absorption costing the application of total expense rates to production automatically carries the fixed expense to products. If standard rates are used, the volume variance must be allocated. But because this is so much smaller than the total fixed expense dollars, errors have a relatively insignificant effect on the profit of any product.

Under direct costing, bases of allocation of fixed expense must be developed. The use of some over-all basis such as total direct cost or direct labor may distort product costs materially. To avoid this, separate allocation of the fixed expense of each productive operation, including its share of service operations, to product lines is necessary. This should be made in relation to the normal volume of each product in each operation expressed in the term which best reflects activity. This may be machine-hours, labor hours, labor dollars, prime cost, etc. In some plants it may not be necessary to take general plant expense to productive operations to allocate it to product lines. In fact, a more equitable allocation may be secured by taking it directly to products. This allocation would be made on the relative effort expended by general plant management and staffs on each product line.

Problem of Setting Sales Prices

The third problem is the determination of costs to be used for sales pricing. Simply taking a greater mark-up on direct costs than that taken on total costs will not provide satisfactory prices. The varying impact of fixed expense on product costs resulting from processing in different combinations of operations or from different processing speeds must be reflected. With fixed expenses allocated to products a satisfactory unit rate may be obtained by dividing the total by the normal sales activity units of each product. This will not be true if there are individual items in the product line which are produced at different speeds. In a fiberboard plant the forming machine runs slower when products with greater density are made. Since this causes substantial variation in the fixed expense cost per square foot, it must be reflected in the sales prices. This may make it necessary to develop expense rates by operations and then apply these to each product; or substantial accuracy may be achieved by weighting the over-all fixed expense rate of the product group according to relative machine speeds.

Problem of Inventory Values in Financial Statements and Tax Returns

The fourth problem is in the use of direct-cost inventory values for certified financial statements and income tax returns. At present some public accountants will qualify their certificate if inventories are valued at direct cost in the balance sheet, even if adequate disclosure is made in the notes to the statements. Other public accountants will not take exception. They support their position by the sentence of the discussion of Statement 3 of Bulletin 29 quoted earlier.

A change from absorption costing to direct costing for inventory valuation for Federal tax returns is a change in accounting procedure which requires approval of the Internal Revenue Service. Securing approval of any change in accounting procedure is always fraught with uncertainty and negotiation.

Because of the advantages of direct costing for internal reporting and analysis of operations, many firms use it within the company but value their inventories for published statements and tax returns on the absorption-costing basis. In this way, they avoid the problems of qualified certificates and of securing approval for changes in accounting procedure, and retain most of the advantages of direct costing.

Separate Control Account for Fixed Expense

When direct costing is used either internally or for both internal and published reports, it is desirable to establish separate expense-control accounts on the general ledger for fixed expenses and variable expenses. Actual expenses are then charged to the proper control account as incurred. No further accounting need be done for the fixed expense. For example, the fiberboard company may use 13100 for variable factory expenses and 13200 for fixed factory expenses. The total of the Fixed Expense Control account is a charge against operations for the period. Variable expenses are applied to production at standard or actual rates, just as total expense rates are applied under absorption costing. The variable expense applied to production is recorded as follows:

> Dr.   Work in Process
> Cr.   Applied Variable Expense

The difference between the Variable Expense Control account and the Applied Variable Expense account is an expense variance resulting from incurring more or less variable expense than allowed in the budget.

Separate expense-control accounts for fixed and variable expense cannot be used if the amount of fixed expense is determined from a scatter chart or other over-all basis. When this is done, all expense is charged to one control account as incurred. The calculated amount of fixed expense is then credited to this account and charged to a Fixed Expense account or directly to Profit and Loss. Variable expense applied to products is credited to a Variable Expense Absorbed account. The difference between this and the net balance of the expense control after crediting it for Fixed Expense is considered to be the unabsorbed variable expense of the period. While this is substantially accurate, it cannot be verified by mathematical calculations.

Alternate Procedure for Using Direct Costs Only in Internal Reports

If a company desires to use direct costing for internal reports and absorption costing for external reports, this can be done without computing and recording absorbed fixed expense on the books each month. At the time direct costing is adopted the amount of fixed expense in the inventory values is computed. This is then charged to a separate account —Fixed Expense on Inventory—and credited to the Work in Process and Finished Stock accounts. No entries are made to this account from month to month. Whenever external reports are to be issued, the number of months' production on inventory is determined. This may be done by units or standard direct-cost value. With a standard direct cost at normal volume of $500,000 per month and standard direct-cost value of inventory of $750,000 the inventory represents the production of 1½ months at normal volume. This establishes the amount of fixed expense which should be on inventory. If the fixed expense of the last month of the period was $48,000 and the next to the last $50,000, the amount on inventory should be $73,000. If this is more or less than the balance of the Fixed Expense on Inventory account, an adjustment is made to the account with a contra entry to Profit and Loss. Such adjustments are not carried back to product lines, job orders, or other internal records and reports. They are made and held at a plant or company level for external reporting purposes only.

The extent of the interest in direct costing will in time require a specific statement as to its acceptability for inventory valuation for certified financial statements, and appropriate tax regulations or legislation. Until that time it can be used most advantageously for internal reporting and profit analysis, with acceptable alternate procedures for external reporting.

REVIEW QUESTIONS

1. Define direct costing.
2. Why is absorption costing used more widely than direct costing?
3. What are the advantages of direct costing?
4. Will profit of a given year be higher or lower under direct costing than under absorption costing?
5. With absorption costing, under what conditions would cost of goods sold be charged with more fixed expense than was actually incurred in the year?

6. Why is it desirable to show the dollars of fixed expense on operating reports?
7. What types of special cost studies do not require the consideration of fixed factory expenses?
8. What problems are created by direct costing?
9. Discuss several methods of determining the amount of factory expense which is to be considered as "fixed" for an accounting period.
10. What is the advantage of a separate expense-control account for fixed factory expense?
11. How can the advantages of direct costing be realized for internal purposes and absorption costing be used for published financial statements and tax returns?

PROBLEMS

1. A small, single-plant company decides to adopt direct costing. It has no expense budgets. For the past year its production and factory expenses were:

TABLE P10-1

Month	Units	Expense
January..........	50,000	$55,000
February.........	55,000	57,600
March...........	60,000	61,000
April............	60,000	60,500
May.............	50,000	55,500
June............	40,000	50,000
July.............	40,000	49,000
August..........	50,000	54,000
September........	55,000	58,000
October..........	60,000	60,000
November........	60,000	61,500
December........	55,000	57,800

What is its approximate fixed expense per month?

2. A company operates one plant and produces one product. It uses absorption costing. Over a 3-year period fixed factory expenses were $50,000 per year and the expense absorption volume was 100,000 units. No processed inventory was on hand on January 1 of the first year. The operating statements and related data are shown in Table P10-2.

a. What would the profits of each year have been if the company had used direct costing?

b. What would the inventory values at the close of each year have been under direct costing?

c. Explain the difference in profits of years 1 and 3 when absorption costing was used.

TABLE P10-2

	Year 1	Year 2	Year 3
Units sold......................	100,000	80,000	100,000
Net sales......................	$300,000	$240,000	$300,000
Standard cost of goods sold.......	240,000	192,000	240,000
Production variance..............	1,100	1,200	800
Volume variance.................	(5,000)*	(10,000)*	10,000
Distribution and administrative expense......................	30,000	30,000	30,000
Profit before income tax..........	$ 33,900	$ 26,800	$ 19,200
Per cent to net sales.............	11.3	11.2	6.4
Production.....................	110,000	120,000	80,000
Inventory, end of year...........	$ 24,000	$120,000	$ 72,000

* Parentheses denote gains.

d. Assuming a constant income tax rate of 50%, how much less income tax would the company pay over the 3 years if it used direct costing and had approval of the Internal Revenue Service to use it for inventory values in tax returns? Why?

CHAPTER 11

Product Standard
Factory Costs

A standard cost accounting system reduces the cost of cost accounting; integrates the management accounting, cost accounting, and general accounting procedures; and facilitates the preparation of special cost studies. Therefore, when standards are developed for cost control, it is advantageous to incorporate them into a standard cost accounting system. This requires the development of product standard factory costs. These are used to measure actual costs and for interim inventory valuation, are applied to units shipped to provide the standard cost of goods sold, and provide basic data for special cost studies and for developing selling prices.

Standard Cost System Expedites Cost Accounting

The application of standard costs to products under a process cost system is particularly advantageous. The compilation of actual costs for each part, pattern, or item in a product line requires a tremendous amount of clerical effort. This delays the closing of the books, because the preparation of reports for actual unit costs must be compiled for each operation in sequence of the flow of production so that the costs can follow the movement of the material. Inventory of work in process at each center must be valued on the basis of the actual costs of that and all preceding work centers, and finally the actual costs must be applied to finished stock and cost of sales. This results in different unit costs for the same article in work in process if more than one period's production is on inventory in a cost center, and of different unit costs of finished products depending upon the period in which the units were produced. With the valuation of inventories at standard, and variances from standard cleared into variance accounts, each item on inventory is always valued at the same unit price, considering its state of completion. This speeds the monthly cost work and substantially reduces the number of calculations required.

Grouping of Products

Under a job-order standard cost system a standard cost is built for each job-order. This is in effect building a standard cost for a specific product, since seldom if ever are several products made on the same job-order.

With a process cost system standard factory costs are built for each product, or for each group of products having approximately the same unit cost. In the fiberboard plant a standard cost would be built for each size and thickness of acoustical tile (12 by 12 inches by ⅜ inch, 12 by 12 inches by ¾ inch, 12 by 24 inches by ⅜ inch, etc.), because the cost per square foot is determined by both size and thickness. For roof insulation, standards would be built for each thickness, but not for each size, since the area of an individual piece has little effect on the cost per square foot. With his knowledge of the product line and of costs, the accountant can group products so as to hold the number of product standard costs to a practical minimum.

Sometimes a standard may be built for a group of items of different dimensions or patterns based on the average mixture of items expected to be produced. This procedure has the advantage of reducing the number of product standard costs which must be built, and the number of calculations in applying standards to production. It has the disadvantage of causing variances from standard due to deviations of the actual mixture of production from that used in building the standards.

Standard Costs for Semiprocessed Materials

The formula, or bill, of materials and the production specifications provide the information as to the raw material used in each product, the operations through which it passes, and the processing methods and speeds. The building of the standard follows these in the sequence of production. A typical product standard cost (acoustical tile) is shown in Exhibit 11-1.

This standard cost starts with the forming operation, since this is the first operation in which the end product can be identified. Chest stock is a processed material, and standard costs were first developed for it. It is used in all the products of the fiberboard plant; therefore, the standard cost for each product includes the amount of chest stock for the specific product at the standard material, labor, and expense cost of this processed material.

In this instance the common processed material enters the finished product early in the production cycle. Sometimes a common product

EXHIBIT 11-1

PRODUCT STANDARD COST

¾-INCH 12- BY 12-INCH ACOUSTICAL TILE

	Quantity	Unit	Material Rate	Material Amount	Labor Rate	Labor Amount	Variable expense Rate	Variable expense Amount	Standard direct cost	Fixed expense Rate	Fixed expense Amount	Total standard cost
331 Forming:												
Chest stock	1,125	lb	0.0105	11.81	0.0052	5.85	0.0020	2.25		0.0033	3.71	
Margose	2	lb	1.20	2.40								
Rekol	3	lb	2.30	6.90								
Labor and expense	0.091	Machine-hours			10.40	0.95	70.00	6.37		90.00	8.19	
Total	1,000	sq ft		21.11								
332 Drying	0.091	Machine-hours			8.00	0.73	30.00	2.73		10.00	0.91	
333 Dry saws	0.091	Machine-hours					2.00	0.18		2.00	0.18	
Total		sq ft		21.11		7.53		11.53			12.99	
Trim loss	2%					7.53		11.53			12.99	
To finishing	980	sq ft		21.54		7.68		11.76	40.98		13.25	54.23
Adjustment for chest stock labor and expense	1,000			12.05		(5.97)		(2.29)			(3.79)	
				33.59		1.71		9.47			9.46	
422 Finishing:												
Paint	2	gal	3.90	7.80								
Labor and expense	1,000	sq ft				1.75		0.85			0.70	
Total	1,000	sq ft		29.34		9.43		12.61	51.38		13.95	65.33
Scrap loss	5%											
	950	sq ft		29.34		9.43		12.61	54.08		13.95	65.33
Packaged	1,000	sq ft		30.88		9.93		13.27			14.68	68.76
Package material	1,000	sq ft		2.10								
521 Warehousing	1,000	sq ft				0.50		0.25			0.33	
Finished stock inventory	1,000	sq ft		32.98		10.43		13.52	56.93		15.01	71.94
522 Shipping	1,000	sq ft				0.50		0.33			0.10	
Cost of sales	1,000	sq ft		32.98		10.93		13.85	57.76		15.11	72.87

proceeds through almost the entire production cycle. For example, if all fiberboard products had the same formula, one standard cost could be built for each thickness of board. Then, when it was cut into a specific product such as acoustical tile, the standard cost for that product would show, as the first item of cost, the quantity of board used at the standard material, labor, and expense cost for large boards.

It is customary to develop separate standard costs for semiprocessed materials or subassemblies which are subsequently used in, or become a part of, two or more finished products. This saves time in building standards in that the detail for such materials need be recorded and the standard cost calculated only once. They are credited to production and carried on inventory at these standard values. When they are used, they are charged to the using operation at this total standard unit cost.

Built by Cost Elements

The identity of each cost element is maintained in the product standard costs. This is desirable in that it permits the determination of inventory values and cost of goods sold by the elements of factory cost. It also facilitates the adjustment of inventory values to the lower of cost or market at the close of each year for the preparation of financial statements.

In the illustration the quantity of chest stock is priced at the standard material, labor, and expense rates per pound determined for it and reflected in the standard cost of acoustical tile by cost elements. The raw materials added at the forming operation are priced at the standard usage rates for these materials. This is the purchase standard rate adjusted for any shrinkage in raw materials which occurs before they are used. Paint and package material used in the finishing operation are priced on the same basis.

Labor and expense for the forming, drying, and dry-saw operations are calculated from the standard machine-hours required per 1,000 square feet and the applicable rates per machine-hour. All other labor and expense rates are established for the respective operations per 1,000 square feet of production and are included as such in the product standard cost.

The procedure for building the standard cost of any product would follow that illustrated for acoustical tile. Direct-material costs are accumulated for the first operation in the production cycle, and the labor and expense per unit of product is computed for that operation. The same procedure is followed for the second operation in the cycle and its standard costs are added to those of the first operation to provide a standard value for work in process completed through the second operation. This procedure is continued for subsequent operations until the unit standard cost of goods sold is established for the product.

Shrinkage in Production

Shrinkage of raw material has already been referred to. This shrinkage was the difference between the quantity of raw material purchased and the quantity measured into production at the initial operation. It is caused by evaporation, spillage, and adherence to containers. Further shrinkage, or sometimes gain, may result in subsequent processing operations. When actual costs are used such gain or shrinkage is automatically reflected in the unit cost of the product by dividing the units produced into the total costs up to the point of cost calculation. When standard costs are used, either the units or the unit cost must be changed to reflect this. Standards are established for this purpose, and actuals are compared with these to assure control. In a textile mill the yards of cloth produced at weaving will shrink in washing, bleaching, or dyeing. If this loss is 5%, it will be reflected in the standard product costs as shown in Table 11-1. In some processes gains occur. For example, linseed oil

TABLE 11-1

	Square yards	Rate	Value
Cloth to dyeing..............	1,000	$0.40	$400.00
Dyeing costs................			18.00
	1,000	$0.418	$418.00
Loss 5%....................	50		
Dyeing production..........	950	$0.44	$418.00

takes on oxygen from the air in the course of being oxidized in the manufacture of linoleum. Here the weight of the oxidized oil is greater than that of the raw oil, and the increase must be added in determining the standard unit cost of oxidized oil. Under these conditions the cost per unit of processed material is less than that of the product entering the operation.

Scrap Losses

Scrap is the result of trim, normal spoilage, splicing, etc. in the production process. As with shrinkage, it is reflected in actual unit costs by dividing total cost by finished units. When standard costs are used, allowances are set for scrap at each operation. These are reflected in the unit column as standards are built and are used for measuring actual scrap, just as are shrinkage allowances. In each instance in Exhibit 11-1 where scrap occurs, the units of board are reduced by the allowable scrap. The unit costs by cost elements are then divided by the square feet after scrap loss to step up the standard cost rates to a 1,000-square-foot basis. This provides standard costs per 1,000 square feet, by cost elements, at all steps in the production cycle for use in costing inventories of work in process.

Material Sold as Seconds

When finished production is graded into perfect material and salable seconds, the production of perfects is costed at a value greater than that of the standard cost to make, so as to provide for a write-down of the value of seconds. Such adjustment is usually made in relation to the sales prices. Under a standard cost system a standard percentage of total production is set as the quantity of seconds expected to be produced. Inventory values are then calculated for perfects and seconds which, when applied to the units of each, as provided by the standard allowance for quantities of seconds, will equal the standard cost of production. This calculation is illustrated in Table 11-2.

TABLE 11-2

Data:

Sales price, perfects................	$1.50
Sales price, seconds................	1.20
Cost to make....................	1.00
Seconds produced................	10%

Units	Sales price	Sales value	Cost to make
90	$1.50	$135.00	
10	1.20	12.00	
100		$147.00	$100.00

Average markup on factory cost is 47%.
$1.50 ÷ 1.47 = $1.020408 inventory value, perfects
$1.20 ÷ 1.47 = 0.816327 inventory value, seconds
Proof:
  90 × $1.020408 = $91.83672
  10 × 0.816327 =   8.16327
                  $99.99999

The procedures for building product standard costs for products which will be graded into perfects and salable seconds are the same as those for any other product up to the point at which the grading is made. At that point the unit product standard cost to make is converted into two standards, one for perfects and the other for seconds. If acoustical tile (Exhibit 11-1) were graded into perfects and seconds, the standard cost of production (either the direct cost of $56.93 or the total standard cost of $71.94, depending upon whether direct or absorption costing were used) would be increased for perfect material and reduced for seconds.

Standard shipping costs would then be added to these standard finished-stock inventory values to arrive at the unit standard product costs of perfects and of seconds.

Absorption and Direct Costing

The procedure for building unit product standard factory costs, recording costs, determining variances, and valuing inventory is the same under both absorption and direct costing. The only difference is in the items included in the standard costs. Under direct costing the fixed portion of the factory expense is excluded. This may require supplementary inventory valuation procedures for fixed expense as discussed in Chapter 10, "Direct Costing."

Sometimes, when direct costing is used, product standard costs are built to show both standard direct cost and total standard cost (Exhibit 11-1). The former is used for internal reports and inventory valuation. The latter is used as basic cost data for setting sales prices and is applied to inventory quantities at the end of an accounting period to arrive at inventory values for published financial statements and income tax returns.

REVIEW QUESTIONS

1. What are the advantages of a standard cost accounting system?
2. Why are product standard factory costs required for a standard cost accounting system?
3. To what extent can standard factory costs be built for groups of products rather than for each product?
4. When is a total unit material, labor, and expense cost used as a material cost?
5. Why should product standard factory costs be built by cost elements?
6. How do product standard factory costs contribute to the cost-control procedure?
7. How is the allowance for shrinkage of materials reflected in standard costs? The allowance for scrap?
8. Why are separate standard costs developed for perfects and salable seconds?
9. What is the basis for marking up the standard cost of perfects to provide for the markdown of salable seconds?
10. What differences are there in product standard factory costs under absorption costing and under direct costing?

PROBLEM

An ice cream manufacturer uses standard costs. The operations up to the hardening rooms are mixing, freezing, and packing.

The standard formula for a batch of mix is milk 600 pounds, cream 240 pounds, and sugar 360 pounds. Flavors are added at the freezing operation where 800 pounds of mix are used per 100 gallons of ice cream produced. Standards include 25 pounds of flavor per 100 gallons of chocolate ice cream and 19.9 pounds of flavor per 100 gallons of strawberry ice cream. Standard material usage prices per pound are milk $0.032, cream $0.08, sugar $0.055, chocolate flavor $0.24, and strawberry flavor $0.40. Package costs are $0.09 per gallon packed.

Standard labor rates are $0.0194 per pound of formula for mixing, $0.08 per gallon for freezing, and $0.15 per gallon packed for packing.

Standard expense rates as percentages of labor are mixing 100%, freezing 150%, and packing 50%.

Of the pounds mixed 3% are lost before freezing. Of the gallons produced at freezing, 2% are lost in packing.

Calculate the total standard cost per 100 gallons of chocolate and of strawberry ice cream transferred to the hardening room. (The identity of cost elements need not be retained through the production cycle.)

CHAPTER 12

Accounting Procedure for Standard Costs

The distinguishing feature of a standard cost accounting system is the use of variance accounts to record the differences between the actual and standard costs of production. Debit balances in these accounts reflect costs above standard, and credit balances reflect costs below standard. The variances show the extent to which costs were controlled and provide for the analysis and interpretation of operating reports.

Since the differences between actual and standard costs are reflected in variance accounts, the inventories are valued at standard cost. These standard values are used for internal reports. For published financial statements they may have to be adjusted to the lower of actual cost or market.

PROCESS STANDARD COSTS

Under a process standard cost system each cost element passes through a variance account before being entered in the inventory accounts. Thus inventories are carried at standard cost and the variances charged against profit and loss of the period or allocated to cost of sales and a separate variance inventory, depending upon the policy of the company. A flow chart of standard cost transactions is shown as Exhibit 12-1. This chart is prepared for the same fiberboard production operations described under the process actual cost procedure.

Material Price Variances

Material price variances are determined when raw material is taken into inventory. Invoices for raw material and freight-in are charged to Materials in Transit and summarized on an inventory ledger card (Exhibit 12-2). Quantities received are also posted to this summary from

140

EXHIBIT 12-1

FLOW CHART OF ACCOUNTING TRANSACTIONS, PROCESS STANDARD COSTS

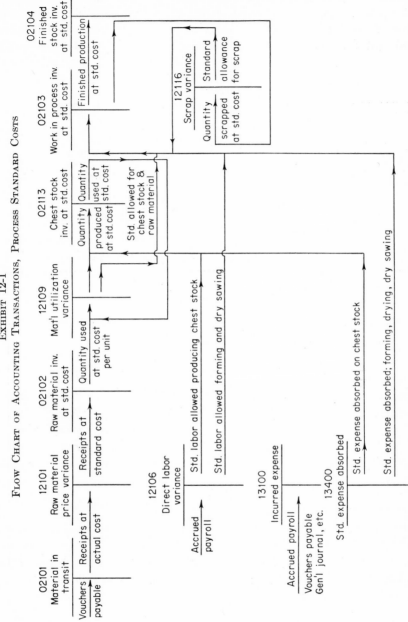

receiving reports (Exhibit 4-3). At the close of the month the quantity of each raw material received during the month and the actual costs thereof are entered on the summary of purchasing variance from standard cost (Exhibit 12-3). Standard cost rates are applied to the units,

EXHIBIT 12-2
INVENTORY LEDGER

INVENTORY LEDGER															No. 19
C.P.D. 122	INVENTORY CONTROL	02101		COMMODITY DESCRIPTION											
YEAR 19--		UNITS Pounds		Margose											
BILLED				RECEIVED				BILLED				RECEIVED			
Date	Voucher Number	No. of Units	Actual Value	Date	Entry Number	No. of Units	Actual Value	Date	Voucher Number	No. of Units	Actual Value	Date	Entry Number	No. of Units	Actual Value
8/2	8-017	500	500 00												
8/3	8-023	Frt	50 00	8/5	43	500	550 00								
8/6	8-070	1000	1000 00												
8/7		Frt	100 00	8/9	92	1000	1100 00								
						1500	1650 00								

EXHIBIT 12-3
PURCHASING VARIANCE FROM STANDARD COST

PURCHASING VARIANCE FROM STANDARD COST

DATE August 19--   PAGE 1

PLANT 122

							Dr. 02101 Cr. 12101	Cr. 02101 Dr. 12101
							Standard Cost	Actual Cost
Code	Description	Quantity	Unit	Rate	Per	Total	Total	
	Margose	1500	lb	1	20	lb	1800.00	1650.00
	Rekol	3000	lb	2	30	lb	6900.00	6952.00
	Wood	4100	cord	15	00	cord	61500.00	59310.00
	Kraft Paper	5000	lb		20	lb	1000.00	1000.00
	Tape	300	Roll		10	Roll	30.00	27.00
	Total						71230.00	68939.00

and the total actual and standard cost of materials received during the month is determined. These totals are used for the following journal entries:

Actual cost:

> Dr. Material Price Variance
> Cr. Material in Transit
> To record the actual cost of raw materials received

Standard cost:

> Dr. Raw Material Inventory
> Cr. Material Price Variance
> To record the standard cost of raw materials received

Debits to Material and Labor Variance Accounts

Material usage reports are prepared in the factory for the usage of raw material, chest stock, and work in process. The quantities of each material used each month are summarized by kinds of material, by operation, and posted to a summary of usages (Exhibit 12-4). This illustration

Month August Year 19—   EXHIBIT 12-4
C.P.D. 122   SUMMARY OF USAGES

Operation	Quantity	Rate	Dr. 12109 Cr. 02102	Dr. 12109 Cr. 02103	Dr. 12109 Cr. 02113	Operation totals
220 Grinding:						
Cordwood.........	6,670	$15.00	$100,050.00	———	———	$100,050.00
331 Forming:						
Chest stock........	9,429,000	0.0210	———	———	$198,009.00	
Margose..........	24,720	1.20	29,664.00			
Rekol.............	18,910	2.30	43,493.00			
Alpod.............	6,400	0.60	3,840.00	———	———	275,006.00
420 Preparation:						
Paint.............	2,110	3.10	6,541.00			
Sealer............	10,000	0.50	5,000.00			
Kraft paper.......	14,750	0.20	2,950.00			
Tape.............	10,000	0.10	1,000.00	———	———	15,491.00
422 Finishing:						
Paint.............	9,720	3.90	37,908.00			
Cartons...........	46,150	0.21	9,691.50	———	———	47,599.50
Total...........	———	———	$240,137.50	———	$198,009.00	

shows two operations beyond the dry saws which were not included in the actual process cost summary. These two operations are for the final processing of roof insulation and acoustical materials after they leave the dry saws. Standard material cost rates are applied and the value posted in the column of the inventory account to be credited. Operation totals on this form show actual material usage at standard cost and provide the detail for certain internal control and other reports. Totals provide the following entries:

> Dr. Material Utilization Variance
> Cr. Raw Material
> Cr. Work in Process
> Cr. Chest Stock
> To record actual quantities used at standard cost

Actual labor is reported as for an actual cost system. Total actual labor is summarized by products in each operation to provide detail for cost control reports. It is debited to the Direct Labor Variance account when the payroll distribution entries are made.

Standard Allowances

From the production reports the quantities of each product processed in each operation are summarized. These quantities are posted to an in-process production summary form (Exhibit 12-5). They are extended at the standard allowances for material, labor, and expense for each product in each operation or group of operations (forming, drying, dry saws), as established in the product standard costs. This provides the standard allowance by products and operations for comparison with actuals for cost-control and reporting purposes. The standard cost used in Exhibit 12-5 for acoustical tile is that developed in Exhibit 11-1. It is in such use that the control and accounting functions are integrated. The standard allowances in each operation are the standard values of the product produced in the operation, which are debited to the inventory accounts.

The first point of measurement of material usage in a fiberboard plant is the production of the dry saws. Therefore, the material usage variance is the difference between (1) the total standard material, labor, and expense cost of chest stock plus the standard cost of raw materials used at the forming operation and (2) the standard material value of boards produced at the dry saws. For this reason the product standard cost is *adjusted* for chest stock (Exhibit 11-1). This removes the standard labor and expense cost of chest stock in finished dry-saw production from total labor and expense and adds it back to material. This adjusted rate of $33.59 is used as the credit to the Material Usage Variance account. The credit to the Labor Efficiency Variance account for forming, drying, and dry saws combined would be the dry-saw production at the adjusted standard labor cost of $1.71. Expense would be credited to the Absorbed Factory Expense account at the adjusted standard expense rates of $9.47 for variable expense and $9.46 for fixed expense.

These adjustments in product standard costs to add back standard labor and expense to standard material rates need be made only at the points where semiprocessed materials are used. They are required because the total standard unit cost of the semiprocessed material is the standard material cost of the operation using it.

In the illustrations it is assumed that a material usage variance for board is not calculated for the finishing operation. For this operation the usage variance is the difference between the standard value of paint and package material actually used and the standard allowance for these

Month August Year 19——
C.P.D. 122

EXHIBIT 12-5

IN-PROCESS PRODUCTION SUMMARY

STANDARD COST OF UNITS PRODUCED BY OPERATIONS

	Operation	Quantity	Material Rate per 1,000	Material Dr. 02103 Cr. 12109	Material Dr. 02113 Cr. 12109	Labor Rate per 1,000	Labor Dr. 02103 Cr. 12106	Labor Dr. 02113 Cr. 12106	Expense Rate per 1,000	Expense Dr. 02103 Cr. 13400	Expense Dr. 02113 Cr. 13400
220	Grinding................	9,500,000	10.50		99,750.00	5.20	——	49,400.00	5.30	——	50,350.00
331-2-3	Forming—drying—dry saws:										
	Roof 24 × 48 × ¾.........	2,147,010	29.69	63,744.73		1.14	2,447.59		14.17	30,423.13	
	Wallboard.............	2,130,300	25.06	53,385.32		1.26	2,684.18		14.16	30,165.05	
	Acoustical stock........	4,858,100	33.59	163,183.58		1.71	8,307.35		18.93	91,963.83	
420	Preparation:										
	Roof 24 × 48 × ¾.........	2,147,010	2.50	5,367.52		0.60	1,288.21		0.60	1,288.21	
	Wallboard.............	2,130,300	3.10	6,603.93		0.50	1,065.15		0.50	1,065.15	
420	Preparation package:										
	Roof.................	2,104,000	0.90	1,893.60							
	Wallboard.............	2,090,000	1.00	2,090.00							
422	Finishing:										
	Acoustical tile.........	4,858,100	7.80	37,893.18		1.75	8,501.67		1.55	7,530.05	
	Acoustical tile package...	4,618,000	2.10	9,697.80							
521	Warehousing:										
	Roof 24 × 48 × ¾.........	2,104,000				0.30	631.20		0.38	799.52	
	Wallboard.............	2,090,000				0.20	418.00		0.25	522.50	
	Acoustical tile.........	4,618,000				0.50	2,309.00		0.58	2,678.44	
	Total........	——		343,859.66	99,750.00		27,652.35	49,400.00		166,435.88	50,350.00

calculated on the square feet painted at $7.80 per 1,000 and the square feet packaged at $2.10 per 1,000.

If a usage variance for board were desired, the material usage variance account of the finishing operation would be charged with the square feet of board delivered to it for finishing at the total standard cost of unfinished board of $53.23 per 1,000 feet. Work in Process would be credited, since this inventory was debited for the standard cost of production at the dry saws. The Material Usage Variance account of the finishing operation would then be credited with the square feet painted, before scrap loss, at the standard value of board, $54.23, plus the standard allowance for paint of $7.80, or a total of $62.03 per 1,000 square feet. Painting labor and expense would be allowed on the gross square feet painted at the applicable rates and credited to the Labor Efficiency Variance and Expense Absorbed accounts. The debits would be to Work in Process. Work in Process would then be credited for the actual quantity of scrap produced at total standard rate of $65.33, and the Scrap Variance account would be debited. The Scrap Variance account would be credited with the production of good painted board at the standard allowance for scrap, $68.76 minus $65.33, or $3.43 per 1,000 feet. Work in Process would be debited and the respective Variance and Absorbed Expense accounts credited for the square feet packaged at the standard material, labor, and expense rates for packaging.

It is to be noted that substantially more calculations are required to develop a usage variance for board at the finishing operation than if this is not done. Actually, no control purpose is served by developing this variance. In the illustration any difference between square feet going to painting and square feet of finished production would be reflected in the scrap account. If there were no allowance for scrap, any actual loss of boards would be charged to the Scrap Loss account. Many accountants endeavor to secure material usage variances at each operation. It is a time-consuming and costly procedure which is not necessary.

Accounting Entries

The totals for the plant as calculated on the in-process production summary are recorded in the ledger by the following entry:

> Dr. Work in Process
> Dr. Chest Stock
>   Cr. Material Utilization Variance
>   Cr. Direct Labor Variance
>   Cr. Applied Expense
> To record actual production at standard allowance for material, labor, and expense

Actual scrap reported is posted to the finished production summary (Exhibit 12-6) as is the good production. The standard allowance for scrap is computed at rates set per unit of finished production, and the entries are as follows:

> Dr. Scrap Variance
>   Cr. Work in Process
> To record actual scrap produced at standard unit cost

> Dr. Work in Process
>   Cr. Scrap Variance
> To record standard allowance for scrap

Finished production is priced at standard cost and the total for the plant is recorded as follows:

> Dr. Finished Stock
>   Cr. Work in Process
> To record finished production at total standard unit cost

This entry transfers the standard value of finished production to the Finished Stock account, and the remaining balance of the Work in Process account is the standard cost value of that inventory. In the illustration the only processed inventory balance is in chest stock.

With the completion of this series of entries the variance accounts reflect the deviation from standard for the period. The difference between the Actual Expense account and the Standard Expense Absorbed accounts reflects the expense deviation for the period. All inventory accounts are at standard cost. Under this procedure variances are reflected in profit and loss in the month in which they occur.

Credit for Salvaged Scrap

If the scrap can be reused in formulation or reworked, the operation creating the scrap should receive credit for the value which it will have when reused. The scrap is then carried on inventory at this value until it is reprocessed. Where the scrap is reworked, a special account is frequently used for recording the Cost of Reworking. This is debited with the inventory value of scrap withdrawn from inventory for reworking and the actual labor and applied expense of reworking. It is credited with the value of good units secured, and this is charged to inventory.

The standard value of scrap which can be reused is reflected in the

EXHIBIT 12-6
FINISHED PRODUCTION SUMMARY

Month August Year 19——   C.P.D. 122

Operation	Size	Net production to finished stock			Standard scrap allowance		Actual scrap		
		Quantity	Rate per 1,000	Dr. 02104 Cr. 02103	Rate per 1,000	Dr. 02103 Cr. 12116	Quantity	Rate per 1,000	Dr. 12116 Cr. 02103
420 Preparation:									
Roof insulation..	24 × 48 × ¾ in.	2,104,000	51.28	107,893.12	1.00	2,104.00	43,010	48.70	2,094.59
Wallboard......	4 × 8 ft	2,090,000	46.94	98,104.60	0.91	1,901.90	40,300	44.58	1,796.57
422 Finishing:									
Acoustical tile...	12 × 12 × ¾ in.	4,618,000	71.94	332,218.92	3.43	15,839.74	240,100	65.33	15,685.73
Total.........				538,216.64		19,845.64			19,576.89

standards and the standard allowance for scrap reduced accordingly. The standard cost entries for scrap which has a salvage value are:

Dr. Scrap Variance
Dr. Scrap Inventory
    Cr. Work in Process
To record actual units scrapped at standard value less inventory value of scrap

Dr. Work in Process
    Cr. Scrap Variance
To record standard allowance for scrap loss in process less standard salvage value

Variance in Per Cent of Perfects Produced

When finished goods are graded into perfects and salable seconds, the variance resulting from the variation from standard in the percentage of perfects produced is recorded in a special variance account. This is not shown in Exhibit 12-1. Finished production is cleared from Work in Process through this variance account into Finished Stock Inventory. The entries are as follows:

Dr. Finished Production Grading Variance
    Cr. Work in Process
To record units produced at the standard cost to make

Dr. Finished Stock
    Cr. Finished Production Grading Variance
To record units of perfects and seconds produced at respective standard values

JOB-ORDER STANDARD COSTS

It is possible and practicable to use standard costs with a job-order cost system. Such use has the advantage of providing a measurement of efficiency of production operations. This is not secured as a part of the accounting process when only actual costs are applied to orders. The actual cost of a job provides only a comparison of actual cost of sales with sales income. It does not tell whether this comparison is satisfactory or unsatisfactory because of too high a cost or too low a sales price. The application of standard costs to the cost sheets results in a standard cost for the order and the comparison of that with the actual cost and the income realized. For this purpose attainable standard costs are used.

The procedure for standard cost building is no different from that followed in building standard costs for a process system where there is a continuous flow of material from operation to operation. Regardless of the type of manufacturing plant, a number of operations are performed on one or more materials. The development of standard costs for individual orders, each of which uses only some of the operations and may have a different production sequence from the others, is no more difficult than it is for developing standard costs for products which pass through all of the operations and always in the same sequence. True, more standards must be built, but these also are needed for price determination and for scheduling production. In filling these latter needs, all the other requirements of standards for cost control are also met.

Applying Standard Costs to Job Orders

For illustration purposes, a cost sheet for the same refrigerator insulation used for the actual job-order cost system (Exhibit 7-6) is used. The accumulation and posting to the cost sheet of the actual costs and production follows exactly the same procedure as outlined for the actual job-order cost system. When standard costs are applied to the order, provision is made for a comparison of actual with standard costs and the calculation of the variances. This is usually made on the cost sheet, but a standard cost summary (Exhibit 12-7) may be attached to the cost sheet (Exhibit 7-6) for this purpose. This latter method is used here so as to tie in with the data and illustrations of the actual job-order cost system. This cost summary replaces the production and cost summary sections of the actual job-order cost sheet.

All production against an order in a given month, as posted to each job cost summary, is added at the close of the month and, when extended at the standard rates, becomes an allowance against the actual costs incurred. In Exhibit 12-7 there was no opening inventory, so that the actual charges to the job during the month represent the total to be measured by the standard allowances. However, inventories must be considered, and therefore a physical inventory of work in process is taken at the close of each month. The description and count for each lot of work in process is recorded, priced at standard, and extended on inventory cards. The total inventory value for each job in process is posted to the cost sheet and also provides an allowance or measure against the actual costs. Thus the opening inventory plus the postings of actual costs, minus the production and closing inventory at standard value, equals the variance from standard cost.

Accounting Entries

The flow of accounting transactions for these procedures is shown in Exhibit 12-8. The forms used and procedures followed which do not have a direct bearing on the standard job-order cost system are not described.

EXHIBIT 12-7
JOB-ORDER STANDARD COST SUMMARY

JOB ORDER STANDARD COST SUMMARY						
		Order No. _59514_				
Production:						
Sept. 10,200		*Oct.* 20,000				
	Material		Labor		Expense	
Std. cost per 1000	$272.00		$2.00		$6.00	
Sept. Opening inventory	—		—		—	
Charges	8287	06	28	50	209	15
Total	8287	06	28	50	209	15
Production	3264	00	20	40	61	20
Closing inventory	5712	00	7	14	73	71
Variance	688	94	(	96)	(74	24)
Oct. Opening inventory	5712	00	7	14	73	71
Charges	—		36	10	54	15
Total	5712	00	43	45	127	86
Production	5440	00	40	00	120	00
Closing inventory	—		—		—	
Variance	(272	00)	(3	45)	(7	86)
Opening inventory						
Charges						
Total						
Production						
Closing inventory						
Variance						
Opening inventory						
Charges						
Total						
Production						
Closing inventory						
Variance						
Total var for order	416	94	(4	41)	(82	10)
Std. value of production	8704	00	60	40	181	20

They are referred to where necessary in following the accounting transactions.

Material price variances are computed and recorded as for a standard process cost system. Raw material and processed material usage reports are summarized, charged to Material Utilization Variance and credited to the respective inventory accounts. Actual direct labor costs are summarized and debited to Direct Labor Variance as the accrued payroll is recorded. Actual expenses are recorded in the expense ledger by control, source, and operation.

Postings of actual material and labor costs and applied expense to the cost sheets are totaled for each month and recorded as follows:

> Dr. Jobs in Process
>> Cr. Variance—Material Usage
>> Cr. Variance—Direct Labor
>> Cr. Applied Factory Expense
> To record costs applied to job orders

The effect of this entry is to give credit in the variance accounts for actual material and labor costs and to credit applied expense for the amount applied against actual labor. Variances must now be removed from the jobs-in-process inventory. These are calculated on the job-order standard cost summaries (Exhibit 12-7) and summarized for the following entry:

> Dr. or cr. Jobs in Process
>> Dr. or cr. Material Utilization Variance
>> Dr. or cr. Direct Labor Variance
>> Dr. or cr. Applied Expense
> To record material and labor variances and adjust applied
> expense:

These entries are shown by the broken lines in Exhibit 12-8. The total standard value of finished production is then debited to Finished Stock and credited to Jobs in Process. After these entries are made the jobs-in-process inventory is at standard cost, and the total of the closing inventory values shown on the job-order standard cost summaries will be in agreement with the ledger account.

It is to be noted that accurate variances would not be recorded by simply debiting Finished Stock and Jobs in Process and crediting Material Utilization Variance, Direct Labor Variance, and Applied Expense for the respective standard values of finished production and inventory of jobs in process. Under a job-order system the value of scrap is not recorded; it appears in part in the Material and Labor Variance accounts and in part in a reduction in the credit to Applied Expense. Thus in Exhibit 12-7 some of the variance in each cost element in the month of

EXHIBIT 12-8
FLOW CHART OF ACCOUNTING TRANSACTIONS, JOB-ORDER STANDARD COST SYSTEM

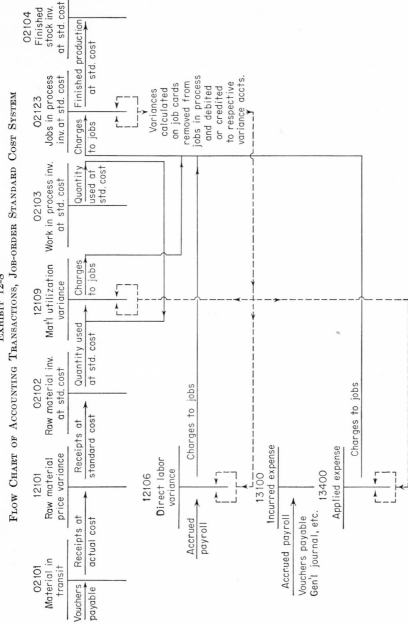

October was due to scrapping of product units which were in the October opening inventory. If production on every order were started and completed in the same month, the accounting procedure could be simplified by simply crediting the standard value of finished production to Material Utilization Variance, Direct Labor Variance, and Applied Expense.

GENERAL PROCEDURES

Standard Costs for Inventory Valuation

The application of attainable standard costs to production provides the debits to the inventory accounts, as well as the comparison of standard costs with actuals for cost control. Thus, inventories are always reflected in the accounts at standard cost. This makes it unnecessary to record prices and extend values on the detailed perpetual inventory records. At any time a pricing at standard cost and extension of the quantities on the perpetual inventory records should result in a value which agrees with the balance of the respective inventory control account of the general ledger. Time is saved in calculating debits and credits to Inventory in that units of each product produced or shipped can be totaled for a month and the total extended at the standard inventory value.

When standard costs used for inventory valuation are in excess of the lower of cost or market, reserves are used to adjust the inventory values to the required level. If the lifo method is used to determine cost of a part of the inventory, it is desirable to have two reserve accounts, one for adjustment of fifo items and the other for lifo items. When standard cost must be written down to the lower of cost or market, the entry is:

Dr.   Inventory Valuation Adjustments
Cr.   Reserve for Valuation of Inventory

The debit is an operating item and the credit a balance sheet item. If standard cost is less than actual, an item would not be written up to actual cost with a resultant debit balance to the Reserve Account. The standard is supposed to represent attainable efficient production. To adjust it upward to actual cost is to reflect inefficiencies in the inventory values.

Inventory valuation reserves are customarily established and recorded only when inventories are listed and priced. For work in process and finished stock, the standard inventory value for each product or group of similar products is compared with the standard cost of production of the months prior to the inventory date to establish the number of months of production on inventory. Material and labor price and efficiency variances from standard are then examined for the same period. If net gains were experienced, actual costs were less than standard, and valuation reserves are required. If net losses against standard were experienced, no reserves are required. For expense the same procedure is followed except that any volume variances are not considered. The objective is to reflect expense in inventory at the lower of standard or actual cost at normal or expense absorption volume.

It is possible that one cost element will show a loss against standard and another will show a gain. Variances by elements should not be offset against each other because different factors influence each cost element. For example, a gain may be shown for material because of very effective utilization control and a loss of labor because of a slowdown by the workers. The former is a true cost reduction, the latter an unusual cost increase which should not be repetitive.

From month to month, between the inventory listing dates, over-all adjustments may be estimated on the basis of price movements and efficiency trends. These are reflected in the accounts and reports in order to minimize the effect on profit or loss at the end of a period when reserves can be calculated with greater accuracy.

Recording Costs by Cost Elements

Some companies carry their work-in-process and finished-stock inventory at standard cost by cost elements on the general ledger. This requires three work-in-process accounts and three finished-stock accounts —Material, Labor, and Expense. Under this procedure the entries for the standard allowance for each element in each operation are debited to the respective work-in-process inventory account. Actual scrap losses and standard allowances for scrap loss are computed and recorded for each cost element. This requires six entries in comparison with the two shown in Exhibit 12-6. Three entries are required to transfer inventory values from Work in Process to Finished Stock and three to relieve Finished Stock and charge Cost of Goods Sold. Since the standard costs are applied to production of each product, in each operation the calculations are also tripled. While this procedure does maintain the identity of the cost elements in the accounts, it is cumbersome and costly.

The more frequently used and simpler procedure is to carry the work-in-process and finished-stock inventories at total standard cost at the stage of completion of each article on inventory. By this method the cost elements lose their identity in the accounts. Also, when processed material is used in a subsequent operation, the Material Variance account will contain some labor and expense of prior operations.

Analysis of Cost by Elements

If product standard costs are built by cost element as in Exhibit 11-1, the cost of goods produced or of goods sold can be determined by elements of cost through analysis. This is less costly than carrying separate cost-element accounts on the books.

The key to the determination of costs by elements through analysis is the pricing and extending of opening and closing inventories at the material, labor, and expense rates for each product. This is a necessary procedure to establish proper lower-of-cost-or-market inventory values for financial statements.

The opening inventory of work in process by standard cost elements plus the actual material, labor, and expense, minus the closing work-in-process inventory by cost elements, will give the material, labor, and expense components of the cost of goods produced. These, plus the opening finished-stock inventory minus the closing finished-stock inventory (both by cost elements), will equal the direct-material, direct labor, and expense elements of the cost of goods sold.

Deferred Variances

If it is usual to have substantial differences between quantities produced and quantities sold in a month, further accounting may be desirable in order not to distort operating results of individual months. This is accomplished by using Deferred Variance accounts, one in the inventory group on the balance sheet and one in the variance group for profit and loss. Referring to the second chart of accounts in Chapter 3, 02105 and 12117 would be added. With production of 10,000 units, sales of 5,000 units, and a net credit variance (gain) of $3,000 for material, labor, scrap, and expense, the entry to defer the applicable portion of the variance would be:

> Dr.　12117 Deferred Variances $1,500
> 　　　Cr.　02105 Deferred Variances $1,500
> To defer production variances applicable to goods on inventory

When sales exceed production, an applicable share of the deferred variance would be withdrawn from the balance sheet account and credited to profit and loss. By this procedure individual variance accounts always reflect performance against standards for the period and are in agreement with the detailed performance reports for the period, while profit and loss reports reflect the variances applicable to material sold.

REVIEW QUESTIONS

1. What additional accounts are required for a standard cost accounting system?
2. What is indicated by a debit balance in a variance account?

3. What is the difference between a raw-material price variance and a usage variance?
4. What is the difference between a yield variance and scrap loss?
5. How is raw material shrinkage reflected in standard costs?
6. Why would standard costs be used with a job-order system?
7. How are variances calculated under a job-order standard cost system?
8. Why are monthly physical inventories of work in process required under a job-order standard cost system?
9. Why are scrap variances usually not calculated under a job-order standard cost system?
10. When and how are standard inventory values adjusted to the lower of cost or market value?
11. What purposes are served by deferring variances?
12. How do the variance accounts of a standard cost system aid management in the control of costs?

PROBLEMS

1. Assume the mousetrap company (Chapter 7, Problem 1), uses a standard cost accounting system and the January 1 unit inventory values were the standard costs.

For base cutting the standard unit cost of $0.012 is a total of the following:

Material............	$0.008
Labor...............	0.003
Expense.............	0.001

Production and costs are shown in Problem 7-1.

a. What were the January variances by elements of cost in the base-cutting operation?

b. What was the standard value of the January 31 inventories?

2. In the mixing operation of the ice cream company (Problem in Chapter 11) 40 standard batches of mix were prepared in a month, and 46,000 pounds of mix were produced for use by the freezing department. The company uses a Loss Variance account to record the difference between the standard and actual mixing loss.

Actual labor costs of mixing were $915.00.

a. Prepare journal entries to record the standard allowances for production and for the mixing loss.

b. Calculate the mixing-loss variance and the direct labor variance.

CHAPTER 13

Control of Material Costs

In many manufacturing companies the cost of direct materials is the largest element of factory costs. Since this is true, the control of material costs should be given relative importance by the accountant. It is the purpose of this chapter to survey the many facets of material-cost control and suggest policies and procedures which can be adopted in this important phase of cost accounting. While the specific treatment will be of direct-material costs, referred to hereafter as material costs, indirect-material costs can, for the most part, be controlled by the same or similar procedures.

Responsibility for Control

The first requisite for the control of material costs is organization, with responsibilities clearly established for all phases of the control problems. The accountant is the keystone in such organization, for control will be no better than the accounting records and data which are established. The accountant's direct responsibility is one of recording, measuring, interpreting, and reporting. His functional responsibility should have no limits, and he should be alert at all times to appraise and report to management the effectiveness with which material costs are being controlled in all areas.

The size and complexity of the control organization as well as the specific assignment of responsibilities will vary with the size and character of the business. In the larger businesses, control responsibility is frequently divided among the production, laboratory, engineering, purchasing, receiving and stores, production-planning, standards-of-production, and accounting departments. In the smaller businesses all these functions may be assigned to one person or may be performed in conjunction with other functions by several persons. The specific organization structure is not important, but the clear assignment and delineation of responsibilities is.

In any large company there must be a central point at which decisions are made and policies established. This coordinating function is usually vested in an inventory-policy committee, or possibly the executive committee. All departments having responsibilities relating to materials, as well as the sales and general production departments, should be represented on an inventory-policy committee. This committee receives reports and recommendations from the staff and operating departments and either approves, disapproves, or sends the recommendation back for further study. Thus, all the material control functions are coordinated and kept in efficient operation. The smaller the company, the less formal the procedure and the fewer the participants in the coordinating and also in the control functions.

Material Specifications

The control of material costs begins with the setting of the specifications for raw material. Since this element of cost is such a major portion of the total factory cost, it is important that the specifications be set for a quality of raw material which is no better than required to produce the quality desired in the finished product. If the raw material used is "too good," costs will be high in relation to competitive prices for the finished product, and the optimum profit will not be realized.

The accounting function with respect to specifications is one of evaluation. Before a specification is finally established, the accounting department should determine its effect on the profit of the product. In many instances this may extend beyond the material cost and affect such things as production speeds, capacity, processing and handling equipment, and even customer acceptance. Therefore, such evaluation cannot be limited to simple application and comparison of unit costs and the addition of these to arrive at comparative material costs of finished products. The accountant must know the production processes, sense the other costs which may be changed by the changes in the material specifications, and question these with staff and production personnel. Indicated changes in these other costs must then be evaluated and considered with the specific material-cost changes. Complete files of specification changes and the work papers developed in the valuation should be maintained to facilitate comparisons of actual costs with those contemplated and the evaluation and interpretation of performance in the usage of materials.

Purchasing

With specifications established, it is the responsibility of the purchasing department to procure materials in accordance with the specifications at the best possible price. Since purchases must be coordinated with production schedules to ensure an adequate working inventory at all times, it is necessary for purchasing and production planning to work very closely in determining what quantities shall be purchased. The material requirements of the next month or months may be for a quantity which will be more costly than standard because of less-than-carload transportation costs, extra packaging, or necessity of placing the order with a distributor rather than the manufacturer. Purchasing brings these matters to the attention of production planning, and in many instances quantities are changed in order to secure a better price. Also, purchasing keeps production planning informed of current price trends and availability of material. Quantities purchased are then governed by these factors as well as by price.

When standard costs are used, the purchasing department sets standard raw-material prices for each standard period. These reflect the best possible estimate of the average price which will be paid for each material over the year or other period for which the standards will be used. Since these standards are used for interim inventory valuation and for accounting, they are approved by the accounting department. The approval procedure requires checking the price against recent purchases, analysis of the f.o.b. and delivered price to establish the inclusion of freight and the method of transportation, determination that the price is based on delivery in the customary form, bulk or package, and appraisal in the light of economic trends and specific industry forecasts.

Accounting control of material costs in the purchasing area is implemented through comparison of actual costs with standard as purchases are made (Exhibit 12-3), and through special material-cost studies. These are not intended to measure the efficiency of the purchasing department but rather to provide detailed analyses of the effect of price variations on profits. Comparison of actual with standard cost is supplemented by determination that the description of the materials on the invoices is in accordance with the specifications and by a system of follow-up of the laboratory tests of inbound materials. Periodically, studies should be made, in conjunction with the engineering or production departments, of alternate methods of receiving and handling raw materials. Thus it may be determined that because of changes in plant layout, labor costs, or market conditions, savings can be effected by changing the purchase specifications.

Receiving and Storage

The physical receipt and storage of raw materials is the responsibility of the receiving and stores departments, and the quantities to be carried are the responsibility of the production-planning department. The inventory records and values are the responsibility of the accounting department. It is in this latter area that the major emphasis of accounting control is frequently placed, all too often to the exclusion of other vital areas.

Costs of receiving, handling, and storing material are frequently of sufficient importance to justify the expenditure of a reasonable amount of control effort on them. It is possible to set labor standards for unloading, moving, and storing materials and for establishing expense rates to be applied to such labor. The material value charged into production should include such costs to the extent of one movement into the standard storage area and from that area to point of usage.

Allowance should not be made for nonstandard movement of materials. Thus, if materials are stored in areas not normally used, the difference between the actual cost of moving them into those areas and the standard allowance for movement into the standard areas should be reflected as a variance. The aggregate of such variances at the close of a period will measure the effectiveness of scheduling purchases, the conformance to standard containers or method of transportation, and the efficiency of handling. While each of these may be computed individually through very detailed application of standards, it is usually unnecessary to do so. Major variances can be spotted on the reports, and the reasons for them can be established by scanning the receiving records and visiting points of storage of inventories.

When costs of storage and handling are studied, it may be found that the provision of storage space at each using operation is desirable. The possibility of more discrepancies in the inventory records, because records cannot be maintained and physical movement controlled as carefully in each such operational storage area as in a central storeroom, may be more than counterbalanced by tangible savings from storing materials adjacent to point of use.

Physical Loss

Physical loss can be detected and controlled if there are adequate records in which management has full confidence. Such physical loss is not limited to pilferage but can also result from deterioration, shrinkage, and damage. To keep each of these at an irreducible minimum requires rather detailed records but not more detailed than the records which are kept of cash. In many businesses the value of the inventories is greatly in excess of the cash of the company. Is there any reason, then, why inventories should not be controlled as carefully as is cash? Probably the only valid one is the general utility of cash as against the more limited utility of inventory items. But this is offset by the fact that employees are more careless in handling inventories than they are in handling cash.

Pilferage can be detected through controlled receipt, storage, and issuance of the raw materials with complete transfer records through production and finished stock into shipments. The records must show quantities entering, on hand in, and leaving each storeroom or operation. Then when shortages occur, it is possible to concentrate vigilance on a small area and thus detect the cause quickly. The very fact that a good system of control through records is in operation will provide a strong psychological deterrent to individuals who otherwise may be tempted to carry some of the products away. It is a major link in the chain of internal control procedures.

Shrinkage

The problem of shrinkage exists in many inventories and particularly with regard to raw materials. Such shrinkage may result from evaporation, seepage through the container, and adherence to the container. The accounting records should show the units received or produced in comparison with the units used or sold. By comparison of statistics of several periods, weighing "empty" containers, test gauging, etc., the amount of shrinkage to be expected can be established. An adjusting factor should be added to unit cost rates so that the units moving out of raw-material inventory will be costed at a higher rate than that at which they were charged in, so as to compensate for these unavoidable losses.

Deterioration

The mere passage of time causes loss in value through deterioration of many materials. If chemical and physical changes do not occur, the accumulation of dust and physical contacts through moving adjacent materials will usually cause damage. Wherever possible, all storage should be in lots or piles which are clearly identified on the inventory control records. Requisitions should be screened by the accounting department and marked to be taken from the oldest pile or lot. Then, if each lot is cleared completely before new material is added, there will have to be turnover. In addition to providing for frequent physical turnover, such records also provide automatic checks on the quantity in each location. As each lot is exhausted, the records are marked accordingly, and thus an automatic continuous check of physical inventories is effected.

Obsolescence

An adequate system of securing turnover will not eliminate all obsolescence of materials. Changes in customer demand, in formulations, and in product design cannot always be anticipated by the production-planning department, either because the causes are outside the enterprise or because other departments did not supply information of trends. If the accounting records indicate that a material is not moving, an investigation should be made immediately to determine whether or not the condition is likely to be permanent. If it is, possible alternate uses or sales outlets should be explored and an estimate made of the value the material would have in each of these. When the best outlet is established, the loss, if any, which will result from using or selling through the alternate outlet should be charged to an account for Loss Due to Obsolescence. If no alternate outlet can be found, the material should be scrapped and its full value charged to the obsolescence loss account. Such charges should have the prior approval of all departments having responsibilities for materials (see Exhibit 4-12).

Valuation

Since inventory valuation directly affects the cost of goods sold, no small part of the control of material costs rests on the method used and the adequacy of the supporting records. Valuation will be determined first by the policy adopted by the company and second by the operations within the policy. It is the responsibility of the accountant to recommend such valuation policies and guide management in their consideration and adoption. The adoption of the lifo basis of valuation can have a marked effect on the profits of any one year. The ideal time to go on to the lifo method is when costs are at a relatively low level. Then, if inventory quantities are maintained, and costs increase, the increase will be reflected in cost of goods sold instead of in inventory values. The opportunities for management in this area are numerous.

After the basis is established, whether it is average cost, fifo, or lifo, the timing of increases or decreases in inventory can have a substantial effect on cost of goods sold. Here the accounting and production-planning departments work hand in hand in operating within the established policies. Inventory valuation policies and procedures should be reviewed and appraised periodically, so that no opportunity for control will be lost. Conditions change constantly, and inventory valuation policies can become obsolete just as the inventories themselves become obsolete. Of course, the basis of valuation as used for published financial statements and tax returns cannot be changed at will. The valuation phase of control is one of long-range rather than current planning.

Current Control Techniques

The control of material costs will be made easier and more effective if standards are established and if the standard material costs are recorded on the books, with accounting segregation and reporting of variances from standard. However, many control devices can be operated effectively if standards are not in use. Specifications must be set for the type and quantity of raw material to be used if there is to be any uniformity of the finished product. These may not be called standards or even thought of as standards, but that is what they are. Therefore unit standards for material are more readily available to the accountant than for the other cost elements. These specifications can be adapted for cost control on the basis of units in any work centers where raw materials are used.

The control of material costs can be effected while production is in progress, the only time that costs can actually be controlled. Acceptable control techniques require daily or even more frequent measurement, comparison, and interpretation. Data on allowable usage relative to units of production should be given to clerks who process usage and production reports, so that they prepare these comparisons and give them to the foreman as a matter of routine. If the clerks are located adjacent to the office of the foreman and have frequent contacts with him, not only will their effectiveness be increased through a better working knowledge of the operation, but also the preparation of the reports will be speeded by avoiding delays in the factory mail.

Formula Variances

In many operations raw material usage must be controlled in accordance with a standard formula. These daily reports (Exhibit 13-1)

EXHIBIT 13-1
FORMULATION REPORT

FORMULATION REPORT

Operation _Forming_   Date _Aug. 11_   Shift _2_

Commodity _Wall Board ½"_

Production _61,440 sq. ft._

Material	Unit	Usage	Current standard	Inventory standard
Chest stock	lbs	44,793	44,544	46,080
Margose	"	186	184.3	184.3
Rehol	"	120	122.9	122.9
Alpod	"	—	61.4	61.4

Comments: _Alpod not used because of high specific gravity of chest stock_

Foreman _A. Hall_

should show the comparison of the actual units of material used with the standard units which should have been used for the actual quantity of production. For control purposes the standards may be revised at any time during a year to reflect changes in formulation. When standards are revised during a year, it may be desirable to show both the inventory (original) and control standard allowance on the daily reports. These reports can be prepared at the end of each shift, or even for each batch prepared during a shift if the detail of material usage is available by batches. The important point is to inform the foreman during a production run, or as soon thereafter as possible, of what actually went into the batch and what should have gone in. If the two are in agreement, it is certain that formula costs will be in line when compiled at the end of the month. If deviations in units are experienced, the cost figures at closing will simply confirm and evaluate a known deviation. Where standard costs are used, formula deviations are usually segregated in a special variance account which is charged with the raw material used and credited with the standard value of the number of batches procured. This standard value is then charged to the Material Utilization Variance account and measured against the yield of product at standard value. This procedure assists in placing responsibility for deviation from total standard cost. For example, if the laboratory has changed formula specifications so as to increase the cost, such increase will be reflected in the formula variance from standard cost, and the effectiveness of the production foreman in securing product from the formula specified will be measured in the Material Utilization Variance account.

Yield Variances

If there are no problems of formulation, there will always be problems of yield. Whether or not standard costs are used, it is essential for the control of material costs to know how many units of product are being produced in relation to the number of units of material going into production. This information is needed by operations. Where there are a series of operations, the material usage of each succeeding one is semiprocessed material. Thus the value of such material used is the total of the material, labor, and expense costs to fabricate the product up to the stage at which it enters an operation for further processing. But, whether it is a raw material or a partially processed material which is being used, the cost-control procedures and reports can be exactly the same. The material entering into production in the operation is counted, weighed, measured, or otherwise determined and recorded in units. Production of either semiprocessed or finished products of the operation is extended at standard unit allowances and compared with usage. A typical control report for this is shown as Exhibit 13-2. As with formula variances, these yield variances in units should be calculated currently or at the end of each shift or day by clerks who work closely with the foremen.

Where operations are performed in sequence with continuous movement by conveyors from one operation to another, the determination of material usage variances for each operation may not be possible because

EXHIBIT 13-2
YIELD REPORT

YIELD REPORT

Operation *Finishing*   Date *Aug. 15*   Shift __2__

Finished product *Acoustical tile 12"×12"×3/4"*

Material used *49"×49"×3/4" boards*

	Standard	Actual
Boards	11,000	11,000
Tile per board *	16	15.98
Yield before scrap	176,000	175,800
Scrap % **	5.00%	2.96%
Scrap tile	8,800	5,200
Finished production	167,200	170,600

Comment: *30 boards not square
** Low humidity resulted in less blister*

Foreman   *E. Rich*

of the inability to measure production between work centers (e.g., forming, drying, dry saws). In such cases the only alternative is to measure the input at the initial operation and output of the final operation in the related sequence and determine variances from standard for the operations as a group. This would be the case in the fiberboard plant from which the illustrations of the process cost system were drawn. Materials are used at the forming machine from which the formed board passes into dryers and from there to the dry saws. In this sequence the first point at which it is practical to measure production is of the sized board at the dry saw. This production extended at standard unit allowances for material provides the total standard quantities to be compared with the actual quantities used at the forming machine. If standards were not met, it may have been because of lack of control at the forming machine, burning or other loss in the dryer, or excess scrap at the dry saws. The comparison with standards would indicate a variance. The leader for each area would have to provide the explanation as to where and why. This is obviously less desirable than measurement at each operation.

Performance against Perfection Standards

When perfection standards are used to measure material-utilization efficiency, performance should be measured daily, or at least weekly. Since these standards do not change from period to period, relative performance can be followed over a period of years. An expedient procedure

EXHIBIT 13-3
PERFORMANCE AGAINST PERFECTION STANDARDS

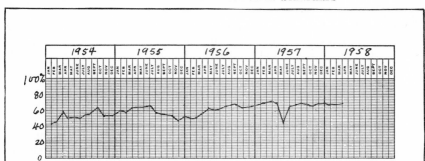

for reporting the ratio of perfection attained is a chart for each significant material or product in each operation (Exhibit 13-3). On these charts actual usage is expressed as a percentage of perfection. With a perfection standard of 0.075 pounds of chest stock per board foot of roof insulation and actual usage of 0.10 pounds the deviation is 0.025 pounds per square foot, or 33%, and the performance is 67%. This comparison, made daily for each type of fiberboard produced, may be charted by product line or as a composite for all products of the operation. The latter of these two methods is less desirable, because the reason for deviations from the trend line usually must be analyzed by product to be of value to the foreman and plant manager.

Summary Variance Reports

While the periodic reports comparing actual and standard units of usage in each operation provide the information for current control, it is necessary to inform the plant manager of the degree of control attained in each operation. This may be accomplished (1) by charting performance against standard as illustrated for the perfection standards,

(2) by preparing monthly summaries of actual and standard units, or (3) by dollar variance reports if standard costs are used. Exhibit 13-4 is an illustration of the latter and is based on the data shown in Exhibits 12-4, 12-5, and 12-6. Since, under a standard cost accounting system, standards are applied against production, the preparation of the dollar variance report requires little additional effort. It is simply a summarization of the data computed and recorded on the monthly closing work papers.

EXHIBIT 13-4
VARIANCE REPORT
MONTH OF AUGUST, 19—

Operation	Material utilization				Scrap produced			
	Actual	Stand-ard	Variance	Var., %	Actual	Stand-ard	Vari-ance	Var., %
220	$100,050	$ 99,750	$(300)*	(0.3)				
331-333	275,006	280,314	5,308	1.9				
420	15,491	15,955	464	2.9	$ 3,891	$ 4,006	$115	2.9
422	47,599	47,591	(8)		15,686	15,840	154	1.0

* Parentheses denote losses.

It is desirable to show the percentage of variance from standard, so that the plant manager can devote his attention to those which are significant. With brief explanations of significant variances accompanying the report, the plant manager will have sufficient information to discuss corrective action with the foreman.

Control by Stock Issued

An expedient method of controlling material costs while an operation is actually being run is to provide in the production order for the issuance of sufficient material from stores to produce the order. This procedure is particularly adaptable to assembly operations but can be used for many others. One of the products of the fiberboard mill is acoustical stock. This is cut into 12- by 12-inch tiles, so that each board coming off the dry saw will, under perfect conditions, yield 16 tiles (see Exhibit 13-2). The standard allowance for scrap is set at 5% of gross production. An order for 167,200 tiles will require gross production of 167,200 ÷ 0.95, or 176,000 tiles. This equals 11,000 boards 49 by 49 inches. When this order is placed in the factory, the storeskeeper releases the 11,000 boards to production. These are charged into process. If usage and scrap are on standard, no further record keeping or charges are required. If more boards are required to complete the order, a special "excess" requisition is given to the storeskeeper for them. This excess is charged to Material Utilization Variance. If all the 11,000 boards are not used, the uncut boards are returned to the storeskeeper, who issues a credit to Material Utilization Variance and charges them back into Semifinished Stock. If there is excess production, as in Exhibit 13-2, a credit is made to material utilization for the value thereof. Foremen can appraise the usage of material by examining the "excess" requisitions, the returns to the storeroom of unused material, and the excess production credits. This procedure is feasible only when there is no great variation in the quantity of material used per unit of finished product.

Salvage

Another important area of material-cost control is the salvage of defective or obsolete material and of scrap and trim. In the larger companies this responsibility is usually placed in a salvage section operating under general supervision of the purchasing department. It is the responsibility of this section to review all requests for obsolescence of materials and equipment and determine whether or not any market can be found. This section is also informed of all scrap and trim losses, for in some production, such as stampings from metal plate, there are frames which can be sold as scrap metal. In others there is scrap, such as ends of rolls and frayed edges of cloth, which can be sold. Thus, while realizable values of these are too low to reflect in the unit cost of the end products, they do have some salvage value. Through a constant search for buyers, the salvage section is able to find outlets and realize substantial income from, and save costs of hauling to the dump of, items which otherwise would be destroyed. The accounting department has the responsibility of determining the net income from salvage and of crediting it to the proper operations or products.

Indirect Costs of Inadequate Control

Inadequate control of material will not only increase the cost of the material component of the finished product but will also result in avoidable indirect costs. If the proper quantities of material are not available, shutdowns or at least expensive machine or production-line changes will be experienced. Inadequate testing of incoming raw materials or poor records of tests may permit substandard materials to be used, causing excessive scrap or completely ruining a lot or batch. Improper inspection of finished products and incomplete records of perfect and imperfect production may result in complaints from customers. Inaccurate finished-stock records may result in unfilled delivery promises and loss of good will. All these need only be mentioned to bring to mind the possible adverse effects on profits.

Then there is the indirect cost of financing the inventory. When commodity prices increase, more and more cash must be converted into inventories just to maintain quantities. The accountant should be able to inform management of the amount of inventory required and carried for each product line and the costs in terms of going interest rates of financing these requirements. The records should provide for the correlation of inventories and sales forecasts, so that inventory requirements and the resulting cash requirements can be reflected in the current and long-term cash budgets.

Summary

Material is the one inert element of cost. It is completely controllable, but because it is inert and inarticulate, it does not force itself upon the attention of management. Other problems demand attention, and it is assumed that material costs cannot go far out of line. Material is cash in another form. It should have the same care and control as cash.

REVIEW QUESTIONS

1. Where should the responsibility for the control of inventory quantities be placed?
2. What are the accountant's functions in inventory control?
3. How do material specifications aid in controlling material costs?
4. How can the purchasing department aid in the reduction of material costs?
5. To what extent are material costs affected by receiving and storage methods?
6. What is the best method of minimizing physical loss of inventories?
7. What is meant by "shrinkage"? Is it avoidable?
8. How can deterioration of stock be minimized?
9. Where should the costs of inventory obsolescence be charged?
10. What is the relationship between the time at which purchases are made and the valuation of inventories? How are profits affected?
11. When must material costs be controlled?
12. What is the purpose of segregating variances due to formulation changes?

PROBLEMS

1. The analysis of factory costs for a month disclosed the following extraordinary items:

a. Purchase of 10,000 pounds of raw material A at a delivered cost of $2.46 per pound. This material was ordered shipped by truck. Purchasing standards call for carload lots at a delivered cost of $2.25 per pound. Truck shipment was ordered because of immediate need for the material to continue production. An inventory-records clerk had failed to notify the purchasing department that stock had dropped to the reorder level.

b. Purchase of 5,000 pounds of material B from a distributor at $5.00 per pound. Purchasing standards call for purchasing from the manufacturer at $4.50 per pound. This material is purchased only as required by orders on hand. An order was received from a major customer who wanted delivery within a week of a product which required raw material B. Shipment of this raw material from the manufacturer takes from 2 to 3 weeks.

c. A charge to Obsolescence for $1,200. Investigation disclosed that this was for a raw material stored in the operation in which it was used. The operator of a lift truck in the operation upset a number of pallets of the material. The $1,200 represented the inventory value of the material which was lost as a result of the accident.

d. An actual cost of $3.00 per gallon for a raw material in comparison with a standard of $2.50. The standard is the sum of the purchase price of $2.00 and an allowance for unloading and storage of $0.50. The actual delivered cost was $2.00. Because of an oversupply of the material, it was necessary to store it temporarily in a finished-stock warehouse and then transfer it to the regular raw-material storage area. The foreman requested the cost accountant to allow costs for the extra movement so that his actual labor would not be in excess of standard. The cost accountant made the extra allowance and charged it to Raw Material Costs.

e. A scrap loss of $11,000 caused by using a raw material which laboratory tests indicated was substandard when received. Because of close scheduling of receipts to hold raw material inventories to a minimum, it was necessary either to use some of the substandard material or to shut down operations for a day. The shutdown would have cost $30,000.

Comment briefly on each extraordinary item both as to whether or not it reflected lack of control and as to possible corrective measures.

TABLE P13-2

Standard Formula

	Pounds	Per cwt	Value
A	1,000	$1.00	$10.00
B	200	3.00	6.00
C	400	2.50	10.00
D	300	2.00	6.00
E	100	4.00	4.00
	2,000	$1.80	$36.00

Actual Usage

A	90,000	$1.00
B	20,000	3.00
C	20,000	2.50
D	30,000	2.00
F	40,000	1.50

2. A finished product is made from a combination of a processed product designated as formula 1 and raw material X. The standard for formula 1 is shown in the upper half of Table P13-2. The finished product standards are 2,000 pounds of formula 1 and 600 pounds of X at $2.00 per hundredweight for each 1,000 units of finished product.

Specifications for formula 1 were changed, and the actual usage of raw materials to make it for a month is shown in the lower half of Table P13-2.

The entire production of formula 1 was used in combination with 60,000 pounds of X to produce 98,500 units of finished product.

Disregarding any labor and expense costs, what were the formula and yield variances in dollars?

CHAPTER 14

Control of Labor Costs

Unlike expenditures for materials, which are usually charged to an inventory account and may be recovered, at least in part, by selling the material, labor costs can be recovered only through the sale of the processed product. Therefore, labor costs should be controlled before they are incurred and must be controlled while they are being incurred. Control in this sense is synonymous with management and supervision. It is the responsibility of the accountant and the industrial engineer through their coordinated efforts (1) to indicate the areas where intensive control is necessary, (2) to determine what the labor costs should be, and (3) to report deviations of actual costs from planned costs and the reasons for the deviations. With this information in hand the supervisor is equipped to do an intelligent, effective job of labor-cost control.

Time was when the most common procedure for controlling labor costs was to lay off workers as soon as there was not enough work to keep each man busy. Fortunately this "out-the-door" control procedure is passing out of the picture rapidly, for unemployment has a depressing effect on a man, his family, and society. Unused raw material in the stock room may deteriorate and become obsolete, but it does so without feeling; not so an unemployed man. Therefore the concept of effective labor-cost control of "efficient utilization of the labor force" has been broadened to include "with the minimum fluctuation in number of workers." The achievement of this requires planning at the top-management level as well as supervision at the operation level. This is implemented through a complete correlation of the budgetary and cost accounting procedures.

Desirability of Standards

It is difficult to control labor costs effectively if standards in terms of man-hours per unit of production or per unit of operating time are not developed. These unit standards may be costed at the appropriate labor rates for use in standard costs and expense budgets. This latter step is desirable and provides a convenient method of reporting the results of control to the upper levels of management through variance reports. It is not essential for control by the foremen in the work centers. If standards are not available, the only alternative is to compare current actuals with past experience. Since past experience may include a substantial amount of inefficiency, such comparisons are valid only as to the trend and not the level of labor hours per unit of product. Also, changes in the type of products produced and in production specifications may be such that even recent past experience is not a fair basis of measurement.

Unit standards should be set for indirect labor as well as for direct labor. These may be either attainable or perfection standards, or a combination of both. Attainable standards can be used for planning the work force, forecasting labor costs, building total standard unit costs, and measuring the performance efficiency. With perfection standards the expected variance must be determined if the standards are to be used for other than the measurement of efficiency. For this reason perfection standards are usually set only for major labor costs, where their use supplements the attainable standards.

Standards for Direct and Indirect Labor

Standards for direct and indirect labor must reflect the different circumstances of control for each of these classes of labor. Direct labor standards are set as a unit of time per unit of product. It is expected that total direct labor costs will vary directly with the number of units produced. Therefore production in units at the applicable standard rates will provide a fair total standard to compare with total actual labor hours or dollars. In contrast, many items of indirect labor will not vary in direct ratio with production, and the standards must be set accordingly. This is usually accomplished by establishing indirect labor requirements for several activity levels within the expected range of activity. From these a fixed and variable component is formulated to arrive at standards which can be applied at any activity level. For example, the industrial engineers may determine that at an activity level of 12,000 units per day 40 hours of material-transfer labor are required and at 20,000 units per day 56 hours are required. This indicates a variable factor of 2 hours per 1,000 units.

$$\frac{56 - 40}{20 - 12} = 2$$

The fixed component is $56 - (20 \times 2)$, or 16 hours. At any activity the standard hours would be $16 + ($ activity units $\times 2)$.

Included in the attainable indirect labor standards will be provision for such unmeasurable items as machine down time, end-of-run cleanup, and idle time due to specification changes. These allowances can be established only on the basis of past experience and informed judgment as to their occurrence in the future. They may be built into the standards as either 100% fixed or as fixed and variable amounts. It must be recognized that failure to keep within standards for unmeasurable items may be due entirely to the inadequacy of the standards under the actual conditions which were encountered. Notwithstanding, the standards provide a basis of measurement, and deviations can be explained, whereas with no standards no measurement or explanation is possible.

Standards Indicate Where Control Is Needed

The very process of setting standards reveals the areas where intensive control is necessary. These are the operations where labor is an important segment of the total cost and output is determined by the worker and not by the speed of the machines. In a steam-electric-generation operation which requires two men per shift to man the controls, there would be no value in reports showing kilowatthours generated per labor hour. In a materials unloading operation, where pounds per hour may range from hundreds to thousands, daily or even shift reports showing weight unloaded per labor hour would provide valuable information to the supervisor. These examples indicate the nature of operations which do or do not require intensive control.

Planning the Labor Force

With unit standards established for direct and indirect labor the information is available for planning for and assigning the labor force. Labor requirements can be anticipated by determining the activity units by operations required to meet a sales or production forecast and extending these at the unit labor standards for the operation. This will provide not only the probable total labor hours and work force but also the requirements as to classes of labor or skills, to the extent that the standards can be identified with the different classes of labor. With this information in hand the foreman and plant manager can plan intelligently to meet requirements for labor and to use excess labor effectively. If there is an indicated future shortage of workers with required special skills, training programs can be established so as to have trained workers ready when needed. If excess labor is indicated, hiring programs can be curtailed to permit normal terminations to eliminate the excess. Or, production schedules can be adjusted through inventory building or reduction to keep the number of men on the labor force at an almost constant level. This long-range planning anticipates and thus avoids many of the problems which cause excessive labor costs.

For close-up planning and control the standard labor units are applied to the production schedules. Exhibit 14-1 illustrates this calculation of labor requirements and allowances for a production schedule for a week. With this information the foreman knows the hours and number of men he should have to produce the scheduled quantities. If he adjusts his work force accordingly, half of his labor-cost-control problem is solved. The other half is to maintain efficiency of production within the standard, and this is purely supervision.

EXHIBIT 14-1
OPERATION 331—FORMING
PRODUCTION SCHEDULE AND LABOR REQUIREMENTS—WEEK OF AUGUST 22

| Commodity | Direct labor | | | | Indirect labor | | |
	Lineal feet	Lineal feet per hour	Scheduled machine-hours	Direct-labor crew	Non-variables Men	Variables Per machine-hour	Variables Hours
⅝-in. Sheathing	22,000	1,000	22	6	2		
Acoustical stock	45,000	900	50	5	2		
¾-in. Roof insulation	19,200	1,200	16	5	2		
1-in. Industrial insulation	25,000	500	50	7	1		
			138			1.25	172.5

Machine Setup

Type	Number	Hours per setup	Allowed hours	Crew
A	3	2	6	6
B	1	3	3	6
			9	

Total machine-hours scheduled.......... 147

In machine-paced operations, such as the board-forming machine in a fiberboard plant, the production will be affected only by idle-machine time. Here labor standards can be set in terms of the number of men of each skill or class per crew. This crew size may be different for different types of products produced on the machine. Thus, if the foreman is using a standard crew for the type of material being run and maintains the established machine speeds, he will automatically control his labor costs. Under these circumstances the application of unit standards to production schedules is not necessary.

The calculation of the number of workers required to man the current production schedules will probably indicate fluctuations in numbers in different operations from day to day. The level of activity and the nature of the products scheduled for production will cause this. In the example shown in Exhibit 14-1 the direct labor crew varies from five to seven for production with six men required for machine setups. Nonvariable indirect labor drops to one man because of slower machine speeds when 1-inch material is run. Variable indirect labor is allowed at 1.25 hours for each operating hour of the forming machine. Obviously, a labor force must be large enough to meet the maximum manpower requirements. With the labor requirements related to the production schedule the foreman can plan his work to utilize his men as crew sizes change.

This can be accomplished by having a number of variable indirect labor jobs such as preventive maintenance, cleanup, rotating inventory counting, etc., planned to be done when labor is available.

In larger plants the varying daily requirements of different operations are covered by carrying a labor reserve. Men are drawn from and returned to this reserve by all operations of the plant. In addition to helping to stabilize the work force such a reserve pool is also an excellent method of training new employees in several operations of the plant.

Performance Reports

Control reports for planning and scheduling must be supplemented by periodic reports comparing actual and standard costs in terms of units or dollars. These show the extent to which the foremen kept within the plan for the labor force and labor hours required for the production schedules and also the degree of efficiency attained. Reports for foremen are usually prepared daily or weekly and show standard and actual labor in terms of hours or number of men. Reports for plant managers and top management are usually prepared monthly and show the results by operations in total for the month. If standard cost accounting is used, these reports show actual and standard labor costs, the dollar variances and the per cent of variance.

There is no one best form for the daily control reports for foremen. The nature of the production processes, the cost system in use, the importance of labor as an element of cost, the possibility of wide deviations in labor costs, the methods of determining earnings, and the wishes of the foremen will all have a bearing on the design of the form and its method and frequency of preparation.

Job-order System Reports

Under a job-order cost system the comparison of actual and standard direct labor hours or production can be made on the labor tickets from which costs are posted to jobs. Exhibit 14-2 shows a time ticket which provides for this. If a set of standards is given to the time clerk, he can place the standard data on the tickets. The foreman can then check on the effectiveness of his supervision by examining the tickets as the work

EXHIBIT 14-2
TIME TICKET

TIME TICKET								
Date _Sept. 7, 19_					Shift __1__			
Name _Amos Miller_					Clock No __1473__			

Job No	Comm No.	Material	Hours	Production		Rate/ piece hour	Labor cost	
				Actual	Standard			
59514	576	143 -1"H	4.0	10,500	10,500	P. .0008	8	40
6301	576	146 - ½"	1.0	2,000	2,100	Hr. 2.00	2	00
6306	576	146 - ½"	3.0	8,100	8,000	Hr. 2.00	6	00

Clerk _W. albert_   Foreman _J. Tone_

EXHIBIT 14-3
INDIRECT LABOR REPORT

INDIRECT LABOR							
Date _Sept. 7, 19_				Shifts worked __2__			
Operation _422 Finishing_				Machine hrs. __321__			

Classification	Std. fixed		Std variable		Total std. hrs	Actual hours	
	Hrs. per shift	Total	Hrs. per mach. hr.	Total			
003 Baling scrap paper			.05	16.1	16.1	—	
004 Scrap removal			.30	96.3	96.3	81.7	
005 Material transfer	8	16	.22	70.6	86.6	83.2	
021 Machine setters	16	32			32.0	40.0	
022 Saw sharpening			.17	54.6	54.6	53.0	
023 Drill sharpening			.11	35.3	35.3	40.1	
040 Inspectors	24	48			48.0	48.0	
051 Down time			.05	16.1	16.1	27.5	
Total					385.0	373.5	

on each job is completed, or daily before the tickets are sent to the cost and payroll departments. Comparison of actual and standard indirect labor hours would have to be made on separate forms, because a composite measure of activity is needed. Exhibit 14-3 is a report for indirect labor designed for this purpose. Here each kind of indirect labor in the operation is shown separately. This provides information for close control by tasks. This amount of detail is desirable only where indirect labor costs are a major item and significant variations from standards are probable.

Process System Reports

In some operations under a process cost system, control information for both direct and indirect labor can be combined in one report. In others separate reports are required. Exhibit 14-4 illustrates a labor con-

EXHIBIT 14-4
OPERATION 331—FORMING
LABOR CONTROL REPORT—WEEK OF AUG. 22, 19—

Date	Shift	Commodity	Lineal feet produced	Machine-hours*			Indirect labor hours		
				Allowed	Actual	Perform- ance, %	Allowed	Actual	Perform- ance, %
8/22	1	⅝-in. sheathing	5,410	5.4	6.2	87.1	34.8†	34.8	100.0
	2	⅝-in. sheathing	7,900	7.9	8	98.8	25.9‡	24	107.9
	3	⅝-in. sheathing	8,200	8.2	8	102.5	26.3¶	28	93.9
			21,510	21.5	22.2	96.8	87.0	86.8	100.2
8/23	1	Acoustical stock	5,400	6.0	5.7	105.3	35.5	43.5	81.6
	2	Acoustical stock	7,100	7.9	8	98.8	25.9	24	107.9
	3	Acoustical stock	7,400	8.2	8	103.5	26.3	24	110.0
			19,900	22.1	21.7	101.8	87.7	91.5	95.8

* Standard number of men used per crew unless otherwise noted.

† Machine setup type A, 1 @ 2 hr—6 men.......... 12
   Nonvariable—2 men........................... 16
   Variable 5.4 hr @ 1.25....................... 6.8
                                               34.8

‡ Nonvariable—2 men........................... 16
   Variable 7.9 hr @ 1.25....................... 9.9
                                               25.9

¶ Nonvariable—2 men........................... 16
   Variable 8.2 hr @ 1.25....................... 10.3
                                               26.3

trol report covering both direct and indirect labor with standards set on the basis of labor requirements in Exhibit 14-1. This type of report can be prepared by a clerk in the production operation from the original production and payroll records. Standard direct and indirect labor rates and fixed indirect labor hours are available from the scheduled labor requirements shown on the production schedule. Upon the completion of each shift the clerk posts production from the production reports and actual labor hours from the labor reports and time cards. Standard hours are then computed by applying the standard rates to the production. The report is kept in the operation for use by the general foreman and the shift foremen until the end of the week, when it is sent to the cost department with pertinent comments so as to provide them with explanations of variances reflected in the accounts for the month.

Exhibit 14-5 is a control report for labor showing the per cent performance against the standard for each operation. This report is pre-

Exhibit 14-5

Atlanta Plant

Per Cent Labor Performance Record—Week of Aug. 22, 19—

Direct Labor or Machine-hours

Operation	8/22	8/23	8/24	8/25	8/26	8/27
220	100.4	98.7	100.9	101.6	99.7	98.3
232	76.2	79.8	74.3	80.1	80.2	76.4
331*	96.8	101.8	100.2	99.3	101.7	102.3
332	90.6	103.2	101.1	99.8	104.2	102.7
333	103.7	100.1	99.3	102.2	100.9	100.0
420	99.8	97.3	96.8	92.1	90.3	90.1
421	101.0	10.29	105.0	106.3	105.9	107.1
422	99.3	70.4	97.6	103.2	101.5	100.2

Indirect Labor

	8/22	8/23	8/24	8/25	8/26	8/27
102	87.6	95.3	70.4	100.8	97.3	95.5
103	100.4	101.0	99.3	98.6	99.5	98.9
220	97.4	100.3	96.5	97.9	91.2	100.5
232	90.6	90.9	89.3	88.7	90.4	80.2
331*	100.2	95.8	100.2	96.0	99.3	100.4
333	95.7	96.9	93.0	98.1	98.0	98.7
421	99.5	90.3	96.2	89.5	87.6	84.2
422	99.6	102.0	100.7	93.5	100.9	102.2

* See Exhibit 14-4.

pared weekly for the plant manager and foremen and is a summary of the data on the daily reports (Exhibit 14-4). It shows the plant manager the trend of performance, and each foreman can also compare his efficiency level with that of the other operations of the plant and the average for the plant. The plant manager can spot operations having bad performance and adverse trends and thus concentrate his efforts on these. To be of maximum value such a report should be accompanied by brief, pointed comments on significant trends or deviations from standards.

Other Reports

When workers are paid piece rates, control of costs is effected through following the make-up pay, that is, the amount which must be added to bring earnings up to a guaranteed minimum per hour. Since this can be the only excess or above-standard labor cost under this system of payment, the report (Exhibit 14-6) can be very simple. It is prepared by the payroll clerks and sent to the foremen daily.

EXHIBIT 14-6
MAKE-UP PAY REPORT

MAKE-UP PAY

Week of _September 19, 19_

Operation	Piece rate direct labor	Make-up	% make-up
420 *Preparation*	430.16	9.20	2.1
421 *Fabricating*	1136.07	~	
422 *Finishing*	2784.44	197.10	7.1
430 *Painting*	861.10	~	
521 *Packing*	910.19	3.10	.4
Total			

Comments: *422 had six new operators being trained*

When perfection standards are used, the actual hours should be charted in comparison with the standard to provide trend information, as illustrated for material (Exhibit 13-3). Here direct and indirect hours may be shown separately and in total as a percentage of the perfection standard hours. These computations are made daily by the time clerks in the work center, and the charts are maintained there. Periodically the charts are sent to the cost section for review, presentation, and interpretation to the plant manager.

Dollar Variance Reports

Dollar variance reports prepared at the end of the month are an important part of the reporting procedure. They are of value in reporting to top management the degree of control attained. They are not control reports, for they cannot be prepared and presented until well after the end of the month. [A typical variance report in dollars would be similar to, and may be combined with, that for material usage (Exhibit 13-4).] They cover direct labor only, since the indirect labor is included with all other expenses in the expense budget reports discussed in subsequent chapters. The total actual cost for all direct labor equals the debits to the Direct Labor Variance account. The application of unit standard costs to production (Exhibit 12-5) provides the credit to the Direct Labor Variance account. Thus, with a standard cost accounting system the total dollar variance on the report is in agreement with the general-ledger account. These reports may also be used to support and supplement profit and loss statements showing the effect of labor variances on profits of products, plants, and the company.

Productivity Indices

In productive operations it is desirable to maintain indices of labor productivity for a period of years. In these the productivity of direct labor and of indirect labor should be charted separately. The reason for this is that the fixed element in indirect labor will cause fluctuations in productivity because of variations in the level of operations. This will not be true for direct labor. The productivity index should be based on units produced per hour of labor. This will provide a continuous record of the trend of cost and help avoid loose standards resulting from building inefficiencies of one year into the standards of the next year.

The calculation of a productivity index is simple where there is a common unit of production, such as gallons frozen in an ice-cream plant. The next best procedure is to convert unlike units to a common unit. Thus, in a fiberboard plant the production of the board mill in square feet of various thicknesses can be converted into square feet ½ inch thick. This then provides a reasonably consistent production unit canceling out differences in machine speed resulting from differences in thicknesses.

In still other operations a purely synthetic production unit must be devised. For example, the productivity index for cutting special parts in the fabricating operation of a fiberboard plant may be based on standard labor hours per 1,000 parts for the year selected as 100. If the base year is 1946, then the productivity index for any other period is the ratio of the actual direct labor hours for that period to the 1946 unit standard direct labor hours applied to the units produced in the period. For items which were in the line in 1946 and are produced in a subsequent year, the 1946 unit standard labor hours are available. For items not produced in 1946, a 1946 standard can be approximated by relating the current year's direct labor standard for the new item to the current year's standard for an item which was in the line in 1946 and is approximately the same. This ratio is then applied to the 1946 standard hours for the old item to secure the 1946 standard hours for the new one. This calculation is shown in Table 14-1. Eventually no 1946 items will be in

TABLE 14-1

(Old item)	Part 107-93-A	Size 20⅛ by 12¾ by ¾
	1946—2.46 hr per 1,000	1952—2.2 hr per 1,000
(New item)	Part 219-63-H	Size 20 by 12⅞ by ¾
	1952—2.31 hr per 1,000	
	2.31 = 105% of 2.2 hr for 107-93-A	
	1946 Standard = 105% of 2.46, or 2.58	

the line, but since all were converted to approximate 1946 standards, the procedure may be continued until another index year is established. If perfection standards are set for all items, the ratio of actual labor hours to perfection standard labor hours will provide an index of productivity.

Control through Incentive Plans

While the simplest method of wage payment is a straight rate per hour for the number of hours worked, this method provides no direct incentive for the worker to produce the maximum units per hour of which he is capable. Production efficiency under this method of payment is governed by the effectiveness of supervision and, in machine-paced operations, by the speed of the machines. In contrast, with an incentive basis of payment, earnings per hour are increased after an established production per hour is passed, and the worker benefits financially when he exceeds this production level.

There is no general agreement as to the desirability and practicability of incentive methods of payment. Many large and successful companies have no incentive plans for hourly workers. Others use incentives wherever work measurement is possible. Still others use incentive payment methods in some operations and plants and straight hourly methods in others. The trend, however, is toward the adoption and use of incentive plans. This is notwithstanding the fact that they are costly to install and maintain and that they complicate and increase the cost of the computation of earnings. When they are used, they must be based on scientific time and motion studies, not past experience, if they are to be successful.

There are innumerable incentive plans and variations of plans for determining earnings. They all have a common objective: to secure the maximum production per unit of time of which the worker is capable at accepted working speeds. The simplest from the standpoint of calculating earnings is the piece-rate plan under which the worker is paid a flat rate per unit of production. All other incentive plans provide for an increase in the effective hourly rate after an established quantity of production per unit of time is exceeded or quality standards are exceeded. Thus, with an incentive to employees to produce at maximum speed there tends to be an automatic control of labor costs.

Summary

Even with incentive plans, in the final analysis labor-cost control is supervision. Supervision will be most effective in this area if (1) the work force is planned for the production level anticipated, (2) the work force is adjusted to daily production schedules with effective utilization of excess labor on work which has to be done but can be done any time, (3) the foreman is informed daily of actual time worked in comparison with standard or past experience, (4) top management is kept informed of the results of control and their effect on profit and loss, and (5) a continuous record of productivity is maintained so that inefficiency is not built into the standards and thus hidden.

REVIEW QUESTIONS

1. How must labor costs be recovered?
2. Why is past experience of questionable value as a measurement of current labor costs?
3. What are the control tools for direct labor cost control? For indirect labor cost control?
4. What types of operations require intensive control procedures for labor costs?
5. How can employment be stabilized over a year?
6. What is the difference between a labor cost control report and a report showing the degree to which control was effected?
7. Should both direct and indirect labor be shown on the same control report?
8. What is "make-up" pay? What does it indicate with respect to labor-cost control?
9. What is the advantage of using hours or number of workers in labor-cost-control procedures?
10. Do productivity indexes provide control information? Explain.
11. How can a productivity index be compiled where there are no common units of production?

PROBLEMS

1. The industrial engineers have established the following hours of indirect labor for a production operation at three levels of activity, measured in standard machine-hours:

Machine time	160 Hours	320 Hours	480 Hours
Routine maintenance......	240	320	400
Material transfer.........	320	640	960
Machine clean-up.........	144	208	272
Janitor service...........	160	160	160

For a given month the schedule calls for 420 machine-hours of production.

In planning his labor requirements, how many hours of indirect labor of each classification should the foreman expect to use?

2. The productive operation of Problem 1 is a single-machine operation. For some types of production a seven-man direct labor crew is required, two of whom are helpers. For other types of production only one helper is required. Helpers are paid the minimum wage of the plant.

For the month in which 420 machine-hours were scheduled (Problem 1) the standard machine-hours were 150 with a six-man crew and 265 with a seven-man crew. Actual machine hours were 160 with a six-man crew and 260 with a seven-man crew.

Actual indirect labor hours for the month were:

> Routine maintenance............ 360
> Material transfer................ 840
> Machine clean-up............... 276
> Janitor service.................. 320

a. What were the variances from standard for direct labor hours, and for indirect labor hours by classifications of indirect labor? (Fixed hours and variable rates for indirect labor were computed in Problem 1.)

b. Comment on any apparent lack of control of labor costs.

CHAPTER 15

Control of Factory Expense

The most significant characteristic of factory expense is that, in total, it is not a constant rate per unit of product as are direct material and direct labor. For this reason there are two designations commonly applied to factory expense, "fixed expenses" and "variable expenses." Fixed expenses are those which are changed only by management decision or external forces. Variable expenses are those which are changed by, and vary in direct ratio to, the volume of production. Some sources of expense contain both fixed and variable components. Because of this behavior pattern of factory expense, the primary control medium is the factory expense budget. This is a predetermined dollar amount of expense, for each source in each operation, which is planned to be incurred at stated production levels and under stated conditions. In implementing control procedures unit rates may be determined and used to measure the variable expenses.

Budget Based on Judgment and Standards

In the development of factory expense budgets judgment and experience are the only bases of determining the amounts for some sources. For example, there is no scientific basis for determining how many supervisors are required. The demands of top management, the nature of the production process, the labor-relations problems, the job hazards, and countless other factors have a bearing on this. Therefore the number and salary level of supervisors provided for in the budget are determined by the judgment of the plant manager, past experience, and company policy. There are, however, many items of expense, primarily indirect material and indirect labor, which can be measured scientifically by chemists, engineers, or industrial engineers. For such expenses the best possible practice should determine the amount to be built into the factory expense budgets. The allowances for these items are in effect standards, and control techniques were discussed in part in the chapters "Control of Material Costs" and "Control of Labor Costs."

186

Responsibility for Factory Expense Budgets

In most plants the plant manager is responsible for the preparation of the factory expense budget and for the control of expense. These responsibilities are, of necessity, delegated to his staff and line organization. In a typical plant the industrial engineers are assigned the responsibility for preparing the budgets for indirect labor, overtime premium, shift differential, and sundry supplies; the plant engineer, for preparing the maintenance and repair budgets; and the plant engineer or power engineer, for preparing the power budgets. The plant controller is responsible for obtaining the remainder of the budget information in cooperation with the respective plant supervisory and general administrative departments.

The plant manager usually delegates to the plant controller the overall responsibility for directing the preparation, analysis, and submission of the expense budget for each budget period. Therefore, it is the plant controller's responsibility to ascertain that the budgets are formulated in accordance with the principles and procedures prescribed by company policy.

The plant manager may also be responsible for computing the budget allowance for each period, comparing this with actual expense, and analyzing and interpreting deviations. Again, as in budget building, these functions would be delegated to his staff, primarily to the plant controller. However, in some companies a separate budget department, sometimes designated as the "control department," may have the responsibility for all budget comparisons and performance analyses. Where such separate departments are established, they usually report directly to the top executives of the company. Such separation has the possible advantage of greater objectivity in reporting but has the disadvantages of two lines of reporting and of probable duplication of functions and records. Where a plant or company controller has the proper objective, professional attitude toward the management accounting processes, it would seem that a separate department is entirely unnecessary.

Supervisors Determine Their Budgets

While reference was made in the preceding section to those having responsibility for preparing the budget, this does not mean that they determine the amounts or rates of expense to be included in the budget. Their function is one of guidance and assistance rather than of determination.

Experience has shown that the most effective factory expense budgets are those which are determined by each supervisor for his own operation. The first step in budget building is for the controller to compile a detailed record of actual costs for past periods and the related activity factors. These are supplied to the staff departments having responsibility for the respective areas of the budget. They supplement these historical data with their knowledge of planned changes. They also determine tentative standard unit rates for those variable items which can be set by scientific measurement. With this information in hand they sit down with the supervisor and help him to build his expense budget for the next period.

The completed budgets are then reviewed by the plant manager or an assistant to whom he has delegated this responsibility. They may be approved as presented, or specific items may be questioned. Those which are not accepted are taken back to the supervisor, and the reasons for their inacceptability are discussed with him. Agreement is reached either on revised figures, the original figures, or compromise figures. The agreed-upon amounts then become the budget allowances against which actual expenses will be measured.

It must be stated that this procedure of having the supervisors build their own expense budgets is not followed in all plants. There are many in which the budget is set by staff departments and the supervisor must accept it. This is at variance with the modern concept that the supervisor is a part of the management team. Planning is a part of the management function, and the supervisor who is not permitted to plan the expenses for his operation does not have full management responsibility.

Fixed and Flexible Budgets

Expense budgets are usually built for a period of a year, although some plants build them semiannually or even quarterly. If the expense budget for a period provides for automatic adjustment to the actual production level and conditions at which a work center operates, it is referred to as a "flexible budget." An expense budget which is developed for a specific estimated production level and operating conditions, and is used for measurement without change during the budget period, is a "fixed budget." In most plants operating conditions and levels vary from month to month. Therefore the fixed budget for a period divided by the months in the period does not provide a fair allowance for expense for any one month. Neither is it likely that monthly variations in conditions will average out so as to make the fixed budget a fair allowance for the full period. Frequent revision of a fixed budget is necessary to make it a useful control tool, and this is time-consuming and costly. For these reasons the flexible budget is more desirable and more widely used.

"Fixed Expense" a Relative Designation

The division of factory expense into two components—fixed and variable—is an oversimplification. In the development of expense budgets it must be recognized that there is no expense which is absolutely fixed. The so-called "fixed" expenses are subject to change by management decision, by marked changes in production levels, and by external forces. A few examples will illustrate this point. Salaries are generally regarded as a fixed expense. However, a salary budget for a plant operating one shift 5 days per week would not be adequate if a second shift were added. The second shift would require more supervisors and more clerks. Rent is a fixed expense only for the noncancellable term of the lease. On expiration of the lease the rent expense can be reduced or eliminated. Depreciation based on the useful life of buildings and machinery can be changed by increasing or reducing the estimated life of the asset. It can be eliminated entirely by selling or scrapping the asset. Property taxes change as tax rates are changed. Fixed expense, therefore, is fixed only for periods of time by management decision and external forces and may even be changed within a given budget period. Therefore, in the building of either a fixed or flexible factory expense budget, recognition must be given to four types of expenses:

1. Those which are expected to be wholly fixed during the budget period
2. Those which are fixed for a given range of activity but change when production levels are above or below that range
3. Those which contain both fixed and variable elements and must be formulated into these
4. Those which are wholly variable

Units of Measurement for Flexible Budgets

The preparation of a flexible budget requires the selection of suitable units of measurement by which to express the activity of each operation. Wherever possible, a single unit should be selected for each operation. However, where necessary, separate units may be selected for different expense sources within the same operation. The following principles should apply in making this selection:

1. The unit is the one whose activity is most closely related to the greater portion of the expense involved.
2. The unit is one that is affected as little as possible by factors other than volume. Units of time or quantity are usually preferable to dollars.
3. Wherever reasonable, the same unit is selected as is used in applying factory expense to the units produced or to job orders.
4. Whenever the activity unit differs from the unit of production, it should represent standard performance. For example, direct labor hours or machine-hours should be standard hours determined by applying standard conversion factors to actual units produced. These standard conversion factors are used to reflect efficient operations. It is recognized

that there are situations where this is not practicable. Consequently, it may be necessary to use the actual activity units but this should be the exception rather than the rule.

Budget Data Sheets

In building a factory expense budget the information is assembled on data sheets which detail each expense item, establish the degree to which it is fixed, and provide explanations as to the amounts included in the budget. These data sheets are prepared by sources of expense (salaries, indirect labor, supplies, electric power, etc.) with the operation to which the expense is applicable indicated. This preparation of work sheets by source of expense rather than by operation makes it possible to divide the budget-preparation work according to responsibilities. After the data sheets for each source of expense are completed, the budgeted amounts are assembled by operations. Illustrative data sheets are shown on following pages for several sources.

Expense Sources—Fixed Budget

The degree of variability of each source of expense will not be the same in all plants nor in all operations of one plant. The following grouping of expense sources is therefore illustrative rather than definitive. The sources are those listed for the fiberboard company used for all illustrations.

Expenses which are customarily budgeted as fixed for a period are:

04	Vacation Pay and Awards	36	Consulting Service
07	Pensions	37	Donations
31	Stationery	38	Association Dues
32	Travel	51	Rent
33	Postage	52	Depreciation
34	Telephone and Telegraph	53	Taxes—General
35	Publications	54	Insurance

While the actual amounts incurred under these sources will not necessarily be the same as the amounts budgeted, no significant deviations should be caused by changes in production levels. They will be due to management decisions. The budgeted amounts will, in most instances, be supported by schedules listing the items anticipated under each source. For example, the travel budget (Exhibit 15-1) would show the expected travelers and destinations and the amount planned to be spent by each.

It may be argued that such detail is unnecessary or that expenses cannot be estimated in advance with such accuracy. Countering this, a budget is of value only if it is the evaluation of carefully developed plans. The detail to be recorded on the data sheets makes it necessary to plan in advance and thus initiates and implements cost control.

If the expense under a source will be incurred in approximately equal amounts over the months in the budget period, it is allowed in the budget in equal amounts per month. If there will be substantial variations from month to month, allowances may be made in each month equal to the actual expense for the source in the month until the total cumulative allowance equals the total amount set up in the budget. Any additional actual expense for the source will be a budget overrun. If, in

EXHIBIT 15-1
BUDGET DATA—TRAVEL
ATLANTA PLANT

	Jan.	Feb.	Mar.	Apr.	May	June	Total for period
001 Works general:							
Manager—General office............			$200			$200	
Richmond................	$50						
Mobile.................					$80		
Engineer—Chicago.................		$300					
New York...............				$250			
Total 001.......................	$50	$300	$200	$250	$80	$200	$1,080
040 Works controller:							
General office.....................		200					
Cost conference....................						200	
Total 040.......................		$200				$200	$ 400
522 Shipping:							
Traffic manager—Conference.........				150			
General office.......		200					
Total 522.......................		$200		$150			$ 350
Total plant....................	$50	$700	$200	$400	$80	$400	$1,830

the last month of the period, these irregular allowances do not equal the total budgeted for a source for the period, the remaining allowance will be reflected in the budget so that the comparison with actual will show a budget underrun. A third procedure, when amounts budgeted vary from month to month, is to allow in each month the specific amount budgeted for that month, without referring to the amount actually spent.

Expense Sources—Step Budget

Salaries are probably the only expense source which would be budgeted for a given range of activity with increments to be added or deducted for production levels above or below the range. This procedure is referred to as "step" budgeting. Salary expense will change with the number of shifts worked, and policy may call for added payments when salaried personnel are required to work a sixth or seventh day. Salary schedules will be prepared for each operation showing position titles or other job designation, and planned salaries for each position for a basic work force for one-shift operation 5 days per week. Increments will then be computed which will be added to the base allowance when extra shifts or days are worked. The salary budget for an operation is illustrated in Exhibit 15-2. The salary-budget allowance for each month will be computed from the budget schedules based on actual shifts and days operated.

EXHIBIT 15-2
MONTHLY SALARY BUDGET
ATLANTA PLANT—OPERATION 331—FORMING

	Jan.–June	July–Dec.
Base budget:		
1　General foreman	$　800	$　850
1　Asst. general foreman	600	630
1　Shift foreman	500	500
1　Mechanical supervisor	500	525
1　Chief inspector	500	500
2　Production clerks	500	500
1　Time clerk	250	265
1　Messenger	180	185
Total	$3,830	$3,955
Add for each additional shift:		
1　Shift foreman	$　500	$　500
1　Inspector	400	400
2　Production clerks	500	500
1　Time clerk	250	250
Total	$1,650	$1,650
Add for sixth day operation:		
30% of base salary up to $500		
Add for sixth and seventh day operation:		
70% of base salary up to $500		

Expense Sources—Fixed and Variable

Expenses which normally contain both fixed and variable elements are:

03	Indirect Labor	21	Fuel
09	Supplies	22	Water
13	Maintenance Material	23	Electricity
14	Maintenance Labor	41	Employee Benefit Programs
15	Maintenance Service	42	Taxes—Payroll

The fixed and variable components of any given source of expense are usually formulated by the straight-line method. Under this method, the total expense for a given source in any operation is determined for the minimum and maximum activity of the usual operating range, and the following formula is applied:

Variable expense per unit of activity = total expense at maximum activity — total expense at minimum activity ÷ maximum activity units — minimum activity units. Fixed expense = total expense at maximum activity — variable expense at maximum activity.

EXHIBIT 15-3
BUDGET DATA, INDIRECT LABOR

Plant........ATLANTA.....

Operation..4 2 1 Fabrication ....   Year............19 - -

Control and Source Account....13103 — Indirect Labor ....   Activity Basis Used..Standard Direct Labor Hours.......

Length of Period Covered: Month....X..... Year ....   Activity Units at 100%....5000.(a)...........................

Normal Work Week: Shifts per Day..1....Hours per Shift ..8....Days per Week ..6..........   Usual Operating Range: From..66.%   To..100.%

Item	CLASS CODE	DESCRIPTION	REQUIREMENTS AT ACTIVITY LOADS			RATE	FORMULATION AT 100% LOAD				VARIABLE RATE PER M ACTIVITY UNITS	
			Min. %66 Standard 3300	Aver. %83 Direct 4150	Max. %100 Labor Hours 5000		Fixed Hours	Dollars	Variable Hours	Dollars	Hours	Dollars
1	043	Clean-up	103	103	103	$1.08	103	111.24				
2	084	Trucking	205	257	310	1.40			310	434.00	62.00	86.80
3	049	Machinery Setup	310	361	413	1.50	110	165.00	303	454.50	60.60	90.90
4	040	Inspection	409	514	619	1.30			619	804.70	123.80	160.94
5	073	Quality Meetings	10	10	10	1.30	10	13.00				
6	041	Inventory Taking	16	16	16	1.15	16	18.40				
7	046	On-the-Job Training	24	24	24	1.10	24	26.40				
			1077	1285	1495		263	334.04	1232	1693.20	246.40	338.64

Specifications and Comments:

Ref. ITEM		Shifts Per Day	Operators Per Shift	Hours Per Shift	Days Per Week	Weeks Per Year	Hours Per Month
	(a) Determination of 100% Activity						
	Direct Labor Hours	1	25	8	6	50	5000

1 & 2 Clean-up and Trucking: (A) When operating at 100% activity load, efforts of two men will be utilized interchangeably 4 hours (1/2 man) for clean-up and 12 hours (1½ men) for trucking.

(B) When operating at 66% activity load, man will be borrowed from labor reserve force for 4 hours.

3 & 4 Machinery Setup and Inspection: At activity loads lower than 100%, machinery setup and inspection skills will be interchanged and supplemented by an operator assigned from General Finishing Operation Crew.

The most effective method for arriving at the formulation is by use of a data sheet for each source and operation (Exhibit 15-3). On these sheets each classification of expense in the source is listed for two or more activity levels. If this listing is in units such as labor hours, kilowatts, gallons of oil, etc., they must be priced after being formulated into fixed and variable to arrive at the dollars of fixed expense and the variable expense rate. The specifications and comments shown at the bottom of the data sheet are of value not only in appraising the soundness of the budget but also in controlling actual expense during the budget period.

Maintenance expense is frequently separated into two groups, routine and major repairs, for budget purposes. The routine-maintenance group includes those maintenance functions which are carried on continuously, such as lubrication, adjustment, minor repairs, etc. This routine group is formulated into fixed and variable components for each maintenance expense source. The major-repairs group includes the maintenance functions which are not repetitive, such as the complete overhaul of a machine or the painting of a building. Budgets for this group are prepared on a fixed basis and comprise a listing of the major maintenance jobs planned for the budget period and the estimated cost of each for material, labor, and service of outside contractors or shops.

The monthly budget allowance for each source containing fixed and variable components in each operation is the fixed dollars per month plus the standard units of activity times the variable rate. If maintenance expense is segregated into routine and major repairs, two fixed sums must be used: the fixed routine and the fixed for major repairs. Because major repairs are not spread equally over the months of a budget period, the budgeted amount is allowed in the months in which the work is done. The allowance is equivalent to the actual cost of major jobs until the entire budgeted fixed amount has been allowed. Any actual cost in excess of the total major-repair budgeted amounts for any operation is a budget overrun. Any unused allowance is added to the budget for the last month of the budget period, so that the underrun is reflected in the reports.

Expense Sources—Variable Budget

There are very few expense sources which are entirely variable in all operations of a plant. A source may be entirely variable in one operation and have fixed and variable components in another. Where a source is entirely variable in an operation a rate is determined per unit of production. The monthly budget allowance is the standard production units times the budgeted variable rate.

Approval of Expense Budgets

Before the budgets become effective, they must be approved by the personnel who are responsible for expense control. Each foreman will finally approve the budgets for his operation. The plant manager will approve all budgets for his plant. The staff departments participating in the budget building will approve those portions of the budget under their direction. Finally, the accountants will approve the budget and submit it to the company officer having responsibility for factory costs. In smaller companies this may be the president of the company; in larger multiplant companies it would be the general production manager. To assist in appraising the soundness of the budget, comparisons with a past period are desirable. Exhibit 15-4 illustrates this comparison, in this instance for the total budget for the plant.

EXHIBIT 15-4
ATLANTA PLANT
COMPARISON OF FACTORY EXPENSE-CONTROL ACCOUNT 13100
BUDGET SUBMISSION WITH PRIOR YEAR FIRST 6 MONTHS ACTUAL EXPENSE

Source account	Prior year first 6 months actual expense adjusted for budgeted current wage and material price levels	Current budget submission adjusted to first 6 months prior year actual activity	Annual variance current budget increase or (decrease) over prior year actual	Explanation of significant variances
02 Salaries..............	$ 93,600	$ 99,800	$12,400	Transfer of four hourly employees to salary
02 Salaries—overtime....	1,700	1,700		
02 Salaries—SWEP......	4,600	4,600		
03 Indirect labor.........	82,700	90,200	15,000	Transfer six men from direct labor
03 Overtime.............	16,500	11,100	(10,800)	Overtime in first 6 months prior year not representative
03 Shift differential......	4,500	3,900	(1,200)	
03 Nonwork holiday pay.	8,600	24,000	30,800	Three additional paid holidays
04 Vacation pay.........	20,500	25,600	10,200	More employees eligible for vacation pay
53 Taxes—general.......	$ 17,100	$ 19,700	$ 5,200	Increased real estate taxes
42 Taxes—payroll........	9,700	9,700		
Total..............	$326,300	$337,100	$21,600	

Budget Allowance Cards

After the data sheets have been prepared and approved for each expense source, a budget allowance card (Exhibit 15-5) may be prepared for each operation. These cards are used as work sheets for calculating budget allowances. They would show all budget allowances in fixed dollars and variable rates, except those on a step basis, and the unit used to measure activity. Space is provided for recording the budget allowances for each month in the budget period. After the allowances are computed they may also be posted in total for each operation in the subsidiary expense ledger or may be posted therein by source for each operation. This provides a permanent record of actual and budgeted expense and provides background information for the preparation of future budgets.

This card shows only those expenses for which the foreman of the operation is responsible. Thus, while sources such as salaries, taxes, insur-

EXHIBIT 15-5
BUDGET ALLOWANCE CARD

Operation 331 Forming
100% activity 575 Std. mach. hrs.

BUDGET ALLOWANCE CARD 19__

				Jan.			Feb.		
Activity — Period to date				413			817		
Activity — Current mo				413			404		
So	Description	Var./hr.	Fix.	V	T	P-D	V	T	P-D
03	Ind. labor	10.50	10,570	4,336	14,906		4,242	14,812	29,718
09	Sund. supp.	.60	10	248	258		242	252	510
13	Maint. matl.	3.00	40	1,239	1,279		1,212	1,252	2,531
14	Maint. labor	1.00	1,100	413	1,513		404	1,504	3,017
15	Maint. services	—	500	—	500		—	500	1000
31	Stationery	—	150	—	150		—	150	300
32	Travel	—	Per data	—	80		—	—	80
	Total	15.10			18,686			18,470	37,156

ance, etc., will appear under an operation in the subsidiary expense ledger, they are not controllable by the foreman of the operation. The calculation of allowances for such sources will be at the general plant level where they probably are controllable.

Monthly Budget Reports

Monthly reports of performance against the budget (Exhibit 15-6) are prepared for all persons having responsibility for expense control. A separate report is prepared for each operation, summary reports for

EXHIBIT 15-6
EXPENSE BUDGET PERFORMANCE REPORT

Operation 331 Forming

Source	Month of February			Period to Date		
	Actual	Budget	Deviation	Actual	Budget	Deviation
03 Indirect labor	$13,910	$14,812	$902	$28,830	$29,718	$888
09 Sundry supplies	250	252	2	540	510	(30)
13 Maintenance material	1,490	1,252	(238)	2,401	2,531	130
14 Maintenance labor	1,610	1,504	(106)	3,097	3,017	(80)
15 Maintenance services	500	500	——	1,000	1,000	
31 Stationery	110	150	40	290	300	10
32 Travel	——	——	——	80	80	
Total responsibility	17,870	18,470	600	36,238	37,156	918
Salaries	7,600	——	——	15,200		
Taxes—payroll	420	——	——	380		
Employee benefits	1,490	——	——	1,210		
Depreciation	4,175	——	——	8,350		
Taxes—general	1,400	——	——	2,800		
Insurance	1,500	——	——	3,000		
Total expense	$34,455	——	——	$67,178		

several operations under the same general foreman, and a summary report for the entire plant for the plant manager. There are many forms for, and much variation in the data presented in, these reports. In the illustration the actual and budgeted expense and deviations are shown for the month and year to date. In some plants the variance is also shown as a percentage of the budget allowance. Still another method of presentation is to show the budget allowance and the deviation from the budget. The form and data shown must be adapted to the requirements of the plant. Where machine accounting is used, the expense ledger and budget allowance may be collated and machine-printed all in one operation on the report form. This form thus is both the subsidiary expense ledger and the budget performance report.

In the illustration (Exhibit 15-6) a total is shown for the sources for which the foreman is responsible. Other sources incurred directly for the operation are also shown to give the foreman the total incurred expense of his operation. A further step may be taken by showing the shares of service-operation expenses allocated to the productive operation. Desires of the plant manager will determine the extent of the information shown on the reports.

While only a form of the budget report is illustrated, an integral part of the monthly performance presentation is a written analysis and interpretation of significant deviations by sources. This indicates the possible corrective action where overruns have occurred. Of course not every overrun indicates bad performance nor every underrun a loose budget. More often the analysis will indicate unusual conditions which could not be foreseen.

Current Control Data Required

It must be recognized that the monthly budget reports simply reflect the degree of control attained. They are a historical record and not control tools. Control is effected by informing all persons having responsibility for expenses of the amounts budgeted for the scheduled production level and providing them with sufficient information from day to day so that they know they are keeping expenses within these limits. The chapters "Control of Material Costs" and "Control of Labor Costs" referred to some of these daily control techniques. Others are suggested in the following paragraphs. In establishing these daily controls the amount and nature of the expense in relation to the cost of maintaining daily control must be considered. For example, telephone and telegraph expense is usually not sufficiently significant in amount to justify a daily control record. The cost of purchased electric power will be determined by the power and light load of the plant. It is controlled by not having machines running when they are not producing, by not having lights burning when not needed, and by watching the peak load which affects demand charges. A daily calculation of what electric cost should be for the scheduled production level would be of little or no value in controlling it. Also, until the billing period is completed and the bill received, the actual charges are not known.

Current Control of Fixed Expense

The budgets for sources such as publications, donations, and association dues show to whom the payment is to be made. Here control is effected by comparing all invoices or requests for payment of these items against the budget before the item is paid. If it is provided for in the budget, it is cleared. If not, it is returned for special approval for a budget overrun or for application against any "miscellaneous" amount budgeted for the source.

Other sources of expense which are budgeted as entirely fixed and are significant and subject to control, such as stationery, may require simple control records. For these a card can be set up for the source showing the allowed amount for the month. Purchase requisitions or stores requisitions are then posted to this, usually at estimated amounts, and a running total kept for comparison with the budgeted amount. Or, actual invoiced amounts and priced stores requisitions may be posted to the card. This latter procedure provides more nearly accurate amounts of expense but has the disadvantage of being recorded after the money is spent.

Control of salary expense is accomplished by checking requests for personnel and salary changes against the positions and salary levels planned in the budget. If all budgeted positions are filled and individual salaries are at budgeted levels, approval for an overrun must be obtained before the person is hired or a salary is raised.

Current Control of Variable Expense

The general control procedure for sources of expense which contain fixed and variable components or are entirely variable is to compute the budget allowance at the level of the production schedule. Incurred amounts are then posted against this from stores requisitions, invoices, labor reports, etc. In these controls the daily figures should be in units rather than dollars wherever possible. Units are usually more comprehensible to the foremen and are available earlier than dollar amounts. This method is particularly applicable to supplies and indirect labor. Control reports for expense material or labor may be consolidated with those for direct material or labor as in Exhibits 14-1 and 14-4.

Current Control of Maintenance Expense

Special control techniques are usually required for maintenance because of the irregularity with which the expenses are incurred. Exhibit 15-7 illustrates a form used for maintenance expense control. Separate cards should be used for the categories of routine maintenance and major repairs if these two items are to be budgeted separately. This provides better control data. However, the two are sometimes combined, as in the illustration. The budget position is built up cumulatively with the fixed and variable allowance of each month. On the first of each month an amount is added to the unreleased balance equivalent to the fixed budget for the month plus the variable allowance for the scheduled activity level. At the close of each month this total budget is adjusted to the allowance based on actual activity. As the foreman signs work orders for maintenance, the estimated amount is posted to the "Funds Released" column and deducted from the unreleased balance. When the job is completed the actual cost is posted in the "Final Cost" column, the difference between the estimate and actual posted in the "Balance" column, and the unreleased balance adjusted to reflect the actual cost. The actual cost of repetitive work such as lubrication and of minor work done without orders is posted weekly or monthly to the "Final Cost" column from the original cost records (invoices, stores requisitions, and labor distribu-

EXHIBIT 15-7
MAINTENANCE EXPENSE CONTROL CARD

JOB NO.	ITEM	DESCRIPTION	BUDGET Date	BUDGET Amount	FUNDS RELEASED Date	FUNDS RELEASED Amount	FINAL COST	BALANCE	BUDGET POSITION OR UNRELEASED BALANCE Date	BUDGET POSITION OR UNRELEASED BALANCE Amount
	Account No. 1313			ACCOUNT NAME Maintenance Material - Forming					1/1	1240
	Division - or Plant Atlanta								1/10	740
									1/5	726
									1/17	626
1-001	Replace screen (major)		1/5	500 00	1/10	500 00	49 000	750 00	1/20	536
	Misc. charges				1/15		1 400	736 00	1/31	422
1-043	Repair head box				1/17	100 00	200 00	536 00		
1-045	Gear charges				1/20	90 00	7 300	443 00	1/31	368.00
	Misc. charges				1/31		1 1400	329 00	2/1	1240.00
							9 1100			1608.00
	Budget adj. to actual activity						39 00			
							368 00			
2-007	Wet saw overhaul (major)		2/1	900 00	2/5	800 00	953 00	655 00	2/3	803.00
	Misc. charges				2/15		127 00	528 00	2/15	681.00
2-091	Electrical control adj.				2/17	500 00	405 00	123 00	2/17	181.00
	Misc. charges				2/28		5 00	118 00	2/28	176.00
							149 00			
	Budget adj. to actual activity						12 00			
							120 00		2/28	130.00
									3/1	1540.00
										1670.00

tions) and deducted from the unreleased balance. Thus the foreman has a reasonably accurate picture at all times of his performance for the year against his cumulative budget. This procedure will not necessarily provide for keeping actual maintenance expense of any one month within the budget for that month but will provide for control of the year-to-date actual. This is the significant figure for maintenance, because these expenses are irregular in amount by months.

Accountant Adapts Control Procedures to Requirements

In control of factory expense, as in all cost control, after-the-fact reports are not control tools. The amount which may be spent must be set in the budget, adjusted to actual activity levels if flexible budgets are used. These allowable amounts must be used by the foremen and other supervisors as their guide in authorizing actual expenses. The procedures for giving them this control information will vary by companies, operations, and sources of expense. The development of the best control procedures is the responsibility of the accountant. It requires more creative thinking and more variation in procedure than for either direct material or direct labor. However, the importance of expense in the total-factory-cost picture justifies these rather detailed control procedures and records. Their development is a challenge to the management sense and ability of the accountant.

REVIEW QUESTIONS

1. Can factory expense be measured and controlled by unit standards or standard costs as are direct material and labor? Why?
2. Who is responsible for the control of factory expense?
3. Why should each supervisor participate in the building of the expense budget for his operations?
4. What are the accountant's functions in building factory expense budgets?
5. Explain the difference between a fixed budget and a flexible budget.
6. What expenses are absolutely fixed?
7. What considerations determine the units of measurement used in a flexible budget?
8. What is a step budget, and for what expenses is it particularly desirable for expense-control purposes?
9. For expenses which contain both fixed and variable items how are the fixed dollars and variable rates determined?
10. What is the purpose of budget allowance cards?
11. Describe the form and content of monthly expense budget reports.
12. What current control techniques can be developed for factory expense?
13. Why are special control procedures required for maintenance expense? How can they be established?
14. When should the amount of allowable expense be given to foremen?
15. Should expense reports show expenses which are not controllable by the recipient of the reports?

PROBLEM

The budgeted activity of a production operation with 12 production machines was 24,000 machine-hours for a 6-month period. This called for operating two 8-hour shifts five days per week.

For expense control purposes the following fixed budget was built to be used for each month of the period:

Salaries—two shift foremen	$1,000
Indirect labor	4,000
Supplies	1,000
Maintenance material	500
Maintenance labor	1,500

In one month of the budget period, which had 22 working days exclusive of Saturdays and Sundays, actual expenses were as follows:

Salaries	$1,075
Indirect labor	4,560
Supplies	1,070
Maintenance material	420
Maintenance labor	1,780

The standard machine-hours computed from units produced were identical with the actual machine-hours of 4,400.

Time and a half is paid for Saturday work and double time for Sunday work. Salaried personnel receive added salary equivalent to 7½% of their base monthly salary for each Saturday and 15% for each Sunday they are scheduled to work.

You are the accountant and are asked to analyze the budget overruns and recommend procedures for effecting closer control of expenses.

In your analysis you find that it was necessary to operate one shift on each of two Saturdays to meet customer demands for products. Direct labor hours on these 2 days were 192, and indirect labor hours were 104. The hourly rate for all direct labor was $2.50 and for all indirect labor, other than maintenance, was $2.00. There are no incentive plans, and no shift differential is paid.

You test 2 prior months' expenses and find the following:

Standard machine-hours	3,000	4,000
Indirect labor	$3,500	$4,000
Supplies	$ 800	$1,000

You find that 90 man-hours of maintenance work is normally scheduled to be done on each of four Saturdays of each month. Because of the production schedule, the maintenance was done on two Saturdays and two Sundays. There were 176 maintenance man-hours of Sunday work. The average hourly rate of the maintenance crew is $2.80, before overtime premium.

What are your conclusions as to whether or not expenses were controlled, and what recommendations would you make for improving control techniques?

CHAPTER 16

Costing By-products and Joint Products

By-products are those products of lesser importance which are secured coincident with the production of a major product and which are not sold through the same distribution channels to the same markets as is the major product. Joint products are products of approximately the same relative importance produced simultaneously and sold through the same distribution channels to the same markets. These two classifications are not absolute. A product which one company in an industry considers to be a by-product and values on by-product costing procedures may be considered as a joint product and valued as such by another company in the same industry.

There are many acceptable methods of costing by-products, but there is only one generally accepted practice for costing joint products. By-product costing is a matter of company policy rather than of accounting procedure. When by-product valuation policies are formulated, there should be no change in their fundamental application, unless there is a marked and probable long-term change in the basic factors pertinent to the material. Otherwise the costs and possibly the sales prices of the major product will be affected temporarily by by-product credits, which may damage its long-range competitive strength and position.

By-products

By-products may be sold to customers in the form in which they are produced, processed further before being sold, or used as a raw material in other products. In a multiunit company the use as a raw material may be by a unit other than the one which produces the by-products. This involves intracompany pricing with the prime consideration the encouragement of the optimum utilization of by-products so as to secure the maximum profit for the company.

GENERAL PRINCIPLES OF VALUATION

The general principles to be followed in by-product values are:

1. The value should provide for an economic costing and consequent competitive pricing of the product which produces the by-product as well as of the commodity which uses it.

2. An incentive should be provided, first, for the development of products which will utilize all the by-products produced by a company and, second, for the finding of sales outlets for any by-product which cannot be used by the company.

3. The established valuation procedure should be based on long-term average conditions and not adjusted for temporary abnormal situations.

For purposes of determining values, by-products fall into three general classes:

1. Those which have an established market
2. Those which are used as substitutes for other materials
3. Those not readily marketable or usable as substitutes for other materials

BY-PRODUCTS WITH ESTABLISHED MARKETS

Certain by-products have established markets with a sufficient volume of sales by other producers of the same products to set going market prices at all times. An example would be cork shavings which are produced when cork stoppers are cut from corkwood. Another would be skim milk produced in the dairy industry when whole milk is separated to secure the cream for butter manufacture and other purposes. If such by-products were not available within a company, they could be purchased on the open market.

The value of these by-products and the resultant credit given to the prime product should be based on the established market prices. This policy would apply if the by-products are used within the company or are sold to outside customers. When used within the company they would not be valued as substitutes for other materials. If they would have a lower net value to the company as substitute materials, they should be sold rather than used. If they would have a higher net value when costed on the basis of substitute materials, they would not be used as substitutes, because the using products would have higher costs than if the alternate raw material were used. The method of arriving at the value of a by-product by working from the established market price would be determined by circumstances within the company.

All of a by-product may be sold to customers, or some of it may be sold and some used as a raw material in other company products. When part or all of it is sold, the value is usually set as the market price less the sum of (1) distribution and administrative expenses incident to its sale, (2) the average transportation costs to customers, (3) the costs of packaging, handling, and storage, and (4) a provision for profit. The latter may be the percentage profit on sales earned by the prime product, the amount required to earn a stated return on the capital employed in the selling function, or an arbitrary rate of profit established by company policy. The company products which use a by-product valued on this basis would be charged less for it than they would pay if they purchased it in the open market. This would be fair to the product which yields the by-product in that it would be receiving credit equal to the amount which would accrue to it if all the by-products were sold. It would provide an incentive to secure maximum sales of the product using the by-product as a raw material, since the cost of it would be less and the profit greater than it would be if the by-product were purchased on the outside.

A company may use all of a by-product with an established market price that it produces and may also buy some of it on the open market. Under these conditions the value is usually set at the market price less the costs of getting the by-product from the point of production to the point of use. This gives more credit to the producer of the by-product than would be received if it were sold. This is equitable because the demand for the by-product within the company exists because of the market for products which use it, rather than because the by-product is available. This demand makes it unnecessary to provide an incentive for the sale of the products which use the by-product.

Some companies follow a policy of dividing the profit advantage on by-products between the producer and the user or seller. This is particularly true when production of the by-product is by a company unit other than the one which uses or sells it. Such division of the profit advantage can only be arbitrary and may result in internal disagreements on the shares given to each unit which must be resolved by top management. The usual method is to split the profit advantage equally. For example, if all of a by-product is used, the costing of it to the user at what would be paid on the open market results in a profit to the producer which is greater than if the producer incurred the costs of selling it on the open market. The producer's cost savings would be split equally between the producer and user of the by-product.

BY-PRODUCTS USED AS SUBSTITUTE MATERIALS

The value of by-products which do not have an established market and can be used as substitutes for other raw materials is based on the value of the raw material which they replace. In determining the value of the by-product it may not be satisfactory to base it on a unit-for-unit replacement of the other raw material. More or less by-product may have to be used than would be of the material for which it is substituted. Other raw materials may have to be added to make it possible to use the by-product, and processing speeds and yield of finished product may be changed. For these reasons the value of the by-product as a substitute material is the difference between total factory cost of production using the specified raw material and the total factory cost of production using the by-product at no value. From this difference would be deducted the costs of getting the by-product from the producer to the user of it as a substitute. The net amount would be the maximum credit to the producing prime product. Company policy may call for this to be split between the producer and the user, so as to provide an incentive to the user to make the substitution.

If sales to customers can be made from time to time of a by-product used as a substitute material, which will return a net amount to the company which is greater than the value of the by-product as a substitute, the by-product should be sold rather than used.

BY-PRODUCTS WITH NO ESTABLISHED MARKETS AND NOT USED AS SUBSTITUTE MATERIALS

Some by-products have no established markets but can be sold either regularly or intermittently. For these the value is based on what the customer is willing to pay. Credit is given to the producer of the by-product only for quantities actually sold. Under these conditions, the by-product, if held on inventory, is carried at no value, and no credits are given to the prime product when it is produced. When it is sold, a credit is determined by deducting from the sales income the costs of selling, of preparing for sale, and of transportation. If the by-product must be processed further before it can be sold, the processing costs would also be deducted from the sales income. If it is sold by a unit of a company other than the one which produces it, a provision for a profit to the seller is also deducted. The profit provision is usually high in relation to the profits realized by the seller on its other products in order to provide an incentive for finding markets for the by-product.

A product may be developed which will use a by-product which could not otherwise be used or sold. When this is done, the using product may be charged only with the costs of getting the by-product to it and no credit given to the prime product which produces the by-product. The prime product would realize some cost advantage, in that it would not have to bear the costs of disposing of the by-product. Or, the profit realized on the product developed to use the by-product may be shared with the prime product, resulting in a greater cost advantage for it.

There is a business risk in investing in facilities to produce, and in developing a market for a product which will use a by-product which otherwise would be destroyed, particularly if the by-product is charged to the new product at the cost of handling. If the market for the product which produces the by-product declines or disappears or if methods of production are developed which will not result in the by-product, the company will have idle facilities and unrecoverable costs. The price of a product developed to use a by-product should be high enough to return all facility and development costs to the company within a period during which it is quite certain that the new product can be sold and that the by-product will be available.

Joint Products

Where joint products are produced, the generally accepted costing procedure is to allocate the costs of production on the basis of the sales prices which will be realized on each product. An example would be a leaf-tobacco company which purchased tobacco from growers, sorted, graded, and packed it, and sold it to manufacturers of tobacco products. The cost of the ungraded tobacco plus the processing costs would be allocated to grades on the basis of the relative sales prices of the grades.

The production processes of a joint-products industry may be referred to as processes of disintegration. Here a bulk or common raw material is separated into grades, or into smaller units or into products with different chemical and physical properties. In contrast, an integration industry takes raw materials and combines them so as to form a finished product. Many of the basic raw materials of integration industries are the finished products of disintegration industries. These are the commodities which, in a free market uncontrolled by price stabilization or other governmental regulation, are most susceptible to the effect of supply and demand. Their price is governed by economic conditions rather than by actual costs. Commodity prices, then, are largely beyond the control of the producer, and he is unable to establish sales prices in relation to the cost of his product.

The integration industries show the opposite tendency. Automobile costs increase as steel prices rise, tire costs are influenced by the rubber market, etc. This is because these industries are building products from basic materials. Their raw material costs are established commodity market values, and as a result they "build" their costs from the basic materials into the finished product. Then they endeavor to cover their costs in their sales prices. Their problems are the control of conversion costs and the creation of a market at a price, i.e., selling.

REQUIREMENTS OF A COST SYSTEM IN DISINTEGRATION INDUSTRIES

If, as in the disintegration industries, the sales price is fixed in the commodity markets and controlled by supply and demand, the problems of management center on purchasing and conversion rather than on conversion and selling. Therefore, costs in such an industry have, in part, a different function than they do in an integration industry. The cost system, to be of the maximum value to the management, must provide the following:

1. A convenient method of determining the price which can be paid for any given lot of raw material
2. The means of measuring actual yields against those anticipated at the time of the purchase of the raw material
3. A comparison of actual conversion costs with those anticipated and used for establishing purchase prices

These requirements can be met successfully by the operation of a standard cost system.

AN ILLUSTRATIVE COMPANY

For purposes of illustration it will be assumed that a company's activity is confined to the purchase, preparation, and sale of a natural product. A year's supply of raw material is purchased in the fall, either at public auctions or privately, from many growers spread over a large geographical area. Thus the material purchased in any one year varies as to quality, depending upon the climatic conditions of the localities from which it is secured. The price paid for each lot is based upon the expected yield of grades as established by test-sorting representative portions before purchase. Since each lot contains some of or all the final grades, the various lots are blended upon entering into process at the factory, so as to offset, in so far as possible, the deficiencies of one lot by the superiority of another. Processing constitutes the removal of dirt and foreign matter, sorting, and packaging.

The material is sorted into six standard grades, one or more of which ordinarily will meet the requirements of the customers who convert it into its final fabricated form. However, there are times when special grades are required. These have no bearing upon the function of the system, since a special grade is necessarily a mixture of existing grades.

SETTING STANDARDS

Because of the peculiarity of this industry in that a year's supply of raw material is purchased near the close of the previous year, the material standards, which in a manufacturing industry are usually considered first, are dependent upon and must wait for their determination until after the development of conversion, administrative, and distribution costs.

Standard labor costs are developed by time studies, and labor-cost control is effected by measuring actual costs against standards for each operation. Expense budgets are used, and standard expense rates are developed from the expense budgets at normal production volumes. Thus, for direct labor and factory expense the cost and budget procedures follow those of any other industry.

Standard administrative and distribution expense rates are developed from the respective budgets. Here the rates are also based on normal volume and may be per unit of product or per dollar of sales. If more sales effort is required to sell the higher grades or if salesmen are paid a

TABLE 16-1

Conversion cost—labor	$2.50 per cwt
—factory expense	1.00
—total	$3.50
Purchase expense	0.50
Administrative and distribution expense	20% of sales
Sales prices:	
Grade 1	$200.00 per cwt
Grade 2	100.00 per cwt
Grade 3	50.00 per cwt
Grade 4	30.00 per cwt
Grade 5	20.00 per cwt
Grade 6	10.00 per cwt

commission on sales dollars, the rates would be per dollar of sales, as used in the illustrations. Otherwise they would be per unit of product.

Since purchasing is such an important function in disintegration industries, a standard is also established for purchasing expense. These expenses are those incurred by the purchasing department and the production department in examining, testing, and buying the various lots of raw material. These expenses are usually reflected in the raw-material inventory values at the standard rates.

With standards developed for these items the accountant is able to develop the standard material costs. For illustrating the building of these assume that the rates shown in Table 16-1 have been established.

CALCULATING ALLOWABLE PURCHASE PRICES

With this information, and an established standard allowance for scrap, the accountant is in a position to furnish the purchasing agent with a schedule of prices which can be paid for the various grades of raw material and permit the business to earn a desired profit on sales, which will be assumed to be 10%. The calculation of allowable purchase prices is shown in Exhibit 16-1.

From this calculation it is evident that raw material which would yield 100% of grade 1 finished product may be purchased at prices up to $122 per hundredweight, material yielding 100% of grade 2 at prices up to $59 per hundredweight, and so on for each grade. However, as previously

EXHIBIT 16–1

CALCULATION OF PURCHASE PRICES

Allowable Purchase Prices of Grades

	Grades					
	1	2	3	4	5	6
Forecast sales price.................	$200.00	$100.00	$50.00	$30.00	$20.00	$10.00
Less:						
Provision for profit, and selling and administrative expense..........	60.00	30.00	15.00	9.00	6.00	3.00
Available for factory cost............	140.00	70.00	35.00	21.00	14.00	7.00
Factory cost before 10% loss........	126.00	63.00	31.50	18.90	12.60	6.30
Conversion cost and purchase expense	4.00	4.00	4.00	4.00	4.00	4.00
Price f.o.b. factory which can be paid for raw material.................	$122.00	$ 59.00	$27.00	$14.90	$ 8.60	$ 2.30

Allowable Purchase Price of a Lot

Grade	Per cent	Allowable grade price	Factor
1	2	$122.00	$ 2.44
2	6	59.00	3.54
3	12	27.50	3.30
4	25	14.90	3.72
5	25	8.60	2.15
6	30	2.30	0.69
Maximum price per cwt f.o.b. factory...........	—	—	$15.84

stated, each lot of raw material will yield some of each finished grade. Thus, when each lot is tested prior to purchase, it is necessary for the purchasing department to calculate the maximum price which may be paid for the lot. This calculation is very simple and for a given lot of material is shown at the bottom of Exhibit 16-1.

With a table of allowable prices and a knowledge of transportation costs, the purchasing department possesses the cold facts necessary to enable it to perform its function satisfactorily. It now becomes its responsibility to secure the quantity of material required for the next year's operations at the allowable prices.

IMPORTANCE OF USING NORMAL VOLUME

The importance of having based all expense rates on normal activity is to be noted. If forecast activity were used in a period of low activity the unit expense costs would be relatively high. As a result it would be well-nigh impossible to purchase at the allowable price. Being hard pressed, the purchasing department would tend to be overhopeful regarding qualities, with resultant poor yields which would increase the material component of the actual factory cost. The enterprise would then not only have to face high unit expense rates but also unduly high material costs. Conversely, in times of peak activity, unit expense rates would be low, thus failing to put the full task on the purchasing department, and consequently not securing the maximum attainable profit for the business.

MATERIAL STANDARDS

Material standards of the illustrative company are not built until after the next year's supply of raw material has been purchased. A record of each lot purchased is presented to the cost accountant. These records show the quantity of material in the lot and the expected yield from the test sorting. These quantities are priced at the allowable price per hundredweight, f.o.b. factory for the lot, the allowable price being considered as the standard. The total standard value for all the lots is adjusted for the expected scrap loss, and this, related to the expected yield in pounds, provides the over-all average standard value.

The next step is to allocate this average standard value to grades. This is accomplished by relating the total material cost of the material processed, assuming all the raw material purchased will be processed during the year, to the sales value of the expected yield by grades (Exhibit 16-2).

In the illustration, the total material cost of $511,500 is 55% of the $930,000 forecast sales value of the expected yield of grades. Therefore, the material cost per hundredweight of each grade is assumed to be 55% of the sales price of the grade. This results in a uniform ratio of material cost to the sales dollar. Under this method, profits are not overstated nor understated in those periods in which the ratio of the grades produced is not relative to the ratio of the grades sold. Neither are the inventory values distorted by the relative proportions of grades remaining in stock. The total dollars of cost distributed are of material cost only. Since grade is the determining factor in the relative sales prices, only the material

EXHIBIT 16–2
CALCULATION OF MATERIAL
COST OF GRADES

Grade	Expected yield in pounds	Forecast sales price	Forecast sales value	Total material cost	Material cost per cwt
1	100,000	$200.00	$200,000.00	———	$110.00
2	200,000	100.00	200,000.00	———	55.00
3	400,000	50.00	200,000.00	———	27.50
4	500,000	30.00	150,000.00	———	16.50
5	500,000	20.00	100,000.00	———	11.00
6	800,000	10.00	80,000.00	———	5.50
	2,500,000	$ 37.20	$930,000.00	$511,500.00	$ 20.46

cost is related to, and allocated on, the sales value, the conversion cost being carried as a uniform rate per hundredweight regardless of grade. As sorting and processing proceeds, the variations from standard material cost are segregated as to cause: purchase price, yield, and scrap. This procedure would follow that of the process standard cost system.

GENERAL APPLICATION

The illustrative procedure assumed that a year's supply of raw material is purchased at one time and that processing costs were the same for each grade of finished product. Where these conditions do not exist, the procedure must be modified accordingly.

If purchases are made continuously, as in the meat-packing industry, current or estimated market prices of the finished product must be used. The allowable purchase prices for raw material would be calculated from these by the same procedure used in the illustration. With each change in market prices of the finished product, new allowable raw-material purchase prices would be calculated.

Where conversion and selling costs vary by grades of finished products, the specific costs for each grade would be used rather than the same rates for all grades.

REVIEW QUESTIONS

1. What is the difference between by-products and joint products?
2. Why is by-product costing a matter of company policy rather than of accounting practice?
3. What are the general principles which should apply in the valuation of by-products?
4. A by-product with an established market can also be used as a substitute

material by the company producing it. When should it be sold, and when should it be used as a substitute material?

5. When a by-product has an established market, what items should be deducted from the market price to arrive at the by-product credit given to the primary product?

6. When a by-product with no established market is used as a substitute material, how is its value determined?

7. What are the business risks in investing in facilities to produce and in developing a market for a product which will use a by-product which otherwise would be destroyed?

8. A certain by-product is sold infrequently. When and how should a value be determined for the by-product and credited to the prime product?

9. What is the generally accepted costing procedure for joint products?

10. What are the differences in management problems in a joint-products or disintegration industry and in an integration industry?

11. What are the basic requirements of a cost system in a joint-products industry?

12. Why should a normal volume of production be used in calculating allowable purchase prices for the raw materials of a joint-products company?

13. What management purposes are served by standard material costs in a joint-products company?

14. In the illustration of joint-product costing, a year's supply of raw material was purchased during a brief period when the crop matured. What changes in costing procedures would be required if purchases were made throughout the year?

PROBLEMS

1. A company produces a by-product in one of its processes which it uses as a substitute material in the formula for another product. It can use all of the by-product produced.

The formulas without and with the by-product are given in Table P16-1.

Costs of transferring the by-product to the operation where it is used are $0.03 per pound.

What credit per pound of by-product should be given to the product which produces it?

2. A cork company buys raw cork and cleans, sorts, and bales it for sale. The cork is sorted into three grades with net sales prices per ton as follows: (1) $225.00, (2) $150.00, and (3) $112.50. Standards provide for 105 tons to be purchased for every 100 tons yield of baled cork. Processing costs are $30.00 per ton of raw cork and purchasing costs are $5.00 per ton of raw cork.

Distribution and administrative expenses are 15% of net sales, and the profit objective is 15% of net sales.

The buyer has an offer of a lot of raw cork at $85.00 per ton. Tests indicate it will yield 60% of grade 1 and 20% of each of grades 2 and 3. Should he purchase the cork?

TABLE P16-1
Formula Using No By-product*

A	2,000 lb	0.145	$290.00
B	400 lb	0.30	120.00
C	200 lb	0.35	70.00
D	150 lb	0.40	60.00
E	1,000 lb	0.18	180.00
	3,750 lb		720.00
Loss 4%......	150		
	3,600 lb	0.20	$720.00

Formula Using By-product*

A	2,000 lb
B	500 lb
C	200 lb
D	50 lb
By-product.........	1,000 lb
	3,750 lb
Loss 4%.............	150 lb
	3,600 lb

* Labor and expense costs are the same for each formula.

CHAPTER 17

Distribution Expense

Distribution expense in the broadest sense includes all costs directly related to the distribution of a product. The specific costs which are included in this category vary from company to company. Some companies consider the costs of warehousing, packing, and shipping at the manufacturing plant as distribution expenses. They are, however, the exception, and distribution expense generally is considered to begin after the products are loaded for shipment from the plant of manufacture. All costs incident to the creation of a market for the products, of securing, recording, and filling orders, and of servicing customers are classified as distribution expense. In addition many companies consider the credit, billing, and customer accounting functions in this category, although some classify these latter costs as general administrative expense. The cost of transporting the product to customers may be considered either as a deduction from gross sales or as distribution expense. "Selling" and "distribution" are both used to designate this type of expense. "Distribution" is preferable because it connotes more than direct sales effort.

Recording Distribution Expense

Distribution expenses are recorded in total in control accounts on the general ledger and in detail in subsidiary ledgers, following the same general procedures used for factory expense. Each of the charts of accounts listed in Chapter 3 provided one control account for distribution expense. This is adequate for many companies, since the subsidiary ledgers contain all the detail required. However, some companies use more than one general-ledger control account. These accounts usually have the same initial digits, if numerical codes are used, so that their relationship is indicated and they appear in sequence in the general ledger. For example, the chart of accounts for the fiberboard company listed in Chapter 3 shows expense account 14100 for Distribution Expense. This might be expanded to 14100 Home Office Selling Expense,

215

14200 District Office Selling Expense, 14300 District Warehouse Expense, 14400 Advertising Expense, and 14500 Sample Expense.

The same source accounts are used for distribution expense as are used for factory expense. This permits the consolidation of all control accounts to arrive at totals for each source of expense for a company. Applying the codes for the fiberboard plant, illustrative controls and sources are Factory Salaries 131-02, Salesmen's Salaries 142-02, Factory Indirect Labor 131-03, District Warehouse Labor 143-03, and District Office Labor (e.g., Janitor) 142-03. The origin of each source of expense is the same as shown for factory expense in Chapter 6.

Beyond the control and source, further detail may be recorded as to location, function, or type of effort. If numeral codes are used, these additional data are coded in the "department," "operation," or "classification" positions of the code. Thus the fiberboard company may have departments 01 Hartford Branch, 02 New Haven Branch, 03 Albany Branch, and 40 Advertising Department; operations 001 Field Selling, 002 Inside Selling, 003 Order Department, 004 Office Display, 005 Warehouse, and 601 Advertising—General; and classifications 003 Stocking, 005 Shipping, 009 Inventory Taking, 604 Magazine Space, and 711 Copy writers. In the industrial-specialties division, New York district, the salary of an office salesman at the Hartford branch would be coded 161-14202-01-002-000 and labor of a warehouseman at New Haven stocking material as 161-14303-02-005-003. For the salaries of copy writers in the general advertising department the code would be 110-14402-40-601-711. The amount of detail recorded will depend upon the extent of analysis, of detailed allocation to product lines, or other management use desired.

Some portion of distribution expense may be recovered through charges for certain services. For example, the advertising department may prepare booklets which are mailed upon request and payment of a nominal charge. Or they may charge dealers for mats, electros, literature, and other advertising material. Such income should be credited to the expense-control account to which the cost of preparing the material was charged, since the amount of material ordered affects the gross expense. An expedient method is to establish a special source to which such income is credited. Thus the actual expenditures by sources are not disturbed, the amount of income is shown, and the control account reflects the true net cost.

Recording Sample Expense

Sample expenses included in distribution expense may require special accounting treatment because of the several areas within a company where they may originate. These expenses include the factory cost of materials used for samples, the labor and expense of sample preparation, the expense of sample distribution, the cost of auxiliary items such as display racks, and if there is a separate sample department, the adminis- trative expense of that department.

A sample department may requisition finished products from the factory and prepare the samples for distribution, or the samples may be prepared in the factory. Also, distribution may be made directly from the factory on requisition by the sample or sales department or may be made from a stock of samples carried in the sample department.

When a factory transfers finished stock to the sample department to be prepared into samples, either Sample Expense or a Deferred Expense account is charged with the factory cost of the material and Finished Stock is credited. The preferable procedure is to make the charge to Sample Expense. This eliminates the necessity for further accounting for the material. The records which are maintained in the sample de- partment of quantities on hand are then used for information purposes only, and valuation is not required.

When the factory converts finished stock into samples, makes up special material for samples, or packs or otherwise prepares samples for distribution, the costs must be accumulated in the factory. A separate operation may be established for this. All materials used for samples and all labor and expense expended on samples are charged to this operation. At the close of each month an entry is prepared charging sample expense and crediting factory cost. The debit and credit need not be by sources of expense; they can be in total only. Another pro- cedure is to issue job orders for sample work in the factory. Direct charges to these are coded directly to Sample Expense as incurred. The job-order number identifies the charges, and being charged to a specific order, they are not included as part of the costs of any operations in the factory. Under this method no entry need be made at the end of the month. For example, material used in the factory for samples for roof insulation would be coded:

MOBILE PLANT	DISTRIBU- TION EXPENSE	EXPENSE MATERIAL	SAMPLE DEPART- MENT	OPER- ATION	ROOF INSU- LATION	JOB NUMBER
124	140	09	41	000	521	0736

When a separate sample department is maintained, all costs incurred in the department and the cost of materials transferred to it from fac- tories are charged to Sample Expense under the appropriate expense source. For example, a coding for sample-department labor could be:

GENERAL OFFICE	DISTRIBU- TION EXPENSE	INDIRECT LABOR	SAMPLE DEPART- MENT	SAMPLE PREPA- RATION	ROOF INSULATION
110	140	03	41	311	521

Generally Treated as Period Cost

The generally accepted accounting practice is to treat distribution expense as a period cost. It is charged against operations of the period in which it is incurred. There are, however, exceptions to this general rule. Where they are made, the accounting is through prepaid or deferred-expense accounts, or in inventory values of stock in district warehouses. Under no circumstances is distribution expense included in inventory values of finished goods at the factory.

When expenditures are made for items which have a life of, and are used over a period of, several years, such as catalogues, they may be expensed immediately or charged to a deferred-expense account. For the latter, cost is then related to the expected period of use of the item and a proportionate amount taken into expense in each accounting period. A separate expense source may be set up for such costs, so as to segregate them from expenses incurred currently and thus subject to closer control.

Costs of transporting products to district warehouses and of handling them into the warehouses are properly includable in the inventory values of material at the warehouses. Under this procedure roof insulation in a district-office warehouse would have an inventory value per 1,000 square feet as follows:

Factory cost	$51.84
Freight to warehouse	1.00
Unloading and stocking at warehouse	0.60
Inventory value	$53.44

When this accounting procedure is followed the actual costs of district warehouses and unloading and stocking at the warehouse may be charged to the inventory account as incurred. A simpler procedure is to charge them to expense as incurred, under the proper control and source accounts, and then credit these accounts for predetermined rates per unit applied to the material placed in the warehouses. Specific rates are used for each warehouse, so as to approximate as closely as possible actual costs of each location. This provides a uniform inventory value for each material in each warehouse. Differences between the incurred and applied costs should be minor and are reflected in profit and loss of the period.

When transportation and handling costs are added to inventory values, they are deferred until the material is sold. There is a question as to whether the effect on profits of a period is sufficiently significant to warrant the accounting effort required. Unless quantities in the warehouses vary considerably from period to period, about the same amount of cost moves into and out of the warehouse inventory value in each period, and the effect on profit is immaterial. For this reason many companies take all costs of transportation to warehouses and of warehouse operation as costs of the periods when they are incurred. Inventories at the district warehouses are then valued at the same unit rates as are used for costing sales at the factory.

Responsibility for Distribution Expense

Some large companies have a general sales manager or a vice-president for marketing who has general responsibility for all distribution costs. He may have division sales managers reporting to him, and they in turn have district managers reporting to them. In addition, an advertising manager may also report to the general sales manager.

In other large companies there is no general sales manager, and each division sales manager operates independently in administering the marketing functions of his division. Each division may have district sales managers reporting to the division manager. With this organization structure the advertising function may be centralized under an advertising manager. He would have direct responsibility for advertising, with each division manager having functional responsibility for the advertising for his division.

In smaller companies there probably would be no division or district sales managers. Also, advertising may be developed by an agency under the guidance of the sales manager. Thus there would be but one level of responsibility for distribution expense—the sales manager.

Where there is an advertising manager, he frequently is also responsible for the preparation and distribution of samples because of the close relationship of the sample and advertising programs. However, there may be a separate sample department reporting directly to the sales manager.

The organization structure of a company determines the placement of responsibility for distribution expense. Over-all responsibility will rest with the top sales executive. In the larger companies he will have direct responsibility for some expenses, while for other expenses the direct responsibility will be placed at the managerial levels where the costs are incurred and can be controlled directly.

Budgetary Control of Distribution Expense

There is no scientific basis for determining how much distribution expense should be incurred. To be effective the marketing programs must be planned in relation to current conditions and long-range objectives.

It is most unwise to attempt to relate the total amount to be spent in any period to the expected volume or profits of the period. More direct sales effort and advertising are usually required in periods of adequate supply of goods and reduced customer demand. This precludes a direct relationship of expenditures to any current activity measurements. In fact, it may be more prudent to reduce some types of these expenditures in periods of good business and increase them during a recession. Conditions within an industry or even within a specific company will effect the extent to which this is possible or desirable. However, experience has shown that companies which maintain their marketing programs in good times and bad secure a definite competitive advantage and usually show a better sales growth trend than others in the industry which substantially reduce them in some years. It has also been shown that companies which tend to cut advertising appropriations as an early step in efforts to improve budgeted profits accentuate their movement into an unfavorable position.

The sales manager must decide how much should be spent for distribution expense. Therefore, the budgets approved by him are the basic measurements for controlling actual expenses during the budget period. Expenses should be planned in detail for each function and area of responsibility and then followed closely to keep actuals within the budget or to justify overruns.

Since distribution expense is considered to be a period cost, the budgets are built as fixed for most of, if not all, the sources. The amount of expense is estimated for each source in each location and function for the budget period, giving effect to general economic conditions and specific company plans and forecasts. If there are items which vary with sales volume, such as salesmen's commissions or clerical salaries in the order department, a variable factor is reflected in the budgets. Otherwise the allowable amounts are fixed by management decision for the period for which the budgets are built.

Here a word of caution is necessary. The fact that distribution expense is assumed to be fixed for a budget period does not mean that it is fixed for a number of periods. It can and should be increased or decreased as changes occur in the specific company, the industry, or the general economic environment. Therefore, in special cost studies, distribution expense cannot be considered as a cost which will neither increase nor decrease regardless of volume, number of products in the line, or general business conditions.

Building the Budgets

In building the distribution expense budgets the expenses are detailed by control, source, location, function, and classification. As in the factory, the budgets are built according to the placement of management responsibility, by the persons who have the authority to control the actual expenditures. Final approval rests with the top sales executive. The accountants should supply basic data to each person building a segment of the budget, assist in developing the budgets, and analyze and appraise them for the sales managers.

Budget data sheets should be prepared for each area of responsibility in the marketing function. These show the sources and classifications of

EXHIBIT 17-1
BUDGET DATA
KANSAS CITY OFFICE
ACOUSTICAL DIVISION

		Actual		Esti-mated	Budget		Notes—next year's budget
		Prior year	8 months, this year	This year, total	This year	Next year	
32	Travel:						
	B. R. Abbott.........	$ 310	$ 193	$ 330	$ 300		
	G. N. Flick...........	1,460	876	1,250	1,475		
	V. G. Heim..........	882	611	920	800		
	F. J. Mast..........	961	413	610	1,000		Includes contractors convention
	J. A. Tierney........	537	162	500	550		
	Total..............	$4,150	$2,255	$3,610	$4,225		
31	Stationery..............	$ 56	$ 27	$ 45	$ 50		
33	Postage...............	$ 112	$ 82	$ 120	$ 120		
34	Telephone and Telegraph	$ 551	$ 342	$ 560	$ 560		
35	Publications:						
	American Architect...	$ 10	$ 10	$ 10	$ 10		
	Building News........	5	———	———	5		
	Wall Street Journal...	10	10	10	10		
	Total..............	$ 25	$ 20	$ 20	$ 25		
37	Donations:						
	Builders Association...	$ 100	$ 100	$ 100	$ 100		
	Police Department....	10	———	10	10		
	YMCA.............	25	———	25	25		
	Community Chest....	100	50	125	125		
	Total..............	$ 235	$ 150	$ 260	$ 260		
38	Association dues:						
	Production Council...	$ 75	$ 75	$ 75	$ 100		
	Associated Architects	50	25	50	50		
	Building Congress....	50	———	50	50		
	Total..............	$ 175	$ 100	$ 175	$ 200		

expense for which the person building the budget is responsible and as guides in budget building may include:

1. The actual expenses for the previous full year
2. The budgeted expenses for the current year
3. The estimated actual expenses for the current year

These data sheets and a statement of anticipated general economic conditions and specific company plans and sales estimates are given to the persons building the budgets. They plan their expenses and insert their figures on the data sheets, showing as much detail as is required to develop budget allowances during the period. They should also supply explanatory comments to guide the manager in his appraisal of the budget.

EXHIBIT 17-2
ADVERTISING BUDGET
BUILDING PRODUCTS DIVISION

	Current budget	Prior year budget	Prior year estimated actuals
Panels and plank:			
General magazines:			
Ladies Home Journal, 6 pp., $1,746, 2%..........................	$ 10,298	$ 9,805	$ 9,805
Woman's Home Companion, 6 pp., $1,450, 2%......................	8,552	9,358	9,358
Collier's, 4 pp., $1,215, 2%...........	4,777	4,424	5,065
	$ 54,116	$62,511	$ 65,025
Preparation on above:			
Room building*....................	$ 2,320	$ 2,500	$ 2,475
Photographs and art work†.........	1,575	1,835	1,800
Engravings, etc...................	3,730	3,900	4,218
Reprints.........................	———	110	25
	$ 7,625	$ 8,345	$ 8,518
Total........................	$ 61,741	$70,856	$ 73,543
Sheathing:			
American Home, 6 pp., $1,200, 2%.....	$ 7,056	$ 6,043	$ 7,056
Better Farming, 6 pp., $450...........	2,600		
Total division....................	$121,060	$97,430	$100,110

* 13 Subjects.
† 6 Commercials.

Exhibit 17-1 is a budget data sheet as supplied to a district manager. It details only those expenses for which he is responsible. Exhibit 17-2 is a completed data sheet for magazine advertising, and Exhibit 17-3 is for sample expense. In each instance the format and extent of detail is different because of the nature of the expenses. These variations illustrate the need for designing each form for the persons and purposes it is to serve.

After all data sheets are completed, they are assembled by the accountants and summarized into budgets for each area of responsibility. Exhibit 17-4 is a summary of the budget of the advertising department.

EXHIBIT 17-3
SAMPLE BUDGET
ACOUSTICAL TILE

	Wholesalers	Contractors
6 by 6-in. Samples	50,000	10,000
Tile @ $72.87 per 1,000 sq ft	$ 911	$ 182
Wrapping paper	100	20
Boxes	50	
Labor—preparation	250	50
Total	$1,311	$ 252
12 by 12-in. Samples	1,000	5,000
Tile @ $72.87 per 1,000 sq ft	$ 73	$ 364
Boxes	10	50
Labor—packing	10	50
Total	$ 93	$ 464
Display stands	$ 300	
Wall racks	$ 200	$ 500
Total	$1,904	$1,216

EXHIBIT 17-4
19— ADVERTISING BUDGET SUMMARY
FIBERBOARD COMPANY

Source	General	Building Products Division	Acoustical Division	Industrial Division	Total
02 Salaries	$41,315	——	——	——	$ 41,315
03 Indirect labor	6,000	$ 2,000	——	$ 1,000	9,000
04 Vacation pay	240	80	——	40	360
09 Supplies	900	100	$ 100	50	1,150
30 Advertising	20,000	121,060	$63,040	27,000	231,100
31 Stationery	2,500	——	——	——	2,500
32 Travel	1,000	——	——	——	1,000
33 Postage	500	1,000	500	100	2,100
34 Telephone and telegraph	500	——	——	——	500
35 Publications	200	——	——	——	200
38 Association dues	250	——	——	——	250
41 Employee benefit program	2,840	120	——	60	3,020
42 Taxes—payroll	450	60	——	30	540
Total	$76,695	$124,420	$63,640	$28,280	$293,035

The completed budgets are then approved by the sales manager, or he secures the agreement of the persons building the budgets to changes which he suggests for their area of responsibility. From the approved data sheets and summaries, budget allowance cards (Exhibit 17-5) are

EXHIBIT 17-5
19— BUDGET ALLOWANCES
KANSAS CITY OFFICE
ACOUSTICAL DIVISION

Source	Budget	Allowance basis
District manager's responsibility:		
31 Stationery..................	$ 60	$\frac{1}{12}$ per month
32 Travel....................	4,500	$300 per month plus $900 for sales meetings as incurred
33 Postage...................	120	$\frac{1}{12}$ per month
34 Telephone and telegraph.....	600	$\frac{1}{12}$ per month
35 Publications...............	25	As incurred
37 Donations.................	300	As incurred
38 Association dues...........	200	As incurred
Subtotal.................	$ 5,805	
Other Responsibilities:		
02 Salaries...................	$40,000	Per schedule
41 Employee benefit programs...	1,600	4% of allowed salaries
42 Taxes—payroll.............	1,200	3% of allowed salaries
51 Rent......................	1,500	$\frac{1}{12}$ per month
52 Depreciation...............	2,500	$\frac{1}{12}$ per month
53 Taxes—general.............	75	As incurred
54 Insurance.................	200	As incurred
Total....................	$52,880	
02 Salaries, per month:		Note: Expense allowed as incurred is not allowable in excess of total budget for the source
Jan.–Mar...............	$ 3,200	
Apr.–July..............	3,400	
Aug.–Dec..............	3,360	

prepared. These are then used from month to month to determine the allowances for comparison with actual expenditures.

Control of Selling Expense

Current control of selling expense (home office and field) is effected for most items through the authorization of the expenditures. Salaries are controlled through the authorized salary roll, with personnel additions or deletions and salary-level changes approved by the sales manager. Rent is controlled through the approval of leases. In the district office stationery costs are controlled by the manager's authorization of purchase orders or requisitions; donations and association dues are controlled by limiting them to specific budgeted items or unbudgeted items approved by the district manager.

The one major item of selling expense which is not subject to specific authorization before being incurred is travel of salesmen. Here the best control tool is the weekly expense report (Exhibit 17-6). Two factors are essential if control is to be implemented through the expense reports: (1) They must be submitted promptly and (2) they must show expenses in detail. With the district manager's knowledge of his territory

EXHIBIT 17-6
WEEKLY EXPENSE REPORT

WEEKLY EXPENSE REPORT

Name Reporting: James O. Poque (Print or Type Name)
Dept Div or Plant: Bldg. Prod. Section or Dist. Office: New York
Period Covered by Report – From 9/6/XX to 9/10/XX
Approved by: ______ Authorized Signatures

Date Report Is Written: 9/12/XX

Advances Received			
Date	Amount	Date	Amount
9/1	200 00		

CASH SUMMARY

1 Balance from Report of 8/31/XX	16	50
2 Advances Received Total from Detail at Left	200	00
3 Total of Lines 1 and 2 Above.	216	50
4 Less Disbursements—Total from Below	111	75
5. Balance on Hand (3 Less 4). Carry Forward to Line 1 of Next Report	104	75

SELLING AND TRAVELING EXPENSES

Date	City	Hotel	Meals No.	Meals Amt.	Tips	Airplane / Railroad	Pullman	Auto	Bus Subway Trolley Taxi	Laundry / Valet	Teleph Phone	Emp Meals	Entertainment Meals	Entertainment Other	Misc.	Remarks	Totals
9/6	Albany	7.00	3	6.20	1.20			4.30									18 70
9/7	"	7.00	3	5.90	1.10			4.35		1.20	2.10		3.00				24 65
9/8	Utica	8.00	3	5.80	.85			5.50			.60						20 75
9/9	Endicott	8.00	3	6.10	1.00			3.80		1.50				5.00			25 40
9/10	Rome	7.00	3	5.60	.90			8.45			.30		3.50				25 75
	Totals	37.00		29.60	5.05			26.40		2.70	3.00		6.50	5.00			115 25

*Total Auto Exp. As per Detail — Less Personal Mileage 70 Miles at 5c per Mile: 3 50
Net Disbursements—Insert This Total on Line 4 Above: 111 75

NOTE: Travel Instructions on Reverse Side

DETAILED AUTO EXPENSES

Date	Gasoline Gals	Gasoline Cost	Oil Qts.	Oil Cost	Storage Parking Tolls	Wash	Repairs Misc.	Tire	Grease	License	Personal Miles	Business Miles
9/6	10	2.80			1.50						60	90
9/7	10	2.85			1.50							120
9/8	12	3.00			1.00	1.50						110
9/9	10	2.80			1.00							140
9/10	10	5.60	1	.35	1.50				1.00		10	230
Totals		17.05	1	.35	6.50	1.50			1.00		70	690

Complete section below once each month and when operating car other than previously reported.

Make and Model | Motor No. | License No.

*Mileage Calculation

1. Reading End of Week	15631
2 Reading Beginning of Wk	14871
3 Total Miles Line 1 minus 2	760
4 Less Personal Miles	70
5 Business Miles	690
Reimbursement	
*Total Auto Exp. Check Against Above Cross Footing	26.40

Items indicated above (*) to be charged to operation ______ for ______

Project No. — This box filled in by the Accounting Office — Man No.

C P D	Ctl	Sr	Dept	Oper	Class	Amount
	141	25				
	141	37				

Extra (carbon) copies may be made for use of individual if desired.

Original only will be accepted by Accounting after approval according to instructions.

and his sales plans he can appraise readily the expenses shown on the reports. If they are out of line, he can take corrective action during a month without waiting for his summary budget report, which is not received until well after the close of the month.

The control of expenses thus effected is but one facet of distribution-cost control. Another important one is the results which are being obtained for the expenditure. Only historical records will establish these, but interim appraisals can be made from call reports of salesmen. These show the customers called upon and the results of each call, with pertinent comments as to the indicated state of the customer's business, his attitude toward the seller, and his future plans. These call reports supplement the travel reports and provide guides to the effective utilization of salesmen's time and travel costs.

Monthly reports (Exhibit 17-7) which show the extent to which control was effected should be prepared for each point of responsibility. These provide guidance to those who control the expenses and inform the upper levels of marketing management how well their personnel are

EXHIBIT 17-7
EXPENSE BUDGET REPORT
KANSAS CITY OFFICE
ACOUSTICAL DIVISION

	April, 19—				Four months, 19—			
	Actual	Budget	Var.	Notes	Actual	Budget	Var.	Notes
Manager's responsibility:								
31 Stationery	$ 3	$ 5	$ 2		$ 27	$ 20	$ (7)*	
32 Travel	310	300	(10)		1,454	1,410	(44)	†
33 Postage	8	10	2		46	40	(6)	
34 Telephone and telegraph	47	50	3		193	200	7	
35 Publications					25	25		
37 Donations	50	50	———		125	125		
38 Association dues	100	100	———		150	150		
Subtotal	$ 518	$ 515	$ (3)		$ 2,020	$ 1,970	$ (50)	
Other responsibility:								
02 Salaries	$3,650	$3,400	$(250)	‡	$13,250	$13,000	$(250)	
41 Employee benefits	146	136	(10)		530	520	(10)	
42 Taxes—payroll	100	102	2		381	390	9	
51 Rent	125	125	———		500	500		
52 Depreciation	208	208	———		816	816		
53 Taxes—general					80	75	(5)	
54 Insurance	50	50	———		50	50		
Total	$4,797	$4,536	$(261)		$17,627	$17,321	$(306)	

* Parentheses denote overruns.
† Actual and budget includes $210 for sales meetings.
‡ Extra clerical help because of sickness.

controlling costs. As with all reports, they should be accompanied by pertinent interpretative comments.

Current Control of Advertising and Sample Expense

Special techniques must be employed to provide current control of the "pure" advertising costs (time, space, literature, and preparation) and sample costs. The other costs in these components of distribution expense are controlled through the authorizations discussed in the preceding section for selling expenses. For pure advertising and sample costs current control is best accomplished through a job-costing procedure under which the budget allowances, commitments, and actual costs are broken down and recorded and controlled by jobs or projects.

An account card (Exhibit 17-8) is set up for each major item for which a separate data sheet was prepared in the budget. In this illustration this is the control card for magazine advertising as budgeted on the budget data sheet shown as Exhibit 17-2. At the beginning of the period the amount budgeted is posted in the "Budget Position" column. As jobs

EXHIBIT 17-8

ADVERTISING-EXPENSE CONTROL, ACCOUNTS

Account No. A-1

Division Building Products

ACCOUNT NAME Panels & Plank General Magazine

Budget Position or Unreleased Balance: Date	Amount
1/1	$61,741
1/5	56,818
2/28	56,813

Job No.	Item	Description	Budget: Date	Budget: Amount	Funds Released: Date	Funds Released: Amount	Final Cost	Balance
1-10	Plates –	March magazine	Feb	500 00	1/5	450 00	445 00	5 00
	Space –	Journal	Mar	1711 00	1/5	1711 00		
		Companion	Mar	1421 00	1/5	1421 00		
		Colliers	Mar	1421 00	1/5	1191 00		
1-11	Prepare room setting		Feb	200 00	1/5	150 00	160 00	(10 00)

EXHIBIT 17-9

ADVERTISING-EXPENSE CONTROL, JOBS

Description of Job Plates for March Magazine

Job No. 1-10 Year 195-

Code 150-14020-40-601-xxx

Division Blg. Products

Funds Released 1/5 450 00

Order Number	Date of Order	Vendor	Description	Estimated Commitments	Artwork & Photos (605)	Engraving (606)	Compos Electros Printing	Author's Alter	Reprints	Misc (690)	Parcel Post Express Freight (680)	Date of Inv	Mo. Paid
1-63	1/10	4318	Color photos of boy's room	200 00	210 00							1/29	Feb
1-72	1/17	2160	Color plates	200 00		195 00						2/16	Feb
1-73	1/17	2160	line cuts	50 00		40 00						2/16	Feb
					210 00	235 00							

are authorized by the advertising manager the job is recorded on the cost control card. The amount included in the budget for the specific job is posted in the appropriate column, and the amount of funds approved for expenditure (released) is also posted. This latter sum is deducted in the "Budget Position" column to show the available balance at all times.

Job cost cards (Exhibit 17-9) are set up for each job. These are filed in back of the account card to which they apply and contain the supporting detail for the account. As purchase orders are placed for the work, they are posted to the job cost card, with the amount of the order shown in the "Estimated Commitments" column. So long as the estimated cost of orders placed does not exceed the amount of funds released, the costs are under control. When they approach the limit of funds released, the cards are brought to the attention of the advertising manager for his review of the job. As invoices are paid, the actual amounts are recorded on the job cost card. When the job is completed, the total actual cost is posted to the "Final Cost" column of the account card and the "balance," or difference betwen the funds released and the final cost, is reflected in the "Budget Position" column to bring the unreleased balance into agreement with the most recent actual cost information. A similar procedure is used for the control of sample expenses.

Through the recording of commitments and actual expenditures by accounts and jobs the advertising or sample-department manager can be kept informed of his budget position at all times. He is able to manage his expenditures and balance overruns on one job by planned savings on another and, conversely, to take advantage of realized savings in the development and preparation of future advertisements. This same management would extend to the major accounts, where savings and excess costs would be balanced to keep total expenditures within the total of the advertising or sample budget. If an unallocated amount were included in the advertising budget, an account card would be set up for it. As it is decided to use it to supplement budgets for planned expenditures or for unanticipated advertising, the amount to be used is transferred from the general card to the respective account cards.

The maintenance of the system of control on advertising and sample expenditures is accomplished most effectively by keeping the records in the areas where the money is being spent. The advertising department and the sample department should have accounting personnel to maintain the records. They would then record purchase orders as placed, receive the invoices, verify them, post them, and then forward the approved invoice to the accounts payable department for payment. They would also receive details of labor and other costs charged to Advertising and Sample Expense which originate in other departments of the company, and post them to the summary cost control records.

If the factory performs work on samples, it should be supplied with account cards for the costs for which it is responsible. Control procedures for these costs are then followed in the factory in the same manner as in the advertising and sample departments for their costs. By keeping the cost cards in the respective areas which exercise control and having personnel located there to process the original records, duplication of effort is avoided, and, more importantly, commitments and expenditures are posted to the cards immediately, so that control information is always up to date.

The account and job cost cards are supplemented by monthly budget reports for the advertising and sample departments. These show the actual and budgeted expenses by sources for each department. The actual expenses are taken from the subsidiary expense ledger. The budget allowances for all sources other than "pure" advertising (source 30) are determined by budget allowance cards which are prepared when the budget is built. Since control is being exercised over pure advertising costs through the account and job cost cards, the monthly allowance for these is the same as the actual up to the time in the period when the total actual exceeds the budget. If that should occur, no further budget allowance is reflected, and overruns are shown for the month and period to date. These monthly reports, with appropriate explanatory comments, are submitted to the persons having responsibility for controlling the costs and to the executives of the company.

Analysis and Comparison of Distribution Costs

Production costing and distribution costing are two entirely different procedures. In the factory the expected output per worker can be established within reasonable limits. Given a quantity of material and processing instructions, an experienced factory worker can be expected to turn out a specified number of processed units per hour. In the factory men are working within a prescribed area with tangible things— machines, tools, and materials—and time and production clerks are assigned to record the material received, the time expended, and the production turned out. All circumstances are conducive to accurate recording of measurable work, and substantially accurate unit costs are secured.

Contrast this with the distribution activity. There are no standard procedures for two of the most costly phases, field sales effort and advertising. Results are dependent upon the judgment and skill of the salesman, copy writer, and creative artist. In addition they are bringing these skills to bear upon the most unstandardized and unpredictable force in the world—human nature. The activities are such that they cannot be observed and recorded by a clerical force. For these reasons, distribution costs per unit of product must be used with full recognition of their limitations.

The inability to develop unit cost rates for distribution expense with the degree of accuracy achieved for factory cost rates should not preclude this step for the distribution function. The analysis of distribution expense and the comparison of unit costs of like functions in different areas will provide valuable management guidance.

The selection of costs to be analyzed and compared will depend upon conditions in each company. It is probable that some costs will be excluded either because they are not significant or because there is no basis of comparison for the item. Areas where costs are significant and unit rates may prove valuable are shown in Table 17-1.

TABLE 17-1
UNIT DISTRIBUTION COSTS

Cost	Related to
Salesmen's salaries	Number of calls
	Gross sales dollars
Salesmen's expense	Miles traveled
	Number of calls
	Gross sales dollars
Order department	Number of orders
Delivery department	Miles traveled by trucks
	Weight delivered
	Ton miles
	Gross sales dollars
District warehouse	Weight or units in and out
	Gross sales from the warehouse

Costs per unit of measurement determined for each area are compared with unit costs of the area for prior periods and with unit costs of other comparable areas. For example, a salesman's salary and travel cost per call could be compared with his cost per call in prior periods and with the cost per call of other salesmen working comparable territories. Order-department costs per order could be compared with those of prior periods. Such analysis provides some measure of effectiveness and shows unit cost trends. These data should guide the sales managers in budgeting cost and in controlling actual expenditures. Exhibit 17-10 illustrates a typical cost analysis report for a district office. Trend is indicated by comparing the month and year to date actual costs with those budgeted. The costs for the office are placed in perspective by comparing them with the average, high, and low offices of the division. Exhibit 17-11 is a similar analysis of district warehouse costs. In this rates are shown only for a 12-month period, because variations in warehouse operations fluctuate seasonally and cause distortion in unit costs of individual months. Budget data are not shown, since the period covers parts of two budget periods. These reports indicate methods of presenting data for distribution-cost control and modifications in the amount of data used as required by special conditions.

Evaluation Based on Results

Many distribution expenses may also be analyzed and evaluated on the basis of the relative profit margins of the several cost areas. Profit

Exhibit 17-10
UNIT SELLING COST DATA
KANSAS CITY OFFICE
ACOUSTICAL DIVISION

	Month		Year to date	
	Actual	Budget	Actual	Budget
Salesman ($1,000 per man):				
District......................	8.56	8.53	8.43	8.46
Division—Average..............	8.69	8.72	8.70	8.73
High..............	9.65	9.60	9.57	9.53
Low................	7.01	7.10	7.15	7.15
Clerical ($1,000 per salesman):				
District......................	1.45	1.15	1.17	1.13
Division—Average..............	1.43	1.42	1.45	1.47
High..............	2.46	2.47	2.33	2.30
Low................	0.81	0.90	0.89	0.92
Cost per $1,000 of sales:				
District......................	27.98	28.00	26.90	28.00
Division—Average..............	31.63	32.00	31.80	33.00
High..............	51.63	50.00	47.20	48.00
Low................	16.96	20.00	17.81	20.00
Sales per salesman ($1,000):				
District......................	356.00	362.00	371.00	362.00
Division—Average..............	342.00	340.00	339.00	345.00
High..............	521.00	530.00	547.00	550.00
Low................	257.00	250.00	253.00	250.00

Exhibit 17-11
UNIT WAREHOUSE COST DATA
KANSAS CITY OFFICE
ACOUSTICAL DIVISION

12 Months to April 30
Data:
Labor............................. $ 3,963
Rent............................. $ 4,797
Space—square feet.................. 10,187
Inventory—monthly average.......... $ 47,904
Warehouse shipments................ $107,022

	Division			Office
	High	Low	Average	
Labor—per $1,000 of shipments......	120.15	2.06	46.43	37.03
Rent—per $1,000 of shipments.......	202.31	4.94	40.03	44.82
per sq ft per year...........	1.03	.12	.40	.47
Space Utilization—square feet:				
Per $1,000 of shipments...........	222.0	22.0	100.0	95.0
Per $1,000 of inventory...........	458.0	76.0	258.0	213.0
Inventory Turnover...............	5.5	1.5	3.2	2.2

accrues from astute business management and is conditioned by all the intangibles which are embodied in the concept of management. There is no basis of measuring the attributes of a good business manager, but in the aggregate he is judged a success or a failure to the degree that he achieves or fails to produce a consistently satisfactory record of profits. Distribution likewise is an aggregate of many components, many of which are in the area of intangibles. The effectiveness of these can best be appraised by comparing the relative profit margins of the resultant sales. Such comparisons may be made by districts or territories, by salesmen, by customer classes, by methods of sale, by branch warehouses, or by product groups. They do not require the allocation of all costs to the particular unit (district, salesman, warehouse, etc.) but instead employ those distribution costs which are specific to the unit. The important point is to get profit margins on a comparable basis rather than on an absolute or complete basis.

The first step is the development of sales statistics. Procedures should be developed to accumulate net sales, before provision for cash discount but after trade discounts and all allowances and other deductions, by the unit or units to be appraised. This can be done economically through the use of punched-card or key-sort equipment, posting machines, or other devices, depending upon the volume of transactions. Factory costs must then be matched with sales income. If standard costs are in use, the standard cost can be recorded for each invoice when the sales are recorded. This provides for the summarization of sales and standard factory cost of sales simultaneously. It has the further advantage of making sure that the standard cost of every sale is recorded. If standard costs are not in use, the actual cost must be accumulated and actual unit rates determined for each product. These are then applied against each sale. This is not a cumbersome job but is a bit more involved than when standards are used. The comparison of sales and factory cost of sales provides a gross margin from which should be deducted the distribution costs specific to the units being studied, to arrive at relative comparable profit margins.

A specific example would be the comparison of the relative profits of sales districts. It is assumed that tabulating equipment is used and standard costs are available. As the plant makes shipments, it places the unit standard cost on the shipping sheet and extends it by the quantity shipped. The shipping sheet is then sent to the general office and the customer's invoice prepared from it. From here the shipping sheet is sent to the sales statistical section, which also receives a copy of the invoice. The standard cost is transferred from the shipping sheet to the statistical copy of the invoice. A master card, prepunched for customer name, state, city, and district office, is taken from the file and sent to the punching section. From these, the complete statistical card is prepared showing, in addition to the data already mentioned, the salesman, customer class, method of sale, and invoice and shipping-sheet number. All credits and miscellaneous charges are coded and summarized in the same manner. Thus it is possible to determine net sales and standard cost of sales for each district. From the standard gross profit is then deducted the specific distribution expense of the district, and the resultant profit margins are relative and comparable for all districts. The same procedure, from the same basic data, would be followed in establishing comparable profit for customer class, method of sale, and salesman.

Another example would be comparison of the desirability of warehousing in branch warehouses and selling direct to customers as against selling through wholesale distributors. Profits of a branch warehouse are first determined by deducting from the gross profit of shipments from the warehouse the costs of operating the warehouse and the freight charges on shipments to it. As an independent operation, the quantities shipped from the warehouse are priced at the manufacturer's lowest wholesale price, delivered, in that city and the standard cost of sales deducted from that figure. If the resultant profit is less than the actual branch warehouse profit, the operation of the warehouse is justified from the profit standpoint.

Allocation of Distribution Costs to Product Lines

In each of the foregoing comparisons only those distribution costs which were specific to the unit under study were considered. Thus there were no problems of cost allocation. However, allocation is necessary if it is desired to report net profits by product lines.

For other than advertising and sample expenses three methods may be used to make such allocations: (1) Actual costs may be allocated on actual activity, (2) Budgeted costs may be allocated on planned activity, or (3) Sales effort, including advertising and samples, may be allocated on planned activity and sales-service costs on actual activity. Any of these will provide better product-line costs than the rather generally used procedure of allocating total distribution costs on actual sales dollars or units. The class of customer and the type of product have a marked effect upon the amount of sales and sales-service effort required. In the fiberboard company it would be expected that less field-sales effort would be required per square foot or dollar of sales to sell wallboard to wholesale distributors than to sell fabricated industrial specialties to manufacturers. For the former, once the wholesaler is established as a customer, the salesman's efforts are directed primarily to product promotion and order taking. A wholesaler does not make frequent changes in the brands he carries. In contrast, a manufacturer who uses fabricated fiberboard pieces in his product is interested in price and engineering advice. He has frequent changes in models, and intensive sales effort is required to hold the business when model changes occur, and even while a model is in the line. Sales dollars or square feet would not provide a fair allocation of sales cost to wallboard and fabricated pieces.

Where actual activity is used for making allocations the salesmen are frequently required to report their time by product lines, and the allocation of their salaries and expenses is made on this basis, with district- and general-sales-office costs applied as overhead. Warehouse expenses are allocated on units or tonnage handled. Orders, invoices, or invoice items are counted for each product, and sales-service-department costs allocated on these. This procedure of allocation on actual activity has the advantage of emphasizing unit costs each month and also of eliminating the judgment factor. However, it is a costly procedure and causes a peak of work at the end of the month which delays the issuance of reports.

Substantial accuracy can be attained by the second method—allocating budgeted costs on the basis of planned activity. The sales manager builds his sales force with certain objectives in mind and directs their efforts to achieve these objectives. He can therefore give to the accountants a reasonable estimate of the portion of each salesman's salary and expense to be assigned to each product line. Other expenses of a district office can then be applied as a percentage of allocated salary and travel costs. Home-office sales expense can also be applied to these as overhead. The costs of the sales-service departments such as order and credit may be allocated separately on forecast sales dollars or units.

The third method differs from the second only in that sales-service-department costs are allocated on actual instead of forecast activity. The reason for this is all other distribution costs may be directed toward product lines as planned, but the service departments' efforts are expended on the products actually sold. Therefore they are allocated on actual activity.

Actual advertising and sample expenses should be charged to the products for which they are incurred. For a substantial portion of the costs this is accomplished by identifying the charges by a commodity code. However, many costs are general in nature. These include the administrative expenses of the sample and advertising departments and institutional advertising. The administrative expenses of the departments are frequently allocated as overhead applied to the specific costs recorded by products, and institutional advertising on actual or forecast sales dollars. Sometimes units of product sold are used for allocating all advertising expenses not specific to products. However, any method of allocation is subject to question, for there is no basis for determining the extent to which any product in the line benefits from these general costs. Accordingly, ratios for allocation are sometimes estimated by the sales or advertising manager. If specific costs are charged to products wherever possible, the unidentified expenses will not be large enough to have any measurable effect on product-line profits.

Equalizing Distribution Expenses

The total distribution expense of a company may vary substantially from month to month. Major causes of such variations are irregular expenditures for advertising, for sales meetings, and for special promotions. If actual costs are allocated to products monthly, material distortion of product profits may occur. This may be overcome if budgeted expenses are allocated on planned activity and, with an annual budget, each product is charged each month with one-twelfth of the total expenses assigned to it. Any difference between the total reflected in product costs and the total actual distribution expense of each month can be held in a suspense account at the company level. At the close of the year the net deviation from the budgeted expense can be applied as an adjusting factor to that reflected in the product costs.

REVIEW QUESTIONS

1. Distribution expense is a broad category. What specific types of expenses does it include?
2. Why is it desirable to use the same expense sources for distribution expense as for factory expense?
3. What purposes are served by recording distribution expense in detail beyond control and source?
4. What costs are included as sample expense?
5. Why is distribution expense generally treated as a period cost?
6. What types of distribution expenses are recorded in a deferred-expense account? Why?
7. How does the organization structure of a company affect the placement of responsibility for the control of distribution expenses?
8. Are the distribution expense budgets generally fixed or flexible budgets?
9. Describe a typical procedure for building distribution expense budgets.
10. To what extent is selling expense subject to current control techniques?
11. What special control techniques may be used for advertising and sample expenses?
12. What factors limit the measurement of the effectiveness of distribution activities?
13. Discuss the unit measurements which may be made of certain distribution expenses and the purposes they would serve.
14. How are distribution expenses evaluated on the basis of results attained? Cite examples.

15. What management purposes are served by allocating distribution expenses to product lines?
16. What bases should be used in allocating distribution expenses to product lines?

PROBLEMS

1. A company has district warehouses in Chicago and Detroit. Each is under the supervision of a district sales manager who reports to the general sales manager. Each warehouse receives customer orders which have been approved for credit in the home office. The warehouses ship the material and prepare the billings to customers, sending copies to the home office, where the customer accounts are kept.

The general sales manager receives reports of the contribution of each warehouse to general expenses and profit and of the actual warehouse expenses. For the period these and related data are shown in Table P17-1. He states that

TABLE P17-1

	Chicago	Detroit
Sales @ $0.75 per lb............	$218,700	$198,450
Cost of sales @ $0.50 per lb.....	145,800	132,300
	72,900	66,150
Warehouse expense.............	25,364	21,661
Contribution..................	$ 47,536	$ 44,489
Expense detail:		
Office salaries................	$ 5,200	$ 2,600
Labor......................	11,664	9,261
Stationery and supplies.......	800	610
Telephone..................	200	190
Rent.......................	7,500	9,000
	$ 25,364	$ 21,661
Orders processed..............	2,430	1,890
Shipments....................	291,600 lb	264,600 lb
Average inventory.............	24,300 lb	29,400 lb
Warehouse space..............	2,000 sq ft	2,000 sq ft
Office space..................	500 sq ft	500 sq ft
Office personnel..............	2	1

with over 10% more sales from Chicago than Detroit the contribution to general expenses and profit of the Chicago warehouse should also have been 10% above that of Detroit.

He asks you as his accountant to analyze the warehouse costs and make recommendations as indicated by your analysis.

2. A district sales office has a manager and four salesmen. The office is located in a large city and salesman Jones covers the city. Salesmen Smith,

Brown, and Green cover outlying territories, which are about the same geographically. Each of these three territories has medium and small towns, and buying-power indexes indicate about equal sales potential. Salesmen average 240 days of field selling per year.

A summary annual report on salary and travel cost and cost per call is shown at the top of Table P17-2. In examining the report the manager questions the differences in the number of calls and cost per call of the salesmen. He expects Jones to have a lower cost because he covers the city with little travel expense and has more accounts because of the concentration of business. However, the manager believes Smith and Brown have too high a cost per call and probably are making too few calls.

Additional data are also shown in Table P17-2.

TABLE P17-2

	Salary and expense	Calls	Salary and expense per call
Jones...........	$12,000	2,000	$ 6.00
Smith..........	17,000	1,000	17.00
Brown..........	16,000	1,250	12.80
Green..........	15,000	1,500	10.00

Annual sales per customer	Jones		Smith		Brown		Green	
	Customers	Dollars	Customers	Dollars	Customers	Dollars	Customers	Dollars
Over $10,000			1	$ 14,000	2	$ 31,000		
7,500–10,000			3	24,000	4	35,000	1	$ 8,000
5,000– 7,500	12	$ 72,000	21	128,000	30	162,000	12	71,000
2,500– 5,000	41	123,000	36	144,000	47	200,000	15	59,000
1,000– 2,500	123	147,000	121	222,000	70	140,000	130	195,000
0– 1,000	224	58,000	68	48,000	97	56,000	192	117,000
	400	$400,000	250	$580,000	250	$624,000	350	$450,000

Prepare supplemental information and comments to aid the district manager in appraising the performance of his men.

CHAPTER 18

Administrative Expense

All costs of an industrial company are incurred either for the production or the distribution of its products. Therefore all expense should be classified either as factory or as distribution expense. However, in any company, and particularly in larger companies, there are many expenses which, for reasons of policy or practicality, are not charged to the production or distribution functions and are grouped and referred to as "administrative" or "general expenses." The broad classification "administrative expense" includes the salaries and expenses of the company's executives and their staffs, and of those general staff departments which serve both production and sales or which serve more than one company plant, division, or other company unit. In representative multiplant and multidivision manufacturing companies the costs of the following are generally considered to be administrative expense: the president's, controller's, secretary's, and treasurer's offices, and centralized staff functions such as personnel, purchasing, traffic, industrial engineering, production planning, and quality control. Also, there may be a general sales manager having responsibility for all marketing functions and a general production manager in charge of all plants, whose salaries and expenses would be included in the administrative-expense grouping.

The broad category of administrative expense also includes research and engineering costs incurred in the development of new products or substantial changes in existing products, or in pure research which may yield knowledge which can be applied in future development work. This type of expense is not to be confused with that of laboratories for testing and controlling quality of raw materials and finished products or preparing formulations for production runs. Nor does it include production engineering costs. Expenses of such laboratories and engineering departments are usually included in, and recorded under, the factory expense control accounts. Research and engineering development expense is customarily recorded in a separate control account and is budgeted separately. This is particularly true in large companies which maintain separate research and development laboratories.

The work performed in such laboratories varies greatly depending upon the nature of the industry and the segment of an industry served by a company. In some companies it is primarily in the area of chemistry; in others, in the area of physics. The scientists carrying on the work may be trained in the several science fields or as engineers. Thus a research department may have a chemistry section, a physics section, an engineering section, and other sections working in specific areas such as plastics, nonferrous metals, and vegetable fibers. These sections may be further subdivided. In the engineering section there may be groups concentrating on power transmission, electronics, or machine design. All this work may be referred to under the general designation of "research."

Recording Administrative Expenses

It is customary to maintain a subsidiary expense ledger for administrative expenses. This supports control accounts on the general ledger. In the chart of accounts of the fiberboard company this is 15100. As with distribution expenses, separate control accounts may be used for different categories of administrative expense. The subsidiary ledger has individual accounts for each area of responsibility for these expenses as indicated by the control, department, or operation sections of the expense codes (e.g., president's office, traffic department, controller, research, etc.). For each department or operation the expenses are recorded by source, using the same expense sources as are used for all other expense-control accounts of the company.

Some sources of expense may be broken down into classifications for control purposes. This is usually done in subsidiary records and not reflected in the administrative expense ledger. For example, in the legal department classifications may be used for source 36—Consulting Service, to segregate costs of patent service, labor-relations service, compensation claims, and liability claims.

Equalizing Accounts

While many sources of administrative expense (such as salaries, travel, and rent) are incurred in approximately equal amounts each month, there are many in which the amounts are incurred irregularly during the year. Donations may be made primarily in the latter months of a year, when the year's income can be estimated more closely. Accounting fees may be incurred early in the year upon completion of the audit of the prior year. Legal fees may be paid as cases arise. These irregularly incurred charges are frequently large enough to cause distortion of monthly profits if they are charged against operations as incurred. Where this condition exists, it is desirable to charge operations each month with one-twelfth of the budgeted or estimated amount of administrative expense for the year. This is accomplished through the use of equalization accounts.

When administrative expenses are equalized during the year, the expenses are charged to the proper sources as incurred, under each department or operation. Then, at the company level, the difference between the total incurred administrative expense and one-twelfth of the total annual budget or estimate is debited or credited to a balance sheet equalizing account, usually included in the deferred-expense group. The contra entry is to an equalization source under the administrative expense control. For the fiberboard company the equalization entry would be:

Dr. or cr.   110-05110 Administrative Expense Equalization
Dr. or cr.   110-15189 Administrative Expense

If during the year a substantial difference between the actual for the year and the original budget or estimate is indicated, the amount to be equalized is adjusted accordingly. In the last month of the year the equalizing account is eliminated, so that actual administrative expense for the year is charged against operations of the year.

Distributing Entries

Because some administrative departments serve all areas of the company, they may be responsible for and incur costs which are properly chargeable to other departments. An example would be the rental of all sales-office and warehouse space by a real estate department under the secretary's office. Rent would then be incurred under, and charged to, this department. Monthly distribution entries would be prepared for such expenses crediting the administrative departments and charging the plants, divisions, or departments which benefit from the cost. This is done under a separate source account. For purposes of comparison with budgeted amounts the expenses of the department responsible for the expense are totaled before this source account is deducted, to provide a total of departmental responsibility. The separate distributing source account is then deducted to arrive at the net amount remaining as administrative expense. The entry for rent incurred by the real estate department of the secretary's office of the fiberboard company and charged to the New York district sales office of the Industrial Specialties Division would be:

Dr.   161-14190-00-000-000
Cr.   110-15190-00-814-000

At the company level the debits and credits to source 90 will balance and thus be eliminated from the consolidated statements of operations.

Capitalizing Research Costs

Without giving consideration to the tax considerations, costs of research may be treated in several ways for accounting. The most conservative treatment is to consider them as expense of the period in which they were incurred. However, these costs could be charged to a deferred-expense account and carried as an asset while projects are in progress. Upon the closing of the projects those which result in products or processes of real value are transferred to intangible assets, particularly if patents are secured, and these intangibles are then amortized over the life of the patent or the expected economic life of the product or process. Those projects which result in nothing of value are charged against operations of the year in which they are closed. This treatment is the least conservative, can well result in an overstatement of assets, and may result in charges to operations several years removed from the one in which the major portion of the cost was incurred. The year in which projects are closed and operations are charged with their cost may be one of unsatisfactory profits. These unfavorable operating results would be accentuated by charges resulting from decisions made in a fairly profitable prior year.

Some companies follow still another procedure in capitalizing research costs. They first charge them against operations of the year in which they are incurred. Then, when usable or patentable products or processes are developed, a reasonable value is assigned to them. This is set up as an intangible asset to be amortized over the estimated life of the product or process, and expense of the period is credited. The major disadvantage of this policy is that an unusual number of, or a few unusually valuable, successful completions in one year could substantially reduce cost and thus distort profits of that year.

Administrative Expense Budgets

Budgets should be prepared for each administrative office or department and, where significant, for segments of the major unit (e.g., the legal and real estate departments of the secretary's office). These provide an estimate of the probable cost of the administrative functions, a measurement for cost control, a basis of equalizing monthly charges to operations, and an amount to be recovered in setting sales prices. Because administrative expenses do not vary directly with volume, they are usually budgeted as *fixed* amounts for the budget period. The head of each administrative department should prepare the budget for his department, assisted by the accountants. Their budgets should be approved by the president or other top-level executive of the company.

While budgets are usually built on a fixed basis, there may be increments budgeted to be added to the fixed sums on the basis of activity. These may be budgeted on a step basis or at a rate per unit of activity. These extra allowances are provided for functions such as customer billing, accounts payable, and payroll, which experience increased work loads when activity increases. The billing department may have a basic force which is adequate to process the normal number of invoices to customers. However, during seasonal peak demand it may not be possible for the basic force to do all the billing in the normal work period. This may be provided for in the budget as a rate per each 100 invoices in excess of a basic number. This variable allowance would thus provide for overtime or added personnel, whichever was the more expedient. Or, the budget for the billing department may provide for the addition of one person for each stated number of invoices over the basic level. This step allowance is less precise and provides less flexibility in selecting overtime or added persons to handle the added work.

When administrative departments have responsibility for expenses which are subsequently charged to another function, such expenses are budgeted under the administrative department having responsibility for them. Following the rent example cited earlier, the real estate department would include in its budget all rent for which it was responsible.

Budgets are built on budget data sheets, already illustrated for other expenses. These are summarized into a budget for each expense source for each administrative department and subdivisions of the departments. The amounts budgeted are determined in relation to the general economic conditions and the company's specific activity forecast for the budget period. Judgment and experience are the only bases for determining the amounts to be included in the budget. No scientific method is known for establishing how much or what types of administrative expense are required for the successful operation of a company.

Controlling Administrative Expense

The expense budgets may include three categories of expenses:

1. Those which are allowed monthly at the rate of one-twelfth of the annual budget, plus increments to cover special situations
2. Those which are allowed in specific months as specified in the budget
3. Those which are allowed as spent, up to the limit of the total amount budgeted for the year

In the first category would be sources such as salaries, rent, depreciation, telephone, and stationery; in the second, contributions and association dues; and in the third, legal and accounting fees, taxes, and travel.

Each month a budget allowance for each source in each department is calculated on the basis of the budget schedule. This is compared with the actual expenses and reported to the department heads and company executives. These reports are accompanied by brief appropriate explanatory comments on significant deviations, to guide management in bringing expenses within budgeted limits.

The monthly budget report is usually adequate as a source of all information which is necessary for administrative expense control. The very nature of the expenses makes day-to-day control impractical. They cannot be related to any daily activity factor, and there is no regularity in the amounts which are spent each day.

Research Project Costs

For research there is not only the problem of keeping expenditures within budgeted amounts but also of directing research efforts toward long-range company objectives. This is best accomplished through a system of numbered research projects.

Under a project cost system for research a project request (Exhibit 18-1) is initiated by supervisory personnel in the research department for

EXHIBIT 18-1
RESEARCH PROJECT AUTHORIZATION

Number: 57-173 Date: May 9, 19—

Title: Evaluation of additives for fiberboard stock

Purpose: It is believed that the quality of all types of board can be improved if certain materials are added to the fiber in the stock chests. The objective is to reduce dimensional changes resulting from climatic additions, increase strength and possibly secure a termite-proof board.

Supervising Chemist: _____

Estimated hours:
Chemists — 500
Technicians—1,200
Pilot plant — 200

Major expenditures:
Equipment: None

Materials: Pulp and additives, $2,000

Outside services: None

Approvals:
Director of research _____
Chief chemist _____
Division manager _____

Costs to be assigned to:
All fiberboard in ratio to
5-year sales estimate.

each specified assignment. It should be approved by the research department head, and some companies require the approval of the division or product manager to whose operations the cost of the project will be allocated. Each project is assigned a number to identify it in accounting and reporting.

The project request indicates the number of hours of effort estimated for the project by classes of technical and nontechnical personnel. It also shows estimates of major specific charges such as equipment, materials, and outside consulting service. Predetermined rates, which include estimated overhead, are applied to the estimated hours. This provides the salary and general overhead cost estimate for the project which, when added to estimated specific charges, provides the total estimated cost. This estimate is posted to a project cost card (Exhibit 18-2), which also

EXHIBIT 18-2
RESEARCH PROJECT COST
Project: 57-173 Evaluation of additives for fiberboard stock

Supervisor: _____

Estimated Cost:

Chemists	— 500 hrs. @ $12.00			$ 6,000.00
Technicians	—1200 hrs. @ 3.00			3,600.00
Pilot plant	— 200 hrs. @ 8.00			1,600.00
Other personnel—None				
Equipment	—			
Materials	—			2,000.00
Outside services—				
Other	—			

Total	$13,200.00

Actual Cost:

Hours reported:	Chem.	Tech.	Pilot Plant	Other
Week of:				

Expenditures:	Equip.	Matl.	Outside Service	Other
Date:				

Assignment of cost:	Estimate	Actual
Building products	$5,280	
Acoustical products	2,640	
Industrial products	5,280	

shows the divisions or products to which the actual project cost is to be allocated.

Salaried technical personnel prepare weekly time reports on which they report their hours of work by projects. Predetermined salary rates, varying as to the technical grade of the employee, are applied to these project hours to determine the salary costs by projects. Hourly personnel also record their time by project numbers, and it is charged specifically in the payroll distribution to the projects on which they work. Major costs, such as material purchased or requisitioned for use on a specific project, are charged to it directly. This is accomplished by following the accounting code with the project number. Each month the specific project costs are determined and deducted from the total costs of the department. The difference is considered to be overhead and is allocated to projects on the basis of reported hours of technical personnel.

If factories do work on research or engineering projects, such as making test runs, they charge the material, labor, and direct expenses to the project for which the work was done. General expense (factory overhead) is usually not added to the cost of this factory test work. Time devoted to tests is not great enough to affect general factory expense, and the application of overhead would serve only to transfer it from one account to another. If work in factories is extensive, it is desirable to segregate it from costs incurred in the laboratory. This can be accomplished by using a separate expense-control account on the general ledger. Thus, indirect labor expended on a research project in the research laboratory would be coded:

GENERAL OFFICE	RESEARCH EXPENSE LABOR	DEPARTMENT	CHEMISTRY SECTION	STRENGTH TESTS	PROJECT
110	15203	00	911	416	54076

If the work were done in the Mobile factory it would be coded:

			PLANT—GENERAL		
124	15303	00	001	416	54076

All factory charges to these controls must be accumulated and added to the research expense to arrive at total costs of individual projects. Another method is to use a department number in the ninth- and tenth-digit positions of the code to designate factories doing research or engineering work. This results in the inclusion of all costs under one expense control, but analysis by department is required to determine where the costs originated.

Total project costs then include specific charges in the research department, overhead of this department, and factory charges to research projects. These should be compared with the estimated costs monthly, and those approaching the estimate referred to the supervisor responsible for the project for his review. If it appears that the project will not be completed within the estimated cost, three steps may be taken: (1) A request for a supplemental appropriation is prepared, (2) the project is revised to keep costs within limits, or (3) it is abandoned.

With the project cost system the comparison of actual and budgeted research costs by source for any one month is purely an informational procedure. It does permit the preparation of a total company figure for actual and budgeted expense for all controls. However, the project system extends beyond the time limits of months or years. It provides a comparison of actual and estimated expense by projects at all times while the project is active. On major projects extending over a period of years this is the only way effective control information can be maintained.

Allocation to Product Lines

Since substantially all the administrative expense is budgeted as fixed for a budget period, sufficient accuracy is achieved if the budgeted, rather than the actual, expenses are allocated to product lines. At the end of the year, or other budget period, the deviations from the budget which occurred may be allocated on an over-all basis as a percentage of the total budgeted amount allocated to each product. This reduces the amount of time and effort required for this work and permits the administrative expense to be shown as a constant amount under each product each month. From month to month any difference between the total actual or equalized administrative expense and the sum reflected against commodities can be taken as a debit or credit at the company level.

The bases used for allocating administrative expense to product lines vary considerably for different companies. The majority use a common base for all administrative expense. This may be sales volume expressed in units or dollars, cost of goods sold, gross profit, or total costs other than administrative expense. It is doubtful if any of these provide more than a "method." Their selection can be rationalized but cannot be defended as representing adequate cost accounting procedure. Certainly the cost of the purchasing department bears no relationship to any of the factors mentioned.

In the factory and distribution areas costs are analyzed by function and allocated to product lines on bases which reflect as nearly as possible the effort expended on each product line. This should also be the procedure used for administrative expense. Since this expense is usually a relatively small percentage of the sales dollar, inequities in allocation cannot distort product profits materially; but they can distort them. To the extent that this can be avoided, procedures should be devised to do so. Also, since the allocations are made only once each year, the amount of effort required is insignificant in relation to the greater accuracy attained and the ability to explain to all interested persons that they were made on well-considered bases.

The first step in allocating administrative expense to product lines is to study the functions of each administrative department or section of a department for which separate budgets are prepared. The functions performed will usually suggest reasonable bases for allocation, and also will indicate that some administrative expenses can be allocated directly to products, others to factories, and others to sales divisions. For the latter two groups further allocation must then be made to products. Some representative administrative departments and sections and logical bases of allocation follow:

Directly to commodities:

Costs of the corporate officers' departments on bases which best measure the demands for their efforts. These may be sales dollars, cost of sales or product units. However, in many companies the ratio of profit to the value of assets assigned to a commodity is being used as a measure of effectiveness. This is discussed in a later chapter. Where it is followed, the allocation of the costs of these departments may be made on the basis of these asset values, since the greater the amount of assets used by a product, the greater will be the demands on management toward earning an optimum profit on it.

Research expenses as indicated by projects.

To factories or sales divisions:

Personnel department on number of employees.

Purchasing department on dollar value of purchases as shown by the accounts payable distributions.

Accounts payable on number of vendors' invoices paid for each company unit.

Internal audit on audit time reports.

Central cost and budget departments on dollars of factory cost and selling expense.

Traffic department on number of freight bills, inbound and outbound.

Central stenographic department on time analysis or number of letters typed.

Tax department on dollars of taxes paid.

Legal department on analysis of effort.

Corporate accounting on number of factories and divisions.

Tabulating department on number of punched cards processed.

To factories:

General production manager on number of plants (a weighting factor may be applied for larger plants), or on number of hourly employees.
Industrial engineering on number of hourly employees.
Property accounting on cost of fixed assets.
Production control on standard factory cost of production.

To sales divisions:

Credit department on number of accounts of each division.
Billing department on number of invoices.
Accounts receivable on number of customer accounts or number of postings to customer accounts.

The administrative expense allocated to factories is in turn distributed to the products produced in each factory, and that allocated to sales divisions to the products sold by each division. In this step, because of the closer relationship to each other of products of a factory or division, broader bases of allocation may be used. For those first assigned to a factory, two bases, material cost of sales and conversion cost of sales, may be adequate. For those assigned to a sales division, the number of customer orders or dollars of sales by product lines may be adequate. Expenses of administrative units assigned to factories or divisions are grouped according to the distribution bases to be used. Each group is then distributed to products as a total rather than separately for each administrative expense unit.

It is important that the management personnel understand the problems of allocation and then agree on the best method. Following such agreement, consistency from year to year is important. Since there is no absolute basis of allocation, frequent change of bases simply creates misunderstanding and lack of acceptance of the product charges and makes allocation more harmful than helpful in providing product operating statements for management guidance.

REVIEW QUESTIONS

1. Define administrative expense.
2. When is it undesirable to charge operations of each month with the administrative expenses actually incurred?
3. Why are administrative expenses incurred in one administrative department sometimes transferred to other departments before allocation to product lines?
4. What factors should be considered in deciding to capitalize or expense research costs?
5. What administrative expenses should be budgeted on a flexible basis?

6. How may monthly administrative expense budget allowances be determined?
7. What management purposes are served by recording and controlling research expense by projects?
8. How should administrative expenses be allocated to product lines?
9. Would it be reasonable to assume that administrative expenses were equal in ratio to the sales or to the cost of sales of each product?
10. Why are administrative expenses generally excluded from costs applied to inventories?

TABLE P18-2

ADMINISTRATIVE EXPENSE

President's office	$ 350,000
Secretary's office	150,000
Treasurer's office	150,000
Controller's office	75,000
Cost accounting and budgeting	131,000
Credit department	40,000
Billing and receivables department	75,000
Accounts payable department	55,000
Payroll department	50,000
Property accounting department	20,000
Traffic department	35,000
Purchasing department	60,000
Personnel department	50,000
Research department	500,000
Total	$1,741,000

Product	Cost of sales	Customer invoices	Research project hours	Sales effort, %	Plant 1, %	Plant 2, %
A	$ 5,000,000	1,000	5,000	20	40	
B	3,000,000	500	10,000	20	25	
C	4,000,000	1,500	10,000	25	35	
D	5,000,000	1,000	10,000	25	——	60
E	3,000,000	1,000	5,000	10	——	40
General	——	——	10,000			
Total	$20,000,000	5,000	50,000			

	Employees	Freight bills	Vendor invoices	Cost of fixed assets
Plant 1	200	1,000	2,000	$ 6,000,000
Plant 2	150	500	1,000	3,000,000
Sales	50	5,000	100	500,000
General	100	500	900	500,000
Total	500	7,000	4,000	$10,000,000

PROBLEMS

1. A company's total administrative expense budget, by months, is as follows:

Jan..........	$516,000	May.........	$570,000	Sept..........	$540,000
Feb.........	500,000	June.........	520,000	Oct..........	530,000
Mar..........	510,000	July..........	490,000	Nov..........	490,000
Apr..........	580,000	Aug..........	500,000	Dec..........	494,000

Policy is to equalize administrative expense charges over the 12 months of the year.

Prepare equalizing journal entries for April and July.

2. The budgeted administrative expense and data for use as bases for distributing the expense to products are shown in Table P18-2.

Vendor invoices are approved by the unit receiving the material or service and sent to the accounts payable department for final checking and payment.

Freight bills are approved by the traffic department and sent to the accounts payable department for payment.

Each plant prepares its own gross payrolls and sends them to the payroll department for calculation of deductions and preparation of payroll checks. The payroll department also maintains the salary roll and prepares the salary checks.

All administrative expense not distributed on other bases is distributed to products on cost of sales.

Using only bases indicated by the data in Table P18-2, prepare a distribution of the administrative expense to products.

CHAPTER 19

Income Accounting

Accounting for income is less complex than accounting for costs, but it is no less important. For control purposes income must be related to the applicable costs, for there is no purpose in incurring costs if they cannot be recovered in the sale of products or services which give rise to them. Also, generally accepted accounting principles require that applicable costs be related to income in order to present fairly the results of operations. It is the purpose of income accounting to record the gross receipts and deductions therefrom by the types of goods sold or services rendered to the customer, by geographical areas and classes of customer, and by units of the company which make the sale. In addition, the requirements of tax and other legislative and regulatory reports must be met. Thus the accounting for income has both internal and external reporting considerations, and the records must be developed so as to cover both of these with a minimum of duplication.

Sources of Income

In the typical manufacturing company income is derived primarily from the sale of the products which it manufactures. If products manufactured by others are purchased and sold along with those of the company, the income therefrom is considered as sales income and treated in the same manner for accounting purposes as is the income from the sale of manufactured products. Secondary, and usually minor, sources of income are payments for services, sale of miscellaneous items such as salvaged materials, and interest, rent, dividends, and similar nonoperating income. The chart of accounts of the fiberboard company, as listed in Chapter 3, provided the basic income and income-deduction accounts required in the general ledger. In large companies these are expanded to record income arising from sales to domestic trade, foreign trade, domestic subsidiaries, foreign subsidiaries, and other units of the company. Accounts would also be provided for recording deductions from each of these gross sales accounts to arrive at net sales income. Such deductions would be classified through the use of separate accounts for sales returns, quantity discounts, trade discounts, price allowances, and freight allowances.

In addition to the accounts required to record net sales income, accounts would also be provided for miscellaneous operating income such as:

Sale of Salvage Material
Refund from Audit of Freight Bills
Group Insurance Premium Refunds
Worthless Accounts Receivable Recovered

and miscellaneous nonoperating income such as:

Interest Earned
Gain on Foreign Exchange
Rent
Royalties
Dividends

Supplementary Income Data

The coding detail given for income in Chapter 3 provides for the accumulation of most of the supplementary income data required for management and reporting purposes. In the fiberboard company a typical invoice for roof insulation would carry the following code: 152-10101-02-521-109. This code indicates the following:

152 · The sale was made by or in the territory of the Chicago district office of the building materials division.
10101 · The general-ledger account indicates a domestic sale to trade.
02 · The product sold was roof insulation.
521 · The specific product was standard insulation.
109 · It was sold to a roofing contractor.

This code could be supplemented with additional information for tax or sales statistical purposes. Thus, if mechanical accounting equipment is used, digits may be added to indicate in code the specific city or county and state location of the purchaser and the customer name. If these data are compiled manually, expansion of the code is not necessary, since the documents themselves show locations and names of customers.

The Customer Order

The accounting sequence for income derived from the sale of products starts with the receipt of the customer's order. This may be a firm order or an inquiry for price if the item ordered is made specially to customer specifications. Some companies prepare a customer order form for all items for which they are asked to quote a price. This provides a control record for having the estimate prepared and submitted to the customer. If a firm order is received, the "quote" order is simply expanded to include quantity, terms, and shipping instructions. After this is done, it has the same characteristics as an order for material sold from inventory at established, published prices.

Exhibit 19-1

Customer Order Acknowledgment

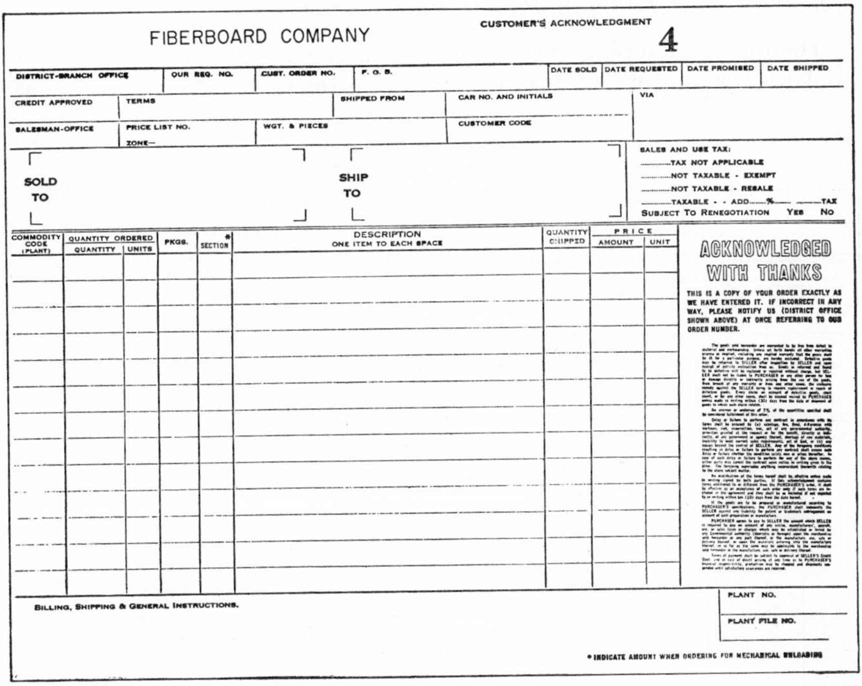
FIBERBOARD COMPANY
CUSTOMER'S ACKNOWLEDGMENT 4
DISTRICT-BRANCH OFFICE | OUR REQ. NO. | CUST. ORDER NO. | F. O. B. | DATE SOLD | DATE REQUESTED | DATE PROMISED | DATE SHIPPED
CREDIT APPROVED | TERMS | SHIPPED FROM | CAR NO. AND INITIALS | VIA
SALESMAN-OFFICE | PRICE LIST NO. ZONE— | WGT. & PIECES | CUSTOMER CODE
SOLD TO
SHIP TO
SALES AND USE TAX:
.........TAX NOT APPLICABLE
.........NOT TAXABLE - EXEMPT
.........NOT TAXABLE - RESALE
.........TAXABLE - - ADD.....%..... ....TAX
SUBJECT TO RENEGOTIATION YES NO
COMMODITY CODE (PLANT) | QUANTITY ORDERED: QUANTITY, UNITS | PKGS. | * SECTION | DESCRIPTION ONE ITEM TO EACH SPACE | QUANTITY SHIPPED | PRICE: AMOUNT, UNIT
ACKNOWLEDGED WITH THANKS
THIS IS A COPY OF YOUR ORDER EXACTLY AS WE HAVE ENTERED IT. IF INCORRECT IN ANY WAY, PLEASE NOTIFY US (DISTRICT OFFICE SHOWN ABOVE) AT ONCE REFERRING TO OUR ORDER NUMBER.
BILLING, SHIPPING & GENERAL INSTRUCTIONS.
PLANT NO.
PLANT FILE NO.
* INDICATE AMOUNT WHEN ORDERING FOR MECHANICAL UNLOADING

The customer order is customarily recorded on the selling company's order forms from the purchase order received from the customer. The number of copies of the order and their distribution will be determined by the organization structure and the internal procedures of the selling company. Exhibit 19-1 is a typical form used for entering customer orders. In this set the distribution of the eight copies is as follows: order department, production planning, shipping, customer's acknowledgment, billing and cost departments, salesman, district office, and home-office sales department. Except for the acknowledgment copy and the shipping copy, all copies are identical. In this illustration the order forms are prepared in the district office receiving the order, or in the home office if it is received there. The district offices send the complete set to the home office. The orders are then given numbers, and all complete sets are routed to the credit department for approval. If credit is approved, the copies are distributed as indicated; if not, the customer and district office are informed and the order is canceled.

Frequently the customer invoice is prepared as one copy of the order-form set. Or, through the use of duplicating processes, a master copy of the order is prepared and other copies and the invoice are prepared from this as required.

The Shipping Documents

The factory shipping copy of the customer order, when completed as to date of shipment and quantity shipped, is the basic record of shipment

Exhibit 19-2
Shipping Copy of Customer Order

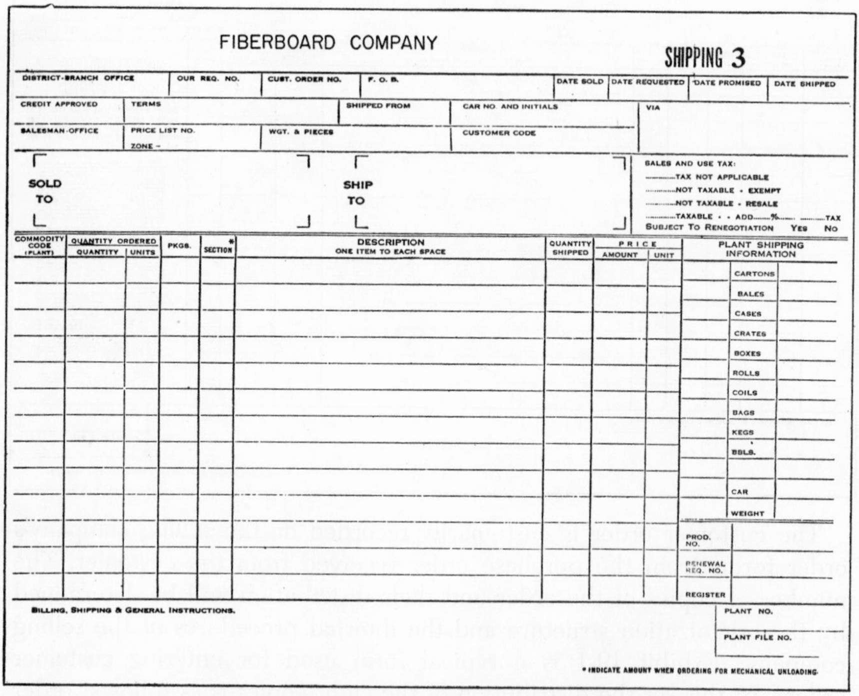

FIBERBOARD COMPANY

SHIPPING 3

DISTRICT-BRANCH OFFICE	OUR REQ. NO.	CUST. ORDER NO.	F. O. B.	DATE SOLD	DATE REQUESTED	DATE PROMISED	DATE SHIPPED
CREDIT APPROVED	TERMS		SHIPPED FROM	CAR NO. AND INITIALS	VIA		
SALESMAN-OFFICE	PRICE LIST NO. ZONE –	WGT. & PIECES		CUSTOMER CODE			

SOLD TO

SHIP TO

SALES AND USE TAX:
........TAX NOT APPLICABLE
........NOT TAXABLE - EXEMPT
........NOT TAXABLE - RESALE
........TAXABLE - - ADD......%...... ....TAX
SUBJECT TO RENEGOTIATION YES NO

COMMODITY CODE (PLANT)	QUANTITY ORDERED: QUANTITY	UNITS	PKGS.	SECTION*	DESCRIPTION ONE ITEM TO EACH SPACE	QUANTITY SHIPPED	PRICE: AMOUNT	UNIT	PLANT SHIPPING INFORMATION
									CARTONS
									BALES
									CASES
									CRATES
									BOXES
									ROLLS
									COILS
									BAGS
									KEGS
									BBLS.
									CAR
									WEIGHT
									PROD. NO.
									RENEWAL REQ. NO.
									REGISTER

BILLING, SHIPPING & GENERAL INSTRUCTIONS. PLANT NO.
PLANT FILE NO.

* INDICATE AMOUNT WHEN ORDERING FOR MECHANICAL UNLOADING.

(Exhibit 19-2). It is used for the preparation of the shipping manifest and bill of lading. It may also provide the basic information for the accounting department to determine and record the cost of goods sold and relieve the specific inventory records of finished stock for the items shipped. When it is received by the billing department, it is the authorization to them to prepare an invoice or to release a previously prepared invoice. If only a part of the order is shipped, the factory will prepare a "partial shipment" sheet and retain the shipping copy of the order until the final portion of the order is shipped. The billing department will then invoice each shipment separately or, if so instructed, will retain the partial shipment reports and invoice the entire order when all items are shipped.

The factory may note the standard or actual cost of materials shipped on the shipping copy of the order. This is then transferred to the cost and billing copy of the order. Or, the cost may be inserted on this copy by a centralized cost department. These costs are then recorded and summarized along with the sales value of the invoice.

For internal control purposes it is desirable that a summary of shipments be prepared in the shipping department. These are a listing of the shipments of each day. Bills of lading, invoices for freight-out, gate passes, car and truck releases are all checked against the summary of shipments to establish that every shipment has been recorded on it. In turn, customer invoices are checked against them to ensure that all shipments have been invoiced which should have been invoiced.

The Customer Invoice

The customer invoice is the final original record in the sequence leading up to the determination of sales income. There is no generally accepted form for the customer invoice. So great is the variation in size and format that a few large companies submit their own form to the vendor, as copies of their order, and require that they be invoiced on their own forms.

The primary requisites in designing a customer invoice are (1) provision for all the information which both the vendor and the customer desire and (2) the arrangement of these data to provide for the most economical transfer of the data to other records and summary forms of the vendor. A typical distribution of copies would be as follows:

> Customer (as many as desired)
> Salesman or sales-office order department
> Accounting department
> Accounts receivable department
> Billing department files

In this set the accounting department copy is used for all accounting and statistical purposes. Separate copies are sometimes provided for the cost department, the general accounting department for the sales journal, and the statistics department for the compilation of statistical data. Copies of the invoices are frequently filed by customer in the accounts receivable department as the subsidiary accounts receivable ledger. When this is done additional space is provided on this copy for recording payments by and credits to the customer.

Exhibit 19-3 is the copy of a typical customer invoice used by the accounting department. In addition to the information which is shown on all copies of the invoice, this copy also provides a block for statistical data. All information on this is shown in numerical code. This provides

EXHIBIT 19-3
CUSTOMER INVOICE

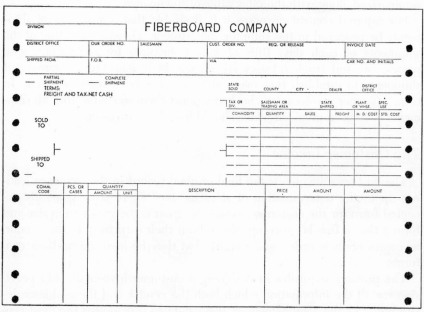

for summarizing the data mechanically. A "Cost" column is also shown in this block. This is to provide for the recording of the standard or actual factory cost of the material covered by the invoice. This factory cost is transferred from the shipping sheet if determined in the factory, or from a copy of the order if it is determined in a central cost department. As tabulating cards are punched or summaries are prepared manually, the cost and sales appear on the same card or the same line of the journal. This permits later comparison of sales income and cost by item shipped, by commodity group, by salesman, by district office, and by sales area. This gross margin analysis provides management with information as to cost-price relationships. Units of products sold are summarized simultaneously with the dollar income.

The summaries of sales and cost of sales, whether made by tabulating equipment or by other means, provide the information for two summary journal entries. For sales the entry is:

> Dr. Accounts Receivable
>   Cr. Sales (by general ledger
>   sales accounts)

For cost of sales it is:

> Dr. Cost of Goods Sold (this may be
>   detailed to parallel the sales accounts)
>   Cr. Finished Stock

This review of accounting for sales income was based on the direct sale of products manufactured or jobbed by the seller. It gives no recognition to the many variations in accounting for income which are required for installment sales, consignment sales, and contracts for installation or erection of the products. Each of these requires special procedures. The difference between these special procedures and those for recording direct sales is in the number of auxiliary records required and in the time when billings are taken into the accounts as sales income. The latter is determined in part by provisions of the internal revenue code. Ultimately sales of any type are taken up as income of some period through a credit to the sales account. Costs must be matched with sales and taken into operations only when and to the extent that income is taken.

Deductions from Gross Sales

Deductions from gross sales should be recorded in as much detail as are gross sales, so that net sales figures will be available for all purposes of management. The net figure is the more significant, for it is the amount of money which a company has available to cover costs and provide a profit. A satisfactory margin between gross sales and cost can be dissipated rapidly by excessive allowances, discounts, and freight.

The illustrative customer invoice had a column in the statistical block for freight. This deduction may be computed on the invoice from the bill of lading and freight rate schedules. Or, the freight bill for freight which is prepaid and allowed may be matched with the respective invoice. By this method freight deductions from gross sales are summarized with the sales. Similarly, any discounts which are computed on the face of the invoice can be recorded and summarized at the same time as are gross sales. When these deductions are computed on the invoice, a combined gross sales and sales deductions entry can be made as follows:

> Dr. Accounts Receivable
> Dr. Trade Discounts
> Dr. Freight Allowed
> Cr. Gross Sales

Other deductions are not known at the time the invoice is prepared. For returns and allowances a credit memo is prepared. These are coded and summarized just as are invoices. The entries are:

> Dr. Sales Returns
> Dr. Sales Allowances
> Cr. Accounts Receivable

A cost entry is also required for returns. Since certain costs (e.g., shipping), which were recorded when the material was sold, represent losses if the material is returned, they must be recognized in the entries recording the cost side of sales returns as follows:

> Dr. Finished Stock
> Dr. Loss on Sales Returns
> Cr. Cost of Goods Sold

Quantity discounts based on purchases over a period and computed at the end of the period would be recorded as follows:

> Dr. Quantity Discounts
> Cr. Accounts Receivable

Cash discounts taken when invoices are paid may be considered as sales deductions or miscellaneous expenses. The preferable treatment is as sales deductions. Payments received on customers' accounts are recorded as follows:

> Dr. Cash
> Dr. Cash Discounts
> Cr. Accounts Receivable

Deductions from sales which are recorded some time after the billing is made are reflected in the same detail as the original sale to which they apply, to the extent that this is possible or practicable. If it is impossible to do this, or the amount of effort required is excessive, the deductions may be allocated to the applicable sales on an equitable basis. Thus, if cash discount terms are the same for all products, cash discount could be allocated to product lines, territories, and salesmen on the basis of gross sales dollars.

Sales Analysis

For sales, as for costs, the primary reason for recording detail and then analyzing, summarizing, interpreting, and reporting it is to assist management in achieving their objective of earning the optimum profit. A secondary, but essential reason is to provide data for tax and other governmental reports. Within each company, and even within each unit of a company, the amount of detail recorded, the extent of analysis and interpretation, and the form of reports will vary if maximum effectiveness is to be achieved. No two businesses are alike, and no two managers work and think alike, so there is no one best sales analysis procedure. Some of the possible uses of sales statistics are suggested in the following:

1. Analysis by product line for:
   a. Gross margin by products
   b. Net profit by products
   c. Comparison with selling effort by product lines
   d. Determining sales trends and seasonal fluctuations by product lines
   e. Planning production
2. Analysis by territory where sold to:
   a. Appraise sales realized in comparison with sales potential
   b. Compare with cost of selling in the territory
   c. Determine territory net profit
   d. Appraise effectiveness of managers of territories
   e. Determine importance of freight allowances
3. Analysis by salesmen to:
   a. Determine dollar and unit volume of each salesman
   b. Measure sales performance on related products
   c. Measure sales secured against specific salesman costs
   d. Provide bases of compensation
4. Analysis by customer to:
   a. Give direction to sales effort
   b. Appraise discount schedules
   c. Direct advertising and promotional campaigns
   d. Determine gross profit by customer
5. Analysis by size of shipment to:
   a. Appraise order handling and billing costs in relation to gross sales or gross margin
   b. Evaluate quantity discount schedules
   c. Determine effect on factory production costs
6. Analysis by unit price to:
   a. Guide pricing policy
   b. Provide price trends
   c. Provide information for selective selling

Other Income

Income from sources other than sales of products is usually insignificant in the typical manufacturing company. Where this is true, the general-ledger accounts listed earlier in this chapter provide all the detailed information needed on such income. If more is required, the miscellaneous income accounts can be expanded by adding codes in the department, operation, or classification positions, to provide it. This would be desirable if the income was related directly to certain product lines. For example, if a factory is realizing income from the sale of scrap which is created by only one product line, and the income from the sale of the scrap is significant in relation to the profit of that product, it should be credited to that product.

The major internal control problem with respect to other income is establishing that all of it is received which should be received. Its very nature makes the usual internal checks difficult to apply. Unless a plant is enclosed with a fence, it is difficult to control the movement of miscellaneous items from the plant. With a fence and guarded gates the guard may know that something was taken out but probably would not be qualified in many cases to determine if the article described on the properly authorized pass was in fact the one taken out. Also, prices realized for salvaged materials are not subject to the usual verification. For these reasons there should be frequent interchange of personnel responsible for miscellaneous income and the participation of two or more employees in each significant transaction, or series of continuing transactions, which in the aggregate are significant.

REVIEW QUESTIONS

1. What is the difference between operating income and nonoperating income? Cite examples.
2. What detail of sales income is required for management purposes? External purposes?
3. What management and record-keeping purposes are served by customer order data?
4. Describe a procedure which will assure that all shipments are billed.
5. Describe the accounting and control uses of the customer invoice.
6. What is the difference between gross and net sales?
7. What are the purposes of sales analysis?
8. Should the analysis be of gross or net sales?
9. How can sales accounting and sales analysis be correlated for maximum efficiency in the office?
10. What is the primary problem in accounting for miscellaneous income?

PROBLEMS

1. The fiberboard company has the following major commodity codes: 02 Roof Insulation, 05 Sheathing, 06 Form Board, 14 Industrial Products, and 21 Acoustical Material. It has the following specific product codes: 521 Standard Roof Insulation, 522 Laminated Roof Insulation, 531 Standard Sheathing, 532 Weatherproof Sheathing, 541 Acoustical Tile, 542 Acoustical Panels, 571 Standard Board, 576 Cut Specialties, and 581 Heavy Form Board. Customer classifications are 101 General Contractors, 102 Acoustical Contractors, 106 Roofing Contractors, 112 Mail-order Houses, 114 Refrigerator Manufacturers, and 121 Lumber Dealers.

Using the codes of the fiberboard company in Chapter 3, code the following sales:

    a. Standard roof insulation to a Los Angeles roofing contractor

    b. Standard board to a refrigerator manufacturer in New York

    c. Acoustical tile by the New York office to an acoustical contractor in England

    d. Heavy form board to a lumber dealer in Birmingham

    e. Acoustical panels to a lumber dealer in Kansas City

    f. Laminated roof insulation to a lumber dealer in Chicago

    g. Waterproof sheathing to a general contractor in New York

    h. Cut specialties by the Birmingham office to a refrigerator manufacturer in Cuba

2. A company deducts trade discounts and freight allowed on its invoices to customers. Rebate credits are issued periodically to customers as their purchases reach or exceed a stated quantity. A summary of the sales and sales deductions for a period follows:

Gross sales................................	$500,000
Trade discounts.............	5,000
Freight allowances.........................	6,000
Allowances for defective material............	1,000
Rebates....................................	3,000
Customer payments.......................	396,000
Cash discounts taken......................	4,000

Prepare journal entries to record these data.

CHAPTER 20

Budgets and Forecasts

Thus far standards, standard costs, and expense budgets have been discussed in relation to their use in the predetermination, measurement, and control of factory, distribution, and administrative costs. In each of these areas these tools of management accounting are very valuable. However, their full value will be realized only when they are integrated into a complete budgetary planning and control program.

Forward planning is vital in a competitive profit and loss economic system. The success of each enterprise in realizing its optimum profit in each year will be determined by the extent to which it establishes its objectives, develops coordinated plans to meet those objectives, and exercises control of all facets of its activity so as to have actual results reach or exceed those planned. This entire process constitutes the budgetary planning and control program. It includes income, costs, profits, working capital, fixed assets, financing, and dividend distribution. It extends throughout the entire organization from the chief executive to the front-line supervisory levels.

Terminology

The planning phase of such a program is generally referred to as budgeting, and the coordinated plan as the budget. The terms "budget" and "forecast" are sometimes used synonymously. However, a rather general usage is to designate the coordinated plans of action for a period as the "budget" and to use the term "forecast" to designate a close-up estimate made during a budget period of the actual results which are then expected to be realized. When used in this sense a forecast reflects expected deviations from the budget. Thus the sales budget built at the beginning of a period may reflect sales income of $950,000 for the period. In the next-to-the-last month of the period a forecast may be made which would anticipate sales of $978,000 for the period, or a plus deviation of $28,000.

262

Another use of forecast is with the term "budget" ("forecast budget") to designate a budget which does not provide for adjustment of the budgeted items as conditions change during a budget period. These forecast budgets are also called "fixed budgets." A forecast budget is contrasted with the flexible budget, which does provide for adjustment to the actual conditions experienced.

A more limited usage of the term "budget" is in reference to expense items only. Companies which use budgets to plan and control factory, distribution, and administrative expenses may state that they have a budget, or budgets. Such budgets are but units of a complete budgetary planning and control program. The companies which limit their budgeting to these areas do not have a budget as the term is used in its broadest sense. Another variation in usage of terms is to use "budget" to designate planned expenses and to refer to the complete coordinated program as a forecast.

Because of the wide variation in the use of terms to designate the components of the over-all program of budgetary planning and control, terminology is extremely confusing. In this and succeeding chapters the term "budget" will be used to designate the coordinated management plans for a stated period and the term "forecast" to designate estimates made during the budget period of the actual results expected. Units of the budget will be preceded by identifying descriptions such as "sales," "expense," and "cash."

Purpose

The purpose of a budget is to provide:

1. A realistic estimate of income and costs for a period and of financial position at the close of the period, detailed by areas of management responsibility
2. A coordinated plan of action to achieve, by the end of the period, the estimates reflected in the budget
3. A guide for management decisions in adjusting plans and objectives as uncontrollable conditions change
4. A comparison of actual results with those budgeted and an analysis and interpretation of deviations by areas of responsibility to indicate courses of corrective action and to lead to improvement in procedures in building future budgets
5. A ready basis for making forecasts during the budget period to guide management in making day-to-day decisions

A budget is a plan of action to achieve stated objectives, based on a predetermined series of related assumptions. To be used effectively it cannot be regarded as an absolute requirement of performance with unfavorable deviations severely criticized and favorable deviations roundly praised. To expect a sales manager to meet a sales budget which was based on expected good business conditions even if there has been a sudden collapse of general business during the budget period would be just as completely unrealistic as it would be to expect a person to make a trip of 300 miles in 5 hours over secondary roads when the trip was planned to be made at that rate of speed over a limited-access throughway which was found to be closed. After being developed as a plan of action a budget is used to evaluate performance under actual conditions in comparison with planned performance under the conditions which it was assumed would apply during the budget period. This evaluation of performance presupposes a flexible budget.

With a "fixed" or "forecast" budget all estimates of income, cost, and financial position are based on stated assumed conditions. Any change from the assumed conditions will result in deviations in at least some of and probably all the budget areas. Because provision is not made in the budget for adjustment to actual conditions, it is difficult to segregate deviations which are the result of management decision from those which are the result of external, uncontrollable factors. Such segregation is a time-consuming process and frequently calls for the exercise of judgment which may be challenged and thus focus attention on questions of judgment rather than on corrective action.

In contrast, the flexible budget is developed from unit prices and costs for those items which vary directly with volume, from ratios for financial position, and from dollar amounts for those items which are not directly affected by volume. Through the application of the rates and ratios to the actual activity units experienced, and adding to the result the appropriate budgeted dollar amounts for items not directly variable, total dollar budget *allowances* are secured which are comparable with the actuals experienced. Any deviations are then the result of management. The differences between the budget as adjusted to actual conditions and the original budget are the result of external factors. Both types of deviations are automatically determined as a part of the measurement and comparison procedure and are readily explainable.

Because conditions do change, and sometimes very quickly, management must have basic data to guide their current decisions so that they will realize the optimum profit and financial position, which may be higher or lower than those budgeted. The correlated plans developed in building a flexible budget will indicate the direction and extent of these decisions. As they are made for one phase of the business, the effects on other phases can be determined from the relationships which were established in the budget. For the fiberboard company an increase in building construction over the level assumed for the budget would indicate higher sales which in turn would affect production schedules, inventories, factory expenses, accounts receivable, and cash. With the higher sales volume forecast, its effects on the other items can be evaluated. Data become available as bases for decisions, and instead of following expediency each move can be planned and correlated.

In appraising the value of a budget system there is a tendency to give first consideration to the degree to which actual results agree with those budgeted. If a record of very insignificant deviation can be shown, budgeting is apt to be considered to be desirable. Conversely, if wide deviations are experienced, the value of the program may be questioned. Achievement of "on-the-nose" budgeting adds to the value of a budget system. Failure to do so does not destroy its other values.

Scope of Budgets

Effective planning of one phase of a business is impossible if all other phases are not planned just as carefully. Therefore, a budgetary planning and control system is made up of many individual budgets. These would include:

1. Sales budgets by areas of responsibility
2. Production volume budgets, based on sales and planned inventory level changes, for each production center
3. Direct-material and labor cost budgets
4. Expense budgets for each area of responsibility
5. Profit budgets by areas of profit responsibility and by major product lines
6. Capital expenditures budgets
7. Working capital budgets

Detail is essential for effective budgeting. Previous discussion of the several expense budgets stressed the importance of detail in budgeting expenses if control is to be effective. This is equally true of all the other budgets. The extent of the detail will be determined by the importance of an item and the extent to which management decisions will be implemented by it. There is no scientific way of determining the amount of detail to be reflected in each budget nor any way of determining it on the basis of generally accepted practice. It will be affected by the type of industry, and more importantly by the personality of the management.

In starting a budget program it is usually desirable to limit the amount of detail. Detailed historical data frequently are not available, and the organization is not experienced in making detailed plans and estimates. A relatively broad approach will have a constructive effect on the business, and experience has shown that the requirements for detailed information increase as management comes to recognize the value of budgets through their use and as the industrial accountants acquire greater experience in administering the budgets.

The Budget Period

The period of time covered by a budget varies considerably between companies and even within a company for each of the individual budgets. There is no "right" length of time to be covered by any budget. If the period is too short, budget building will become excessively time-consuming and costly. Also, the value of real forward planning will be lost. If the period is too long, those who build the budgets will feel that there are so many unpredictable factors that it is useless to attempt to budget accurately. The longer the period, the more general must be the approach to budget building.

Some budgets must cover a period of from 6 to 12 months if they are to be useful rather than restrictive. It would obviously be impossible to budget advertising expenditures on a monthly or even a quarterly basis. Space and time commitments must be made, copy and script must be prepared, and a continuing program developed if the maximum value is to be realized from the advertising expenditures. For these reasons advertising budgets are customarily built for a 12-month period.

A capital expenditures budget must give consideration to future facilities requirements and the time required for their construction or acquisition. Therefore, it may cover a period of several years. In contrast the budget of inventory position may be for a month or quarter with plans adjusted thereto and changed from period to period as close-up forecasts are made.

Some companies prepare a complete set of budgets for each calendar or fiscal year. During the year shorter-range forecasts are made by adjusting the annual budget figures. Others prepare a complete set of budgets twice each year. Still others prepare budgets each quarter with each budget covering the next 12-month period. Another procedure is to have a moving budget: each month the past month is dropped and the sixth or twelfth future month is added.

The budget period must be adapted to the requirements of the persons who are to use the budgets, the purposes to be served by the budgets, and the conditions peculiar to the industry in which a company operates. Also, general economic or other conditions may make it necessary to deviate from the customary budget periods from time to time in order to give management sharper and more informative data. Budgets prepared in the fall of 1941 for 1942 probably became worthless with the attack on Pearl Harbor, because the entire business picture was changed.

General Principles

Those budgets which relate to income, costs, and profits may be grouped and designated as the operating budget. In summary it is a budgeted profit and loss statement, developed from, and supported by, such detailed supporting budgets and schedules as are required to meet the purposes of a budgetary planning and control program. The general principles which govern the preparation of operating budgets and their administration are:

1. Budgets are to reflect costs which are attainable by efficient operations and income which can be realized under the conditions which are expected to prevail during the budget period.

2. Budgets are to be prepared from basic data such as unit sales prices, wage rates, operating speeds, manpower requirements, and raw-material prices. These data are to be developed from a thorough study and knowledge of the probable requirements and the conditions expected to prevail for the budget period.

3. Those responsible for the execution of each segment of the budget are to participate in its preparation and approval.

4. Budgets are to be prepared in sufficient detail to permit adequate explanation of variations from the planned results, and the adjustment of plans to meet changed conditions.

5. All budgeted and actual income and expenditures are to be classified, organized, and assigned in accordance with responsibility for control or execution.

6. Actual performance is to be compared regularly with the established budget in each area of responsibility. Significant variations are to be analyzed, appraised, interpreted, and reported.

7. Expense control budget allowances are to be applied so that only those variations from the budget will be reflected which are within the control of a particular level of responsibility. When necessary, special allowances are to be made to cover costs which result from policy decisions and cannot be directly controlled by the respective operating executive.

8. Flexible budgeting techniques are to be applied wherever practicable. The flexible budgets are to be designed so that they provide a ready means for adjusting budget allowances to varying levels of activity.

The general principles which govern the preparation of capital expenditures budget are:

1. Budgets are to reflect (*a*) expenditures in the current period against authorizations for expenditures approved in prior periods which will be uncompleted at the beginning of the current period, (*b*) estimated

authorizations for expenditures to be approved in the current period, and (c) estimated carry-over into future periods of unexpended authorizations of prior periods and the current period.

2. Budgets are to be prepared in detail by specific planned capital acquisitions, with a practical minimum included for miscellaneous capital expenditures.

3. Budgets are to be prepared for each area of responsibility.

4. Persons who will have responsibility for the capital assets to be acquired shall participate in the preparation and approval of the budgets.

The general principles which govern the preparation of working capital budgets are:

1. Budgets are to be based on the approved operating and capital expenditures budgets.

2. Budgets are to reflect planned changes in inventory levels and estimated changes in accounts receivable and payable.

3. Budgets are to reflect planned short- and long-term financing.

4. Budgets are to reflect planned dividend payments.

Responsibility of Budgeting

The responsibility for the administration of the budgetary planning and control program of a company should rest with the chief accounting officer. This facilitates the complete integration of the budgeting and accounting procedures. Many records can be used for both purposes, and work loads can be distributed among a larger number of personnel. As a result, the cost of accounting and budgeting is lower than if the two functions are administered by separate departments. However, in some large companies the budget department is independent of the accounting department, and the budget officer reports directly to the president. The arguments for this are independence, objectivity, and freedom from the effects of the periodic accounting functions. In setting the budget responsibility these intangibles must be weighed against the tangible savings which result from a combined responsibility.

The specific line and functional responsibilities of the budget officer are to:

1. Define the policies and procedures under which the budget plan is to operate

2. Define the form and manner in which the necessary budget detail is to be prepared

3. Aid and advise in the preparation of budgets and forecasts

4. Schedule the time for submitting the required data

5. Assemble and publish budgets and forecasts

6. Provide for the accounting for actual income and expenditures in the details necessary for the operation of the budget plan

7. Analyze, report, and interpret comparisons of actual and budgeted results and position

Budget Committee

While the budget officer should have the responsibility for administering the budgetary program of the company, he should not be solely responsible for the assumptions upon which a budget is built nor for the appraisal of the budget data. The responsibility for these latter functions should rest with a budget committee. The members of this committee should be company executives who do not have operating responsibilities in either the sales or production sides of the business. A typical committee would be made up of the executive vice-president, controller, treasurer, and economist.

It would be the responsibility of the budget committee to develop general and basic concepts as to economic conditions expected during the budget period, trends in price and wage levels, and other relevant data. These would provide the basic assumptions which would underlie the entire budget. During the course of the building of the budgets the committee would be available for consultation and advice on specific problems. After the budgets are built and are reviewed by the budget staff for conformance to basic principles and for completeness, they would be submitted to the budget committee. They would appraise each budget in the light of the basic assumptions for the period and the specific considerations applicable in each budget area. If they feel changes are necessary, they would recommend them to the person who developed the budget, who may or may not agree to revise the budget. Finally the committee would submit the budgets in summary form to the company executives together with interpretative comments and any recommended revisions which were not accepted by the persons building the budgets. Final acceptance would rest with top management.

The budget committee would also develop possible long-term patterns of change in general economic conditions which will affect the demand for, or the cost of, products of the company. These would be designed to:

1. Assist management in the development and evaluation of long-range plans

2. Make possible a long-term projection of cash and working-capital position

3. Indicate probable facilities requirements

4. Evaluate financing requirements

5. Indicate opportunities for the profitable investment of capital

6. Provide management with the basis for making changes in organization structure and personnel to meet changing economic conditions

7. Indicate fields of commercial research which should be undertaken

Basic Assumptions

Because effective budgeting requires coordinated planning, it is essential that all persons participating in the building of the budget are planning toward the same objectives and are contemplating the same company, industry, and general economic conditions. This can be accomplished by issuing a statement of basic assumptions prior to the start of the budget building.

These basic assumptions would state the company objectives for profits, growth, and financial position for the budget period. Where there are operating divisions within a company, separate objectives may be set for each division, and if there is product-line diversity, they may even be different for each line.

They would also set forth a rather detailed explanation of contemplated general economic and specific industry conditions. Where sales of a product are correlated with indices or with activity of another industry the assumptions as to these would be stated so that correlations can be made. Information would also be supplied as to conditions which may influence sales prices, raw-material availability and costs, wage and salary levels, and building and equipment construction and acquisition cost trends. In short, they would cover all factors which would affect planning for the budget period.

In a small company the statement of basic assumptions may be prepared by the chief accounting officer and approved and issued by the president. Or, it may even be prepared by the president. In a large company employing an economist it would probably be prepared by his staff, approved by the budget committee, and finally approved and issued by the president.

Specific Budgets

The development of the expense budgets and their use in measuring and controlling actual expenses has been discussed in preceding chapters. Those procedures are an integral part of the budget system of any company. They should be reviewed for correlation with the general procedures and principles stated in this chapter and the other specific budgets to be discussed in subsequent chapters.

REVIEW QUESTIONS

1. Describe the scope of budgetary planning and control.
2. What are the five purposes of a budget?

3. Why is a flexible budget more desirable than a fixed budget?
4. How does a well-developed budget aid management in day-to-day decision making?
5. Is failure to meet a budget an indication of unsatisfactory performance?
6. Name the major individual budgets found in a complete budgetary planning and control program.
7. What considerations govern the length of the budget period?
8. Should all budgets be built for the same period of time?
9. What is the operating budget?
10. What are the general principles for building and administering the operating budget?
11. Describe the capital budget.
12. Describe the working capital budget.
13. What are the responsibilities of the chief budget officer?
14. What are the functions of a budget committee?
15. What is meant by "basic assumptions" for the budget period? What purpose do they serve?

CHAPTER 21

Sales Budgets

The sales budget for a company is an estimate of sales to customers for a budget period. For a unit of a company the budget includes sales to other units of the company, in addition to sales to customers. Budgets are prepared in detail by product lines and by areas of sales responsibility such as divisions or districts. The purpose of a sales budget is to:

1. Establish sales objectives for the period and months of the period with which actual sales can be compared and appraised

2. Provide basic data for use in budgeting profit or loss for the company and each of its component units

3. Serve as a guide in the preparation of working capital and capital expenditures budgets

4. Provide basic data for determining future requirements for inventories, raw-material purchases, production facilities, and personnel

5. Facilitate forecasts within the budget period of operating and financial position which will indicate desirable and necessary changes in plans during the budget period

In building the sales budget consideration must be given to the method of sale, e.g., direct, installment, construction contract, etc., and to company practice. Some companies budget customer orders, particularly when there is normally a substantial time lag between the date of receipt of an order and the date of shipping and billing the material. A budget for installment sales would probably be for the initial transactions rather than for estimated collections during the period. The sales budget for construction contracts may be for contracts booked, for progress billings on contracts, or for contract completions. Whenever the sales budget is for other than sales to be reflected as income during the budget period, it must be adjusted to a sales-income basis before it can be used to budget profit.

Historical Data

Historical sales data should be used as bench marks in building the sales budget. These supplement but do not replace current information, and they provide bases for correlating past experience with indices and other data which originate outside of the company. The sound sales budget must recognize the past sales record, the present position, and the speed and direction of movement from the current position. These factors should be considered for the company as a whole, and for divisions, plants, territories, and product lines of the company.

Two sets of figures are useful for this purpose, the totals for each year for a long period of time and a 12-month moving average for at least each of the past 12 months. The first shows the long-term trend and intermediate fluctuations, the second the immediate trend. If these are converted into index numbers relative to a base period or are plotted on logarithmic charts, the speed of movement will be indicated. When they are correlated with other statistical data, they provide a basis for budgeting sales for the immediate future.

Coupled with the consideration of historical sales records will be the consideration of historical production records. Obviously, the budgeted sales cannot be in excess of the ability to produce, plus any reduction which can be made in inventory. These production records should show monthly achieved production levels by product lines for a period of several years and also the theoretical or rated production capacity. This will indicate the maximum limits of the sales budget.

Sales Budget Period

Sales must be budgeted for a period which is at least as long as the longest period for which a budget of profit and loss is required. Sometimes they are budgeted for even longer periods, with interim profit budgets prepared as required for management guidance and planning.

The extent to which sales budgets are built by months of the budget period varies substantially from company to company. The most desirable practice is to budget by months with the total for the period being the sum of the months, rather than to budget for the period and then divide by the months in the period to arrive at the monthly figures. The number of business days in a calendar month will vary by more than 10%. This alone will cause substantial deviations from a budget which is spread evenly by months. Seasonal fluctuations, vacation periods, holidays, model or pattern changes, and similar factors will cause further fluctuations in the monthly sales figures. All these must be reflected in the sales budget by months to permit effective planning and to provide a fair basis for measuring and appraising actual performance.

A common practice is for a company to prepare a detailed budget for each 6-month period and a less detailed budget for each ensuing 6-month period. Where this is followed, a budget would be prepared in the last quarter of each year for the ensuing year. The data submitted in this budget would include the following sales data:

1. The second half of the current year by months and in total. Sales shown for this period may consist of the actual sales for the months of July, August, September, and October, and estimated sales for the months of November and December. This would provide a close-up sales estimate to be used in appraising the budget.

2. The first half of the ensuing calendar year, with sales budgeted for this period shown by months and in total.

3. The second half of the ensuing calendar year, with sales for this period shown by quarters and in total.

A midyear budget would then be prepared during the second quarter of each year. This budget would show sales for the following periods:

1. The first half of the current year by months and in total. Sales shown for this period may consist of the actual sales for the months of January, February, March, and April, and estimated sales for the months of May and June.

2. The second half of the current year, with sales budgeted for this period shown by months and in total.

3. The first half of the ensuing calendar year, with sales budgeted for this period shown by quarters and in total.

Other companies prepare sales budgets in each quarter for the next 12-month period. Where this is done, sales may be budgeted by months for the full period. Or, monthly figures may be budgeted for the immediately ensuing quarter or half with totals shown for the remainder of the period. Another practice is to maintain a "rolling" budget for 6 months or a year in which each month is dropped as it is passed and the next sixth or twelfth month is added.

As with all budgets, there is no one "right" length for the period for which sales are budgeted. Company preference, industry conditions, and the general economic situation will determine the length of the periods and the frequency of revisions.

Basic Assumptions

The sales budgets would be prepared in the light of the statement of basic assumptions issued for the budget period. It would be expected that in general the level of sales to be budgeted would be related to the expected general industry and economic conditions. However, there are many factors which do not follow the general patterns and which have marked effects upon specific products. For this reason the basic assumptions which will apply to sales must be stated in detail.

It would be expected that the sales of a fiberboard company would be influenced primarily by the level of building construction. However, repair and modernization would provide a substantial market for its products. This market would be influenced primarily by the level of personal income which may be expected to be high in the budget period while new construction may be dropping. Thus the adverse effect of a decline in new construction may be offset by an increase in the amount of repair and modernization. To the extent that it sold products for other than building, its volume would be affected by conditions in those markets. If the industrial specialties of a company were sold primarily for use in automobiles, the budget for those products would be based on estimated production of cars.

Another consideration in budgeting sales is the factors which are peculiar to a specific company or product. If a company has been doing considerably more advertising and sales promotion than its competitors and has been increasing its share of the market, the probable continuation of that trend must be considered in the sales budget. If it has developed a unique product which has high customer acceptance, sales of that product may be expected to run ahead of, or counter to, general business or industry conditions.

It follows then that basic assumptions on factors affecting sales are required for:

1. General business conditions
2. Conditions in each industry or market area served
3. Conditions peculiar to the company
4. Conditions peculiar to specific products

Correlation with Other Data

Sound business judgment influenced by the basic assumptions, rather than mathematical computations, must be relied upon in building the sales budget. However, correlation of sales with other data is a valuable aid in appraising conditions and arriving at sound conclusions. These data, in the form of index members or absolutes, should be used as guides whenever they are available, and constant research should be carried on to find correlations between sales and general economic data, industry statistics, or other external factors.

If a fiberboard company establishes that sales of its interior-finish materials for houses lag housing starts by 3 months, it has an excellent bench mark for budgeting sales of these products. The number of houses actually started is published, and many estimates of future starts are always available in trade and business publications. Thus sales for the immediate 3 months ahead can be forecast with reasonable certainty. For periods beyond this they can be related to the consensus of opinion as to new housing starts.

In selecting any series of data for use in sales forecasting it is essential to establish the correlation between sales and the data for a long period of time. This period should include periods of high and low general business activity. The most valuable data for budgeting sales are those for which the trend leads that of the sales being budgeted by from 3 months to a year. The number of new automobiles actually produced would be of little value to a manufacturer of automobile wheels as a guide in sales budgeting. The purchase and usage of the wheels is roughly coincident with the completion of the car. However, the estimates of cars to be produced could be used as a basis for budgeting sales.

Approximately coincident factors and inverse ratios to lagging factors are of interest and value in appraising actual sales performance. They are of little or no value in budgeting.

In establishing the correlation of sales to a leading indicator it is also necessary to establish the period of the lead, the consistency of this period, and the extent of deviation of the sales trend from that of the indicator. If the number of housing starts leads the sale of fiberboard interior finish by 3 months in the summer when the weather is favorable for construction, it may lead by 4 or 5 months in the winter when construction delays are common. Such variation in the lead period must be reflected in the sales budgets. Also, since some of the products are used for repair and renovation, some portion of the sales potential will not be affected by changes in housing starts. A drop of 10 points in housing starts may result in a change of only 7 points in the sale of fiberboard interior finish. Therefore correlation must be established as to direction, lead, and degree of variation from trend for a long period if the data are to be of real value in budgeting.

Unit Volume

The first step in building a sales budget is to establish the number of product units which will be sold. To the extent possible, correlation with outside data and historical statistics should be in terms of unit volume. This removes the effect of price variation from consideration and thus provides a more consistent basis of appraisal. Where no common unit of measurement exists for a product line, as for automobile gaskets which may range from spark-plug to oil-pan size, some sales unit must be derived. It may be that gross sales dollars are the only units which can be used. When this is true, correction to a common historical price level is necessary in order to show volume realistically.

Unit volumes would be budgeted by product lines and by divisions, territories, or other units of the company. Exhibit 21-1 illustrates a sales budget summary in terms of units of product.

EXHIBIT 21-1
19— SALES BUDGET SUMMARY—1,000 UNITS
BUILDING PRODUCTS DIVISION

	Exterior construction products		Interior finishes			Foundation board	Form board	Total
	Roof Insulation	Sheathing	Tile	Plank	Wallboard			
Budget:								
First 6 months:								
January	9,000	15,000	1,000	2,000	4,250	5,000	6,000	42,250
February	10,000	17,000	1,500	3,000	4,250	5,000	6,150	46,900
March	10,000	17,000	1,500	3,000	4,250	6,200	6,150	48,100
April	15,800	26,350	2,100	4,200	5,400	6,200	6,150	66,200
May	17,200	26,650	2,100	4,200	5,400	6,200	6,250	68,000
June	17,500	27,000	2,100	4,200	5,400	6,200	6,500	68,900
Total—first half	79,500	129,000	10,300	20,600	28,950	34,800	37,200	340,350
Third quarter	60,000	70,000	6,000	12,000	16,200	15,000	18,900	198,100
Fourth quarter	30,000	30,000	4,000	8,000	12,000	12,000	18,000	114,000
Total—second half	90,000	100,000	10,000	20,000	28,200	27,000	36,900	312,100
Total year	169,500	229,000	20,300	40,600	57,150	61,800	74,100	652,450
Prior Year Actual or Estimate:								
First half	80,000	127,300	11,600	21,900	26,300	32,100	8,900	308,100
Second half	85,000	106,000	9,200	18,700	24,100	29,400	22,400	294,800
Total	165,000	233,300	20,800	40,600	50,400	61,500	31,300	602,900
Five-year average:								
First half	71,600	110,700	12,500	22,100	23,900	31,800	——	272,600
Second half	82,300	97,600	10,000	19,300	21,100	30,200	——	260,500
Total	153,900	208,300	22,500	41,400	45,000	62,000	——	533,100

Product Mixture

A product line usually is made up of various sizes, gauges, colors, or qualities of the product, and these are sold at different prices per unit. It is indeed rare if a line consists entirely of a single product. Therefore, after the number of units of a line have been budgeted for a period, the second step is to estimate the mixture of products. Here, again, past experience will be a valuable but not infallible guide. Plans may call for the introduction of new items which will have a marked effect on the average mixture. Customer preferences may be changing. Equipment on which the products are used or with which they are sold may be changed in design. All these factors which influence mixture must be evaluated and reflected in the unit forecast. Reliance on a consistent averaging of mixture year after year could result in budgets which were completely unrealistic and unattainable.

This detail by specific items in a line is usually considered to be supplementary. It is not carried forward onto the budgets as submitted to the budget committee or executives.

Gross Sales Dollars

After unit volume and product mixture are budgeted, the next step is to estimate the gross sales dollars. Where prices are established, this step is simply the pricing of the specific items budgeted for each product line at the applicable list prices. When established prices are not available, the gross sales value of the units must be determined by reference to historical records or through the sales manager's estimate of prices which can be realized for each item. It could be that such an estimate would be delayed until cost estimates or the complete cost budgets are available and then be based on a markup on cost.

If budgets were developed in terms of gross sales dollars, because units could not be used, the initial determination stated in terms of a common price level must be brought into line with expected price levels. This is a work-sheet calculation, and the budget summary would show only the gross sales at the expected price level for the period.

Budgets by Territories

Budgets of gross sales dollars may be developed for the total company and for each product line, with these then allocated to sales territories. Or the budgets may first be built for each product line in each territory. These would then be added to arrive at totals for the company.

When figures are first developed by territories, judgment rather than external and internal data is the major determinant of the quantities, mixture, and prices to be budgeted. The territory manager is in close personal contact with his sales force and customers, and his budgets will tend to reflect their opinions. Also, external data with which budgets for the territory could be correlated are usually less readily available and less closely related to any one territory than they are to totals for the company. Thus, with a narrower approach and less guiding information the territory managers tend to inject either excessive optimism or excessive pessimism into their budgets. However, this is not necessarily true, and some companies have had excellent results with budgets built by their territory managers. It is not uncommon to accept the territory managers' budgets as goals and then modify them to bring the total to a realistic level for the company.

If the gross sales dollars are budgeted in total for each commodity at the company level they must be broken down to territories in order to measure individual performance in each area. This breakdown may be made on the basis of the ratio of actual sales realized in each territory. However, better territorial budgets are secured if the basis used to determine the share of the budget assignable to each territory gives recognition to the sales potential of a territory as well as to the actual performance in the territory. Many data are available for this purpose, such as buying-power index, bank clearings, construction awards, population, and Bureau of the Census statistics.

When total company sales are broken down to territories, consideration must be given to specific influences in each territory which could cause substantial deviation from average company product mixture. If none are uncovered, the better procedure is simply to break down the budgeted gross sales dollars. If substantial deviations do occur, the budget developed first at the company level should be limited to units. The determination of mixture and the application of prices would then be done for each territory.

Sales Deductions

With the exception of freight allowances, the budget of sales deductions must be based primarily on past experience and judgment. The amount of freight which will be allowed can be determined with relative accuracy on the basis of the sales budgeted for each territory. Other deductions would be budgeted in ratio to gross sales according to recent past experience. Modifications would be made for expected changes, such as tight money supply increasing the average credit period and reducing the cash discount taken. Usually sales deductions are budgeted in total for the company or a major unit of a company such as a division. They are then applied in equal ratio to the gross sales of each product. However, there may be circumstances when specific sales deductions budgets by product lines are necessary. This would be true if terms of sale were substantially different for different product lines.

Responsibility for Preparing Budgets

The sales manager has the direct responsibility for building sales budgets. He may seek advice and assistance from staff personnel, the economist, and the budget committee. However, the budget as submitted should be his budget.

In budgeting sales there is no exception to the fundamental principle of budgeting that those who are responsible for performance shall participate in the preparation of and approve the budgets for their area of responsibility. If a district manager is responsible for sales in his territory, the budget for that territory should be his budget, just as the total sales budget is the sales manager's. He should be given the basic assumptions for the budget period and data sheets showing such indices as are available and the historical record for his territory. With these data as background he would build the budget for his territory. If this is approved by the sales manager, it becomes the budget for the territory. If it is not, it is reviewed with the district manager, and an effort is made to secure his approval of changes. If he does not approve, the budget should be accepted as submitted and used for the measurement of his performance. When this occurs, adjustments should be made by product lines at the division or company level, so that the total sales budget will be one with which the sales manager agrees.

Approval of Budgets

The submission for review by the budget committee and company executives would be in summary form (Exhibit 21-1). In order to provide perspective for the appraisal, supplementary data sheets may be submitted with the budget. These may contain external data with which the budget was correlated or internal historical data.

If there is a budget committee, they should appraise the sales budgets before they are submitted to the company executives for final approval. If the budget committee does not agree with the budget, they may influence the sales manager to change it. However, since it is his budget, they should not, and would not, have the authority to order a change made. They would submit their recommended adjustments to the executives with the budget as prepared by the sales manager. The executives may or may not agree with the recommended adjustments of the budget committee. If they do not, the sales manager's budget will be used. If they do, company policy will determine the procedure to be followed. They may direct that the adjusted budget be used for all purposes during the period, or the sales manager's budget may be used for measuring his performance and the adjusted budget used for planning and control at the company level.

Reports and Comparisons

Actual sales by product lines, territories, salesmen, and classes of customers are secured from the records compiled as actual sales are recorded. These will be compared with the budgets and reported periodically to those having management responsibility. The number of internal reports and comparisons and the frequency of issuance will vary materially between companies, depending upon the needs and desires of management. The following would be the minimum reports for effective control:

1. *Daily net sales report* (Exhibit 21-2)

This report shows the actual net sales (gross billings less deductions) for the day and the month to date. It shows the estimated net sales for the month, which is an arithmetical projection of net sales to date in the month modified by known or expected circumstances. The final column shows the budget for the month. In the illustration the report is prepared by divisions of the company and for the total company. It may be pre-

EXHIBIT 21-2
DAILY NET SALES REPORT
MONTH OF MAY, 19—
(In thousands of dollars)

Billing days in month: 23   Billing days reported: 10

	Today	Actual to date	Estimate for month	Budget for month
Building Products Division.............	196	1,280	2,960	2,820
Acoustical Division....................	140	1,695	3,900	3,900
Industrial Specialties Division...........	248	1,204	3,230	4,590
Total............................	584	4,179	10,090	11,310

Comments: Sales of the Industrial Specialties Division will be lower than budgeted because of strikes at the plants of two major customers in the first week of the month. These strikes are now settled, and shipments are now being made at slightly above the expected levels.

pared by product lines, plants, or other units of the company. Its purpose is to inform the sales and production managers and company executives of the current sales level and trend. It also provides basic data used by the controller to prepare estimates of profit and loss during the month.

2. *Gross sales report* (Exhibit 21-3)

This report is a listing of the actual and budgeted gross sales for the current month (omitted in the illustration) and the year to date. Sales units and unit prices are shown for each product line having a common unit. Actual gross sales are secured from manually or mechanically prepared summaries of invoices. The budgeted figures are obtained from the approved sales budgets. The purpose of this report is to inform the sales manager and company executives of the ratio of actual to budgeted sales and localize the cause of deviations as to unit volume or price. It may also be used as a guide in scheduling production. It would also be used as a source of statistical data to provide background for budgeting future sales.

In addition to these two basic reports others showing actual and budgeted gross sales would be prepared as required by the extent of the breakdown of responsibility for sales and by the production organization for production scheduling and inventory control. These reports would provide data such as sales by salesman, geographical area, district office,

EXHIBIT 21-3

THE FIBERBOARD COMPANY

GROSS SALES REPORT

FIRST 4 MONTHS, 19—

	1,000 Units		Price		$000 Gross Sales	
	Actual	Budget	Actual	Budget	Actual	Budget
Building Products Division:						
Roof insulation..............	42,670	44,800	$64.00	$64.00	$ 2,731	$ 2,867
Sheathing..................	67,570	75,350	66.00	66.00	4,460	4,973
Tile......................	5,640	6,100	75.00	75.00	423	457
Plank.....................	11,470	12,200	70.00	70.00	803	854
Wallboard.................	16,780	18,150	65.00	65.00	1,091	1,180
Foundation board...........	20,710	22,400	59.00	59.00	1,222	1,322
Form board................	22,600	24,450	58.00	58.00	1,311	1,418
Total....................	187,440	203,450	———	———	$12,041	$13,071
Acoustical Division:						
Tile......................	120,110	122,100	$91.00	$95.00	$10,930	$11,600
Board.....................	56,050	34,880	86.00	86.00	4,820	3,000
Total....................	176,160	156,980	......	......	$15,750	$14,600
Industrial Specialties Division:*						
Automotive.................	127,250	......	$73.57	......	$ 9,362	$ 8,000
Refrigeration..............	116,530	......	52.06	......	6,066	11,000
Transportation.............	78,400	......	50.00	......	3,920	4,000
Other.....................	16,000	......	51.00	......	816	1,000
Total....................	338,180	......	......	......	$20,164	$24,000
Total company.............	701,780	......	......	......	$47,955	$51,671

* Units not budgeted.

class of customer, specific customer, and warehouse or factory from which shipment was made. The codes as applied to the invoices would provide for the summarization of all required data by code number. A similar coding of budget data would permit the preparation of all sales budget reports by mechanical methods. This is usually one of the first applications of machine accounting in a company and the one which provides the most evident opportunity for cost savings in comparison with manual summarization. Extensive use of charts and graphs is also made in this area for reporting and summarizing performance.

Long-range Budgets

In addition to the sales budgets prepared for each current budget period long-range budgets are also required for management planning. These are less precise and detailed than the current budgets. They will usually be set as to ranges of activity (probable high, average, and low) rather than as specific units or dollars for each year or the period of years. This indicates the possible extremes within which management must plan and indicates alternative courses of action which may be required if either the high or low level is reached. Also, long-range sales budgets are usually prepared only for the total company or for major units of the company, and not by product lines. Keeping the long-range budget on a broad basis as to major units of the company provides for an averaging out of sales of items within the unit. Of course the unit must not be so broad that it makes definite planning impossible. For example, if two or more plants produce products for one sales division, a sales budget for that division would be of little value in considering the probable range of operating activity of each of the plants.

The sales budget for the current period or for a span of years is intended to set the tone of the basic planning in all areas of a company. In its development and use a fine balance must be struck between usefulness of detail for management purposes and the cost, delay, and confusion of recording and analyzing excessive detail.

REVIEW QUESTIONS

1. What are the purposes of a sales budget?
2. To what extent is the sales budget based on past experience?
3. What factors influence the length of the period for which sales are budgeted?
4. How are external data used to determine and appraise the sales budget?
5. Why are sales units better than sales dollars for correlation with external data and historical trends?
6. To what extent should sales be budgeted by individual products rather than by product lines?
7. Is it better to build budgets by territories and combine these for the company sales budget or to budget the total company sales first and then allocate them to territories?
8. Why should gross sales and sales deductions be budgeted separately rather than simply net sales?
9. Who should build the sales budget?
10. What procedures can be followed in using the budgets if management does not approve the budgets as submitted by the sales organization?
11. What management purposes are served by a daily report of net sales?
12. Why should both units and dollars be shown on sales budget reports?

13. What are the purposes of a long-range sales budget?
14. To what extent is the amount of detail different in a short-range sales budget from that in a long-range budget?

PROBLEMS

1. The budget committee of the fiberboard company has prepared the following basic assumptions for next year:

National growth plus the momentum of current heavy buying by business and consumers assures continuation of at least present sales levels for business generally through the first half of next year, but the "confidence" factor will assume major proportions in shaping developments thereafter. There is a growing belief that the recent upsurge in general business will reach its highest point no later than July of next year, to be followed by a period of leveling or slight decline during the closing months of next year. The slow-up in business is expected to result from a fairly abrupt halt in inventory accumulation next spring or summer, leading to reduced orders and production.

In summary, over-all buying and output will continue at, or at no more than, 1 to 2% above present levels through next year. The expected improvement in sales opportunities will be at a lower rate than during the past year, when general business increased more than 5%.

Further general economic expansion will be limited by (*a*) capacity operations in many industries, (*b*) moderate declines in automobiles and new-home building, (*c*) some restraint on business expansion of new facilities because of concern over narrowing profit margins, (*d*) some adverse consumer reaction to advancing prices, and (*e*) relatively tight money and credit conditions.

Consumer spending, however, holds the real key to next year's business. Despite some general credit restrictions, total consumer purchasing power will increase slightly to a new record level. Hence the coming year will see further opportunities for expanded sales and profits but on a much more selective basis than during recent months. Uncertainty, surprises, and shocks, especially on the political front and in the securities markets, will disturb business confidence from time to time but will not interfere seriously with the progress of companies geared to "growth" markets and offering new and improved products. Substantial further gains in sales and especially profits, however, will require a high degree of management skill in the absence of a rapidly expanding national economy.

DETAILED ASSUMPTIONS:

a. Total Construction (new plus "fix-up") will increase slightly to establish another record level.

(1) *Nonfarm housing starts* (1,500,000 in this year) will show a moderate decline to 1,400,000 next year, largely because of mortgage and construction credit restrictions. The dollar volume, however, should compare favorably with this year's level, because more larger homes will be built and building costs and selling prices will be somewhat higher.

(2) *Nonresidential building* (schools, churches, hospitals, commercial structures, industrial plants, etc.) will hold at about present levels through next year.

(3) *Fix-up activity* also will increase 10% or more, because more property owners will recognize the need to modernize and repair homes to offset obsolescence and declining values induced by the growing volume of new homes and the public acceptance of modern styling in home building.

b. *General Cost-Price Relationships* will not improve, particularly where any adverse volume trend develops. Further increases in raw material and labor costs will occur, but competitive pressures and consumer resistance will limit increases in final product prices.

GENERAL OBSERVATIONS:

The general business outlook points to the need for:

a. Unusually close attention to changing market trends and prompt action to reflect them in operations throughout next year

b. New and improved products and allied merchandising-promotion programs ready for prompt introduction

c. Redoubled efforts to:
(1) Reduce costs
(2) Adjust prices promptly to reflect unavoidable cost increases
(3) Correct, if possible, or weed out unprofitable situations
(4) Capitalize fully on the most profitable sales opportunities
Historical data are shown in Table P21-1.

TABLE P21-1

Past years	Gross national product, billions of dollars	Housing starts	Millions of square feet		
			Building products	Acoustical products	Industrial products
5	390	1,100,000	132	160	92
4	380	1,000,000	130	170	89
3	395	1,000,000	135	175	93
2	405	1,500,000	195	180	95
1	425	1,500,000	200	200	100

The company's building-products sales are about 40% for new homes, 30% for repair and modernization, and 30% for nonresidential construction.

The following sales budget, in millions of square feet, is submitted for next year: building products, 225; acoustical products, 210; and industrial products, 102.

In the light of the basic assumption and the historical record, does the forecast for each group appear to be reasonable? Explain.

2. A gross sales report for a month is shown in Table P21-2.

TABLE P21-2
GROSS SALES

Product	Budget			Actual		
	Units	Price	Dollars	Units	Price	Dollars
A	20,000	1.50	$ 30,000	12,000	1.50	$ 18,000
B	60,000	1.25	75,000	80,000	1.25	100,000
C	50,000	2.00	100,000	40,000	2.00	80,000
D	10,000	3.00	30,000	12,000	2.50	30,000
E	10,000	3.10	31,000	8,000	3.00	24,000
Total.....	150,000	——	$266,000	152,000	——	$252,000

Analyze and explain the reasons why the budgeted sales were not achieved.

CHAPTER 22

The Factory Cost Budget

The factory cost budget is a compilation and analysis of the factory costs planned to be incurred during the budget period. To the extent that changes are planned in quantities of processed inventory, the factory cost budget will differ from the budgeted factory cost of goods sold. Standard costs and factory expense budgets should provide the basic data for developing the factory cost budget. For the development of a well-coordinated management plan for the budget period, it is essential that the factory cost budget be built in detail by work centers, by areas of responsibility for costs, and by the detailed components of cost in each center or area.

It is unlikely that a company which does not develop standard costs and expense budgets would have a budget program which would include a factory cost budget. In such unusual circumstances the factory cost budget can only be based on past experience modified by expected or planned changes.

Level of Activity

The first step in the building of the factory cost budget is to calculate the volume of production expected in each work center and for each commodity or product group. Two factors determine this: (1) the budgeted sales volume and (2) planned changes in quantities on inventory.

The units of finished product as contained in the sales budget are adjusted for planned changes in inventory and for scrap losses in the production cycle to calculate the budgeted activity for each operation. This calculation is illustrated in Exhibit 22-1. It is an oversimplified illustration in that only three product lines are included. In practice the computation would be made for individual products of each product line. Groupings can be made only to the extent that all items in a group have the same raw material, scrap and production specifications. However, the procedure would follow the illustration, working from the budgeted sales of each product.

If it is expected that activity during the budget period will be approximately the same from month to month, the operational activity can be determined in total for the period. However, if there are marked variations in the figures of each month, it will be necessary to calculate operational activity by months. This will indicate the months when overtime,

EXHIBIT 22-1

MOBILE PLANT

BUDGETED ACTIVITY BY OPERATION

Operation		Unit	Wall-board	Roof insu-lation	Acous-tical tile	Total
522	Shipping (Sales budget)	1,000 sq ft	30,400	10,600	29,000	70,000
	Less: Estimated opening inventory	1,000 sq ft	5,000	2,000	4,000	11,000
			25,400	8,600	25,000	59,000
	Add: Planned closing inventory	1,000 sq ft	6,000	2,000	6,000	14,000
521	Warehousing (finished production)	1,000 sq ft	31,400	10,600	31,000	73,000
520	Wrap and pack	1,000 sq ft	31,400	10,600	31,000	73,000
423	Paint—Finished production	1,000 sq ft	31,400	——	31,000	62,400
	Scrap—4%					
	Gross production	1,000 sq ft	32,708	——	32,292	65,000
422	Sand and bevel—Finished production	1,000 sq ft	——	——	32,292	32,292
	Scrap—5%					
	Gross production	1,000 sq ft	——	——	33,992	33,992
	—Blanks—opening inventory	1,000 sq ft	——	——	500	
	—Blanks—closing inventory	1,000 sq ft	——	——	33,492	
					1,000	
					34,492	
420	Preparation	——		10,600	——	10,600
333	Dry saw—Finished production	1,000 sq ft	32,708	10,600	34,492	77,800
	—Trim loss—2%					
	—Gross production	1,000 sq ft	33,376	10,816	35,196	79,388
331-2-3	Forming, drying, dry saw—Hours per 1,000 sq ft		0.0278	0.0436	0.0333	
	Forming, drying, dry saw	Hours	928	472	1,172	2,572
220	Grinding—lb pulp per 1,000 sq ft	——	500	950	400	
	Grinding	1,000 lb	16,688	10,275	14,078	41,041

extra days, and extra shifts will be required to achieve the required production level. It will also prove valuable in planning for building and reducing inventory during months of the budget period so as to level production as much as possible.

Another purpose of the determination of activity by operations by months is to indicate bottlenecks. The production budget for the period, in units, may be well below the over-all rated capacity for the same period. However, when product-line mixture in the budget is considered, it may be found to place demands on one or more operations which cannot be met. This calls for a revision of the sales forecast to secure a mixture which can be produced and a redirection of sales effort so as actually to sell the necessary mixture. Or, capacity of some operations may be inadequate only in some of the months. Higher production must then be planned in preceding months so as to build inventory to meet the demands in the peak months of the period. This inventory building may be of finished products or of semifinished products if the bottleneck exists in operations at the beginning of the production sequence. It may also be possible that some portion of the peak requirements cannot be met even if inventory is built to maximum levels in prior months. Plans will then have to be made to purchase semiprocessed material, component parts, or even finished products. Such prior planning and provision to meet the peak requirements will provide the only possibility of meeting the budgeted sales volume.

Exhibit 22-2
Mobile Plant
Raw Material Budget

	1,000 sq ft	Per 1,000 sq ft	Quantity required
Pulpwood—41,041,000 lb pulp—yield 1,428 lb per cord..........................	——	——	28,740 cords
Margose—Wallboard.....................	33,376	3.0 lb	100,128
Acoustical tile..................	35,196	2.0 lb	70,392
			170,520 lb
Alpod—Wallboard......................	33,376	1.0 lb	33,376
Roof insulation...................	10,816	2.0 lb	21,632
			55,008 lb
Rekol—Wallboard......................	33,376	2.0 lb	66,752
Acoustical tile..................	35,196	3.0 lb	105,588
			172,340 lb
No. 4 Paint—Wallboard..................	32,708	1.0 gal	32,708 gal
No. 1 Paint—Acoustical tile..............	32,292	2.0 gal	64,584 gal
Sealer—Roof insulation...................	10,600	5.0 lb	53,000 lb

Direct Material

The budgeted usage of direct materials is calculated by applying standard or experienced formulas or quantities of each material to the gross production quantities as determined for each operation (Exhibit 22-2). Summaries of budgeted usage are then prepared from these calculations and the usage is adjusted for planned changes in raw-material inventory to arrive at the quantities to be purchased during the budget period (Exhibit 22-3).

The exercise of many of the elements of material-cost control discussed in earlier chapters is in large measure dependent upon these usage and purchase determinations. When production is expected to be fairly constant during the budget period, the direct-material requirements can be computed for the entire period and assumed to be even by months. With marked fluctuations in production budgets, usage and purchase must be calculated for each month. In either case, these data are used to plan quantities to be purchased on each order, the purchase of bulk or pack-

EXHIBIT 22-3
MOBILE PLANT
PURCHASE BUDGET

Material	Unit	Planned closing inventory	Budgeted usage	Total	Estimated opening inventory	Budgeted purchases
Pulpwood..........	Cords	2,000	28,740	30,740	2,100	28,640
Margose............	Lb	10,000	170,520	180,520	9,020	171,500
Alpod..............	Lb	5,000	55,008	60,008	6,195	53,813
Rekol..............	Lb	10,000	172,340	182,340	9,360	172,980
No. 4 paint........	Gal	3,000	32,708	35,708	4,008	31,700
No. 1 paint........	Gal	5,000	64,584	69,584	4,584	65,000
Sealer.............	Lb	3,000	53,000	56,000	2,000	54,000

aged materials, storage methods and space requirements, and sources of supply. They are also essential in determining inventory planning for valuation purposes, particularly if lifo valuations are used.

Finally, the quantities of material to be used, priced at expected purchase prices, will provide the material cost of production, and the planned purchases will provide the raw-material costs to be reflected in the development of a cash budget.

Direct Labor

The activity computed for each operation is also the basis for budgeting direct labor costs. In many instances the product units must be expressed as time units before they can be used for planning labor costs. This is accomplished through the application of standard or experienced machine speeds or output per man-hour to the production units at budgeted activity levels. Where special worker skills are required, the computations must be made for these individually, both to plan the work force properly and also to secure accurate costs. Exhibit 22-4 illustrates the computation of the direct labor requirements for the board-forming operation of the Mobile plant of the fiberboard company. Here square feet of production are first converted into hours of machine operation. These hours are then converted into direct labor hours for each skill or job classification represented in the forming-machine crew. These budgeted direct labor hours, when priced at the respective job rates, provide the budgeted direct labor cost for this operation. These calculations for

EXHIBIT 22-4
MOBILE PLANT
DIRECT LABOR BUDGET
FORMING OPERATION

	Wall-board	Roof insu-lation	Acous-tical tile	Total labor hours	Rate	Direct labor cost
Machine-hours...............	978	950	400			
Labor crew:						
Machine tender............	1	1	1			
Pulp operator..............	1	1	1			
Wet-saw operator..........	1	1	1			
Helpers...................	3	2	2			
Direct labor hours:						
Machine tenders...........	978	950	400	2,228	2.10	$ 4,679
Pulp operators.............	978	950	400	2,228	1.90	4,233
Wet-saw operators..........	978	950	400	2,228	1.80	4,010
Helpers...................	2,934	1,800	800	5,534	1.60	8,854
Total...............						$21,776

all of the operations are summarized to arrive at the total direct labor budget for the plant.

Factory Expense

When flexible factory expense budgets are available, the budgeted dollars of factory expense are calculated by expense components from the flexible budget data for each operation. These calculations are made for both the productive and service operations and are summarized into the factory expense cost for the budget period. The procedure is the same as that of calculating factory expense budget allowances as illustrated in Chapter 15, "Control of Factory Expense." If factory expense budgets are not developed it is necessary to build an estimate of expense by operations for the budgeted levels of activity on the basis of past experience or engineered studies of requirements. Such calculations result in fixed budgets.

While the development of the cost of factory expense by expense sources at the budget level is adequate for budgeting total factory cost, it should be supplemented by more detail to be of maximum value for management purposes. For example, the budgeted indirect labor cost should be detailed as to types of indirect labor for use in planning the work force for the budget period.

Total Factory Cost

The detailed calculation of direct material, direct labor, and factory expense costs provides both the total budgeted factory cost and specific data for management planning. If the program of budgetary planning and control has not developed to the point where such detailed data would be used for planning, the procedure can be simplified. This is accomplished by applying unit total product costs (Chapter 11) to the budgeted production of each product for the period. If unit standard product costs are not developed, adjusted experienced unit costs must be used. In either case the budgeted factory cost may be calculated in total or by cost elements.

When standard costs are used, either by operation or by products, consideration must be given to probable variances from the standards. This raises the question as to why variances should be expected, since in discussing attainable standard costs it was stated that they should reflect efficient production and cost levels expected to prevail on the average for the period for which they were set. Variances from attainable standards may be budgeted because of:

1. Changes in production or product specifications which were not known when the standards were built
2. The extent to which cost reduction was anticipated, which may not be realized in the budget period
3. Unexpected changes in raw-material prices or wage rates
4. Difference between budgeted volume of production and expense absorption volume

Also, basic standards may be used for a period of years for accounting and reporting purposes with perfection standards or current unit standards used to implement cost control. Here again, it would be necessary to budget expected variances from such basic standard costs to arrive at the total budgeted factory cost.

Budgeted Material Variances

In connection with raw materials, the first consideration is expected deviations in quantities used. These may result from a consistent histori-

cal record of failure to meet standard quantities, from anticipated variations in the quality or characteristics of raw materials, from tighter
inspection standards causing more scrap losses, etc. The accountants
working with the production supervisors and their staffs determine these
expected variances in quantities of material. The quantities required at
standard specifications are then adjusted upward or downward to arrive
at the quantities to be reflected in the cost budget.

Expected purchase prices at the time the cost budget is built may also
be different from those used for the material rates built into the unit cost
standards. Such differences would be caused by substantial changes in
market conditions resulting from external and uncontrollable factors such
as strikes, crop failures, or government regulations. They would have to
be of importance in the profit of a product line to be reflected in the cost
budget. The standard purchase prices were based on judgment. At the
time of building the cost budget, judgment again must be used. Both sets
of prices will be different from those which will actually be experienced.
Therefore, unless substantial deviations are indicated, no purpose is
served by making changes.

The budgeted material usage and price deviations are reflected by
product lines so as to provide for the preparation of a profit budget by
product lines.

Budgeted Labor Variances

Standard labor costs would be appraised in the light of performance
experience in each operation, planned changes in production methods,
and known changes in wage rates. Where there has been a definite record of failure to attain standard efficiency, it would be unrealistic to
budget costs at standard. A factor should be added to bring the labor
cost to the efficiency level which is expected to be achieved. Where
changes in production equipment or process specifications are planned
which have not been reflected in the standards, they should be incorpo-
rated in the cost budgets. Wage rates reflected in the budget should be
those in effect when it is built. If a change in wage levels has occurred
since the unit standard costs were built, it should be reflected. However,
changes in wage levels should not be anticipated. The wage rates incor-
porated in a factory cost budget tend to become known rather generally
through the factory. Reflection of an increase or decrease could cause
embarrassing and difficult labor-relations problems.

Budgeted Expense Variances

Expenses reflected in the cost budget would be adjusted for differences
in wage rates, price levels, and factory volume. Any changes in wage
levels, as reflected for direct labor, would also be reflected for the indirect labor component of the expense standards. Changes in price levels

which would affect the cost of expense materials and purchased services are usually not sufficient to require adjustment to these expense components of attainable standard costs. However, if there has been a marked change since the standard costs were built, an adjustment should be made.

Factory volume is the most significant factor to be considered as a cause of expected expense deviations in the cost budget. With absorption costing the expense rates which are included in the unit standard product costs are determined at expense absorption volume. Therefore, to the extent that production is higher or lower than expense absorption volume, the standard costs as applied to the budgeted units of production will result in the application of more or less expense than will be allowed in the expense budgets or than should be incurred if expense control is effective. In Exhibit 22-1 the activity is calculated for the dry-saw operation of the fiberboard plant at 2,572 hours for the budget period of 1 year. Assuming the activity level used for expense absorption for this operation is 2,080 hours per year, the excess of budgeted activity over standard activity, or 492 hours times the standard fixed expense rate of $2 per hour, equals the budgeted overabsorption of expense, a volume gain of $984.

Expected Variances Related to Sales Volume

All the expected or budgeted variances are calculated on the budgeted volume of production. To the extent that this differs from the budgeted sales volume, they will be high or low in relation to the standard cost of goods sold. If it is the policy of the company to reflect variances in the period in which they occurred, then no adjustment of the budgeted variances calculated on production volume is required in calculating factory cost of sales. If it is the policy to reflect variances in inventory values until the material is sold, then if the budget contemplates an increase in inventories, the portion of the variances applicable to the increase must be removed from budgeted profit and loss of the period.

Period Expense under Direct Costing

If direct costing is followed, with the fixed or period factory expense excluded from inventory values, the dollars of period expense expected to be incurred during the budget period must be calculated. This requires a breakdown of the production budget by months to determine the number of shifts to be worked in each month, the amount of overtime work, and the amount of sixth- and seventh-day work required to meet the production budget of each month. From these activity levels of each factory operation, the dollars of period expense are determined by applying the period expense budgets to the respective activity levels. Exhibit 22-5 is based on direct costing.

Budgeted Cost Reduction

Consideration has been given, up to this point, to budgeting variances for relatively specific factors—price changes, wage-rate changes, historical efficiency variance trends, and volume variances. In many cost budgets an additional variance is reflected, the variance expected to result from cost-reduction programs. The necessity for this and the extent to which such variances are budgeted depends upon circumstances peculiar to each company. If the technical and production staffs have a consistent record of methods improvement, estimated variances may have to be reflected in the budgets to provide a realistic profit budget. Also, at times these will be reflected at the request of top management if the profit budget is not acceptable. In this instance they will represent "tasks" for the production department.

These variances expected to result from cost-reduction programs usually cannot be reflected by cost elements nor by individual factory operations. They are unknown and indefinite, or they would have been reflected in the standards or in the budgeted variances by cost elements. It is customary to reflect them in total only for each plant.

Responsibility for Building Factory Cost Budgets

The building of factory cost budgets should be under the direction of the person responsible for the accounting and budgeting functions in the factory. In a small single-plant company or a company having its budget functions centralized, this would be the chief accounting officer. In multiplant decentralized companies, it would be the plant controller or chief works accountant.

While the budget building is under the direction of the accounting or budgeting personnel, it requires the active participation of the production supervisors and factory-staff personnel. They are the only ones who are qualified to estimate what actual costs will be if standards are not used, or what deviations may be expected if standards have been built. As with the development of all budgets, the persons responsible for meeting them should participate in building them. For this reason, much effectiveness is lost if the general-office accounting or budgeting staff attempts to build a plant cost budget in the general office on the basis of data secured from the plant.

Summarization and Approval

Whether factory costs are budgeted as direct material and labor and expense cost elements by operations or as total standard factory costs adjusted for expected variances, they must be summarized for presentation to, and approval by, those having cost and profit responsibility. The summary form will be determined by the wishes of those who are to approve the budgets and by the nature of periodic reports to be made of actual performance. An example is shown as Exhibit 22-5 illustrating a summary of the budgeted standard costs of production and sales, of budgeted variances from standard direct cost, and of the dollars of period expense. This summary may also contain comparable data for one or more prior periods to provide a basis for appraising the budgeted costs and variances.

EXHIBIT 22-5

MOBILE PLANT

SUMMARY OF BUDGET FOR 19—

Square feet finished production	73,000,000
Square feet sales	70,000,000
Standard direct cost of production	$3,239,496
Standard direct cost of sales	3,229,134
Budgeted variances:	
Raw material usage	$ 6,000
Scrap	(8,000)*
Direct expense	48,000
Total production	$ 46,000
Raw material prices	(450,000)
Total variance from standard direct cost	$ (404,000)
Period expense	$3,759,000

* Parentheses denote gains.

The summaries provide the factory costs included in the profit budget. They are also used from month to month during the budget period in reporting and interpreting factory-cost performance in reports to top management.

REVIEW QUESTIONS

1. What purposes are served by the factory cost budget?
2. What two factors determine the level of activity for which the factory cost budget is built?
3. Why is it desirable to calculate the budgeted activity for each month of the budget period?
4. How does the use of standard costs expedite the building of the factory cost budget?
5. Discuss the relative merits of two methods of determining budgeted factory costs.

6. Why would variances from standard costs and expense budgets be budgeted?
7. What effect does direct costing have on the budget-building procedures for factory costs?
8. What effect will variations from budgeted sales volume have on budgeted factory costs?

PROBLEMS

1. A plastics molding company budgets the following unit sales for a quarter: product A, 50,000; product B, 100,000; and product C, 10,000. Inventories of finished stock at the beginning of the period are: A, 4,000; B, 12,000; and C, 2,000. It is planned to increase the inventory of A 1,000 units, to reduce B 2,000 units, and to make no change in C.

The seven factory operations in sequence of production are preforming, flat-bed molding or rotary molding, finishing, inspecting, packing, and shipping. For flat-bed molding the plastic molding powder is formed into pellets in the preforming operation. Products made by the rotary-molding process are molded directly from powder. A and C are rotary-molded and B is flat-bed-molded.

Standards allow for a 2% loss between the molding and finishing operations for all products. An allowance of 5% is provided for all products for scrap after inspection. Products are packed before being placed in finished-stock inventory.

Determine to the nearest 100 units the budgeted production of each product in each operation.

2. Production time standards are given in Table P22-2 for the plastics company of Problem 1.

TABLE P22-2

	A	B	C
Units per machine-hour:			
Preforming.................	———	200	
Flat-bed molding..........	———	50	
Rotary molding............	10	———	5
Units per labor hour:			
Finishing.................	12	30	10
Inspecting................	50	200	50
Packing..................	100	500	200

The company has four flat-bed presses, seven rotary-molding machines, and one preforming machine. All other operations are handwork.

Determine for the quarter (*a*) the operating schedules for preforming, flat-bed molding, and rotary molding and (*b*) the labor requirements of the finishing, inspecting, and packing operations, for the activity calculated in Problem 1.

CHAPTER 23

The Operating Budget

The operating budget is the coordinated plan of operations of a company for a budget period. It provides the profit budget for the company and for its units and product lines through consolidating the sales, factory cost, distribution expense, and administrative expense budgets and including all other items of income and expense which have not been reflected in the other budgets. However, it is not limited to the budgeting of profit, since it includes the plans for purchasing and for changes in inventory levels. It is developed concurrently with the other budgets rather than from them after they are completed. To a degree it affects the building of other budgets, particularly the factory cost budget.

An operating budget which is built in total for a period of 6 months or a year does not provide sufficient detail for planning purchasing, production, and inventories. The differences in quantities sold in different months will affect the amount of finished-stock inventory which must be available in some months to meet peak customer demands. Production schedules must be set so as to level production for the budget period in so far as possible, rather than have it fluctuate with sales. This requires inventory building in some months and inventory reduction in others. If because of limitations in warehouse space or other reasons it is not possible to build sufficient inventory to meet demands in peak months, overtime work must be scheduled. Major maintenance work must be scheduled for months when equipment will be available. Purchases of raw materials should be made at opportune times but must be geared to usage and to available storage space. All these factors make it necessary to build an operating budget for each month of the budget period rather than in total for the full period.

Responsibility for Inventory Quantities

The placement of responsibility for quantities of inventory varies greatly from company to company. In small companies the president or general manager may decide how much inventory will be carried. In larger companies there may be a production planning manager who makes the decisions, or a multiunit company may place the responsibility with a production planning manager in each unit and have no centralized responsibility. Large companies frequently have an inventory-policy committee (sometimes the budget committee) which formulates the basic inventory policies, which are then administered by the production planning manager or managers.

Those responsible for inventory planning formulate the policies in the light of (1) the basic assumptions for the budget period, (2) the sales budget, (3) stabilization of the labor force, (4) past experience in raw-material markets and transportation, and (5) available storage space.

Planning Raw-materials Inventories

The basic assumptions for the budget period as to expected general business and specific industry conditions will indicate the extent to which raw-material prices may be expected to change. This will influence the plans for changes in quantities of raw material on inventory so as to realize the lowest average prices. If prices are expected to decline, minimum quantities would be carried, and conversely maximum quantities would be carried if prices are expected to increase.

Past experience with respect to raw-material markets also influences the quantities planned to be on hand at any one time. Seasonal factors would have a marked bearing. For example, a fiberboard company located in the South may build inventory of pulpwood during the summer, fall, or early winter to meet its requirements during the spring when rains interfere with or prevent the cutting of timber.

The time required to receive materials after an order is placed would determine the minimum stock levels at which orders are placed. This would be at the quantity which would be needed to service production from the date of placing the order to the date of receipt of the material. In practice some quantity above this minimum is usually specified to provide insurance against unusual delays in delivery.

In the preceding chapter Exhibit 22-1 illustrated the breakdown of planned production to operations. The raw-material requirements are determined from this schedule by applying the formula, or bill, of materials to the units indicated for each product. The planned inventory level then is the number of days' supply required to service production plus quantities for protection against seasonal influences and changes in prices.

Turnover (usage divided by inventory) is frequently used as a measure of inventory control. It is an adequate guide only if raw-material inventories are to be held at a constant ratio to usage. If this is not done because of market conditions, separate goal turnover ratios must be established for each month, or comparisons must be made of actual with planned quantities expressed in units or dollar values.

Planning Processed-materials Inventories

The sales budget usually has the greatest influence on decisions as to the quantity of finished stock on inventory. Stocks must be adequate to ship customer orders at least as promptly as they would be shipped by competitors. Also, periods of peak sales may be in excess of production capacity, and thus stocks must be built up in other periods to meet the peak demands. Or, if the sales budget indicates lower volume than is being experienced, it may be desirable to reduce inventories. All such decisions must be made in the light of their effect on the labor force. If production is to be stabilized over a year so as to avoid layoffs and hirings, plans must be made to produce at approximately the same level throughout the year with variations between sales and production covered by building and reducing inventories.

Inventories of work in process will be determined for the most part by the length of the production cycle. However, semiprocessed inventories may be carried to compensate for unbalance in production equipment or for customer service where the specifications of the finished product are determined by the customers' orders. In a fiberboard plant the speed of the forming machine may be in excess of that of certain units of the finishing operations. Under that condition board may be processed through the dry saw and carried on inventory in large blanks for subsequent finishing. For industrial specialties stocks of large boards of different thicknesses may be carried to be cut to customers' specification as orders are received, so as to service customers without waiting until the required board could be scheduled for production on the forming machine.

Finished-stock or semiprocessed-material quantities will also be influenced by expected changes in raw-material prices or in processing costs. Building inventories prior to cost increases will result in lower average costs for a period. Also, it is frequently possible to overcome limitations in raw-material storage space by "storing" the materials in work in process or finished stock.

As for raw material, turnover provides a measurement of control but is an inadequate measurement when changes in quantities are planned which are not in ratio to changes in sales volume.

Budgets Required by Company Units

Unless a company is manufacturing only one product in one plant, an operating budget for an entire company will not require sufficient detailed planning nor provide adequate bases for measuring performance to be of maximum value as a tool of management. Each manager who has profit responsibility should have an operating budget for his division or factory. This will set forth the plans for his unit as if it were a separate business and thus permit him to manage effectively and to receive reports which show specifically how his unit is performing in relation to its budget.

Frequently reference was made in preceding chapters to the determination of income and costs by product lines. Complete operating budgets cannot be built by product lines because of the usage by several lines of the same raw materials and the manufacture of different products on the same production line. Reasonably accurate profit budgets can be developed for each product line, and these are essential to effective planning and control. It is most unusual for two product lines to have the same ratio of total factory cost or of direct factory cost to net sales. Therefore deviations from the sales budget of a product line will affect the composite gross profit.

Demands of product lines on production facilities vary because of the use of different equipment or because of different production speeds. Also, distribution and administrative expenses are not uniform by product lines. Some products require more selling effort, or more advertising, or more research, or more engineering than others. Therefore, only a full allocation of all factory, distribution, and administrative expenses will provide true product-line profits.

A composite budget or a budget which does not reflect the allocation of all expenses will provide no explanation of deviations in the gross-profit or net-profit ratios. Neither will it provide guidance for management decisions on pricing, sales promotion, selective selling, product-line changes, or expansion.

It follows then that an effective operating budget is supported by detailed inventory plans for each unit where inventories are controlled and by profit budgets by areas of profit responsibility and by product lines within those areas.

Sales Income

Since the sales budget is developed for both gross and net sales for the budget period, it can be used without modification in preparing the profit budget. In the multiproduct company the sales budget for the company or for a unit of the company is usually rather detailed as to sizes, patterns, models, colors, etc. It is usually neither practicable nor desirable to develop profit budgets for each of these. Instead they are grouped into product lines and profit budgets built for each line. For example, the fiberboard company may prepare a sales budget for each of three patterns of acoustical tile. They may have slightly different sales prices and direct factory costs but would be produced on the same equipment and be marketed through identical channels. For the profit budget these would be grouped as a product line.

The number of product lines for which profit budgets are built will be determined by the extent to which specific products can be grouped logically and by the relative importance of the specific product. Frequently there are a number of specific products which are not related and individually are not significant as to sales income or profit. It is usually expedient to bring these together as a product line in the profit budget with a designation such as All Other or Miscellaneous.

Factory Costs

The factory cost budget reflects the expected costs of producing commodities at the budgeted level of production activity. If no changes in processed inventory are planned, these costs will also be the ones which are included in the profit budget. However, if there is a difference between the quantities to be produced and the quantities to be sold, adjustment of the budgeted factory costs is necessary in building the profit budget.

Exhibit 23-1 is a typical data sheet for summarizing the cost of sales of a product line for the profit budget. It is to be noted that it is set up for a company using direct costing. A data sheet for absorption costing is shown as Exhibit 23-3.

The "standard direct cost of sales" is determined by applying the product standard costs to the units budgeted to be sold. Where more than one product is included in a product line, the application of costs should be made by specific products as detailed in the sales budget. These product costs would then be summarized by the product lines of the profit budget (Exhibit 23-2). This provides a standard cost of sales which is related directly to the budgeted sales income. If this is not done, some averaging of standard costs is necessary to reflect the unit average standard cost of the product line. Such averaging usually requires as much time as the detailed application of standard costs and is less accurate.

If it is company policy to reflect variances in profit and loss of the period in which they occur, the variances in the factory cost budget can be taken directly into the profit budget. If it is the policy to defer variances applicable to quantities added to inventory, then if inventory is to be increased, the portion of the variances in the factory cost budget which are applicable to the quantities added to inventory must be removed from the costs included in the profit budget. If inventories of processed materials are to be reduced and there are deferred variances at the beginning of the budget period, the portion applicable to the quantities to be sold or used from inventory must be added to the budgeted cost of sales for the budget period.

Variances from the standard purchase prices of raw materials are sometimes treated differently from production variances. Even though no other variances are deferred, those due to purchase prices may be. They are then reflected in profit and loss when the raw materials are used, rather than when they are purchased. When purchase variances

EXHIBIT 23-1

BUDGETED FACTORY COST OF SALES—SECOND 6 MONTHS, 19—
BUILDING PRODUCTS DIVISION
EXTERIOR CONSTRUCTION PRODUCTS
(Direct costing)

	Quantity	Unit	Rate	Amount
Standard direct cost of sales:				
Roof insulation............................	10,600,000	sq ft	$40.27/M	$ 426,862
Sheathing...............................	12,900,000	sq ft	41.00	528,900
Total.................................	23,500,000	——	——	955,762
Budgeted production variance—(gains) losses:				
Material—6.7 % less Margose in roof insulation.	10,600,000	sq ft	$ 0.322/M	$ (3,413)
Labor—5 % increase in forming speed—sheathing......................................	12,900,000	sq ft	0.0355/M	(458)
Scrap—1 % instead of standard 2 % roof insulation at preparation.....................	109,010	sq ft	37.62/M	(4,101)
Direct expense (see labor).................	12,900,000	sq ft	0.238/M	(3,070)
Total.................................	——	——	——	$(11,042)
Purchasing—pulpwood usage..............	18,140	Cords	0.25	$(4,535)
package materials—5 % increase	——	——	——	1,521
Total.....................	——	——	——	$(3,014)
Period expense:				
Base budget.............................	——	——	——	$ 262,915
Unbudgeted machine overhaul..............	——	——	——	4,033
Added by production on two Saturdays.......	——	——	——	2,947
Total.................................	——	——	——	$ 269,895
Total factory cost.....................	——	——	——	$1,211,601

are significant and there are substantial differences between the quantities purchased and those used in some months, this is the more desirable procedure. It eliminates gains or losses which are not relative to the production of a month.

Under direct costing the total dollars of factory period expense reflected in the factory cost budget will be taken directly into the profit budget, since period expenses are charged to operations of the period in which they are incurred.

All of the foregoing discussion was based on using standard costs. Where these are not used, the factory costs reflected in the profit budget can be based only on past experience modified by known or planned changes. When this procedure is followed factory costs are usually determined as a percentage of net sales income.

Distribution and Administrative Expenses

If there are no variable costs in the distribution and administrative expense budgets, the budgeted expenses as distributed to product line are carried directly into the profit budget. If there are variable items, such as commissions, the variable rates are applied to the budgeted sales to determine the variable costs to be reflected in the profit budget. These are then added to the fixed costs by product lines to arrive at the total distribution and administrative expense reflected in the profit budget for each line.

Other Income and Expense

If other income and expense items, which are not included in the sales or cost budgets, are significant either in total or for a product line, they should be reflected in the profit budget. Some of these can be budgeted rather accurately; others can only be estimated roughly on the basis of experience. However, the best possible estimate should be reflected in the profit budget.

An example of an item which could be budgeted rather accurately would be the income from the sale of scrap metal by a company producing metal-clad automobile gaskets. As gaskets are die-cut from sheets or rolls, there is trim from the edges and scrap from bolt holes and other openings. The weight of such scrap varies directly with production, and experience will indicate the weight which will be produced at the budgeted volume. This weight, priced at the expected sales price, would determine the amount of income from this source to be reflected in the profit budget.

If a company has excess cash invested in securities, the income is determinable. Likewise, if there are bank loans or funded debt, the interest expense is determinable.

Frequently the items of other income and expense which can be budgeted rather accurately are the only ones which are significant, and all others can be ignored in the profit budget. However, if experience indicates that other items are usually realized or incurred, an estimated net amount may be added to give greater accuracy to the budget.

Taxes on Income

It is generally accepted that taxes on income are a cost. True, they are a cost which is incurred only if a profit is realized, but if the objective of business is to earn the optimum profit and if this objective is achieved, the income tax cost will be incurred. The treatment of tax as a cost is recognized in the Accounting Research Bulletin of the American Institute of Accountants, which states, "Income taxes are an expense that should be allocated, when necessary and practicable, to income and other accounts, as other expenses are allocated."

Income taxes, like other costs, can be recovered only in the selling price of the product and so must be included in costs used to set selling prices. There is one difference, but it is only a difference of time: As income tax rates change, there tends to be a greater lag in reflecting the cost changes in selling prices than is experienced when other costs change. For example, when the excess profits tax expired at the end of 1953, most companies which had been subject to the tax gained an after-tax profit advantage. But as competition intensified, sales prices were reduced to the extent of part or all of the tax relief; or, as other costs increased, sales prices were not increased. Gradually over a relatively short period the effect on after-tax profits of the demise of the excess profits tax was lost.

Since taxes on income are a cost of doing business successfully, they should be reflected in the profit budget as well as in reports of actual earnings. At the corporate level this presents no problem, for income tax rates are known or can be anticipated on the basis of pending tax legislation. For units of a company—divisions, plants, or product lines—the problem is a bit more involved. State taxes on income will vary by states and must be computed for each unit of the business specifically as that unit gives rise to taxable income. Since the basic data must be assembled to file the state tax returns, these data provide an equitable basis for budgeting state taxes on income by company units. One further factor must be considered, both for state and Federal taxes on income, and that is products which show a loss. Since taxes are assessed for the corporate entity, its taxable profits are the net of gains and losses of its units. It follows then that units for which a loss is budgeted should receive a credit for the amount by which such losses reduce the tax of the corporation. Assuming a Federal tax rate of 50% and no state taxes on income, a unit which shows a profit before tax of $1,000 will have a profit after tax of $500, and a unit which shows a before-tax loss of $800 will show an after-tax loss of $400.

Interpreting the Profit Budget

The profit budgets are placed in perspective and can be explained more readily to management if they are related to actual experience of some past period. In Exhibit 23-2, a profit budget for the second 6 months of a year, the budget is related to actual experience for the first 4 months of the year projected to 6 months. This period was selected

Exhibit 23-2
Comparison of Budget with Prior Period
Building Products Division
Exterior Construction Products
(Direct costing)

	Budget—2d 6 months		Actual—first 4 months projected to 6 months	
Unit sales......................	23,500,000		21,000,000	
Average net sales price per 1,000....	$ 63.87		$ 64.52	
Net sales.......................	$1,501,000	100 %	$1,355,000	100 %
Standard direct cost of sales........	955,762	63.6	853,700	63.0
Variance (gain) loss—production....	(11,042)	(0.7)	6,119	0.4
—purchasing....	(3,014)	(0.2)	(2,997)	(0.2)
Actual direct cost of sales.........	941,706	62.7	856,822	63.2
Gross margin (marginal contribution)	559,294	37.3	498,178	36.7
Period expenses—factory...........	269,895	18.0	262,915	19.4
—distribution.......	105,010	7.0	108,012	8.0
—administrative....	59,891	4.0	58,897	4.3
Miscellaneous (income) expense.....	——	——	(8,112)	(0.6)
Profit before tax..................	124,498	8.3	76,466	5.6
Profit after tax...................	62,249	4.1	38,233	2.8

Budget (Higher) Lower than Projected Actual

Net sales........................	$ (146,000)	
Profit before tax—total...........	$ (48,032)	
Due to:		
Sales volume...............	(59,675)	
Sales price.................	15,900	
Sales mixture..............	(163)	
Efficiency.................	(13,128)	
Purchase prices.............	(17)	
Production volume...........	2,947	
Distribution and administrative expense.................	(2,008)	
Miscellaneous income expense...	8,112	

in this instance because it is the most recent period for which actual figures are available when the budget is prepared, and it was not affected by seasonal or other factors. If seasonal or other factors make it inadvisable to use a recent period for comparison, then a period should be selected in which conditions more nearly approximate those anticipated in the period for which the profit budget is being prepared.

COMPARISON WITH PRIOR PERIOD

The right-hand columns of the form show the actual income, cost, and profit for the period selected for comparison. These are taken directly from internal reports for that period. On the lower portion of the illustration the effect of the difference in sales is shown, and the difference in profit before tax is analyzed as to causes. The material for this analysis is taken from the data sheets supporting the budget and from the work papers for the period with which the comparison is made.

The illustration is for a product line, Exterior Construction Products, of the building products division of the fiberboard company. This product line is assumed to include two specific products, roof insulation and sheathing, with different cost-price relationships. The detailed sales budget and the actual sales detail are shown in Table 23-1. The standard

TABLE 23-1

	Budget			Projected actual		
	1,000 Units	Per 1,000	Amount	1,000 Units	Per 1,000	Amount
Roof insulation ..	10,600	$62.50	$ 662,500	10,000	$64.00	$ 640,000
Sheathing.......	12,900	65.00	838,500	11,000	65.00	715,000
Total.........	23,500	———	$1,501,000	21,000	———	$1,355,000

direct costs are shown in Exhibit 23-1 as $40.27 for roof insulation and $41.00 for sheathing. These were applied to the product units for the two periods to calculate the standard direct costs of sales for the two periods shown in Exhibit 23-2. The standard gross margin dollars are $545,238 for the budget period and $501,300 for the projected actual, an increase of $43,938. This added contribution to profit is separated into that due to volume, to price, and to mixture.

The average standard gross margin for the projected actual period is $23.87 per 1,000 units ($501,300 ÷ 21,000,000). The increase in unit volume is 2,500,000. This unit increase at the experienced average standard gross margin gives a contribution of the higher volume to profit of $59,675.

Sales prices on roof insulation are budgeted at $1.50 per 1,000 lower than those experienced. For the budgeted volume of 10,600,000 units of this product this results in an adverse effect on profits of $15,900.

The combined effect volume and price is $59,675 minus $15,900, or $43,775. The difference between the increase in standard gross margin of $43,938 and the $43,775, or $163, is due to mixture. In the budget

TABLE 23-2

	Increased sales units	Standard gross margin	Volume contribution
Roof insulation............	600,000	$23.73	$14,238
Sheathing.................	1,900,000	24.00	45,600
Total.................	——	——	$59,838
Total at actual margin......	2,500,000	$23.87	$59,675
Difference due to mixture....	——	——	$ 163

EXHIBIT 23-3
BUDGETED FACTORY COST OF SALES—SECOND 6 MONTHS 19—
BUILDING PRODUCTS DIVISION
EXTERIOR CONSTRUCTION PRODUCTS
(Absorption costing)

	Quantity	Unit	Rate	Amount	
Standard cost of sales:					
Roof insulation.......................	10,600,000	Sq.Ft.	51.84/M	$ 549,504	
Sheathing...........................	12,900,000	Sq.Ft.	52.87/M	682,023	
Total............................	23,500,000			$1,231,527	
Budgeted variances (gains) losses:					
Material—6.7 % less Margose in roof insulation...........................	10,600,000	Sq.Ft.	0.322/M	$ (3,413)	
Labor—5 % increase in forming speed—sheathing..........................	12,900,000	Sq.Ft.	0.0355/M	(458)	
Scrap—1 % instead of standard 2 %—roof insulation..........................	109,010	Sq.Ft.	37.62/M	(4,101)	
Direct expense (see labor)...............	12,900,000	Sq.Ft.	0.238/M	(3,070)	
				$ (11,042)	
Purchasing—Pulpwood Usage...........	18,140	Cords	0.25	(4,535)	
Package material—5 % increase.................	——	——	——	1,521	(3,014)
Fixed expense—Base budget overabsorbed*	——	——	——	(12,850)	
Unbudgeted machine overhaul.................	——	——	——	4,033	
Added by production on two Saturdays.........	——	——	——	2,947	(5,870)
Total factory cost...................	——	——	——	——	$1,211,601

* Calculation of overabsorbed fixed expense:

Absorbed—Roof insulation.....................	10,600,000	$11.57	$122,642
Sheathing........................	12,900,000	11.87	153,123
			$275,765
Base budget—standard fixed expense............	——	——	262,915
Overabsorbed (volume gain).................	——	——	$(12,850)

approximately 54.9% of the units are sheathing, while in the prior period sheathing accounted for about 53.3% of the total. The greater percentage of sheathing, which has a better standard gross margin, yields a profit contribution due to mixture of products sold. This was calculated above by deduction. It can be proved as in Table 23-2. It is to be noted that the standard gross margin for roof insulation in this calculation is based on the experienced price of $64.00, not on the lower budgeted price. The effect of price on volume is segregated in the specific calculation of the effect of the price change on profit.

EXHIBIT 23-4
COMPARISON OF BUDGET WITH PRIOR PERIOD
BUILDING PRODUCTS DIVISION
EXTERIOR CONSTRUCTION PRODUCTS
(Absorption costing)

	Budget—2d 6 months		Actual—first 4 months projected to 6 months	
Unit sales....................	23,500,000	———	21,000,000	
Average net sales price per 1,000....	$ 63.87	———	$ 64.52	
Net sales........................	$1,501,000	100 %	$1,355,000	100 %
Standard cost of sales.............	1,231,527	82.0	1,099,970	81.2
Variance (gains) losses:				
Production efficiency............	(11,042)	(0.7)	6,119	0.4
Purchasing....................	(3,014)	(0.2)	(2,997)	(0.2)
Fixed expense.................	(5,870)	(0.4)	16,645	1.3
Actual cost of sales..............	1,211,601	80.7	1,119,737	82.7
Gross profit....................	289,399	19.3	235,263	17.3
Distribution expense..............	105,010	7.0	108,012	8.0
Administrative expense............	59,891	4.0	58,897	4.3
Miscellaneous (income) expense.....	———	———	(8,112)	(0.6)
Profit before tax.................	124,498	8.3	76,466	5.6
Profit after tax..................	62,249	4.1	38,233	2.8

The effects of efficiency, purchase prices, and production volume on profit are calculated from the data shown in Exhibit 23-1. The changes in distribution and administrative expenses and miscellaneous income are taken from similar supporting schedules which are not illustrated. In presentation the reports would be accompanied by appropriate interpretative comments.

The illustrations (Exhibits 23-1 and 23-2) for the profit budget and the analysis of the causes of changes in profit were based on a direct-cost system. If absorption costing were used, the procedures for analysis would be almost identical. In each instance, where standard direct cost is used under direct costing, total standard cost would be used under absorption costing. A factory volume variance resulting from the difference between absorbed and standard fixed expense would be calculated for each period (Exhibit 23-3). In this illustration it as assumed that there was no difference between production and sales volumes in either the budget period or the actual period. The difference between the unit standard direct costs in Exhibit 23-1 and the unit total standard costs in Exhibit 23-3 is the standard fixed expense rate per unit.

Exhibit 23-4 illustrates the comparison of the budgeted and actual operating statements under absorption costing. In the actual period the only fixed expense variance was an underabsorption of $16,645 due to the lower-than-expense-absorption volume of production. The analysis of the difference between budgeted and actual profit would be exactly as shown under direct costing in Exhibit 23-2. The determination of the contribution of the added sales volume in Exhibit 23-4 is shown in Table 23-3.

TABLE 23-3

CONTRIBUTION OF ADDED VOLUME TO PROFIT

(Absorption costing)

Difference in standard gross profit......................	$(14,443)
Add back effect of price reduction......................	15,900
	(30,343)
Deduct contribution from mixture.......................	(163)
	(30,180)
Add difference in fixed expense volume variance...........	(29,495)
Profit contribution of added volume.....................	$(59,675)

REVIEW QUESTIONS

1. Describe the operating budget.
2. What factors must be considered in planning the quantities of raw-material inventories?
3. When should semiprocessed and finished-stock inventories be correlated with raw-material inventories?
4. Why should an operating budget be built for each unit of a company?
5. To what extent and why are operating budgets required by product lines?
6. What differences may exist between the budgeted factory costs and the cost of goods sold reflected in the profit budget?
7. What advantages are gained by applying standard costs to specific products rather than to product lines to determine the budgeted standard cost of goods sold?
8. Why should taxes on income be included in the profit budget?
9. What management purposes are served by comparing the operating budget with actual results of a prior period?

PROBLEMS

1. A company uses two raw materials, X and Y. They are purchased in carload lots of 40,000 pounds each. The operating budget indicates a level usage over the next 6 months of 120,000 pounds per week of X and 480,000 pounds per week of Y. The budget reflects an expected price increase of 10% for X as of April 1 and of 5% for Y as of July 1, with these prices to hold for the remainder of the year.

Inventories are estimated to be 480,000 pounds of X and 1,440,000 pounds of Y at January 1, normal amounts to service operations. Maximum storage capacity is 1,000,000 pounds of X and 2,400,000 pounds of Y.

What should the purchasing plan be to minimize the effect of the price increase without creating unnecessary problems in unloading and storing the raw materials and for the suppliers in producing and shipping them?

TABLE P23-2

	Budget, first 6 months, 19—			Actual, last 6 months, 19—		
	Units	Rate	Dollars	Units	Rate	Dollars
Net sales..........................	1,000,000	$11.00	$11,000,000	900,000	$10.00	$9,000,000
Standard direct cost of sales:						
Material......................	———	2.70	2,700,000	———	2.20	1,980,000
Labor........................	———	1.05	1,050,000	———	1.00	900,000
Expense......................	———	.65	650,000	———	.60	540,000
Total.......................	———	$ 4.40	$ 4,400,000	———	$ 3.80	$3,420,000
Standard gross margin............	———	6.60	6,600,000	———	6.20	5,580,000
Production variances..............	———	———	(10,000)	———	———	30,000
Purchasing variance..............	———	———	———	———	———	50,000
Adjusted gross margin............	———	———	6,610,000	———	———	5,500,000
Factory period expense............	———	———	3,400,000	———	———	3,200,000
Distribution expense..............	———	———	1,000,000	———	———	950,000
Administrative expense............	———	———	500,000	———	———	450,000
Other (income) expense............	———	———	60,000	———	———	(10,000)
Profit before tax.................	———	———	1,650,000	———	———	910,000
Provision for income tax...........	———	———	825,000	———	———	455,000
Profit after tax...................	———	———	825,000	———	———	455,000
Period expense detail:						
Salaries......................	———	———	210,000	———	———	200,000
Indirect labor.................	———	———	630,000	———	———	500,000
Maintenance labor.............	———	———	651,000	———	———	600,000
Other........................	———	———	1,909,000	———	———	1,900,000

2. Table P23-2 shows a single-product company's operating budget for the first 6 months of a year in comparison with actual operating results for the last half of the prior year.

Supplemental data are:

a. Purchase prices of a raw material are budgeted at $0.05 per pound higher than the standard cost of the prior period. Ten pounds of this material are used per unit of finished stock.

b. Wages were increased 5% as of the first of the year for which the budget is built.

c. Standard direct expense in the actual period included $0.20 of indirect labor per finished unit of product.

d. Unit standards are the same for both periods.

e. The volume of both periods falls within an operating schedule of three 40-hour shifts per week.

f. No changes are planned in inventory levels.

Prepare an analysis of the difference in before-tax profit of the two periods.

CHAPTER 24

Measurement and
Control of Profit

The ultimate objective of a budgetary planning and control program is the measurement and control of profit. Thus far the emphasis has been on building sound budgets for income and costs and managing the enterprise so as not to have deviations from these which would affect profit adversely. With this concept profit is a residual. It may be appraised as satisfactory or unsatisfactory on the basis of judgment and past experience, but it is not subjected to any definitive measurement. Such residual profits are not apt to be optimum profits. The probability of realizing optimum profits is substantially greater if they are planned as a percentage of return on the capital employed to produce them and the business is managed with the objective of achieving this planned ratio.

A few American corporations have used return on investment or capital employed for measuring and controlling profits for many years. As a result they have been unusually successful. Their employees at all levels have enjoyed relatively high incomes; their stockholders have received high dividends and have had substantial appreciation in their equity. These companies have had outstanding growth records, supplying more and more products at competitive prices which contributed to the improvement of the economy of the nation and the general standard of living. With this demonstrated record of the effectiveness of profit measurement and control it is difficult to understand why companies have been so slow in using it. It is only recently that it has been receiving increased attention and has begun to be used by a growing number of companies.

The importance which companies are placing on return on investment and profitable growth is indicated in the following quotation from the May, 1955, Federal Trade Commission *Report on Corporate Mergers and Acquisitions:*

The General Foods Corp.'s aggressive acquisition policy appears to be matched by an equally active divestment policy based on continuing survey of the rates of return on its capital investments. In a statement made by a spokesman for the corporation in November 1953, it was pointed out that the firm's pattern for development required that it achieve growth through profitability rather than merely through increased sales, and that it is interested in acquiring other companies with long profit margins rather than those with large sales and short profits. In this connection, in the corporation's 1953 annual report it is pointed out that as a business grows and acquires new product lines, its character constantly undergoes changes, and that the company must examine itself periodically to make sure that each operation continues to contribute its share to the company's profitability and growth. It is pointed out further, that, as a result of such a study during the previous year, General Foods decided to dispose of several businesses whose rates of earnings on the funds invested were below the level considered adequate for growth.

Bases of Measurement

The best basis of measurement of business profits for management purposes is the ratio of profit *after tax* to total assets. It reflects the effectiveness of management for any business in which capital is significant. It would not be applicable for a business such as a law firm where personal ability is the determinant of income and capital is insignificant.

Per cent profit on sales is the profit measurement most frequently used in reports and analyses. This varies between industries—the food-processing industry has a low ratio of profit on sales and the chemical industry a high ratio. Within a company with different products it will vary between products. Also, the ratio of profit to sales gives no consideration to the amount of capital used to produce the sales and profit. Prolific investment in a product or a company may produce a high ratio of profit to sales, but the ratio of profit to investment would be relatively low.

To meet the failure of the ratio of profit to sales to give recognition to investment and in an endeavor to equate between industries, the ratio of profit to tangible net worth is frequently used. Profit measured by this gauge indicates how effectively the funds which have been provided by the owners, through both investment and undistributed earnings, have been employed. This is a sound basis of appraisal for the equity investor. However, it does not consider capital provided by other sources. One company will elect debt financing and another equity financing. Both may be using the same amount of total assets in relation to their sales or to their profits; yet the ratio of profit to net worth would be quite different. In a recent year two companies in the same industry showed returns on net worth of 11.5% and 24.0%. The first had used equity financing; the second had used debt. The leverage from debt at a low interest rate resulted in the high return on net worth of the second. When profits were related to total assets, the first showed a return of 6.8% and the other 7.9%, more nearly comparable ratios. Profit accruing from the use of nonequity capital is the one source of funds which can be used to retire loans and increase working capital coincident with an increase in stockholder equity.

For management purposes the source of funds is not important in measuring and controlling profit. What is important is how profitably all funds are being used irrespective of whether they were supplied by stockholders, borrowing, or trade creditors. The use of total assets as the basis of measurement accomplishes this.

Capital Employed

The capital employed by a company is the sum of its assets as shown on its balance sheet. Some companies refer to this as "investment" and refer to the ratio of profit to investment as "return on investment." This tends to be misleading, for it may be interpreted as the return on the stockholders' investment.

Use of the total assets shown on the balance sheet means that each asset account is taken after deducting the applicable valuation reserves. Accounts receivable are net of provision for bad debts. Inventories are at the balance sheet values, and a company using the lifo basis of determining cost would probably have a lower capital employed than one with the same quantities of the same materials costed on the fifo basis. Fixed-asset accounts are taken as net of the provision for depreciation.

The use of gross asset values as capital employed would mean that profits of a period, which have been reduced by the additions made to the respective valuation reserves during the period, were not being measured against comparable assets. Additions to reserve provisions are costs, and the transfer of any amount from an asset account to a cost account reduces the asset.

Some companies use net asset values for all except fixed assets. For the latter they use cost. Two reasons are given for this: First, in periods of rising prices original cost is closer to replacement cost than is depreciated value. This is simply compromising a situation. If they desire to measure return against replacement values of the assets, they should state all assets at replacement values. This may be of value for company purposes but could not be used for comparison with returns of other companies, since it would be impossible to determine the replacement values of assets of others. Second, fixed assets are taken at cost, because it provides a better basis of comparison of units of the company, some of which may have new assets and others older and well-depreciated assets. This too is correcting only one phase of a problem. Older production facilities are generally less efficient and require more maintenance than new ones. The use of original cost penalizes the unit using older facilities, in that it has higher costs and thus lower profits. If these are measured against depreciated values, its return is more nearly comparable with that of a newer unit.

At the company level the use of the cost of fixed assets results in a doubling of some part of capital employed. The depreciation which has been recovered in costs is in some other asset account. It may be in inventories, accounts receivable, or cash; or it may have moved into cash and then been invested in other fixed assets. The use of the depreciated value of the fixed assets provides a much fairer basis of measurement.

Assets used for calculating return on capital employed should be averaged over the period in so far as possible. Year-end figures may be high or low because of management decision or because of peculiarities and seasonal influences of the industry. Within a company a 12-month moving average provides a very satisfactory basis of measurement and removes the pressure of units of the company to have low inventory or other asset accounts at the end of a year and to ignore asset values during the year. When comparisons are made with the returns of other companies their assets should also be averaged in so far as possible, considering the number of times during a year at which they publish balance sheets.

Formula for Return on Capital Employed

While the return on capital employed is the ratio of profit after tax to total assets, it is usually shown as the result of its component factors—per cent profit on sales and turnover. The formula for return on capital employed is:

$$\frac{\text{Profit}}{\text{Sales}} = \text{per cent profit on sales}$$

$$\frac{\text{Sales (annualized)}}{\text{Total assets}} = \text{turnover}$$

Per cent profit on sales $\times$ turnover $=$ return on capital employed

Both the per cent profit on sales and turnover are significant ratios. They help to localize the sources of changes in return and can be used in making comparison with operations of similar businesses.

It is evident from the formula that the intensity of use of capital, turnover, is just as important as profit on sales in determining the return achieved. In a recent year a food-processing company had a profit on sales of 2.3% and a turnover of 3.90, giving them a return of 8.97%; a chemical company had a profit on sales of 12.0% and a turnover of 0.74, resulting in a return of 8.88%. Both were using their capital with approximately equal effectiveness but achieving their return differently because of the different nature of their business.

Within an industry individual companies will achieve their returns by different methods. Those with the best returns will usually show both a high profit and a high turnover ratio. However, some will have a relatively low ratio for one of the factors and compensate for this with a high ratio for the other.

What Is a Satisfactory Return on Capital?

If profits are to be measured and controlled, there should be some method of determining the optimum and the maximum return on capital employed. Unfortunately, no formula has been developed which will do this. Judgment, based on comparisons with other companies and the experience of the company, is the only method of selecting optimum and maximum return-on-capital-employed objectives. The major factors to be considered are:

1. The best and the average returns of all companies
2. The best and average returns of similar industries
3. The company position in the industry
4. The competitive value of patents or secret processes of the company
5. The possibility of new businesses entering the field and becoming significant competitors

The Federal Trade Commission and Securities and Exchange Commission publish reports of profits, assets, and equity of all companies by asset value of the companies and by industry groups. The 1954 average return on capital employed for all manufacturing companies was 6.55%. The return on capital employed of some well-known companies for the years 1952, 1953, and 1954, listed in the sequence of their 1954 return on capital, is shown in Table 24-1.

There is sufficient evidence in published corporate reports that the type of industry does not determine the return on capital employed which may be expected in that industry. Companies with high, average, and low returns are found in every industry. The return achieved is the result of management, and no company should feel that its return is satisfactory until it is in the upper quartile of all companies. However, there is evidence that companies which have a very small percentage of an industry do not usually realize a high return. There is also evidence in some industries that the average return for the industry is low and only a very few companies are achieving a high return.

A company with patent protection on its products and processes or with secret processes should realize a higher return than its competitors who do not have these advantages. This higher return is the reward for developing or purchasing these advantages.

The possibility of new businesses entering the field and becoming significant competitors is determined by industry rather than by individual company considerations. In recent years it has proven virtually

TABLE 24-1
PER CENT RETURN ON CAPITAL EMPLOYED

	1952	1953	1954
E. I. du Pont	13.5	13.2	18.2
General Motors	14.6	14.2	16.9
International Paper	11.3	13.1	13.9
Eastman Kodak	9.7	9.9	12.9
General Electric	9.6	10.1	12.5
Texas Company	11.0	10.9	12.1
J. C. Penney	10.8	10.8	11.9
Phelps Dodge	10.4	11.4	11.7
Kennecott Copper	12.4	12.2	10.5
Caterpillar Tractor	8.7	7.9	9.6
Continental Oil	11.3	10.6	9.4
Crown Zellerbach	9.3	10.0	9.2
B. F. Goodrich	8.3	8.4	8.6
International Business Machines	7.3	7.2	8.6
Merck & Company	7.0	7.4	8.5
Borden	6.2	7.0	7.6
Union Carbide & Carbon	9.6	9.1	7.4
Westinghouse Electric	6.2	6.0	6.5
Monsanto Chemical	7.5	7.4	6.4
Dow Chemical	5.4	4.6	5.0
Deere & Company	8.6	5.7	4.8
American Viscose	7.4	4.6	3.9
Chrysler	9.4	8.3	1.9

impossible for a new company to achieve success in the manufacture of automobiles. In contrast a number of new food-store chains have been started and have achieved marked success.

Because of these varied influences on return on capital employed, a company with a broad product line should not expect to realize the same return on all products. Separate objectives need to be established for each line and for the total company.

The maximum average return over the period of a business cycle should not be so high that it subsidizes inefficient competitors or invites new competition. As a rule of thumb, it would appear that a return on capital of 20% in a product line is almost the maximum that should be expected to be held over a period of years, even with patent protection. For total company return, the historical pattern is a range of from 10% to 15% for companies which are generally considered to be successful growth companies.

Allocation of Capital Employed

Throughout the discussion of income and costs emphasis was placed on reporting profits by product lines as a guide to management. With return on capital employed used as a measure and control of profits, it is necessary to allocate assets to product lines to calculate the return for each line. For internal purposes this establishes each product line as a separate business.

Cash is usually allocated to product lines on sales or cost of sales. Cost of sales more nearly reflects the demands for cash, since it is not necessary to finance profit. The actual dollars of cash and government securities shown on the balance sheet may be distributed, or a standard ratio of cash to sales or cost may be applied. In the latter procedure there may be a residual or deficit of cash at the company level. Consideration is sometimes given in manufacturing companies to different products on the basis of whether they are manufactured and sold, purchased and carried on inventory for resale, or shipped from suppliers' stocks as they are sold. The first would carry the highest ratio of cash, the second a lesser ratio, and the third the least.

Accounts receivable are usually allocated on sales dollars, giving consideration to different credit terms on each product line.

Inventories of finished goods are specific by product lines. Semiprocessed materials may be used for a specific line or for several lines. In the latter case they are allocated on the basis of usage. Raw materials and supplies are allocated on usage.

Fixed-asset values are first assigned to the operations of the company according to the location of the assets and then allocated to product lines on the same bases used to allocate the fixed expenses of those operations. This procedure is followed for production operations, sales offices, and general-office items.

Prepaid expenses may be considered to be covered in the ratios used for cash or may be allocated specifically according to their character, e.g., prepaid property insurance on the basis of insurable values.

Miscellaneous assets which may be applicable to product lines can usually be assigned specifically. If not, some general allocation base is selected, or they are carried at the company level as unallocated.

Approach to Building the Profit Budget

The measurement and control of profit through the use of return on capital employed requires a special approach to the building of the profit budget. After the basic assumptions are available, estimated attainable goal percentages of return on capital would be set for each product, plant, division, or other unit of the company for which profit is measured, as well as for the total company. These goals would be based upon the long-range return objective of the company, weighted by:

1. The present level of return
2. The historical trend of return
3. The future outlook in general and as specifically applied to the unit of the business for which the goal is developed

When the goals are developed, accepted, and approved, they become the guides for the remainder of the budget-building procedure. The result is a rather marked change in the attitude toward the elements of the budget. The objective return on capital is constantly influencing the planning in each area. Instead of budgeting sales which could be secured through established marketing techniques, promotions and other sales stimuli are planned for certain products so as to secure the best possible average margin. Costs are considered in the light of what can be incurred, rather than as what should be allowed to provide a "comfortable" budget. Capital expenditures are weighed against the increase in capital and the resultant decline in turnover, and their potential contribution to higher profits. In short, the setting of the goals has a psychological effect throughout the company, and attitudes in the final analysis are the determinants of success.

As the profit budgets for units of the company are completed, the budgeted return is compared with the goal. If it is lower, management at the division or plant level can take action to revise the plans to achieve the goals or will have a detailed explanation as to why the goal appears to be unattainable. When the budgets are presented for top-management approval, they may be expected to be realistic and not contain "padding" which can be removed if top management is not satisfied with the profits budgeted.

Another consideration is the possibility of budgeting too high a return on a product line. When the budget indicates a return which is above the optimum or the maximum considered to be safe, it can be examined as to the reasons for it. These may indicate that the high return should be accepted for the budget period because of unusual circumstances, for example, a high volume of business which is not likely to be continued over a long period of time. On the other hand, if the budget reflects sound plans for lower costs, which will result in exceptional margins, consideration may be given to planning certain price reductions so as to retain or increase the share of the market. If planned, the effects would be reflected in the sales budget before it was finalized for the period.

Long-range Planning

Profit measurement and control should not be limited to the span of the budget period. Long-range objectives for return on capital should be set. These would then provide a guide for planning to add products to, or drop products from, the line, for market research and development, for capital expenditures, for cost reduction and expansion, and for corporate financing. They would change the desire to grow for growth's sake to a planned growth for profits' sake. In this connection the return on capital employed will have a marked effect on the capital appropriations and expenditures budget as discussed in the next chapter.

REVIEW QUESTIONS

1. Why is the per cent profit on sales an inadequate ratio for profit measurement?
2. What is the principal use of the ratio of profit to tangible net worth?
3. Define capital employed.
4. What are the reasons for and against including property, plant, and equipment in capital employed at cost rather than at depreciated value?
5. Why are total assets as of any one date not a proper base for determining return on capital employed?
6. What is meant by turnover as a factor in return on capital employed? Why is it important?
7. What factors determine the return on capital employed that should be set as the objective of a company?
8. Should a company expect to earn the same return on capital employed each year? Why?
9. Can each company unit be expected to realize approximately the same return on capital employed?
10. How may fixed asset values be allocated to product lines or company units?
11. How does return on capital employed as a measurement of profit tend to change the approach to budget building?
12. How does the return-on-capital-employed ratio aid in determining the optimum profit of a company or unit of a company?

PROBLEMS

1. The monthly balance sheets of a company show average total assets for a year of $100,000. Sales for the year were $160,000, and profit after tax was

$9,760. For the next year sales are budgeted at $186,000 and profit after tax at $11,532. The budgeted balance sheets show average total assets of $120,000.

If the budgeted amounts are realized, what will be the change in return on capital employed, and what will be the reasons for the change?

2. For a year a company had sales of $600,000. Its variable costs were $300,000, and its fixed costs were $240,000. Its income tax rate was 50%. The capital employed was $500,000.

The president wishes to establish an objective of 1½ percentage points improvement in return on capital employed. What change would be required to achieve his objective:

   a. In sales volume with no change in variable cost rates or capital employed?

   b. In costs with no change in sales income or capital employed?

   c. In capital employed with no change in costs or sales volume?

CHAPTER 25

Capital Expenditures and Financial Budgets

The capital expenditures budget represents the plans for the appropriations and expenditures for fixed assets during the budget period. The financial budget is the plan of financial operations developed to assure adequate funds to meet the requirements for the budget period indicated by all the other budgets. Since the capital expenditures budget may call for substantial funds, it is developed, at least tentatively, prior to the building of the financial budget. However, as a matter of sound business management, no capital expenditure which will yield a return on capital employed equal to, or in excess of, the company objective should be omitted because of a shortage of cash. On the other hand, desirable but nonessential capital expenditures may be deferred if there is a shortage of cash. Therefore, the two budgets are closely interrelated, and neither can be finalized until each has been prepared on a tentative basis and evaluated in the light of the other.

CAPITAL EXPENDITURES BUDGET

Purpose

The purpose of the capital expenditures budget is to provide:

1. A basis for the evaluation of proposed capital expenditures and the establishment of priorities in the execution of the capital program so that essential needs will be met and the optimum return on capital employed will be realized

2. A means of controlling capital expenditures

3. A basis for planning the financing of the capital-expenditures program

4. A valuation of fixed assets for the budgeted balance sheet

Capital expenditures are an immediate transfer from working capital to fixed assets of funds which will flow back into working capital over a relatively long period of time through the recovery of depreciation in the prices of goods or services sold. Therefore, they must be considered both as to their immediate and their long-range effect on the company. Such consideration is largely in the area of management judgment, but the judgment will more often be sound if it is based on careful evaluation of expected results. The capital budget, as a plan of capital expenditure, details the expected expenditures so that each can be appraised. Control is then effected by relating actual expenditures to those budgeted and by comparing actual results attained with those stated as the justification of the expenditures.

Responsibility

The final approval and acceptance of the capital budget rests with top management. This may be the president of the company, the treasurer, the executive committee, or the finance committee. Even with a divisional organization structure it is the usual practice to require approval at a level above the division manager. The demand for funds and the provision of funds is a corporate problem and centers on the utilization of available company funds to the best advantage of the company, which, at times, may be disadvantageous to a particular unit of the company.

The building of the capital budget must start at the lower levels of the organization structure and follow a consolidating and coordinating process until the complete company budget is assembled. Assuming a divisional organization with each division having several plants, the procedure would be to start the budget-building process at the plant levels for capital expenditures for plants, at the district-office levels for their expenditures, and at the office-manager level for capital expenditures for the general office. Following these assumptions and further assuming that there is a central engineering department, a typical assignment of responsibility for preparing and administering a capital budget would be as follows:

1. The chief engineer is responsible for directing the preparation of the capital budget, for assembling budget data, for presenting the budget to the president's office for approval, and for preparing it for publication. Members of the general engineering department will give their counsel to all those involved in submitting proposals for the capital budget. The chief engineer is responsible also for making periodic comparisons between the actual amounts appropriated and spent with the budget.

2. Each division manager is responsible for appraising and selecting the projects to be included in the budget for the plants, district offices, and warehouses of his division. In the case of office furniture and fixtures

for district offices, district-office and warehouse improvements, and passenger cars, the division manager's responsibility is exercised by submitting proposed projects to the company office manager, the manager of the real estate department, and the general purchasing agent, respectively.

3. Each plant manager is responsible for submitting to his division manager the proposals for his plant during the budget period. The plant manager should contact the general engineering department to be certain that he considers items for his plant which may be recommended by the general engineering department.

4. The company office manager is responsible for appraising, selecting, and approving projects to be included in the budget for general-office facilities, and for office furniture and fixtures for the general office and district offices.

5. The manager of the real estate department is responsible for appraising and approving the projects to be included in the budget for improvements to district office and warehouse facilities other than office furniture and fixtures.

6. The general purchasing agent is responsible for appraising and approving proposed purchases of passenger cars for all units of the company.

Obviously, with a less involved organization structure fewer persons would participate in the development of the capital budget, and in a small, single-plant company the president may actually develop the budget himself. The organization structure and placement of responsibility will determine the steps to be followed and their sequence.

Classification by Purpose

A broad capital budget which lists only total sums for each unit or area of responsibility cannot be appraised adequately and stimulates no creative thinking or forward planning. Therefore the budget should list specific items of proposed expenditures, commonly referred to as "projects." Each project would be described adequately and show the amount budgeted for it (Exhibit 25-1).

For the purpose of perspective and final selection and approval it is desirable to group the individual projects according to their basic purposes. These may be as follows:

1. Rebuilding and replacement of existing facilities—those expenditures which will restore existing facilities to their original state or equivalent or will be for a complete replacement in kind

2. General plant improvement—those expenditures for items such as roads, sewer lines, parking areas, and railroad sidings, which will add to or improve the factory as a unit

3. Safety, health, and working conditions—those expenditures which

EXHIBIT 25-1
19— CAPITAL APPROPRIATIONS AND EXPENDITURES BUDGET
RICHMOND PLANT
(Dollar figures in thousands)

	Project number	Unexpended appropriations January 1	Appropriations to be requested	Total	Budgeted capital expenditures	Unexpended appropriations December 31
Rebuilding and replacement:						
Rebuild paint machine...............	56013	$ 47		$ 47	$ 47	
Replace laminating press..............	57112	———	$ 36	36	36	
Safety and health:						
Install dust-collector system...........	56220	277	———	277	193	$ 84
Improve locker-room ventilation.......	57317	———	17	17	17	
Cost reduction:						
Purchase fork-lift trucks for warehouse	56010	36	———	36	36	
Purchase carton sealer...............	57119	———	12	12	12	
Capacity:						
Increase length and decks of dryer.....	57012	———	1,380	1,380	604	776
Miscellaneous........................		———	25	25	25	
Total.............................		$360	$1,470	$1,830	$970	$860

provide for protection from harm, injury, and sickness; alleviate the effects of dust, gas, heat, and other physical discomforts; or add to comfort and convenience, such as locker rooms, showers, and smoking rooms

4. Cost reduction—those expenditures for which the primary objective is the reduction in costs of producing products already in the line

5. Quality improvement—those expenditures for which the primary objective is improving the quality of existing products

6. Additional capacity—those expenditures made to increase productive capacity for products already in the line

7. New products—those expenditures for facilities to manufacture products not currently being made by the company

The above seven classifications fall into two general categories: The first three cover those expenditures required to maintain satisfactory operations and working conditions. They normally do not increase the earning power of a company, at least not to a measurable degree. Expenditures under the latter four classifications normally would be expected to increase the earning power of the company and should be appraised on the basis of the ratio of the improvement in earnings to the investment required.

Preparation of the Budget

Capital budgets are usually prepared for each fiscal year of a company, so that a budgeted balance sheet as of the end of the year can be prepared. Obviously, there are many major items which are planned for years in advance of the time when appropriations and expenditures will be made. These are part of the long-range program of a company and are not reflected in the capital budget until the year that initial specific action is expected to be taken on the item.

For planning and control purposes two factors must be considered in building the budget: (1) the planned authorizations of capital expenditures or appropriations during the budget period and (2) the planned expenditures against appropriations of prior periods and of the current period. To be of maximum value to management the budget submission (Exhibit 25-1) should show:

1. Estimated unexpended capital appropriations to be carried into the current year
2. Estimated appropriations to be requested during the current year
3. A total of 1 and 2
4. Estimated expenditures to be made during the current year
5. Estimated unexpended appropriations to be carried into the next year (3 minus 4)

Each person having responsibility for originating a part of the capital budget should prepare a data sheet (Exhibit 25-2) for each item to be

EXHIBIT 25-2
DETAIL OF APPROPRIATION INCLUDED IN CAPITAL BUDGET

Plant: Richmond

Project: 57119—Purchase Carton Sealer

Purpose: Cost Reduction

Explanation: Cartons of acoustical tile are now sealed by hand at the end of the packing line. To assure a positive seal, kraft-paper tape is placed over the flaps of each carton. With an automatic sealer, labor could be eliminated, and the longer period under pressure in the automatic sealer would eliminate the necessity for using kraft-paper tape.

Estimated Cost: $12,000

Estimated Return on Added Capital: 25%

Recommended:

_____ Plant Manager

_____ Division Manager

_____ Chief Engineer

included in his budget. Each sheet would include a statement of the reason for recommending the item and the advantages to be derived from it. Those items which are expected to increase the earning power of the company would show the estimated return expected on the new capital required. These data sheets are then listed by classification on the summary for the respective unit of the company (Exhibit 25-1). These may be further summarized by division or other management responsibility and finally into an over-all company summary (Exhibit 25-3). The recommended appropriations would be screened at each level of responsibility, so that the tentative budget submitted to the person or committee having final company approval would have been approved by all

EXHIBIT 25-3
THE FIBERBOARD COMPANY
19— CAPITAL APPROPRIATIONS AND EXPENDITURES BUDGET SUMMARY
(In thousands of dollars)

	Unexpended appropriations January 1	Appropriations to be requested	Total	Budgeted capital expenditures	Unexpended appropriations December 31
General office..................	———	$ 340	$ 340	$ 340	
Harrisburg....................	$ 130	710	840	600	$ 240
Atlanta.......................	1,490	290	1,780	1,480	300
Richmond.....................	360	1,470	1,830	970	860
Mobile.......................	27	930	957	900	57
Building Products Division......	———	17	17	17	
Industrial Specialties Division....	———	24	24	24	
Acoustical Division............	———	9	9	9	
Total......................	$2,007	$3,790	$5,797	$4,340	$1,457

lower levels of management. For example, the budget of a plant manager reporting to a division manager would be approved or revised by the division manager before being submitted to top management as a unit of the company capital budget.

Items in the first three classifications, which do not increase earning power, can be selected for inclusion only on the basis of judgment. Consideration must be given to their desirability in relation to the investment required, the effect on the composite return on capital employed of the unit of the company, and the availability of funds. Items which are expected to increase earning power would be selected in relation to their relative return on capital and to company policy on the minimum acceptable return. This latter guide would not necessarily remain the same year after year but would be set prior to the building of the budget, considering the composite company return and the availability of funds for expenditure.

While it is necessary to build the capital budget by specific items if it is to be a sound plan for appropriations and expenditures, it is usually impossible or impracticable to plan every single capital expenditure. Therefore the budget should include a general amount for small capital expenditures or unforeseen needs. Sometimes the unspecified amount is limited to a percentage of the annual depreciation of the company or each unit of the company, but more often it is simply a matter of judgment. However, the greater the unspecified amount, the less precise and valuable the capital budget as a plan of action.

Approval of the Budget

The capital budget must be correlated with the financial budget so as to determine the funds which will be available or must be secured to cover it. Therefore the budget of a unit of the company as approved by the manager of the unit is, in most companies, not the accepted budget for that unit until it has been approved at the top level of the company. This final approval may require action by either the directors, the executive committee, the finance committee, the budget committee, the treasurer, or the president, depending upon company policy.

Usually, the tentative capital budget is included in a tentative financial budget, and the effect on working capital is determined. If it is found that the funds are adequate, the capital budget is submitted for final approval without revision. If funds are not adequate, items may be deleted on the basis of their relative desirability for those not increasing earning power, and the relative return on capital employed for the others. Such deletions should be made in consultation with the respective managers who submitted the budgets. After such deletions the remaining essential items plus those showing the possibility of a high return may still exceed the available funds. This condition would indicate the need for borrowing or for securing more equity capital. Again, top management must decide on the action to be taken; the accountant can only evaluate the capital requirements, the effect on earnings, and the effect of alternate courses of action, and make recommendations based on his findings.

Appropriation Requests

The approved capital budget should be regarded as the plan for capital expenditures for the year, but it is most undesirable to regard it as an approval to proceed with every new item included therein. Rather, for

EXHIBIT 25-4
REQUEST FOR APPROPRIATION

REQUEST FOR APPROPRIATION

Job No._____   Date **3/19/--**

Supersedes "D"
Order No._____ Plant **Richmond** Bldg. **43**   Proj. No. **57119**

Est. Cost $_____ Obsolescence _____ —   Est. Comp. Date **51.1--**

Reason for Request **Cost Reduction**

Data in This Block to Be Inserted by Division Controller

	Summary of Estimated Economics	
Efficient Productive Period	**5+** Yrs.	Average Added Profit After Tax $ **2,330** /Yr.*
Period for Recovery of Cost	**3.5** Yrs.	
Return on Average Total Added Capital Employed	**26.1** % •	*NOTE: Before Charge for Expense and Obsolescence Of $ **500** After Tax in First Year

Title:

Purchase Carton sealer (Budgeted)

Plant Mgr.	Date	Dept. Mgr.	Date
Chief Architect	Date	Div. Gen. Mgr.	Date
Asst. Chf. Engr.	Date	Prod. Mgr.	Date
Chief Engr.	Date	V.P. Mfg.	Date
Gen. Prod. Planning Mgr.	Date	Controller	Date
Dir. of Research	Date	Exec. Comm.	Date Granted
Assoc. Dir. of Research	Date	Account	**123-03203**

Purchase and installation of carton sealer will save $800 per year in kraft tape which will no longer be required to assure a positive seal. One may now hand sealing cartons can be eliminated and the runways attached to the sealer will carry the cartons directly to the skids for removal by the trucker, reducing handling time. Labor saving-sealer 2000 hrs. @ 1.85 - $3700 and handling 650 hrs. @ $2.00 - $1300

new items, it should be used as a basis for determining priority of engineering work required on the new items. Time limitations usually make
it impossible to engineer many of or all the items included. Thus only
preliminary evaluations can be made of those expenditures which will
increase earning power. Also, detailed engineering may indicate that
certain planned items are undesirable and should be eliminated and that

EXHIBIT 25-5

ESTIMATES OF RECOVERY PERIOD AND RETURN ON CAPITAL EMPLOYED

ESTIMATES OF RECOVERY PERIOD AND RETURN ON CAPITAL EMPLOYED

TITLE			DATE *Mar. 17 19--*
Purchase carton sealer			PROJECT NO. *57119*

PLANT *Richmond*	P. & L. STATEMENT COMMODITY *Acoustical Tile*

(1) Total Funds Requested $ *12,400*	(2) Obsolescence Requested $
(a) Capital $ *11,900*	(3) Estimated Efficient ⎰ 5 or More Yrs. ☒
(b) Expense *500*	Productive Period ⎱ _____ Yrs.

Use lines numbered (4) through (21) to support any estimated cost reduction indicated in any request regardless of category if line numbered (1) is $2,000 or more.

	AVG. YEAR DURING E.E.P.P. ☐	5 YRS. ☐
	A. PRESENT FACILITIES	B. PROPOSED FACILITIES
(4) Material	$ *65,960*	$ *65,160*
(5) Labor	*21,860*	*16,860*
(6) Scrap		
(7) Salaries	–	–
(8) Employee Benefits (15% x (#5 ╪ #7))	*3,279*	*2,529*
(9) Power	–	*200*
(10) Repairs and Maintenance	–	*500*
(11) Depreciation		*1190*
(12)		
(13)		
(14) Total Costs Affected (#4 Thru #13)	*91,099*	*86,439* •
(15) Savings Before Tax (#14A - #14B)	——————	*4,660* •
(16) Savings After Tax (*50* % of #15B)	——————	*2,330* •
(17) Add: Dep'n. Difference (#11B - #11A)	——————	*1,190*
(18) Total Recovery (#16 ╪ #17)	——————	*3,520*
(19) Recovery Period (#1 ÷ #18)	——————	*3.5* Yrs.

The Division Controller will use lines numbered (22) through (39) in accordance with the procedure outlined in Section 13.2, Paragraph "e" of the Accounting Manual.

	FORECAST FOR CURRENT YEAR	AVG. YEAR DURING E.E.P.P. ☐	5 YRS. ☒
		A. PRESENT FACILITIES	B. PROPOSED FACILITIES
(20) Sales Units	*2,100,000*	*2,000,000*	*2,000,000*
(21) Net Sales	$ *203,700*	$ *194,000*	$ *194,800* •
(22) Plant Direct Cost		*115,520*	*108,970* •
(23) Plant Period Cost		*47,920*	*44,810* •
(24) Selling Expense		*13,580*	*13,580*
(25) Administrative Expense		*6,790*	*6,790*
(26) Profit before Tax		*10,190*	*14,850* •
(27) Profit After Tax @ *50* %		*5,095*	*7,425* •
(28) Additional Profit after Tax (#27B - #27A)		——————	*2,330* •
(29) Add: Dep'n. Cost in #23B Less Dep'n. Cost in #23A		——————	*1,190*
(30) Total Recovery (#28 ╪ #29)		——————	*3,520*
(31) Recovery Period (#1 ÷ #30)		——————	*3.5* Yrs.
(32) Cash		*11,640*	*11,640*
(33) Receivables		*16,200*	*16,200*
(34) Inventories		*32,700*	*32,700*
(35) Property, Plant, and Equipment		*63,820*	*72,745*
(36) Miscellaneous			
(37) Total Capital Employed		*124,360*	*133,285*
(38) Return on Capital Employed (#27 ÷ #37)		*4.1%*	*5.6%* •
(39) Return on Added Capital (#28 ÷(#37B - #37A))			*26.1%* •

*Note: Before Charge for Expense and Obsolescence of $ *500* After Tax in First Year.

Comments on Estimated Efficient Productive Period:

_____	PLANT INDUSTRIAL ENGINEER	⎱ Lines numbered
_____		⎰ (4) through (19)
_____	PLANT CONTROLLER	⎱ Lines numbered
_____	DIV. CONTROLLER	⎰ (3) and (20) through (39)

others will require substantially more money than anticipated in the budget.

As an item is about to be studied by the engineers, it is customarily assigned an identifying number, referred to as a "project number." When the engineering work is completed and detailed estimates or quotations are available, the project should be submitted to the appropriate managers for their approval, and projects above an amount determined by company policy should be approved by the person or group which had final approval of the capital budget.

A typical request for approval of an appropriation for capital expenditure is shown in Exhibit 25-4. This summary form is supported by a complete description of the project, the reasons why the appropriation is being requested, and supporting schedules for any indicated improvement in earnings (Exhibit 25-5). When items not budgeted specifically are presented for approval, a statement should be made as to whether they are to be applied against the unspecified amount or substituted for other items, or considered as an addition to the budget.

Periodically a summary report (Exhibit 25-6) should be submitted,

EXHIBIT 25-6

· FIRST 4 MONTHS, 19—

COMPARISON OF ACTUAL CAPITAL APPROPRIATIONS AND EXPENDITURES WITH AMOUNTS BUDGETED

(In thousands of dollars)

		Appropriations				
			Actual			
	Annual budget	Budgeted items	Un-budgeted items	Total	Balance available	Estimated under (over) budget for year
General office...............	340	210	———	210	130	
Harrisburg.................	710	200	100	300	410	(100)
Atlanta....................	290	40	———	40	250	
Richmond..................	1,470	330	———	330	1,140	
Mobile.....................	930	310	240	550	380	(100)
Buiding Products Division....	17	5	———	5	12	
Industrial Specialties Division.	24	19	———	19	5	
Acoustical Division..........	9	4	———	4	5	
Total...................	3,790	1,118	340	1,458	2,332	(200)

		Expenditures				
General office...............	340	130	———	130	210	
Harrisburg.................	600	300	50	350	250	
Atlanta....................	1,480	230	———	230	1,250	500
Richmond..................	970	245	———	245	725	(300)
Mobile.....................	900	210	———	210	690	
Building Products Division....	17	4	———	4	13	
Industrial Specialties Division.	24	19	———	19	5	
Acoustical Division..........	9	2	———	2	7	
Total...................	4,340	1,140	50	1,190	3,150	200

showing the cumulative appropriations and expenditures in comparison with the amounts budgeted. This would show not only the status of the budget but the most recent estimates of deviations from the budgets. The latter would not necessarily be the actual appropriations and expenditures to date for unbudgeted items. These may be provided for against the unspecified amount in the budget or through substitutions. For expenditures, delays or acceleration in procurement or construction would also affect the amounts to be spent and cause deviations. The report would be accompanied by explanations of the expected deviations.

Control of Capital Expenditures

For control purposes, as well as to provide cost data for setting up the property accounting records, all capital expenditures should be recorded by the project number to which they apply. This procedure is the same as that used for a job-order cost system for production. Cost cards should be prepared showing the appropriation for the project in total and the engineers' estimate of the breakdown to units of the project when it covers more than a single item of buildings or machinery.

Actual commitments and expenditures should be posted to the cost cards as made. When commitments and/or other costs equal a percentage of the total appropriation as established by policy, say, 80%, the person having responsibility for the control of the expenditures should be notified. If it is evident that costs will exceed the appropriation, a supplemental appropriation request should be presented for approval. Upon completion of each project a report should be prepared showing the deviation from the amount appropriated. These reports would provide information for estimating deviations from the capital expenditures budgeted.

Make-good Reports

Since capital expenditures which are expected to improve earnings usually receive more favorable consideration than those which are not, it is desirable to examine the actual improvement achieved at some time after a project is completed. The waiting period between completion and the study of the results achieved will be determined by the size and nature of the project. For example, the purchase of a second machine, of a type already in use, to increase capacity could probably be studied 6 months after installation to determine if the additional volume were being produced and sold. A new plant to make a new product could probably not be evaluated until several years after it was in operation.

Frequently company policy will require make-good reports only for major capital expenditures, say, $10,000 and over. This reduces the demands on accounting, engineering, and production-management time for making the studies and on top-management time in examining the reports.

The form of the make-good report would follow that used to evaluate the estimated earnings improvement when the appropriation was requested (Exhibit 25-5). It would contain a complete explanation of any significant differences between the actual results and those contemplated.

FINANCIAL BUDGET

Purpose

The financial budget brings together the effects of the operating budget and the capital expenditures budget on the financial position of a company. It also incorporates the effects of financing, dividend disbursement, prepayment of expenses, and other financial transactions not reflected in the operating budget. The purpose of the financial budget is to:

1. Determine when and in what amounts funds will be available
2. Indicate if, when, and to what extent additional funds will be needed
3. Guide the chief financial officer in procuring and administering company funds

Preparation

To be of real value in financial planning the financial budget must show the transactions and balances budgeted for each month of the year. A budget for a year would give no indication of the effect of variations from month to month in sales, inventories, collections, tax payments, dividend payments, and many other items which are not constant from month to month. Also, because financial planning must always be for some months ahead, the original budget for a year is of little value in the latter months of that year. Thus, even if all other budgets are prepared only once or twice a year, a financial budget must be prepared each month for some period of future months, preferably 12.

Rarely, if ever, is the responsibility for financial planning placed anywhere below the company level. Units of a company will have varying demands for funds and will make varying additions to funds, but they are working from the company treasury. Therefore, the preparation of the financial budget must be at the company level and incorporate the effects on the treasury of all the units of the company.

Since the financial budget is a company budget, it is prepared under the direction of the chief accounting officer. All budgets and plans which will affect financial planning are secured from the respective staff and operating managers and evaluated as to their contribution to, or demand for, funds. These include the tentative capital budget. The first draft of the financial budget is usually regarded as tentative. Financial plans and modifications of the capital budget are made on the basis of this tentative budget, and a final budget is then prepared which reflects these. Each month a new budget is prepared which reflects the effects of the deviations from other budgets or financial plans and projects the budget for 1 more month so that it always covers the same number of months.

Form of the Budget

Varied approaches can be used to develop the financial budget. It may be prepared as a series of related statements of source and application of funds. These do provide the information as to the availability of funds but are not sufficiently detailed to provide adequately for interpretation of deviations. A statement of working capital balances and planned changes (Exhibit 25-7) is more useful for planning, for analyzing and interpreting deviations, and for revising the budget for future periods.

This form of financial budget requires the budgeting of working-capital account balances, other than Cash, as of the end of each month or period of months within the budget period for which information is needed. Accounts Receivable are budgeted on the basis of budgeted sales and collections. Inventories are determined from the purchase plans and production budget. Prepaid Expenses are secured from the schedule of insurance-premium dates, rent schedules, etc. Notes Payable balances are supplied by the treasurer's plans for borrowing money and for paying notes. The Provision for Income Taxes is calculated from the taxes applicable to profits as earned and the payments of taxes on the dates established by regulations. Dividends are determined by the corporate dividend policy. Profit and Depreciation are taken from the operating budget and Capital Expenditures from the capital budget. With these amounts budgeted the changes in Cash are calculated.

Budgeted Balance Sheet

A budgeted balance sheet as of the end of the budget period can be prepared from the data developed in the capital and financial budgets. However, with these budgets in use there is actually no additional management guidance provided by a budgeted balance sheet. For this reason it is usually not prepared or considered to be a part of the budgetary control program.

EXHIBIT 25-7

THE FIBERBOARD COMPANY

FINANCIAL BUDGET

(In thousands of dollars)

Working Capital Account Balances

	Jan. 1	Jan. 31	Feb. 28	Mar. 31	Apr. 30	May 31	June 30	Sept. 30	Dec. 31
Current assets:									
Cash and securities	$ 7,510	$ 7,422	$ 8,704	$ 6,637	$ 9,909	$14,024	$12,465	$21,253	$27,198
Accounts receivable (net of reserves)	11,216	11,250	11,250	11,750	12,250	12,500	12,500	12,000	11,500
Inventories (net of reserves)	20,950	22,500	23,900	25,400	25,000	24,000	23,000	22,000	21,000
Prepaid expense	1,618	2,600	2,500	2,400	2,300	2,200	2,100	1,900	1,700
Total	41,294	43,772	46,354	46,187	49,459	52,724	50,065	57,153	61,398
Current liabilities:									
Notes payable			2,000	2,000					
Accounts payable and accrued expense	18,540	18,600	18,750	19,000	20,000	19,000	19,000	20,000	20,000
Provision for taxes on income	3,000	4,000	5,000	3,000	5,000	7,000	4,000	5,000	5,000
Dividends declared but not paid		2,000	2,000		2,000	2,000			
Total	21,540	24,600	25,750	24,000	27,000	28,000	23,000	25,000	25,000
Net working capital	$19,754	$19,172	$20,604	$22,187	$22,459	$24,724	$27,065	$32,153	$36,398
Current ratio	1.9-1	1.8-1	1.8-1	1.9-1	1.8-1	1.9-1	2.2-1	2.3-1	2.4-1

Additions to or deductions from net working capital during period

	Jan. 31	Feb. 28	Mar. 31	Apr. 30	May 31	June 30	Sept. 30	Dec. 31
Add: Net profit after income taxes	1,013	967	1,168	1,807	1,900	2,031	5,813	4,920
Provision for depreciation and amortization	715	715	715	765	765	765	2,445	2,500
Miscellaneous						45		
Deduct: Dividends declared	2,000			2,000			2,000	2,000
Capital expenditures	300	250	300	290	400	500	1,150	1,150
Miscellaneous	10			10			20	25
Net increase (decrease) in working capital	(582)	1,432	1,583	272	2,265	2,341	5,088	4,245

REVIEW QUESTIONS

1. What are the purposes of a capital expenditures budget?
2. Who should build the capital expenditures budget?
3. What management purposes are served by building the capital expenditures budget in detail by items of expenditure? By categories, as to purposes of the expenditures?
4. Why should the capital expenditures budget show both planned appropriations and planned expenditures?
5. How are capital expenditures influenced by the use of return on capital employed as a measurement of profit?
6. What would be considered to be justifiable causes of an overrun of an appropriation for capital expenditures?
7. What management purposes are served by make-good reports on capital expenditures?
8. How does the financial budget assist in management planning?
9. Why should a financial budget be built by months of the budget period?
10. How are the capital expenditures and financial budgets interrelated?

PROBLEMS

1. The Lansing plant manager submits the following as his proposed capital expenditures to be included in the budget:

a. Rebuild turret lathe no. 41–012............................$15,000
This lathe is 12 years old. It has been used on a three-shift basis since it was installed. It is difficult to meet required tolerances on many jobs. A new lathe would cost $30,000. This rebuilding will place this lathe in like-new condition.

b. Expand locker rooms and provide improved ventilation..........$35,000
Since present locker rooms were built and equipped, the number of employees has increased 23%. Foremen are receiving many complaints about overcrowded conditions, and it is almost impossible to keep the rooms clean because of overcrowding.

c. Purchase and install 10 rotary molding machines..............$530,000
Present schedules in the molding department are 6⅓ days per week. Addition of these machines will permit the production schedule to be reduced to 5 days, and capacity will be available to meet surges in orders and thus improve service. Elimination of overtime premium will reduce costs and provide a return on this investment of 24%. Eight of these can be purchased and installed next year. Placing a firm order now will avoid a possible price increase.

d. Replace five punch presses................................$500,000
These presses are 12 years old. New presses have many features which result in easier operation. Purchase of these presses will reduce maintenance costs $30,000 per year.

e. Purchase and install five injection molding machines............$100,000
The sales department has developed outlets for polystyrene injection-molded food cups. This is a new product. Estimated sales will add $35,000 of profit after tax. Delivery schedules of the manufacturer will permit the delivery of only three machines next year.

f. Rebuild roofs on buildings nos. 8 and 10.....................$30,000
These roofs are 20 years old, and frequent repairs are required to stop leaks. Inventories have been damaged as a result of these leaks. It is proposed to remove all of the existing roof surface, replace rotted planks, and install new built-up roof surfaces.

g. Build new gatehouse......................................$20,000
The present wooden gatehouse is 37 years old. It does not create a good impression on visitors entering the plant. It is proposed to demolish it and replace it with a brick building of modern design.

h. Purchase and install automatic carton sealer...................$18,000
Cartons are presently sealed and taped by hand. This machine will seal automatically and provide a better seal, eliminating the use of tape. Labor and material savings will yield a return of 32% on the investment.

i. Add one bay to shipping platform...........................$12,000
The increase in shipments is causing overcrowding at the shipping platform. Trucks are delayed as much as 3 hours waiting for loading space. The addition of one bay will reduce these delays to a minimum.

j. Purchase and install spray coating unit.......................$20,000
There is a market for products with finishes which cannot be produced with known molding powders. Spray coating of brown phenolic molded pieces will provide these finishes and open a new market. These will be wide-margin items, and the estimated sales will add $15,000 of profit after tax.

k. Rebuild three flat-bed presses............................$ 9,000
These presses are 16 years old, and maintenance is excessive. They have not been rebuilt previously.

l. Provision for unspecified items............................$10,000

Last year essential but not anticipated capital expenditures totaled $12,918.
Total property, plant, and equipment at cost is $12,376,000, and annual depreciation is $495,040.

The company classifies capital expenditures in five categories: rebuilding and replacement, plant improvement, cost reduction, production capacity, new products.

Approved but uncompleted projects at the close of the year are as follows: build new warehouse—appropriated $200,000, expended $160,000; and purchase and install six lining machines to increase capacity—appropriated $60,000, expended $12,000.

Prepare a summary capital appropriations and expenditures budget which you would recommend to the executive committee. (Company profits are satisfactory, but it is expected that there will be a shortage of cash.)

2. Working capital accounts of a company, as of January 1, are Cash, $52,000; Accounts Receivable, $176,000; Inventories, $302,000; Prepaid Ex-

pense, $17,000; Accounts Payable, $229,000; and Provision for Taxes on Income, $29,000.

The operating budget for the year shows Profit after Taxes of $128,000, Depreciation $59,000, Dividend Payments $30,000; and end of the year balances for Inventories $325,000, Accounts Payable $260,000, Prepaid Expense $20,000. Sales budgeted for the latter months of the year are November, $200,000, and December, $240,000. Normally 45 days' sales are outstanding.

The capital expenditures budget is $78,000.

The income tax rate is 50%, and 75% of the year's provision for taxes is paid during the year.

Prepare a tentative working capital budget for the year, and comment on the management action which it indicates.

CHAPTER 26

Reporting to
Top Management

There are two types of reports which should
be prepared for top management: (1) periodic reports of performance
by areas of responsibility which provide information for operating decisions and (2) special reports to implement planning and policy making.

Those of the first type are an integral part of the budgetary planning
and control program. They show the deviations from the budgets in each
area of management responsibility, the effect of these deviations on other
areas, and the possible courses of action which should be taken as a result of the deviations. An acceptable budget is of no value if it is not
met, and poor performance in one area cannot be overlooked when it is
offset by superior performance in another area. Each supervisor and
manager must be held responsible for meeting his budget, unless it can
be shown that his failure to do so was due to factors clearly beyond his
control. The control phase of budgeting is of greater importance than the
planning phase, for ultimate success is measured by results, not by plans.

Special reports are used to present detailed analyses of special problems which are indicated by the periodic reports, to evaluate alternative
courses of action, and to suggest areas of exploration for expansion or
profit improvement. They are not a part of the budget program but are
a function of management accounting.

Integrated Periodic Reports

The system of periodic reports must be integrated to be of maximum
value. A performance report at the lowest level of management must support a segment of the performance report to the next highest level, and
so on, up to the top level. An accumulation of all reports will not do this,
for it would be necessary for top management to study each individual

report in detail to determine the areas to which they should direct their attention. The ideal report for a manager who has others with management responsibility reporting to him is one which tells him at a glance the achievements of each of his subordinates against their plans.

An integrated system of performance reports permits management by exception. In a company having several operating divisions, the president can tell from his reports which divisions, if any, failed to achieve budgeted performance. The division manager, from his reports, can localize the failure as to production, sales, advertising, research, etc. The production manager can tell from his reports the specific plants which did not meet budgeted performance, and the managers of those plants will know from their reports which of their operations caused the deviations. In each instance from the president to the front-line supervisor each person can direct his attention to the specific subordinates or areas where the deviations occurred and initiate corrective action.

The data on periodic reports are more readily comprehended and interpreted if they are presented in the same form and the same arrangement from period to period. For this reason, particularly in larger companies, preprinted forms are used for periodic reports. However, the need for revision as conditions change must not be overlooked. Also, a change in format will often direct attention to a report which has become routine and has not been generating the management action which its contents indicate to be desirable.

Reports which contain interpretative and explanatory comments will save the time of management in report analysis and will be more likely to generate action. The managerial accountant is trained to analyze, interpret, and evaluate operating data; management frequently has neither the time nor the technical training to do this. Therefore, the text of the periodic report should present the important conclusions to be drawn from the data and direct attention to the exceptional items which require management attention. The data are presented only to support the conclusions and to provide a complete picture of operations.

In writing the comments for a periodic report the managerial accountant must visualize himself in the position of the manager who is to receive the report. He must sense what is important and what is not important to the manager and limit his remarks to the important facts. Restatement in the text of figures and comparisons which are obvious in the data section detracts attention from the significant comments and is a waste of time. Repetition in period after period of the same comments on the same items is a sedative rather than a stimulant to management action. To achieve maximum attention the comments in each periodic report must be brief, essential, and different—a challenge to the creative ability of the managerial accountant.

Information Reports versus Performance Reports

A clear distinction must be made between those periodic reports which are presented only for the information of the recipient and those which are to be used by him in discharging his management responsibilities. A report on the profits of a plant which is presented to a plant manager who has no responsibility for sales is an information report. A profit report for a division presented to the divisional manager who is responsible for the profit of his division is a performance report.

Information reports are not intended to generate direct management action. They are a part of the communication system of a company, and provide valuable background information for decision making. They permit the recipient to participate more intelligently in staff and other management meetings. More importantly, they enable the recipient to exercise a general stewardship responsibility through suggesting to those responsible for other areas of management possible approaches to the improvement of the final composite results. Some companies do not submit information reports to supervisors and managers and limit the reports given to each person to those specific items for which he is directly responsible. This would seem to be bad psychologically. There is no satisfaction in playing on a team if you do not know the score of the game. It precludes the possibility of receiving ideas from other management areas, and it inhibits the development of men for broader and more important management responsibilities.

Performance reports are intended to implement and generate direct management action. As such they must contain complete data and comments on the performance in the area for which the recipient has responsibility and must not be cluttered with extraneous material. They are adapted to the special needs of each recipient, and while it is customary to use the same format for like management levels (e.g., all division managers), it is seldom used for all management levels. A performance report is intended to present and interpret for a manager the results of operations in his area of responsibility and of those who report to him. It is not intended also to inform the next higher level of management of the manager's performance. Reports designed for, and adapted to, the needs of that management level will do that.

However, copies of performance reports of one level are frequently used as information reports to the next higher level and thus supplement the performance reports for that level. The danger in this is that a manager will endeavor to analyze these performance reports, intended primarily for his subordinates, and thus become involved in minutiae. As with all phases of management accounting the extent of the use of performance reports as information reports for higher management will be determined by the desires of management. Since management accounting is a service to management, that service extends to giving each manager all the reports which he wants and not only those which the accountant thinks he should receive.

Reports to Directors

In a corporation the highest level of management is the board of directors. Since the chief executive officer is the only person reporting

EXHIBIT 26-1
THE FIBERBOARD COMPANY
REPORT TO THE BOARD OF DIRECTORS—SUMMARY
MONTH OF APRIL, 19—
(Dollar figures in thousands)

	Current month		Prior month		Four months, current year		Four months, prior year	
Net Sales.............	$10,090		$11,427		$45,616		$43,212	
Cost of goods sold.....	7,315	72.5%	8,239	72.1%	32,524	71.3%	31,415	72.7%
Distribution expense...	837	8.3	840	7.4	3,350	7.4	3,179	7.4
Administrative expense	414	4.1	416	3.6	1,661	3.6	1,430	3.3
Other (income) expense	——		——		5			
Profit before income taxes..............	1,524	15.1	1,932	16.9	8,076	17.7	7,188	16.6
Profit after income taxes	762	7.6	966	8.5	4,038	8.9	3,594	8.3
Capital employed......	$89,028		$88,412		$89,028		$88,114	
Turnover and return on capital.............		1.36 10.3%		1.55 13.1%		1.54 13.6%		1.47 12.2%

At End of Period

	Current month	Prior month	Four months, current year	Four months, prior year
Cash.................	$ 5,918	$ 4,015	$ 5,918	$ 6,340
U.S. government securities.............	4,000	2,000	4,000	3,500
Total cash and equivalent.............	$ 9,918	$ 6,015	$ 9,918	$ 9,840
Working capital.......	22,978	22,610	22,978	22,419
Current ratio..........	1.9–1	1.8–1	1.9–1	1.7–1

Capital Appropriations and Expenditures

	Current month	Prior month	Four months, current year	Four months, prior year
Unexpended appropriations at beginning of period.............	$ 1,843	$ 2,046	$ 2,007	$ 817
Appropriations during period.............	719	117	1,458	765
Total.............	$ 2,562	$ 2,163	$ 3,465	$ 1,582
Expenditures during period.............	287	320	1,190	519
Unexpended appropriations at end of period.............	$ 2,275	$ 1,843	$ 2,275	$ 1,063

directly to the board and all other officers and managers of the company report to or through him, the report to the board is an information report rather than a performance report. The accountant's report to the directors should contain all the information needed for the formulation of corporate operating and financial policies. In many instances this is limited to data on corporate sales, profits, working capital, capital expenditures, funded debt, and equity (Exhibit 26-1), with interpretative comments as to levels and trends.

EXHIBIT 26-2
THE FIBERBOARD COMPANY
REPORT TO THE BOARD OF DIRECTORS—DETAIL
4 Months
(Dollar figures in thousands)

	Total company	Building products division	Acoustical division	Industrial-specialties division
Current Year				
Net sales..................	$45,616	$11,319	$14,720	$19,577
Profit after tax............	$ 4,038	$ 1,109	$ 1,663	$ 1,266
Capital employed..........	$89,028	$25,920	$40,890	$22,218
Per cent profit to net sales......	8.9%	9.8%	11.3%	6.5%
Turnover..................	1.54	1.31	1.08	2.64
Return on capital employed......	13.6%	12.8%	12.2%	17.1%
Prior Year				
Net sales..................	$43,212	$12,615	$13,806	$16,791
Profit after tax............	$ 3,594	$ 1,249	$ 1,518	$ 827
Capital employed..........	$88,114	$27,992	$40,113	$20,009
Per cent profit to net sales......	8.3%	9.9%	11.0%	4.9%
Turnover..................	1.47	1.35	1.03	2.52
Return on capital employed......	12.2%	13.4%	11.3%	12.3%

While the board of directors is primarily interested in figures at the corporate level, they should be, and usually are, concerned with the operating results of each of the units of the company. A typical summary report of operations by divisions is shown in Exhibit 26-2. These data and ratios would be shown for at least the year to date and the same period of the prior year. They may also be shown for the current month, but there can be unusual factors affecting the operating results of a unit of a company in any one month which tend to confuse rather than clarify an appraisal of results. The section of the report on the operating results of company units would also contain pertinent interpretative comments.

In some companies the directors approve the budgets, and where they do, they should be shown a comparison of actual with budgeted results. In others the budgets are regarded as tools of operating management, and no budget information is presented to the directors.

Frequently the financial section of the directors' report is followed by a section containing both comments and statistics on supplementary information. Such a section would present order backlogs, units produced, units sold, percentage of capacity operated, wage rates, overtime, hours worked, etc. It may also contain progress reports on, or results achieved on, special matters approved by the board, such as a major capital expenditures program.

Reports to the Chief Executive

The report presented to the directors is in effect the performance report of the chief executive. However, it usually does not contain sufficient data to guide him in directing his attention to those areas which require corrective action. This is particularly true if it does not contain comparisons of actuals with budgets. For this reason more detailed reports are prepared for the chief executive which show the actuals and budgets for all parts of the budget program. These contain analyses and explanations of deviations. The organization structure and placement of responsibility will determine the form and content.

In a company which has several divisions, the managers of which have profit responsibility, the company statement of performance in comparison with that budgeted (Exhibit 26-3) would be supported by like statements for each division. The accompanying text would then cover the effect of each division on the company results.

In the illustration the deviation in profit before tax is analyzed at the company level. There were no changes in sales prices from those budgeted. Sales dollars were $4,094,000 below budget, which, at the standard gross margin budgeted of 47%, had an adverse effect on profit of $1,924,-000. The difference between this and the total deviation in standard gross of $1,935,000 was due to the mixture of products sold. The ratios of 53.0% of standard direct cost to net sales would indicate that mixture was as budgeted. However, if the percentages are carried to more decimal places, it will be found that the standard gross margin realized was slightly lower than that budgeted. An unfavorable production variance of $95,000 was budgeted, but actually a favorable variance of $12,000 was

EXHIBIT 26-3
THE FIBERBOARD COMPANY
ACTUAL AND BUDGETED OPERATING STATEMENT
4 MONTHS, 19—

	Actual		Budget	
	Thousands	Per cent	Thousands	Per cent
Units sold......................	701,780	——	765,000	
Net sales......................	$45,616	100.0	$49,710	100.0
Standard direct cost of sales.........	24,176	53.0	26,335	53.0
Direct-cost variances—production....	(12)*	——	95	0.2
Direct-cost variances—purchasing....	(603)	(1.3)	(510)	(1.0)
Actual direct cost of sales...........	23,561	51.7	25,920	52.2
Gross margin...................	22,055	48.3	23,790	47.8
Factory period expense.............	8,963	19.6	8,950	18.0
Total factory cost...............	$32,524	71.3	$34,870	70.2
Distribution expense...	3,350	7.4	3,260	6.6
Administrative expense............	1,661	3.6	1,670	3.3
Other expense...................	5	——	——	
Profit before income tax............	8,076	17.7	9,910	19.9
Profit after income tax.............	4,038	8.9	4,955	9.9
Capital employed..................	89,028	——	89,760	
Turnover........................		1.54		1.66
Return on capital employed........		13.6		16.5
Deviation from budgeted profit before tax...........................	$ 1,834			
Due to:				
Sales price...................	——			
Sales volume.................	1,924			
Sales mixture.................	11			
Production efficiency...........	(31)			
Production volume.............	(63)			
Raw-material prices............	(93)			
Distribution expense...........	90			
Administrative expense.........	(9)			
Other.....................	5			
	Prior Year Actual			
Net sales......................	$43,212			
Profit after tax...................	3,594	8.3%		
Capital employed and turnover......	88,114	1.47		
Return on capital employed........	——	12.2%		

* Parentheses denote gains.

realized, so that the effect was a $107,000 contribution to profit. Factory period expenses were $13,000 over budget, but at the actual production level caused by the lower sales they should have been $63,000 lower (assumed). Thus $76,000 more factory period expense was incurred than allowed in the budget adjusted to the actual production level. This $76,000 is deducted from the $107,000 effect of production direct-cost variances to arrive at the $31,000 favorable deviation in profit due to efficiency. Gains over standard costs of raw materials purchased were $93,000 greater than budgeted.

The comparison of the actual with the budgeted operating statement for the company gives the chief executive a picture of the operating factors which caused the deviation from budgeted profit. The supporting statements for each division show the extent to which each contributed to these. These divisional statements are analyzed and interpreted, as was the company statement.

If responsibility for sales and production is divided, with a sales manager and a production manager reporting to the chief executive, the reports supporting the company operating statement would be for management areas instead of for divisions. Exhibit 26-4 illustrates, in summary form, the information which would be supplied for each area of responsibility. It is to be noted that in this illustration the sum of the division deviations due to sales mixture equals the total for the company. In practice this would not necessarily be true. To the extent that the percentage deviation of actual from budgeted net sales varied by divisions, there would be an additional mixture deviation at the company level.

The chief executive would also receive budget comparisons for all the other budgets not reflected in the sales and profit budget. These would include capital appropriations and expenditures and working capital. Each budget report would be so designed and include appropriate interpretative comments that the items demanding corrective action would be highlighted. The chief executive could then direct his reviews of performance with the respective managers reporting directly to him to the specific items in each area which required corrective action.

Reports to Division Managers

When a division manager has profit responsibility, he is the chief executive of his division. The performance reports which he receives for the division would be similar to those which the company chief executive receives for the company.

The operating statement for the division would be in the form illustrated in Exhibit 26-3. It would be supported by product line operating statements in the same form and with the same analysis of deviation from

EXHIBIT 26-4
THE FIBERBOARD COMPANY
SUMMARY OF DEVIATIONS FROM SALES AND PROFIT BUDGETS
FIRST 4 MONTHS, 19—
(In thousands of dollars)

	Sales Responsibility			
	Total com- pany	Building products division	Acoustical division	Industrial- specialties division
Net sales......................	$4,094	$981	$1,280	$1,833
Standard gross margin:				
Sales price...................	$	$	$	$
Sales volume.................	1,924	459	631	834
Sales mixture................	11	20	(7)*	(2)
Total......................	$1,935	$479	$624	$832
Distribution expense............	90	(17)	———	107
Total—sales responsibility......	$2,025	$462	$624	$939

	Production Responsibility				
	Total com- pany	Harris- burg	At- lanta	Rich- mond	Mobile
Direct-cost variances:					
Material......................	$ (89)	$(76)	$ 13	$(11)	$(15)
Labor........................	4	———	(2)	7	(1)
Scrap........................	19	(7)	(17)	21	22
Direct expense................	(41)	(11)	(4)	(20)	(6)
Total......................	$ (107)	$(94)	$(10)	$(3)	
Raw-material prices.............	(93)	———	(46)	(3)	(44)
Factory period expense:					
Efficiency....................	76	54	(7)	9	20
Volume......................	(63)	(3)	(18)	(20)	(22)
Total......................	$ 13	$ 51	$(25)	$(11)	$(2)
Total—production responsibility...	$ (187)	$(43)	$(81)	$(17)	$(46)

	General Office				
Administrative expense...........	$ (9)				
Other income and expense........	5				
Total deviation from budgeted profit.....................	$1,834				

* Parentheses denote favorable deviations.

budgeted profit for each product line. These product line reports would be information reports, since at the product-line level profit results are the combined result of production and sales effectiveness.

Causes of profit deviation would be shown by areas of responsibility in the division, as they are for the company in Exhibit 26-4. Deviations from the budgets under sales responsibility would be shown in total for the division and by product lines. Those under production responsibility would be shown in total and by the plants of the division.

Reports to Sales Managers

Sales managers have responsibility for sales volume and distribution expense of a company or of a division. If they set the sales prices, they are responsible for net sales income, and if they do not, they are responsible only for unit sales. Their performance reports would be designed to show in detail the comparison of actual with budgeted sales units or net sales dollars, and distribution expense.

The daily net sales reports (Exhibit 21-2) provide a sales manager with interim information as to achievement against the sales budget. At the end of each month he should receive a detailed report of budgeted and actual sales and of the effect on profit of deviations from budgeted sales (Exhibit 26-5). If the sales manager is responsible only for volume, this report is an information report; otherwise it is a performance report. Where there are division or product-line sales managers reporting to a general sales manager, the report would show the totals for each of these managers' responsibility.

The sales reports should be supplemented by reports on orders received and order backlogs when there is a significant lag between the date orders are booked and the date they are filled.

The sales manager's performance reports for distribution expense would be designed to show actual and budgeted expenses of each district office, the general sales office, and sales-service functions under the line responsibility of the sales manager. If he has direct responsibility for advertising, these expenses would be included in his performance reports. If he does not, he should receive as an information report a copy of the advertising manager's performance report together with an analysis of the deviations from the budgeted advertising expense which affect his products. For example, with a central advertising department in the fiberboard company the sales manager of the industrial-specialties division would be informed of the deviations from the amount of advertising budgeted for the industrial-specialties division. All these budget reports would follow the forms and procedures discussed under the control of distribution expense in Chapter 17.

Exhibit 26-5
Building Products Division
Comparison of Actual and Budgeted Sales and Effect of Deviation on Profit
4 Months, 19—

Sales

	1,000 Units		Gross price		$000 Gross sales		$000 Deductions		$000 Net sales	
	Actual	Budget	Actual	Budget	Actual	Budget	Actual	Budget	Actual	Budget
Exterior construction products:										
Roof insulation	42,670	44,800	$64.00	$64.00	$2,731	$2,867	$161	$172	$2,570	$2,695
Sheathing	67,570	75,350	66.00	66.00	4,460	4,973	263	298	4,197	4,675
Interior finishes:										
Tile	5,640	6,100	75.00	75.00	423	457	25	27	398	430
Plank	11,470	12,400	70.00	70.00	803	868	59	52	744	816
Wallboard	16,780	18,150	65.00	65.00	1,091	1,180	64	72	1,027	1,108
Foundation board	20,710	22,400	59.00	59.00	1,222	1,322	72	79	1,150	1,243
Form board	22,600	24,450	58.00	58.00	1,311	1,418	78	85	1,233	1,333
Total	187,440	203,650			$12,041	$13,085	$722	$785	$11,319	$12,300

Sales Deductions

	Actual	Budget
Allowances	$ 12	
Freight	451	$492
Cash discount	259	293
Total deductions	$722	$785

Sales deviations reduced (increased) profit due to:

Price	$	459
Volume		20
Mixture		
Total	$	479

Some companies have product-line managers who are responsible for the sales of a product line and who report to the sales manager. Each such manager would receive a report of the sales of his product line. The form of this report would follow that of Exhibit 26-5. It would, of course, be limited to sales of the product line managed by the recipient.

Reports to Production Managers

The production manager's performance report would show the actual and budgeted cost of production for each area of his responsibility. If deviations from standards and budgets are taken into operating results in the period in which they occur, the deviations shown on the production manager's report would support and explain the factory cost deviations shown on the operating statements of either the chief executive or the division manager. If variances are related to production going into sales and into inventory, the disposition of variances would be shown on the report, so that it could be reconciled with the deviations shown on the operating report.

Exhibit 26-6 is a typical summary performance report for a production manager. It shows the amounts allowed in the standards or budgets, the actual amount and percentage of deviations, the budgeted deviations, and the effect of the difference between the actual and budgeted deviations on company profits. It is to be noted that the standard and budget allowances cannot be added to arrive at the budgeted cost of goods sold. This is because of duplication of figures in allowances. Raw-material purchase price variances are based on the standard value of material purchased, and part of or all the purchased material is again included in the actual amount used at standard value which developed the raw-material usage variance. Also, the standard allowance for scrap is the sum of the material, labor, and direct expense cost up to the point in the production cycle where the scrap occurred. This value was allowed in the standards or budgets of the preceding operations as material, labor, or direct expense. This report directs the attention of the production manager to those areas where significant unfavorable deviations were experienced and also to those where the actual deviations were significantly different from those budgeted. It would be supported by the reports of each plant on performance against standards or budgets.

Information reports showing the actual and budgeted operating results of divisions and product lines should also be given to a production manager. These would be copies of the reports of the division and product-line managers. In addition, the results of the product lines manufactured in each plant may be added to provide information on the profit contribution to the company of each plant's products. These should not be

EXHIBIT 26-6

THE FIBERBOARD COMPANY

COMPARISON OF ACTUAL AND BUDGETED FACTORY COST

FIRST 4 MONTHS, 19—

(In thousands of dollars)

	Standard or budget	Actual deviation		Budgeted deviation	Effect on budgeted profit
		Amount	Per cent		
Direct-material usage:					
Harrisburg...........	$ 1,563	$(76)*	(4.9)		$(76)
Atlanta..............	4,120	7	0.2	$(6)	13
Richmond...........	4,547	(21)	(0.5)	(10)	(11)
Mobile..............	3,980	(11)	(0.3)	4	(15)
Total..............	$14,210	$(101)	(.7)	$(12)	$(89)
Direct labor:					
Harrisburg...........	$ 1,091				
Atlanta..............	1,418	$(2)	(0.1)	———	$(2)
Richmond...........	1,582	7	0.4	———	7
Mobile..............	1,364	(1)	(0.1)	———	(1)
Total..............	$ 5,455	$ 4	0.1	———	$ 4
Scrap:					
Harrisburg...........	$ 121	$(7)	(5.8)	———	$(7)
Atlanta..............	132	(3)	(2.3)	$ 14	(17)
Richmond...........	147	21	14.3	———	21
Mobile..............	126	17	13.5	(5)	22
Total..............	$ 526	$ 28	5.3	$ 9	$ 19
Direct expense:					
Harrisburg...........	$ 1,334	$ 10	0.7	$ 21	$(11)
Atlanta..............	1,734	(33)	(1.9)	(29)	(4)
Richmond...........	1,937	53	2.7	73	(20)
Mobile..............	1,665	27	1.6	33	(6)
Total..............	$ 6,670	$ 57	0.9	$ 98	$(41)
Raw-material prices:					
Harrisburg...........	$ 1,606	$(13)	(0.8)	$(13)	
Atlanta..............	4,234	(301)	(7.1)	(255)	$(46)
Richmond...........	4,672	57	1.2	60	(3)
Mobile..............	4,088	(346)	(8.5)	(302)	(44)
Total..............	$14,600	$(603)	4.1	$(510)	$(93)
Factory period expense:					
Harrisburg...........	984	———	———	$(51)	$ 51
Atlanta..............	2,596	$ 13	0.5	38	(25)
Richmond...........	2,864	———	———	11	(11)
Mobile..............	2,506	———	———	2	(2)
Total..............	$ 8,950	$ 13	0.1	———	$ 13
Total company.........				$(415)	$(187)

* Parentheses denote favorable deviations.

viewed as showing the effectiveness of the plant manager, since the profit realized is the result of the combined effectiveness of production and sales.

Special Reports

A program of budgetary planning and control and the related performance and information reports provide the basic information for management decisions. However, more detailed information may be required in some areas before final decisions can be made. Also, there are many long-range decisions in areas such as expansion, product-line revision, changes in distribution methods, and revision of sales territories for which information for management guidance is not available in the periodic reports. Special studies are required to develop this information, and it is presented in special reports.

There can be no established format for, or content of, special reports. Each is designed specifically for the purpose it is to serve. For some a one-page memorandum will be adequate. For others extensive text supported by many tables and schedules is required.

A special report should cover only those items of income, cost, and capital which will be affected by the decision to be made. At the same time the managerial accountant must be certain that nothing is omitted which will be affected. Special reports for make or buy and lease or buy evaluations are discussed in Chapter 27. There the effect of the omission of items of cost and the inclusion of extraneous items on the results of a special study is discussed and illustrated in detail.

Special studies and reports should not be limited to those initiated by proposed changes or requested by others. The managerial accountant should be alert at all times to detect significant changes or the development of trends. As these are observed through his analysis of periodic reports, he should initiate studies and submit reports thereon for management guidance.

REVIEW QUESTIONS

1. Describe the features and content of an adequate budget performance report.
2. Why should a performance report at one level of management support a segment of the report to the next higher level?
3. What is the difference between a performance report and an information report?
4. How do information reports contribute to management planning and control?

5. Why should the reports to the board of directors contain information on the results of divisions, plants, and departments of a company?

6. Should the chief executive receive copies of the detailed performance reports of each company unit or a summary report showing only the totals for each unit?

7. When a sales manager has no responsibility for production, what reports should he receive?

8. If a plant manager has no responsibility for sales, is the return on capital employed for his plant a fair measure of his performance?

9. An integrated system of performance reports permits management by exception. Discuss the advantages and disadvantages.

10. Why must the periodic reports to management be supplemented by special reports?

PROBLEM

A company has three divisions, each of which has a manager with profit responsibility for his division. Each divison has a sales manager and a production manager. The latter has line responsibility for the plants of his division. Each plant has a plant manager, and there are product sales managers in each division reporting to the sales manager of the division. Executive and staff departments in the general office report to the president. Summaries of certain of the integrated reports are given in Tables P26a and P26b.

Following the principle of management by exception, discuss the contacts to be made by each level of management to initiate corrective action as indicated by the reports.

TABLE P26a
PRESIDENT'S REPORT
(Dollar figures in thousands)

	Division 1		Division 2		Division 3	
	Actual	Budget	Actual	Budget	Actual	Budget
Net sales..................	$4,680	$4,510	$9,440	$9,390	$7,480	$8,220
Factory cost...............	2,760	2,700	6,197	5,803	5,013	5,610
Distribution expense.........	493	500	860	917	769	815
Administrative expense......	211	196	419	396	398	363
Profit before tax...........	1,216	1,114	1,964	2,274	1,300	1,432
Profit after tax............	608	557	982	1,137	650	716
Capital employed...........	3,017	3,000	5,841	5,870	3,980	4,110
Profit on sales.............	13.0%	12.4%	10.4%	12.1%	8.7%	8.7%
Turnover..................	1.55	1.50	1.62	1.60	1.88	2.00
Return on capital employed..	20.2%	18.6%	16.8%	19.4%	16.3%	17.2%

TABLE P26*b*
DIVISION MANAGER'S REPORT
DIVISION 2
(Note: Dollar figures in thousands. Division total is shown in Table P26*a*)

	Product A		Product B		Product C	
	Actual	Budget	Actual	Budget	Actual	Budget
Net sales..................	$2,850	$2,700	$3,596	$3,300	$2,994	$3,390
Factory cost................	1,965	1,890	2,310	2,145	1,922	1,768
Distribution expense.........	247	265	346	360	267	292
Administrative expense......	154	135	196	171	69	90
Profit before tax............	484	410	744	624	736	1,240
Profit after tax.............	242	205	372	312	368	620
Capital employed...........	1,863	1,800	1,262	1,245	2,716	2,825
Profit on sales..............	8.5%	7.6%	10.3%	9.5%	12.3%	18.3%
Turnover..................	1.53	1.50	2.85	2.65	1.10	1.20
Return on capital employed..	13.0%	11.4%	29.5%	25.1%	13.5%	21.9%

PRODUCTION MANAGER'S REPORT

	Plant X		Plant Y	
	Actual	Budget	Actual	Budget
Standard direct cost of sales...........	$1,859	$1,340	$1,702	$2,129
Purchasing variances (gain)...........	(100)	300	95	
Production variances (gain)...........	597	600	164	(325)
Period expense......................	764	722	1,116	1,037
Total cost........................	$3,120	$2,962	$3,077	$2,841

CHAPTER 27

Make or Buy and
Lease or Buy Decisions

The evaluation of the alternatives in make or buy and lease or buy decisions are special studies which are among the most important that the managerial accountant is called upon to make. Frequently they are related to, or are a part of, an evaluation of expanding productive capacity or adding new products to the line. However, make or buy decisions may be limited to products already being sold or used as raw materials or component parts; and lease or buy decisions may be limited to the replacement of existing facilities.

There is no finality to make or buy and lease or buy decisions. Competitive pressures, production methods and capacities, available working capital, and costs of borrowing are changing constantly. These changes make it desirable to make frequent appraisals of past decisions in the light of experience since the decisions were made and of current conditions. In some instances capital expenditures, long-term leases, and like factors will make it impossible to change the decision or will delay the change for some time. Other decisions can be reversed immediately. Therefore, the managerial accountant should initiate studies in these areas when he knows that changes in conditions have taken place.

Basis for Decisions

There are both tangible and intangible considerations in these two decision areas. The evaluation studies can reflect only the tangible factors. The intangibles are in the areas of management policy. However, the weight of evidence can be so heavy in certain studies that it will result in a modified or revised policy. The accountant as a member of the management team will have to consider policy, but it should not influence the evaluation studies. They should be completely objective.

The determining factors in make or buy and lease or buy decisions are the effects upon the balance sheet and on profits. These can be measured and appraised by the return on capital employed. Considering only the tangible factors, the alternative which will result in the higher return on capital employed or in increasing total profits without affecting the return on capital employed adversely is the one which should be selected.

The return on capital employed is increased by (1) increasing sales income without an equal increase in cost, (2) reducing costs without an equal reduction in sales income, (3) reducing capital employed, and (4) shifting capital to more profitable uses. Certain decisions, such as that to make a product rather than buy it, may make it necessary to bring more capital into the business. This would be justified only if the return on the new capital would equal the rate which the company was earning or, if the company return were high, would be at the minimum level which it considered acceptable. Thus, the addition of capital to produce more dollars of profit would not necessarily improve the company return on capital employed.

Effect on Company and Units of a Company

In decisions of this type it must be recognized that the effect on a unit of a company can be in the opposite direction from that on the total company. The studies should be carried through to the company level, so that top management can appraise the studies from their level. Where the results are indicated to be favorable to a company unit but unfavorable to the company, they must decide if the effect on the morale of a unit which could improve its results is more important than the adverse effect on company results. This is a long-range matter, and the intangible factors will weigh heavily in the decision.

An example of opposite effects at the unit and company level would be a proposal of division A to buy from an outside supplier a product of major significance which was being made for it by division B. The purpose of buying on the outside would be to get a lower cost and thus improve profits. Division B would lose the volume, and its profits would be affected adversely. If the total dollar savings which division A would realize were less than the total dollar costs which division B could eliminate on loss of the business, the company profits would be reduced.

MAKE OR BUY DECISIONS

Areas in Which Decisions Are Required

Make or buy decisions are required for processed raw materials, supplies, component parts or subassemblies, and finished products.

Any processed raw material which a company is using provides an opportunity for making it instead of buying. A user of cartons may want to know if it should make them or buy them. The carton manufacturer may have the same question about the paperboard which he uses to make the cartons. The paperboard manufacturer may want to know if it should buy pulpwood or buy land and grow the trees. Spanning the entire cycle, the carton user may carry its make or buy study back to the growth of the trees. Make or buy decisions relative to raw materials are decisions as to the extent of integration of a company.

For component parts and subassemblies the make or buy decision may be for total requirements or for the top quantities needed to service seasonal or other peak production levels.

For finished products an item may be needed to complete a product line. If it can be purchased from another manufacturer, the alternatives of investing in facilities to produce it must be evaluated. Or, the market for a product may have declined to the point where a company cannot produce and sell it profitably. Here the alternatives may be to live with the situation, to convince another manufacturer to discontinue production and buy from the company, or to discontinue production and buy from another manufacturer. Also, the question of making or buying finished products to service peak sales demands must be answered.

In all these areas consideration must be given to both long- and short-range factors. The effect on profit and return on capital employed in any one year should not be permitted to obscure the net effects over a period of years. This is particularly true if the decision is to make rather than buy. The capital investment will most likely result in continuation of manufacture, even though it is less profitable in later years.

Rates and Ratios Are Misleading

A frequent error in make or buy evaluations is to calculate readily evident changes, such as direct-material and -labor costs, and then apply existing rates and ratios to these to determine the effect on other areas. It must be recognized that total dollars of expense, allocations to product lines and productive operations, fixed capital and working capital will all be changed by a change from buying to making or vice versa. There are no short cuts which can be taken safely in evaluating a make or buy decision.

Exhibit 27-1 is an illustration of a typical quick and erroneous evaluation of the desirability of buying component parts which are presently being manufactured. At the top is shown the data under present conditions with the parts manufactured. The accountant was informed that parts could be purchased for $1.50 each and asked if this would result in a saving. He took his unit costs from the cost records and determined that the parts cost $1.70 each while all other factory costs of the finished product were $2.80 per unit. This showed a saving of $0.20 per unit or

Exhibit 27-1

ERRONEOUS EVALUATION OF MAKE OR BUY DECISION

Present costs—parts made

Net sales—100,000 units @ $6.00	$600,000
Costs—Direct material @ $1.75	175,000
Direct labor @ $1.25	125,000
Factory expense 120%	150,000
Selling expense	60,000
Administrative expense	30,000
Total	$540,000
Profit before income taxes	$ 60,000
Profit after income taxes of 52%	$ 28,800
Per cent to net sales	4.8
Capital employed—Cash	$ 50,000
Receivables	50,000
Inventory	100,000
Property, plant, and equipment	200,000
Total	$400,000
Turnover	1.50
Return on capital employed	7.2%

	Parts	Other	Total
Analysis of unit factory costs:			
Material	$0.60	$1.15	$1.75
Labor	0.50	0.75	1.25
Expense 120%	0.60	0.90	1.50
Total	$1.70	$2.80	$4.50

Cost and profit if parts are purchased

Unit cost of manufactured parts	$1.70
Unit cost of purchased parts	1.50
Cost saving per unit	0.20
Present profit before tax	$60,000
Add saving on 100,000 @ $.20	20,000
Profit before tax if parts are purchased	$80,000
Profit after tax if parts are purchased	$38,400
Per cent to net sales	6.4
Turnover	1.50
Return on capital employed	9.6%

$20,000. The revised profit after tax was calculated and related to sales income, showing an improvement in the profit-on-sales ratio from 4.8% to 6.4%. The 6.4% was multiplied by the turnover experience of 1.5 to arrive at the new return on capital employed of 9.6%. On the basis of these calculations the purchase of the parts appears to be most advantageous.

The results of the study shown in Exhibit 27-1 are incorrect because the accountant failed to consider all the items of cost and capital employed which would be affected by changing from manufacturing to purchasing.

Costs and Capital Affected by Decisions

The alternatives of making or buying will usually have an effect on direct material and direct labor, factory expense, administrative expense, cash, inventories and property, plant, and equipment. It is unlikely that they will affect sales income, selling expense, or accounts receivable.

The fact that direct material and direct labor will be affected is evident. If products are being made, these direct costs will be eliminated if they are purchased, and vice versa. If the consideration is to purchase rather than make, the direct-material and -labor costs of making should be the actual costs. Where standard costs are used, the variances from standard due to price and efficiency must be analyzed to ascertain those which are specific to the product under consideration. The use of average or percentage deviations by operations will result in erroneous evaluation if other than the product under consideration is processed in an operation. If the consideration is to make instead of buy, careful estimates must be made of the direct-material and -labor costs. Consideration must be given to the degree of accuracy attained in estimates prepared for other studies. If experience shows that estimates are consistently high or low, the estimates should be adjusted accordingly either specifically by items of cost or through an over-all provision for variance.

Factory expense must be examined by source in each operation which will be affected. The use of existing expense rates as a percentage of labor, or as rates per labor hour, machine-hour, or unit of product will distort the study. Certain expenses can be reduced if products are bought and will be increased if they are made. Others would not be expected to change.

Exhibit 27-2 illustrates the basic cost data for evaluation of the purchase of component parts which was shown as an erroneous evaluation in Exhibit 27-1. In Exhibit 27-2 consideration was given to closing the parts-making operation and disposing of the equipment. As a result almost all sources of expense will be lower. Particular attention should be given to payroll tax and employee benefits. These will be affected not

EXHIBIT 27-2
COST DATA FOR MAKE OR BUY DECISION

Factory Cost

	Make	Buy
Material—Parts	$ 60,000	$150,000
Other	115,000	115,000
Total	$175,000	$265,000
Labor—Parts	$ 50,000	
Other	75,000	75,000
Total	$125,000	$ 75,000
Expense—Salaries	$ 30,000	$ 22,000
Indirect labor	35,000	29,000
Payroll tax and benefits	19,000	12,600
Repairs	30,000	25,000
Power and light	10,000	7,700
Fuel	10,000	9,000
Stationery	2,000	1,800
Depreciation	9,000	8,000
Taxes	3,000	3,000
Insurance	1,000	900
Other	1,000	1,000
Total	$150,000	$120,000
Total factory cost	$450,000	$460,000

Administrative Expense

	Make	Buy
Salaries	$ 20,000	$ 17,500
Payroll tax and benefits	2,000	1,750
Other	8,000	8,000
Total	$ 30,000	$ 27,250

Allocation of Costs

	Unassigned	Parts	Other	Total
Parts made:				
Material	——	$ 60,000	$115,000	$175,000
Labor	——	50,000	75,000	125,000
Expense	——	60,000	90,000	150,000
Total	——	$170,000	$280,000	$450,000
Parts purchased:				
Material	——	$150,000	$115,000	$265,000
Labor	——	——	75,000	75,000
Expense	$30,000	——	90,000	120,000
Total	$30,000	$150,000	$280,000	$460,000

Added factory cost if parts are purchased .... $10,000 only by the change in direct labor but also by the changes in salaries and indirect labor. Depreciation and insurance will be lower because equipment is being sold or scrapped, but depreciation and insurance on buildings would continue. Property taxes probably would not change unless there was a substantial reduction in valuation for personal property tax purposes. Local conditions would determine this. These illustrations point up the necessity of examining each item of expense in relation to such factors as company policy, the tightness of expense control, and local conditions.

The study of factory expense (Exhibit 27-2) shows that, while there would be a reduction of $30,000, the parts production has absorbed $60,000. This leaves another $30,000 of general expenses which are unassigned. These could, of course, be applied to the remaining production processes. To do so would distort those costs. The better procedure is to carry them as "unassigned" to provide a continuing picture of the effect of discontinuing production of the parts and to serve as a stimulus to management to secure other production to absorb these expenses.

Administrative expense is a cost which is often omitted in evaluating make or buy decisions. However, certain administrative expenses are susceptible to change. The reduction in the number of workers will affect the costs of processing payrolls. Purchase will eliminate all cost and record keeping up to the point where the purchased items will come into inventory. At the same time costs of the purchasing department may be increased. While administrative expenses are less sensitive to the effects of make or buy decisions than are factory expenses, they should not be ignored in the evaluation studies.

Exhibit 27-3 illustrates the changes in capital employed if the parts are

EXHIBIT 27-3
BASIC CAPITAL EMPLOYED DATA FOR MAKE OR BUY DECISION

	Make	Buy
Cash	$ 50,000	$ 50,000
Accounts receivable	50,000	50,000
Inventory—Raw material	40,000	62,000
In-process	10,000	8,000
Finished	50,000	50,000
Total inventory	$100,000	$120,000
Property, plant, and equipment—Land and buildings	75,000	75,000
Machinery	100,000	90,000
Tools and equipment	25,000	20,000
Total property, plant, and equipment	$200,000	$185,000
Total capital employed	$400,000	$405,000

purchased. The purchased parts are classified as raw materials, and a substantially heavier inventory must be carried to avoid production interruption due to delays in the plant of the producer of the parts and in shipping. Some reduction is achieved in inventories in process because of the elimination of parts manufacture, but since the parts are issued from stores early in the production cycle, this is not significant in relation to the increase in raw materials. The investment in machinery and tools and equipment is reduced by disposal of those formerly used in the parts-production operation. As with costs, every item of capital employed must be examined to determine the effects on it of a change in practice.

Presentation of Reports

The format of the reports presented on make or buy decisions will vary according to the nature of the study and number of areas affected. They should show both the effects on the unit of a company and on the total company if these are different. In the illustrations on making or buying component parts, it is assumed that there are no separate managerial units, so that the presentation is for the total company. Exhibit 27-4 is a

EXHIBIT 27-4
EVALUATION OF MAKING OR BUYING PARTS
EFFECT AFTER YEAR OF CHANGE

	Make	Buy	Higher (lower) if bought
Sales......................	$600,000	$600,000	
Factory cost..............	450,000	460,000	$10,000
Selling expense...........	60,000	60,000	
Administrative expense.....	30,000	27,250	(2,750)
Total cost..............	$540,000	$547,250	$7,250
Profit before tax..........	60,000	52,750	(7,250)
Profit after tax...........	28,800	25,320	(3,480)
Per cent to net sales.....	4.80	4.22	(0.58)
Capital employed..........	$400,000	$405,000	$ 5,000
Turnover................	1.50	1.48	(0.02)
Return on capital.........	7.20%	6.25%	(0.95%)

summary presentation of the effects of changing from making to buying. It presents these for the years after the year of change. In the year of change it may not be possible to reduce costs immediately, and the obsolescence on disposal of equipment would have to be absorbed. It will be noted that the evaluation using rates and ratios (Exhibit 27-1) indicated a profit advantage in buying. The evaluation which was made using total dollars indicates that net profit and return on capital employed would be reduced. These are hypothetical figures presented to show the possibility of error if dollar amounts of all items of cost and capital are not considered. They are not intended to be indicative of the direction and extent of the effects of such a decision on any of the asset or cost items.

A hypothetical evaluation of making or buying a product to complete a product line is shown in Exhibit 27-5. The significant points in this

EXHIBIT 27-5

EVALUATION OF MAKING OR BUYING A PRODUCT TO COMPLETE A LINE

	Make	Buy	Higher (lower) if bought
Sales of the product..............	$1,000,000	$1,000,000	
Cost of goods sold..............	750,000	770,000	$ 20,000
Selling expense.................	90,000	90,000	
Administrative expense..........	50,000	40,000	(10,000)
Total cost....................	$ 890,000	$900,000	$10,000
Profit before tax...............	110,000	100,000	(10,000)
Profit after tax.................	$ 52,800	$ 48,000	$(4,800)
Per cent to net sales...........	5.28	4.80	0.48
Capital employed...............	$ 675,000	$ 570,000	$(105,000)
Turnover......................	1.48	1.75	0.27
Return on capital employed......	7.82%	8.42%	0.60%

illustration are that costs would be higher if the product were purchased but capital employed would be sufficiently lower to result in an improved return on capital employed. The increased cost of the purchased product is partially offset by lower administrative expense resulting from less accounting and related record keeping than would be required if it were manufactured. Capital employed is lower because there would be no investment in equipment and in inventories of raw material and work in process. Here the lower potential profit dollars would have to be appraised in relation to the higher return on capital. The study shows that more capital must be secured. For a company unit this would probably come from unused company funds. Under these conditions the study would be extended to the company level to establish the effects there and to appraise other possible uses of the capital.

Any report on such a study should contain the recommendation of the managerial accountant. This would be supported with interpretative comments and by supporting schedules. An important part of this would be the evaluation of the effects in the year the change is made. It is possible that these may be great enough to cancel out the advantages of the change for a period of several years. Thus the immediate effects can have a marked bearing upon the decision, even when the long-range effects are favorable.

LEASE OR BUY DECISIONS

Lease or buy decisions are required for buildings and equipment. There has been a definite trend toward leasing factory buildings. This, coupled with the more general practice over many years of leasing office and warehouse space, has increased the demands for accounting evaluations of leasing or buying buildings. These evaluations may be required for proposed new buildings or for a proposal to sell an existing building to a buyer who will lease it back to the seller. The leasing of equipment is not a new practice but today the types of equipment which are available for lease and the number of companies offering equipment on lease are substantially greater than they were 5 or 10 years ago. There are some plants in operation today where neither the buildings nor the machinery are owned by the operating company.

The evaluation of the tangible factors in lease or buy decisions will center on the comparative return on capital employed. Leasing either buildings or equipment will increase the profit potential by freeing capital for other uses, or providing facilities without increasing the capital employed. Cost of leasing may be more or less than the cost of ownership. If it is less, all the tangibles will favor leasing. If it is more, the increased cost must be compared with the potential added profit or the effect on the return on capital employed of operating with less capital.

Tax Considerations

An argument advanced frequently in favor of leasing is that the rent is deductible for income tax purposes. If this is to be accepted as a reason for leasing buildings or equipment, it must follow that costs of ownership are not deductible. This is not true. Taxes, insurance, depreciation, and interest (if money must be borrowed to make the purchase) are deductible for income tax purposes. Therefore, tax considerations are not a determining factor in lease or buy decisions. The alternative which has the higher costs will result in the lower before and after tax profits.

Assuming that leasing is more costly, the after-tax effect on profits will be reduced in dollar amount by the lower amount of tax payable which results from having lower profits. At the same time the after-tax profits produced in the alternate use of funds provided by leasing may more than offset the lower after-tax profits on products manufactured with leased facilities. Or, the lower capital employed may offset the lower profits in the effect on the return on capital employed.

Apart from Federal income taxes, leasing can have an effect on certain state taxes. For many states some taxes on companies operating both within and outside the state are assessed only on that portion of the business which is determined to be applicable to the taxing state. To the extent that the ratio of fixed assets owned in the state to those owned outside the state is used in the factor which sets the assessment base, the base can be changed by leasing equipment. A company which leases all its buildings and equipment in a state would have a zero factor for fixed assets in the setting of the assessment base. This may not have a significant effect on profits, but it should not be ignored in making evaluations.

Illustrative Evaluation Study

A typical evaluation for a lease or buy decision is illustrated in Exhibits 27-6 and 27-7. This is for the lease of machine tools with a useful life of 10 years and an estimated salvage value at the end of the tenth year of one-third of the purchase price. Rental payments include in-

EXHIBIT 27-6

MACHINE TOOLS

COMPARATIVE ANNUAL COSTS PER $10,000 OF LIST PRICE IF PURCHASED OR LEASED

Year of use	Average book value	Annual cost if owned					Annual cost if leased		Net profit advantage (disadvantage) of ownership
		Depre-ciation	Insur-ance	Interest on average value @ 3½%	Total	Total after tax at 52%	Rental before tax	Rental after tax at 52%	
1	$9,667	$ 667	$ 36	$ 338	$1,041	$ 500	$ 3,900	$1,872	$1,372
2	9,000	667	36	315	1,018	488	3,000	1,440	952
3	8,333	667	36	292	995	477	2,100	1,008	531
4	7,666	667	36	268	971	466	1,600	768	302
5	6,999	667	36	245	948	455	1,200	576	121
6	6,332	667	36	222	925	444	800	384	(60)
7	5,665	667	36	198	901	432	500	240	(192)
8	4,998	667	36	175	878	421	360	173	(258)
9	4,331	667	36	152	855	410	240	115	(295)
10	3,664	667	36	128	831	399	100	48	(351)
Total 10 years....	———	$6,670	$360	$2,333	$9,363	$4,492	$13,800	$6,624	$2,132

surance of the machine. All other costs, including maintenance, are born by the lessee. Rental rates are quoted per $10,000 list price of the machine tools. It is assumed that, if the machines were not leased, money would have to be borrowed to buy them, so interest is included in the cost of ownership at $3\frac{1}{2}\%$ of the average book value of the equipment in each year. This average was computed as the book value at the beginning of the year less one-half of the depreciation for the year.

In the illustration in Exhibit 27-6 there is a profit advantage in owning during the first 5 years of the lease and a profit disadvantage during the second 5 years. Over the 10-year period net profits will be higher by $2,132 per $10,000 of list price if the machine is purchased instead of leased, and the company will have a machine with a book (and salvage) value of $3,330. Assuming the machine is sold for book value at the end of the tenth year, the company will have a net profit and a net cash advantage of ownership of $2,132.

This illustration reflects depreciation on the straight-line method. Other methods of computing depreciation would change the comparative annual and total costs. Also, a uniform tax rate is used. Higher tax rates in the earlier years than in the later ones would also change the comparative costs because of the declining scale of rental fees.

To go further and to determine the effect of machine-tool rental on return on capital employed, it is assumed in the study, as developed in Exhibit 27-7 that a plant found it necessary to replace a machine which

EXHIBIT 27-7
MACHINE COSTING $10,000
COMPARISON OF EFFECT ON RETURN ON CAPITAL EMPLOYED OF PURCHASING
OR LEASING

Year	Purchased			Leased			Difference in net profit	
	Average capital employed	Net profit	Return on capital employed, %	Average capital employed	Net profit	Return on capital employed, %	Advantage (disadvantage) of ownership	Ratio to difference in capital employed, %
Before acquisition	$5,000,000	$350,000	7.0000	$5,000,000	$350,000	7.0000		
1	5,009,667	349,500	6.9765	5,000,000	348,128	6.9626	$1,372	14.2
2	5,009,000	349,512	6.9777	5,000,000	348,560	6.9712	952	10.6
3	5,008,333	349,523	6.9788	5,000,000	348,992	6.9798	531	6.4
4	5,007,667	349,534	6.9800	5,000,000	349,232	6.9846	302	3.9
5	5,007,000	349,545	6.9811	5,000,000	349,424	6.9885	121	1.7
6	5,006,333	349,556	6.9823	5,000,000	349,616	6.9923	(60)	
7	5,005,666	349,568	6.9834	5,000,000	349,760	6.9952	(192)	
8	5,005,000	349,579	6.9846	5,000,000	349,827	6.9965	(248)	
9	5,004,333	349,590	6.9857	5,000,000	349,885	6.9977	(295)	
10	5,003,666	349,601	6.9869	5,000,000	349,952	6.9990	(351)	

was fully depreciated. If cash is assigned to plants of the company as a percentage of their sales and other assets are specifically assigned, the effect of the purchase of a machine for $10,000 would be to increase by that amount the plant's capital employed. Before acquisition of the new machine, the plant is asumed to have capital employed of $5,000,000 and net profit of $350,000, or a return of 7.0%. All other assets and costs, except those incident to the purchase or lease of the replacement machine, are assumed to remain constant over the 10-year period.

Reflecting these assumptions, capital employed, net profit after tax, and return on capital employed are shown in Exhibit 27-7 for the $10,000 replacement machine, first as a purchased and then as a leased item. The added capital employed and the changes in net profit were based on the schedule shown in Exhibit 27-6. The comparison of return on capital employed shows that, if the machine is leased, the return is lower for the first 2 years and higher thereafter than it is if the machine is purchased. This is the result of the ratio of the profit advantage of ownership to the amount of capital required for ownership. These ratios for each year are shown in the "Difference in net profit" column of the illustration.

This study reveals a peculiar situation. There was a net-profit advantage of ownership in total over the 10-year period, profit advantages in the first 5 years more than offsetting profit disadvantages in the last 5 years. On the other hand, ownership results in a better return on capital employed in only the first 2 years of the period. Over the 10-year period of ownership, the average additional capital employed shows as $6,670, and the net-profit improvement is $2,132, a ratio of 32%, or a straight arithmetical average of 3.2% per year. Since this is less than the average return experienced before replacement, it obviously results in a reduction in the average return after replacement of the machine by purchase. In this case, the weight of evidence is slightly on the side of leasing.

Costs and Capital Affected

The illustrative evaluation study involves fewer items of cost and capital than are considered in make or buy decisions. This is true because the alternatives are limited to either lease or buy. When alternate use of funds is to be evaluated, the study would be extended to include sales income, all costs, and all capital employed. This would be true if the facility being considered were a building or a machine.

There are relatively few costs which are specific to the possession of equipment, since most are incident to its operation. In most instances the costs specific to ownership will be insurance, depreciation, and interest. This is not intended to imply that interest is a cost which should be added for cost accounting purposes. However, it is a cost which must be considered in lease or buy evaluations. If a company had to borrow money to buy a machine, the interest would be a cost which it would not have if the machine were leased. If it had funds which could be used to buy the machine, they could be invested and earn interest if the machine were leased. The loss of this interest income through purchase of the machine is a cost of ownership. Property taxes would also be a cost of ownership of buildings and in some localities of equipment. It was assumed in the illustrations that there were no property taxes assessable on machinery.

Intangible Factors

Purchase of equipment usually permits selection from a wider field of makes and types than is offered for lease. Purchased equipment and owned buildings can be modified to meet changed operating conditions after their acquisition, without the necessity of bringing an outside party into the picture. All these factors tend toward greater efficiency of operation.

For equipment requirements of uncertain duration, it may be most desirable to avoid the possibility of high obsolescence by leasing the equipment. Obsolescence can turn an apparent cost advantage of ownership into a disadvantage. On a cost-plus contract, rental costs may be higher than ownership costs, but since they are recoverable, there is no actual advantage of ownership. These intangible advantages of leasing equipment demand full consideration, along with the cost studies, before any decision is made to lease or purchase.

REVIEW QUESTIONS

1. What are the four ways to increase the return on capital employed?
2. How does the use of the return on capital employed as a profit measurement affect make or buy and lease or buy decisions?
3. How could a make or buy decision improve the profit of a division of a company and at the same time reduce total company profit?
4. "Make or buy decisions relative to raw materials are decisions as to the extent of integration of a company." Discuss.
5. Which would usually require the longer-range planning, a decision to make or a decision to buy? Why?
6. How can the use of rates and ratios result in erroneous evaluations of make or buy decisions?
7. A company which has been buying a component part decides to make it. What items of factory expense would be affected?
8. In a change from making an item to buying it, how should the factory expense which had been charged to the item and cannot be eliminated be treated?
9. How would the dollars of capital employed be affected by make or buy decisions?

10. In a change from making to buying, what costs would be incurred in the year of change which would not be incurred in subsequent years?
11. How can the leasing of buildings or equipment increase the profit potential? The return on capital employed?
12. Which will be the more favorable from the standpoint of deductions for income taxes, leasing or ownership?
13. Why should interest be considered in evaluating lease or buy decisions?
14. Under what conditions would it be necessary to consider sales income and all costs and capital in evaluating a lease or buy decision?
15. What are the intangible factors which should be considered in lease or buy decisions?

PROBLEMS

1. A company manufacturing bottle crowns is purchasing the cork discs used as liners in the crowns. Its sales, costs, and capital employed are shown in the upper part of Table P27-1.

It investigates the possibility of buying ground cork and manufacturing the discs. The results of the engineering and accounting studies of the cost of manufacture, and of production equipment for the discs, are shown in the lower part of Table P27-1.

The treasurer finds that cash is inadequate to purchase the equipment. He can borrow the money on a ten-year note at 4%.

TABLE P27-1

Annual sales	10,000,000 gross
Per gross:	
Net sales price	$0.25
Material cost—other than disc	0.07
—disc	0.04
Direct labor	0.03
Direct expense	0.02
Plant period expense	$400,000
Distribution expense	150,000
Administrative expense	100,000
Capital employed:	
Cash	$ 125,000
Accounts receivable	200,000
Inventories	275,000
Property, plant, and equipment	650,000
Total	$1,250,000

Direct costs of disc manufacture:	
Material	$0.01 per gross
Labor	0.005 per gross
Direct expense	0.005 per gross
Added expense:	
Plant period expense	$100,000
Administrative expense	10,000
Cost of production facilities for discs	$100,000

The production planning manager examines the inventory requirements and finds that $50,000 of raw-material inventory will be required to service disc production. Lower inventories of discs will be required if they are being produced by the company, and this reduction amounts to $40,000.

Prepare an evaluation of the make or buy decision for the first year in which discs would be made, and state your recommendations.

2. A company is short of cash and does not have unlimited borrowing capacity. It is financially sound and has a good earnings record, and can do some borrowing at 4%.

It needs trucks for hauling material between the plant and a leased warehouse located in another part of the city.

Trucks will cost $18,000 each and have a 5-year life and a salvage value of $2,000 at the end of 5 years. The trucks can be leased for $4,100 each per year, with the lessee paying the license, insurance, maintenance, and operating costs.

The company can expand its facilities and earn 18% before tax and interest costs on the average capital invested for the expansion over the next 5 years.

Should the company buy the trucks and limit its expansion, or should it lease the trucks and take full advantage of its market potential?

CHAPTER 28

Break-even Analysis

The break-even point of a company or a unit
of a company is the level of sales income which will equal the sum of its
direct costs at that level and its period expenses. These costs are also
referred to as "out-of-pocket costs" and "fixed expenses." Break-even information is frequently presented in chart form plotted either on unit
income and costs or total dollars of income and costs (Exhibit 28-1).
The break-even chart is not a recent development. The *Encyclopaedia
of Accounting*, edited by George Lisle and published in Edinburgh and
London in 1904, contained a break-even chart and a discussion of the
procedures for its preparation. All too often the chart is emphasized
rather than the income-cost-volume relationship which it pictures.

The conventional break-even chart which presents income and costs
as straight lines from zero to 100% of capacity is erroneous and is apt to
be misinterpreted by management. The relationships will be true only
within a limited range of activity above and below the level for which
the data were computed. Also, they will be applicable only for the
average prices, product mixture, and costs which were used in developing the data for plotting the chart.

Limitations and possible misinterpretation of the break-even chart
should not preclude the development of break-even studies by the
managerial accountant. They provide valuable information for the
guidance of management if they present the assumptions on which they
are made and state the limits of their applicability. The presentation of
a break-even analysis study should include charts only when they will
serve a real purpose in facilitating interpretation.

Not a Sharp Tool

Break-even analysis is not a sharp tool of management. Only if a company were making and selling a single product at the same price to all
customers with prices f.o.b. factory could a sharp break-even point be

EXHIBIT 28-1
UNIT RATE AND DOLLAR CROSSOVER CHARTS

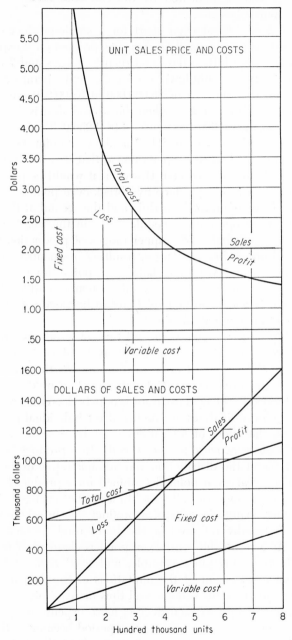

EXHIBIT 28-1
UNIT RATE AND DOLLAR CROSSOVER CHARTS

calculated. Even then, the relationship of costs to income would not follow the even pattern indicated by the conventional break-even chart from zero activity to capacity.

Exhibit 28-2 is a break-even chart for a single-product company. It shows the added increments of fixed cost as production is expanded from one to two to three shifts 5 days and then to 6 days and 7 days. It also differentiates between shutdown fixed costs and operating fixed costs. Here it is seen that the loss of $6,000,000 at 3,500,000 units of production and sales becomes greater when the second shift is added and does not fall back to the $6,000,000 figure until 4,250,000 units are made and sold with two-shift operation. The break-even point falls within the production limits of two-shift operation, so that it is not changed by the number of shifts or days worked. However, it would be possible to have a condition which would produce two break-even points, the first at the upper limit of one operating schedule and the second at the lower level of the next longer operating schedule. Also, in this chart consideration is given to the fact that as the upper ranges of production are reached the individual orders become larger, resulting in quantity discounts and lower average income per unit. This chart points up the fact that so-called "fixed costs" are not the same dollar amount at all levels of activity and that there is not a constant relationship between variable costs and sales income at all levels of activity.

In a multiproduct company the mixture of products produced and sold will have an effect upon the company break-even point unless all products have the same cost-price relationship. As the mixture of products changes, the break-even point will move up or down as the percentage of total sales of wider-margin products decreases or increases.

When break-even analyses are prepared for individual products or for product lines, the effect of allocations must be considered. Substantial amounts of factory expense are not specific to a product line, and even greater portions of the distribution and administrative expenses must be allocated. The break-even point determined for a product line will hold only so long as the expenses allocated to it are not changed. Any marked and continuing change in sales of a product line in relation to sales of other lines is usually reflected in the bases used for making expense allocations. As a result the break-even point is changed. A product manager who is given his sales, variable, and fixed costs and break-even point without a statement of the limitations of the data may decide to reduce prices, increase his volume, and thus increase his dollars of profit. If he is successful to a marked degree, more expense may be allocated to his product line in the next accounting period because of the relatively greater activity of the line. As a result the profit of the next period could be lower, even with the higher sales volume.

EXHIBIT 28-2
CROSSOVER CHART, STEP BUDGETS

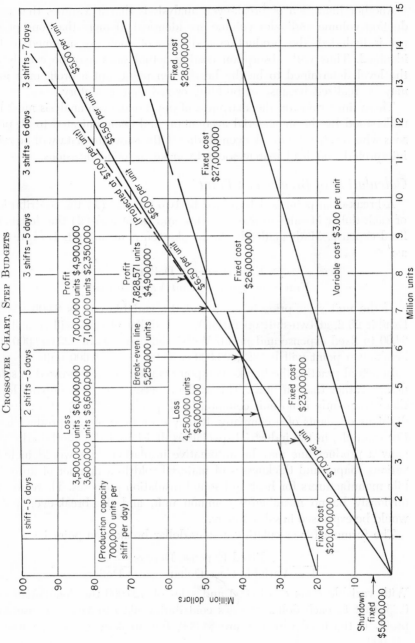

Another limitation of break-even analysis is that it assumes that production volume and sales volume are identical. If more than one product is included, the production and sales of each are assumed to be identical. Thus with absorption costing actual sales may be exactly at the level determined to be the break-even point, but a profit or a loss may be realized because of building or reducing inventory.

These limitations on the sharpness of any break-even analysis must be understood by the managerial accountant and communicated to all persons who receive the break-even studies. Otherwise, the data will be misinterpreted and lead management to make unsound decisions.

Calculation of Break-even Point

A break-even point is determined by two factors: (1) the contribution of each dollar of sales to fixed expense and profit and (2) the dollars of fixed expense. Mathematically the break-even point in units is expressed as:

$$\frac{\text{Fixed Expense Dollars}}{\text{Unit Sales Price} - \text{Unit Variable Cost}}$$

If the unit sales price is $7.00 and the variable cost is $3.00 (as in Exhibit 28-2, at two-shift operation), each dollar of sales will contribute $4.00 to fixed expense and profit. With fixed expenses of $23,000,000 the break-even point will be $23,000,000 ÷ $4.00, or 5,250,000 units.

In actual practice the break-even point is more often expressed in sales dollars rather than in units. This is done because at the company level there frequently is no unit common to all products. This is also true for divisions or plants of a company. It may even be true of a product line. For example, in the industrial-specialties division of the fiberboard company a product line may be automative insulation. This would include various shapes and thicknesses of material sold to a number of automobile manufacturers for heat and sound insulation purposes. There would obviously be no meaningful common unit, and the break-even point would be expressed in sales dollars.

The formula for calculating a sales-dollar break-even point is:

$$\frac{\text{Fixed Expense Dollars}}{1 - \text{Variable Cost Dollars/Sales Dollars}}$$

With variable costs of $15,000 and sales of $20,000 the denominator is 0.25; that is, each dollar of sales contributes $0.25 to fixed expense and profit. If the fixed expenses are $4,000, the break-even sales volume is $16,000.

The mathematical calculation of a break-even point requires that costs be separated into their fixed and variable components. Where flexible budgets are used, this information can be secured from the basic budget data. If unit variable costs are to be used, the fixed and variable components of expense must be segregated in building the product costs. With an adequate budget and cost system such segregation is provided from established records. Mathematical calculation of the break-even point can be supported by these data and is preferable to any other method of computation.

Determination by Charting

An approximate break-even point can be determined by charting if sales and total costs are known for at least two activity levels. The more

EXHIBIT 28-3
DETERMINATION OF BREAK-EVEN POINT BY CHARTING

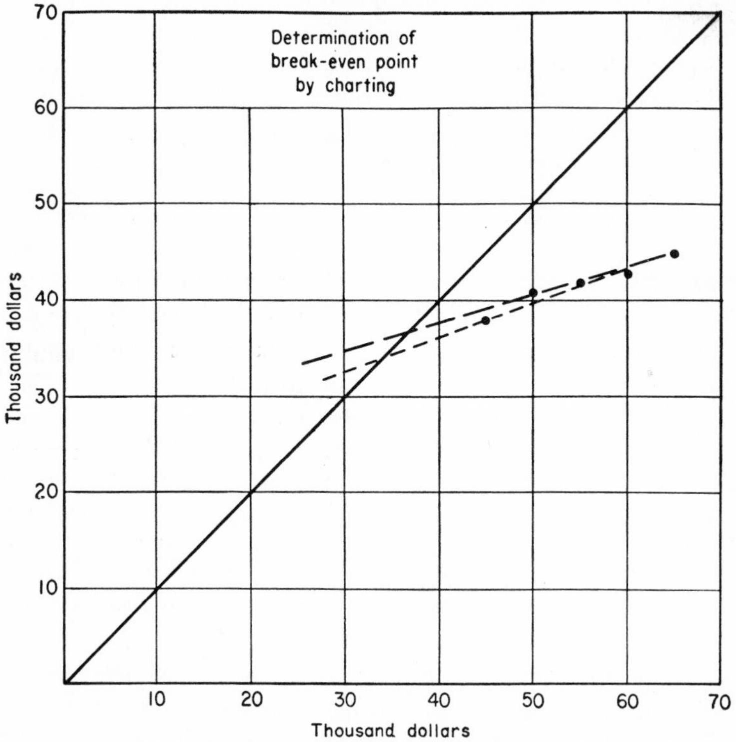

levels for which these are known, the better will be the approximation of the break-even point. The determination is made by this method when information as to the fixed and variable components of cost is not available.

Exhibit 28-3 is an illustration of the determination of an approximate break-even point by charting. Here it is assumed that only sales and before-tax profits are known. Total costs are calculated by deducting profits from sales. Both axes of the chart are in dollars, and a sales line is projected from zero to $70,000 as a straight line. For five periods the respective sales and total costs were $60,000 and $43,000, $45,000 and $39,000, $50,000 and $41,000, $65,000 and $45,000, and $55,000 and $42,000. These costs are spotted on the chart by dots. A cost line is then projected which crosses the maximum number of dots and has approximately the same number above and below the line. In the illustration costs for $50,000, $55,000, and $65,000 of sales were almost in a straight line and were used for the broken line and indicate a break-even point at between $36,000 and $37,000 of sales. If costs were projected on the highest and lowest cost points, the break-even point, determined from the dotted line, would be between $34,000 and $35,000 of sales. Neither is precise, and it may be concluded that it is in the range of from $34,000 to $37,000 of sales.

If index numbers are available to adjust both sales and costs to an approximate constant price level, the plotting of the points would be made on the basis of such adjusted figures. This would provide a more useful break-even point in that it would not be affected by changes in sales prices which were not proportionate to changes in prices paid for materials, services, wages, and salaries.

Computation Facilitated by Direct Costing

When a company is using direct costing, the information for break-even analysis is readily available from the internal reports. Exhibit 26-3 was presented as an illustration of an operating report of a company using direct costing. On such a report the direct (variable) costs are shown separately both at standard and as adjusted for variances from standard. Here the gross margin as a percentage of sales is the contribution of each dollar of sales to period (fixed) expenses and profit. If the total dollars of factory period, distribution, and administrative expenses are divided by the gross-margin ratio, the result will be the break-even sales income. This is, of course, the break-even point for the conditions actually experienced in the period for which the data apply.

Break-even points can be calculated in the same manner from the budgeted operating statements. A comparison of these break-even points with those established by the actuals experienced during the period will provide management information on the effect on the break-even points of deviations from the budget.

It is evident that with direct costing the internal reports provide the data at all times for calculating the break-even points. Allocations are made to produce lines, plants, and divisions of a company as a part of established procedures. The managers are familiar with the basic data and can readily visualize and understand the relationships of income.

direct cost, and period expense which combine to establish the break-even points.

Margin of Safety

The decline which would occur in sales from actual or budgeted levels to the break-even point is referred to as the "margin of safety." A company with sales of $1,000,000 and a break-even point of $700,000 has a margin of safety of 30%. Its sales could decline that much, and, other conditions remaining equal, it would break even.

Unless there is a very narrow margin of safety, it is unlikely that the ratio of direct costs to sales income, and the total dollars of period expenses, would remain the same during a period of decline in sales to the break-even point. Sales prices may be reduced which would move up the break-even point. Period expenses may be reduced which would move it down. Direct costs may also be changed. Thus the margin of safety is a theoretical ratio not likely to hold if conditions occur which cause it to be invaded. However, a substantial margin of safety does indicate that a company or a unit of a company is less vulnerable to a decline in sales than one which has a very narrow margin of safety.

Income-Cost-Volume Relationships

Thus far the emphasis has been placed on the break-even point. While this is significant management information, the more important use of the basic data in break-even analysis is to indicate income-cost-volume relationships at any level of activity. In fact, break-even analysis is income-cost-volume relationship analysis. From the basic data the effects on profits can be computed for any change in any of the three factors, or for any combination of changes.

Exhibit 28-4 is an evaluation of a proposal to reduce sales prices, reduce direct costs, and increase sales volume. A reduction in sales price of 10% is estimated to increase volume 20%. Sales income at the present volume with a 10% price reduction would be $900,000 but would be increased to $1,080,000 by the 20% increase in volume. At the same time it is proposed to change the raw-material specifications to effect a $30,000 reduction in direct costs, or to $620,000 at present volume. This $620,000 would become $744,000 with a 20% increase in volume. It is assumed that this change in raw materials will not affect the quality of the product to such an extent that its acceptance will be affected adversely when the lower sales price is considered. Period expenses and capital employed are not expected to be changed sufficiently to affect the operating ratios.

By using the break-even or income-cost-volume relationship formula, the effects of the proposals were evaluated in total without a tedious and time-consuming working-through of unit costs and sales prices of individual products. In the illustration the effects are definitely unfavorable. The favorable effects of higher volume and lower direct costs do not offset the adverse effect of a 10% reduction in prices. All the operating ratios are lower, except turnover. This result would probably give rise to the question as to how much sales prices could be reduced, with a 20% increase in volume, without reducing the return on capital employed.

EXHIBIT 28-4

EFFECT OF CHANGE IN INCOME-COST-VOLUME RELATIONSHIP ON
OPERATING RATIOS

Current data:

Sales income	$1,000,000
Direct costs	650,000
Period expenses	200,000
Capital employed	500,000
Break-even point	570,000

Current operating ratios:

Gross margin	35%
Margin of safety	43%
Profit on sales, before tax	15%
Turnover	2
Return on capital employed, before tax	30%

Proposed changes:
1. Reduce sales prices 10%
2. Increase volume 20%
3. Reduce direct costs $30,000 by change in raw-material specifications

Basic data if proposals are effected:

Sales income	$1,080,000
Direct costs	744,000
Period expenses	200,000
Capital employed	500,000
Break-even point	437,000

Operating ratios after reflecting effects of proposal:

Gross margin	31.1%
Margin of safety	40.5%
Profit on sales, before tax	12.6%
Turnover	2.16
Return on capital employed, before tax	27.2%

The answer is that sales income must equal the sum of (1) a 30% return on capital or $150,000, (2) period expenses of $200,000, and (3) direct costs of $744,000 or $1,094,000. At the current prices, with a 20% increase in volume, sales income would be $1,200,000. The difference is $106,000, or approximately 8.8% of $1,200,000, and this is the percentage price reduction which would yield the same return on capital employed. Profit on sales of 13.7% would still be lower than the 15% currently being realized, but turnover would be increased to 2.19, which would offset the adverse effect on the return on capital of the lower profit on sales.

Use for Internal Control

Small companies with a single product or a very limited line of closely related products would find income-cost-volume data as plotted on charts useful as internal control information. Such charts would not be an adequate substitute for standard costs and budgets. They would provide some guidance to management if management were not receptive to the installation of an adequate control system.

EXHIBIT 28-5
BREAK-EVEN CHART FOR CONTROL

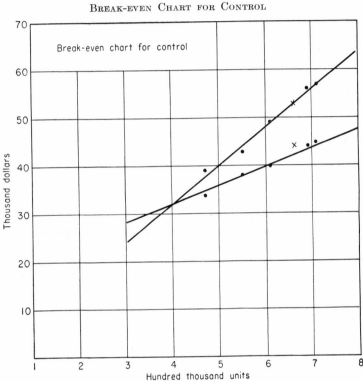

When break-even charts are used for this purpose, they are drawn from experienced income and costs. The form and procedure is as illustrated in Exhibit 28-3. Charting may be done on a quarterly, semi-annual, or annual basis. However, any period shorter than a year is likely to result in distortions in the relationships because of seasonal or other interim factors.

On the basis of prior years' experience a "goal" cost line may be drawn on the chart. When costs of other years fall above this line, there is an indication of need for corrective action. This could be either sales price increases or cost reduction. Unfortunately, in the absence of detailed cost information, there will be no basis for determining what should be done.

If there is a single product or a common unit for all products, the horizontal axis of the break-even chart should be in units and the vertical axis in dollars (Exhibit 28-5). Sales and costs are first plotted on the chart for the assumed experience shown in Table 28-1. It is evident that

TABLE 28-1

Sales, units	Sales, dollars	Costs
550,000	$43,000	$38,000
470,000	39,000	34,000
610,000	49,000	40,000
690,000	56,000	44,000
710,000	57,000	45,000

the average sales price is approximately $0.08 per unit, and a sales line is drawn for this average price. An approximate cost line is then drawn, based on the experienced costs at the several volumes. This chart is now accepted as the basis for future control. It is assumed that income-cost-volume relationships should remain constant over the next several years.

When the first subsequent years' experience is available, it is noted on the chart with different symbols (x). Sales are placed on the dollar sales line, ignoring the units actually sold. Costs are marked in the same vertical line as sales. If costs fall on the line drawn as the cost goal, the income-cost-volume relationship has been maintained. Prices may have averaged more or less than $0.08 per unit, but price changes would have been offset by cost changes. In the illustration this was not the case. Costs were well above the target. However, the chart provides no information as to the reasons why the relationships were not maintained. There may have been increases in raw-material prices or wage rates which were not recovered in sales-price increases. Period expenses may have been allowed to increase. Efficiency may have deteriorated. Special price concessions may have been made. The management's knowledge of the business would be the only basis for isolating the problem in the absence of adequate costs and budgets.

Profit measurement through the medium of a break-even chart is very broad and is after the fact. The most that can be said for it is that it is better than no measurement.

Use for Financial Analysis

Approximate income-cost-volume relationships can be determined for any company which publishes financial reports if data are available for more than one period. These can be calculated mathematically, but more often they are determined by charting. This information is of value in appraising the strengths and weaknesses of competitors. It is also used by potential investors in equities.

A company should know the margin of safety which each of its competitors has, the effect which changes in sales prices will have upon their margins and break-even points, and the contributions to profit of each dollar of sales. This information can then be used to plan more intelligently the competitive tactics and strategy. It can be compiled and analyzed from year to year if the competitors' financial statements are available. It will be broad and will give no information on any product line. It will, however, provide indications of the areas of strength and weakness of the competitors.

Prospective investors in equities of a company frequently determine its break-even point and margin of safety to appraise the degree to which its profits are affected by changes in volume. They also compare the income-cost-volume relationships for a period of years to determine the effectiveness of pricing and of cost control. The break-even chart provides a valuable tool for such analyses and appraisals.

A Typical Analysis

Exhibit 28-6 is an illustrative schedule showing the data for and the results of an analysis of income-cost-volume relationships. It is for a company with two operating divisions, the manager of each of which has profit responsibility. The following are interpretative comments which would be made for the president of the company when the budget for next year is presented:

To appraise the budget for next year it has been compared with the actual results for last year. Trends are indicated by showing on the supporting schedule [Exhibit 28-6] both the estimated results for the year and the actuals for last year with which the comparisons are made.

Profit of $1,487,000 is budgeted. This compares with $1,016,000 estimated for this year and $1,233,000 realized last year. Next year's budgeted profit is 20.6% higher than that of last year and 46.3% higher than that estimated for this year. This improvement is not as great as it should be. The reason for this is found in the income-cost-volume relationships.

For the Company, sales are 12.6% higher but total period expenses are 14.2% higher. Factory period expenses are 9.9% higher, in part due to budgeted overtime premium required for the budgeted production levels. Distribution expense is 21.3% higher and administrative expense 18% higher, in comparison with an increase in sales of 12.6%. In short, period expenses are increasing more rapidly than sales income. The reasons for this will be found in the analysis of the two divisions. The adverse effect on profit of the increased period expense

EXHIBIT 28-6

ANALYSIS OF INCOME-COST-VOLUME RELATIONSHIPS

(Dollar figures in thousands)

	Company			Division A			Division B		
	Next Year Budget	This Year Estimate	Last Year Actual	Next Year Budget	This Year Estimate	Last Year Actual	Next Year Budget	This Year Estimate	Last Year Actual
Net sales	$25,538	$23,016	$22,670	$14,580	$13,063	$12,020	$10,958	$9,953	$10,650
Direct cost	15,136	14,110	13,700	7,810	6,954	6,565	7,326	7,156	7,135
Contribution to period expense and profit	$10,402	$8,906	$8,970	$6,770	$6,109	$5,455	$3,632	$2,797	$3,515
Factory period expense	$4,110	$3,862	$3,741	$2,332	$2,112	$2,018	$1,778	$1,570	$1,723
Distribution expense	2,110	1,914	1,739	1,040	1,015	960	1,070	899	779
Administrative expense	1,208	1,098	1,024	736	672	609	472	426	415
Total period expenses	$7,428	$6,874	$6,504	$4,108	$3,799	$3,587	$3,320	$3,075	$2,917
Profit (loss) *after* income tax	$1,487	$1,016	$1,233	$1,331	$1,155	$934	$156	$(139)	$299
Break-even sales	$18,251	$17,315	$16,424	$7,664	$7,141	$6,570	$10,030	$10,943	$8,839
Capital employed	$14,989	$13,010	$11,076	$10,813	$8,977	$7,089	$4,176	$4,033	$3,987

Per Cent Increase (Decrease) over Last Year

	Company			Division A			Division B		
	Next Year Budget	This Year Estimate	Last Year Actual	Next Year Budget	This Year Estimate	Last Year Actual	Next Year Budget	This Year Estimate	Last Year Actual
Net sales	12.6%	1.5%	—	21.3%	8.7%	—	2.9%	(6.5)%	—
Direct cost	10.5	3.0	—	19.0	5.9	—	2.7	.3	—
Factory period expense	9.9	3.2	—	15.6	4.7	—	3.2	1.6	—
Distribution expense	21.3	10.1	—	8.3	5.7	—	37.8	15.4	—
Administrative expense	18.0	7.2	—	20.9	10.3	—	37.8	2.6	—
Total period expenses	14.2	5.7	—	14.5	5.9	—	13.8	5.4	—
Profit	20.6	(17.6)	—	42.5	23.7	—	(47.8)		—
Break-even sales	11.1	5.4	—	16.6	8.7	—	16.5	18.7	—
Capital employed	35.3	17.5	—	52.5	26.6	—	4.7	1.1	—

Ratios

	Company			Division A			Division B		
	Next Year Budget	This Year Estimate	Last Year Actual	Next Year Budget	This Year Estimate	Last Year Actual	Next Year Budget	This Year Estimate	Last Year Actual
Gross margin	40.7%	39.7%	39.6%	53.6%	53.2%	54.6%	33.1%	28.1%	33.0%
Margin of safety	28.5%	24.8%	27.6%	47.4%	45.3%	45.8%	9.5%	(1.4)	18.0%
Per cent profit to sales	5.8	4.4	5.4	9.1	8.8	7.8	1.4	2.47	2.8
Turnover	1.70	1.77	2.05	1.35	1.45	1.69	2.62	(3.4%)	2.67
Return on capital employed	9.9%	7.8%	11.1%	12.3%	12.9%	13.2%	3.7%		7.5%

is partially offset by a better gross margin, 40.7% budgeted for next year in comparison with 39.6% last year. As a result of these combined factors sales of $18,251,000 will be required to break even in comparison with a break-even point of $16,424,000 last year, an increase of 11.1%. It must be recognized that budgeted period expenses include items such as overtime premium payments which would be reduced as sales dropped toward this calculated break-even point. However, with these readily reducible period expenses eliminated the break-even point will still be above that of last year. The margin of safety is greater because of the higher sales budgeted and the better gross margin ratio. The increase of 35.3% in capital employed reduces turnover and more than offsets the improvement in profit on sales. As a result the budgeted return on capital employed is 9.9% in comparison with 11.1% last year.

Division A has budgeted sales for next year which are 21.3% higher than those of last year. Budgeted profits are 42.5% higher than those of last year. Total period expenses are up 14.5% in comparison with an increase in sales of 21.3% so this division will realize some profit benefit from volume. Factory period expenses include approximately $300,000 of overtime premium pay which is necessary to produce the higher volume. This cost will be eliminated in the future when the new productive facilities, already included in part in the capital employed, are completed. Administrative expenses are budgeted at 20.9% over those of last year as a result of the accelerated research program. Gross margin is one percentage point lower due to the fact that it is not planned to increase sales prices to cover the budgeted higher raw material costs. The higher period costs and lower gross margin combined to increase the sales required to break even 16.6% over those required last year. The margin of safety is higher because of the substantial increase in sales. The contribution of volume to profits more than offsets the adverse effects of higher period expenses and the lower gross margin ratio and will result in a 9.1% profit on sales in comparison with 7.8% last year. Turnover is substantially lower because of the capital employed in construction in progress. As a result of the lower turnover the budgeted return on capital is 12.3% in comparison with 13.2% last year. The less favorable income-cost-volume relationships of this division are due in part to temporary conditions which will be corrected when the new production facilities are in operation, and in part to the increased research program which should result in marked profit improvement in future years.

Division B has budgeted sales which are only 2.9% above those of last year. Their total period expenses are 13.8% higher. Factory period expense is up 3.2%, due entirely to increases in wages and salaries. Distribution expenses are 37.4% higher, reflecting the intensive promotional expense budgeted with the objective of gaining a larger share of the market in future years. Administrative expenses are 37.8% higher, reflecting the increased engineering effort planned to be expended in the design and development of new models. Gross margin is budgeted at essentially the same rate as last year. The substantially higher period expense has increased the budgeted break-even sales level to $10,030,000 in comparison with $8,839,000 last year. This increase coupled with the modest increase in sales results in a margin of safety of 9.5% in comparison with 18% last year. Some benefits are already being realized from the more intensive promotion and development programs and these, coupled with price increases which improved the gross margin over that realized this year, account for the budgeted profit in comparison with an estimated loss for this year. In comparison with last year, the higher period expenses reduce the profit on sales to 1.4% from 2.8%. Turnover is slightly lower and return on capital employed is budgeted at 3.7% for next year in comparison with an estimated loss this year and a return of 7.5% last year. This division's budget reflects a marked deterioration in its income-cost-volume relationships which can only be justified if the higher budgeted expenses result in substantial increases in the volume and profit of future years.

REVIEW QUESTIONS

1. What is a break-even point?
2. What are the major weaknesses of a break-even chart?
3. What two factors determine the break-even point?
4. Under what conditions could a company have several break-even points?
5. What is the mathematical formula for calculating a break-even point?
6. Describe a procedure for determining an approximate break-even point when data are not available to calculate it mathematically?
7. How does direct costing facilitate break-even analysis?
8. What is meant by "the margin of safety"?
9. What is the difference between break-even analysis and income-cost-volume relationship analysis?
10. How can internal control data be provided by charting income-cost-volume data?
11. In view of the problem of allocating common costs, is income-cost-volume relationship analysis by divisions or other company units of value to management?
12. What steps could management take to increase the margin of safety?

PROBLEMS

1. A company's budget shows sales of 300,000 units and net sales income of $2,400,000. Variable costs are $1,200,000 and fixed costs are $900,000.

   a. What is the break-even volume in units and net sales dollars?

   b. What is the margin of safety?

2. A company does not have standard costs or budgets. You are asked to analyze its operations for the current year and determine if income-cost-volume relationships are being maintained.

   For the past five years sales and costs respectively were $46,000 and $37,000, $40,000 and $34,500, $54,000 and $40,000, $50,000 and $38,000, and $48,000 and $37,000. Projecting the first 6 months of the current year indicates sales of $56,000 and costs of $44,000.

   What conclusions do you draw from the historical data and projection?

CHAPTER 29

Setting Sales Prices

The perfect sales price is the sum of all costs plus the profit which will yield the goal return on capital employed. Unfortunately, perfection is seldom if ever attained in setting sales prices. Competition is the most potent force in pricing. Company management can control its costs and capital and hold them at or below the level of any competitor. They cannot control the profit margins of competitors, nor unsound and uninformed competitive pricing which covers losses or low margins on some lines with excessive margins on others. Nevertheless, total unit cost plus profit to yield the desired return on capital employed should be developed for each item in the line to serve as a guide to pricing, to cost reduction where margins are inadequate, to marketing emphasis, and to product-line revision. These "target prices" must then be modified by management judgment to meet competitive conditions or to capitalize on unusual market opportunities.

Placement of Pricing Responsibility

It is a fundamental rule that pricing responsibility must rest with the person or persons who are responsible for profits. For this reason it is customary practice for the chief executive or a division manager who has profit responsibility for his division to make the final decisions on prices. At these management levels it is possible to appraise most objectively the relationship of price, cost, and volume, and the relative importance of each on the profitability of the business. Pricing decisions should be based upon the objective of securing the most profitable volume and assortment of sales over a long period of time rather than on meeting the prices of all significant competitors on every product simply to secure volume and retain or gain position in the industry.

Where sales and production responsibility are divided, the sales manager does not usually have final responsibility for sales prices. In these companies the chief executive sets pricing policies and approves prices, or these functions are performed by a pricing committee.

Salesmen are frequently given some latitude in quoting on a specific order. This may be accomplished by giving them a list of minimum and maximum prices and permitting them to decide where in the price range they can get the business. The desirability of this is questionable. In his eagerness to get volume the average salesman is likely to offer price concessions sooner than he should, and maximum possible income will not be realized. Where nonstock items are sold, the salesman may set the price by costing the available order from sales-manual data and then adding an established markup. Here there is danger that costs of minor items in the specification will be omitted intentionally or in error. Unless time is of essence, the salesmen should be required to submit the specifications to the home or district office, where trained cost estimators can establish costs and management can approve the prices.

What Is Cost?

Costs to be used in setting sales prices will not necessarily be the same as any costs developed for any other purpose. It is a generally accepted principle of management accounting that different costs are required for different purposes, and costs for setting sales prices are no exception. The basic data will be secured from existing cost and budget records, especially where standard product costs are developed, but they must be modified and adapted for sales-price determination.

The basic rule is that the unit product cost to be used as a basis for pricing shall reflect the prices of purchased materials and services and wages and salary rates expected to be in effect when the product is delivered to the customer, with unit direct costs based on the most efficient methods of production and unit period expense costs based on normal volume. It is obvious that costs for setting sales prices will not be the actual costs of any period. It is unlikely that they will be the standard product costs used for cost control or for inventory valuation under a standard cost accounting system.

The time lag between the quoting of a price and the delivery of the product has an important bearing upon the development of costs for pricing. The longer the time lag, the greater the importance of sound forecasting in determining the costs. This problem is avoided at times by inserting escalator clauses in sales contracts which permit the recovery of material- and labor-cost increases up to a stated maximum. However, in a competitive market the seller who quotes a firm price has a definite competitive advantage over one who demands escalation provisions.

Customers cannot be expected to pay for inefficient production or for carrying excess productive capacity. Therefore the possibility of recovering total actual unit costs must be weighed against the possibility of losing the business if sales prices are based on such costs. Frequently a company appears to have a competitive-pricing problem when it actually has a cost-reduction problem. The managerial accountant can direct attention to the true problem by developing sound costs for pricing and then comparing them with the actual or budgeted costs.

Raw-material Costs

The prices paid for raw materials change more frequently than do any other components of the cost of the delivered product. Also, direct-material costs are in many cases the largest cost element. Except in integrated companies, a company's sources of raw materials are usually available to its competitors. But it cannot be assumed that the prices it pays for materials will be the same. The timing of purchases, quantities purchased, and purchasing policies can have a marked effect on raw-material costs. All these factors must be considered in deciding upon the raw-material cost rates which will be reflected in product costs for pricing.

Sales prices should reflect the replacement cost of raw materials at the time of the sale of the product. If they are based on costs which are lower, the company working capital is being impaired, since the replacement of the raw material in inventory will require more cash than was provided by sales income. If they are based on higher than replacement costs they probably will not be competitive. Protection can be secured to the extent that it is possible to make advance purchases or fixed commitments for the raw materials required to produce quoted business and order backlogs. When this cannot be done, a forecast of raw-material prices must be made. Since frequent sales price changes are undesirable, the forecast should provide for an averaging over a reasonable period.

Close coordination of purchasing, production planning, and cost accounting is essential to secure the minimum raw-material costs. The purchasing department must be informed of the quantities of materials which will be required and when they will be required. Here good sales and production budgets are vital, and the managerial accountant must develop the raw-material requirements from these. With this information in hand the purchasing department can develop a program for buying to secure the lowest costs for the specified material. The managerial accountant will then consider these in developing costs for pricing, but may use higher costs if a definite company purchasing advantage is known. If the raw material prices change, the accountant should be informed immediately, so that he can determine if new costs should be submitted to management for consideration of sales price adjustments.

In an integrated company the raw-material costs should be based on what would be paid for the material if it were purchased, not on what it costs to produce it. All the cost advantages of integration can be dissipated by passing them on to the customer in lower prices. For example, if the fiberboard company owned woodland and grew its pulpwood, it would be unrealistic to price the finished board on the basis of the cost of growing and cutting pulpwood if market prices of pulpwood were higher.

Because of the relatively frequent changes in raw-material prices, forms should be devised which show the standard quantities of raw materials used in each stock product. A number of columns would be provided for prices and extensions. As prices change, new direct-material costs would be calculated on these forms, thus reducing the amount of clerical work involved. The importance of a raw material relative to total cost and the extent of the cost change would determine how frequently these calculations would be made.

Direct labor Costs

Wage rates present fewer problems in determining costs for setting sales prices than does the level of efficiency of labor. Wage rates and related benefit costs are usually established by contracts or informal agreements with employees which extend for a period of a year or more. The wage-rate problem is encountered when the production of the order will occur after the current labor agreement expires. If there is no provision for escalation, the wage rates must be estimated for the period or periods during which the order will be produced.

Since costs for setting sales prices should be based on maximum production efficiency, the standards used for labor-cost control may not be usable for costs for pricing. Two questions must be answered: (1) Do the control standards represent maximum attainable efficiency and (2) what variances from standard are being experienced? If perfection standards are being used for cost control, they cannot be used for cost determination for pricing. They are not attainable. If current standards are being used, they may include allowances for unusual and temporary conditions, and these would not represent maximum attainable efficiency. If the standards do reflect maximum attainable efficiency, they are acceptable for cost determination for price setting. If they do not, the variances must be analyzed to determine the attainable efficient labor cost of production.

There may be one exception to using labor costs at maximum attainable efficiency for pricing bases, and that is when an entire industry is in a sold-out position. Under these conditions it is usually necessary to hire inexperienced workers and to use nonpreferred equipment. It is perfectly reasonable to attempt to cover the cost of the resultant inefficiencies in the sales prices, since competitors are faced with the same problems. Care must be taken, however, to bring costs and sales prices into line with efficient operation when the period of peak demand ends.

The Volume Factor

Direct-material and -labor costs, except during periods of peak production, should not be affected by the level of production activity. In contrast, expense rates will be affected by volume because of the many expense items which do not vary in direct ratio to changes in volume. For this reason the volume factor must be considered before the factory, distribution, and administrative expense rates, which will be included in the costs for pricing, are determined.

The basic rule for calculating unit expense costs for pricing purposes is that they shall be determined at the normal volume of production. In most instances the normal volume will be the same as that selected for the application of expense to production when absorption costing is used. If a company is using direct costing, normal volumes must be set for calculating unit expense rates. These volumes would be based on the ability to produce and sell over the period of a business cycle.

After a long period of relative business stability or constant increase, the selection of a normal volume becomes increasingly difficult. In the 1920s and 1930s a period of years could be selected which included both peaks and valleys in general business activity. Here an average volume could be taken which would have resulted in the failure to recover all period expenses in sales prices in some years and to more than recover them in other years. The wars in the 1940s and the release of deferred demand and industrial expansion of the 1950s presented a new problem. There were no sharp or prolonged declines in general business. As a result the volumes at which period expenses were expected to be recovered in sales prices were relatively higher than in the prior decades. Probably a contributing factor was that expenses were increasing during the same period and the moving up of the volumes tended to remove some of or all the impact of these increases on sales prices. The result was a sales-price structure which was more vulnerable to declines in activity than that of the earlier decades.

If experience does not provide an average level of production which is usable for unitizing period expenses for determining costs for pricing, the only alternative is to select a percentage of production capacity. In no case should practical capacity be used. Prices based on costs at practical capacity would have to be increased as soon as volume declined, if profits were to be protected. Price increases at a time of declining demand have an adverse effect upon the ability to compete for available business and tend to accelerate the decline. The percentage of capacity which should be used will vary from industry to industry and company to company, depending upon the demonstrated stability of volume. However, experience has shown that any percentage above 70 is too high. The higher the activity level in relation to practical capacity, the greater the possibility of passing the benefits of peak volume on to customers and the greater the vulnerability of prices to declines in volume.

When expense rates to be used in costs for pricing are set at a percentage of capacity, the capacity should not include that of nonpreferred equipment. Such equipment is marginal. Its use entails higher direct costs. The exclusion of this marginal capacity will result in higher expense rates which, when recovered in sales prices, will provide an increment to cover the higher cost of operating the nonpreferred equipment when this is necessary.

Distribution and administrative expenses are customarily unitized in costs for pricing at the same volumes used for unitizing factory period expenses. Selling activity and production activity cannot be out of balance for any extended period. Unusual distribution or administrative expenses should be eliminated in the determination of the dollars of expense to be unitized rather than through the use of a different activity level.

Thus far reference was made to an activity level, rather than to activity levels. If more than one product is produced, separate normal sales levels should be determined for each, or for each group of closely related products. The normal volume of each productive operation would be calculated from these, following the procedures illustrated in Exhibit 9-1. Expense rates are then based on these volumes, following the same procedures used in building expense rates for absorption costing in accounting for expense. The product or product-line normal volumes would also be used for unitizing the distribution and administrative expense allocated to each product or product line.

Factory Expense

In developing the factory expense rates to be used for pricing, the major problem is that of determining how much expense should be incurred at normal volume. When flexible factory expense budgets have been built, they provide a starting point. However, the sum of the fixed and variable expense dollars at that activity will usually have to be adjusted before it can be used for costs for pricing. Factory expense budgets are built for purposes of expense control and profit planning.

They may include costs which will be incurred and which should be reflected in the profit budget but which should not be included in the same amounts in costs to be used for pricing. An example would be major maintenance items. In a given year the cost of a major overhaul of a large piece of equipment may be included in the expense budget. Assuming this major overhaul is performed every other year, neither the budgeted expense of the year it is made nor of the year it is not made would be usable for cost determination for pricing purposes. The proper amount to be included would be one-half of the average cost of an overhaul. A similar situation would arise when maintenance work is planned to be deferred during a year of peak production and then budgeted for a year when it can be performed without losing sales through shutting down machines for maintenance. Here too an average amount of maintenance expense would be reflected.

Depreciation also may require special consideration. If the company is using other than the straight-line method of depreciation, the amount taken in any one year may be unusually high or low, unless there is an almost constant annual level of acquisitions. Also, more rapid depreciation than that provided under the straight-line method can, when reflected in sales prices, have an effect upon the ability to compete for business. Suppose two companies began operations in 1954, the first year that declining balance and sum-of-the-years-digits depreciation were made available in the internal revenue code. The first elected to use declining-balance depreciation and the second to use the straight-line method. Each has identical costs other than depreciation, has the same equipment, and uses a markup on cost of 20% to cover selling and administrative expenses and profit. In the first year, the first has a unit depreciation cost of $8 and the second of $4. Other factory costs are $96. The first arrives at a total cost of $104 and a selling price of $124.80. The second has total costs of $100 and a selling price of $120. Who will get the business in a competitive market?

Now, suppose instead of two companies these were two plants of the same company, one which began operations prior to 1954 and the other in 1954. Which cost should be used as a basis for pricing? If the plants are selling in different territories, possibly one could have a higher sales price than the other. If it did, and since each was taking the same markup on cost, the one with the higher cost would have the higher dollars of profit. Would that mean that it is the better plant from a management appraisal viewpoint? In the second year, the difference will be less, and in time the costs of the first plant will be lower than those of the second. Should its sales prices be reduced as depreciation costs decrease?

The above questions do not have a ready answer, even though the preceding suppositions are oversimplified in that two separate plants

were used. The problems become more acute when facilities are added
to existing operations. Thus, in one production center there can be equipment acquired prior to 1954 which is being depreciated on the straight-
line method and other equipment acquired in or after 1954 being depreciated on one of the more rapid methods permitted under the 1954
code. Thus depreciation calculated under two or more methods becomes
intermingled and inseparable in the cost picture.

The problem of which method of depreciation to reflect in product
cost cannot be ignored on the basis of immateriality. A survey of the
published reports of a number of corporations showed that depreciation
ranged from about 2% to about 8% of total factory cost. For those in
the lower ranges the increase in cost, resulting from more rapid depreciation of new acquisitions, when averaged with the substantial amount
of fixed assets acquired prior to 1954, may be insignificant. For those in
the higher ranges, it would be noticeable and would have an effect on
costs used for pricing. But in both instances corporate averages are being
considered. In actual practice the impact would be on specific production units and specific product lines, and most likely in new and growing lines. In these it would be material. If other than straight-line depreciation is reflected in the budgeted and actual expense, because of
tax considerations or because of policy decisions, its effect on costs for
pricing must be considered.

In general the dollars of factory expense which should be unitized
in the costs to be used in setting sales prices will be those which should
be incurred on the average in each year at normal volume with effective
cost control. There are exceptions which arise when unusual conditions
make it possible to recover more expense in sales prices. When sales
levels require capacity operation, more overtime and other expenses
are incurred than when production is at normal volume. If the demand
is expected to continue for a long period and there would be no adverse
long-range effect on relations with customers, these higher expenses
should be recovered in the sales prices.

Distribution and Administrative Expenses

As with factory expense, the amounts of distribution and administrative expenses budgeted for any one year are not necessarily the amounts
to be unitized in building costs for setting sales prices. They too should
be averaged for a period of years. Advertising may be high in a given
year because of a special promotion which will not be repeated for
several years. Research cost may be high because of special product
development. Field selling expense may be low because of inability to
secure salesmen. These and similar situations would affect the amount

of distribution and administrative expense budgeted for any one year. They would have an even greater effect on the amounts allocated to product lines as advertising, research, or other emphasis is shifted from one product line to another from year to year. Sales prices should not be changed from time to time because of such changes in direction or amount of effort. The amounts should be determined in relation to long-range plans and then revised only for changes in cost levels, such as a salary increase.

Costs of Representative Products

It is an arduous task to develop costs for pricing every product in the line. The cost of doing this is seldom justified by the degree of preciseness attained. A better procedure is to develop costs for selected representative products. Sales prices are then set for these, and prices of all similar products are adjusted in relation to the adjustment of the sample.

The selection of the sample and the determination of the other products for which the sample is representative must be made very carefully. Basically the sample must be representative of the group in the kinds and quantities of raw materials used, must be produced in the same operations, and must have the same ratio of material, labor, and expense to total cost. In the fiberboard company 1-inch-thick material could not be priced on costs determined for $\frac{1}{2}$-inch material. The ratios of material cost to total cost are quite different. In contrast, the cost of 1-inch roof insulation would be satisfactory as a basis for pricing 1-inch industrial insulation if both have essentially the same formulation.

Bases of Applying Markup on Cost

There are many theories as to the cost on which the markup sales price should be based. Some companies apply a percentage markup on total cost, others on conversion costs, and others on direct costs. Some add dollar amounts per unit of product to one of these cost bases.

When conversion cost is used as a basis of applying markup, it is common practice to calculate the desired profit on conversion cost and then add unit direct-material cost and distribution and administrative expense to the total. This presupposes either that no profit should be earned on direct material or that the markup on conversion cost is high enough to provide a profit on material. It does not seem reasonable that a company should only swap dollars on its direct-material costs. If the markup on conversion cost is intended to provide the profit on material, then to the extent that the ratio of direct-material cost to conversion cost varies, the profit will be too low on some items and too high on others.

Applying the markup to direct cost assumes that factory period, distribution, and administrative expenses have the same relationship to direct cost for every product. If this were true, it would be necessary neither to allocate these expenses to products nor to set normal volumes for unitizing them. An adequate cost accounting system will show that this is not true. Some proponents of this method will agree that, even though the period expenses do vary by product lines, the amount which cannot be recovered on one product must be recovered on another, and therefore allocation is a useless procedure. Unless management knows the total unit cost of each product on which sales prices should be based, they do not know if one product is subsidizing another or why their prices on some products are not competitive.

The questions which can be raised regarding any base other than total cost for applying markup all point to total cost as the best base. This is confirmed by the fact that it is used by the majority of companies. Any other base should be examined very critically before it is accepted.

Pricing for Return on Capital Employed

Return on capital employed is the best basis for the measurement and control of profit. Therefore, the markup on cost for setting sales prices should be the percentage which will yield the desired return on capital employed. Since this measurement is usually made for a product line rather than the individual products, the same rate of return on capital would be used for all products in a line.

Since capital employed has a portion which varies with sales dollars, for example, accounts receivable, the price will in part determine the amount of capital employed, and capital employed will determine the profit and the sales price. This presents the problem of two interrelated variables. It can be solved by using the following equation to calculate sales prices:

$$\text{Net unit price} = \frac{(C + RF)/V}{1 - RW}$$

The symbols indicate the following:

$C \cdot$ Total of factory cost, selling, and administrative expense.

$R \cdot$ Percentage return desired on capital employed.

$F \cdot$ Fixed portion of capital employed, e.g., property, plant, and equipment.

$W \cdot$ Variable capital employed expressed as a percentage of sales volume.

$V \cdot$ Annual sales volume in units.

If this formula is used, the period expenses need not be unitized. The total dollars allocated to the product are used in the formula. The use of the formula is illustrated in Table 29-1.

TABLE 29-1

Assuming that $C = \$100,000$, $R = 15\%$, $F = \$20,000$, $W = 30\%$, and $V = 200,000$, the sales price would be

$$\frac{(\$100,000 + 0.15 \times \$20,000)/200,000}{1 - 0.15 \times 0.30} = \frac{0.515}{0.955} = 0.539267$$

This is proved as follows:

Sales 200,000 @ 0.539267...............	$107,853.40
Cost...................................	100,000.00
Profit...............................	$ 7,853.40

Capital employed:

Variable, 30% of $107,853.40..............	$32,356
Fixed....................................	20,000
Total...................................	$52,356

15% Return on capital employed......... $ 7,853.40

Discounts

After net sales prices are set as cost plus the desired profit, the effect of discounts must be considered. The desired net sales prices are increased to gross prices to cover the discounts to be allowed to customers.

Where cash discounts are allowed, the net sales prices may be increased by the full amount of cash discount allowed on the assumption that all customers will take the discount. More frequently, the experienced rate of cash discount is used rather than the full rate. With a cash discount of 2%, experience may show that the average actual discount is 1.5%. A target net sales price of $1.97 would then be increased to a gross price of $2, so that on the average the desired net price will be realized.

Discounts other than cash should be based on differences in cost. Strictly from the cost accounting point of view (not considering laws, governmental regulations, and court decisions) the cost differences may occur in the manufacturing or distribution areas. An order for 100,000 units of a product manufactured to customer specifications, not for stock, will incur less special tool and setup cost per unit than would an order for 10,000 of the same item. Sales effort per dollar or unit of sales to a large chain of stores will be less than to a single retail store which buys small quantities. Such differences would make it necessary to develop different costs for setting prices for different customers or classes of customers. This is usually accomplished by adjusting the basic costs or the net sales prices for such known differences.

The objective in providing for discounts in setting gross sales prices is to have the net price realized provide the desired return on capital employed regardless of the class of customers or the size of individual orders. Competitive and general economic conditions will not always permit this. However, the managerial accountant should calculate the discount structure which will do this, so that management will know what the gross prices should be. They must then decide what the prices will be.

Delivery Costs

It is not unusual for a manufacturer to absorb part of or all the cost of delivering products to customers. Freight is a cost which, like all other costs, can only be recovered in the sales price. The net sales price must be realized after freight costs are absorbed.

Pricing policies, as they apply to delivery costs, range from f.o.b. mill, under which the customer pays all the freight, to delivered prices, under which the seller absorbs all the freight. Between these two extremes there are many pricing systems which result in the seller's absorbing part of the freight cost. An example could be f.o.b. mill with freight equalized to the nearest competitive point. For example, Indianapolis is the location nearest to Chicago of a seller located in Pittsburgh. In selling to customers in Chicago he will absorb the difference between freight from Pittsburgh to Chicago and from Indianapolis to Chicago. Another method is the setting of zone prices in which each customer in a geographical area pays the same price and each zone price includes the average cost of delivery into that zone. Here freight absorption arises when the freight increment in the zone price does not cover the average actual cost of all deliveries into that zone. Also, freight equalization may be coupled with zone pricing, so that the customer pays zone prices with freight equalized to the nearest competitive point in the zone.

Delivery costs must be added to the net sales prices to arrive at gross prices. The amount per unit of product will be determined by a company's pricing policies and the experience or forecast as to the locations to which the products will be delivered. If discounts are allowed on delivered prices, the added increment for delivery costs must be increased so that the costs will be covered after allowing discounts.

Special Considerations

While the managerial accountant's first responsibility in pricing is to calculate sales prices which will yield the desired net sales price after all discounts and allowances, a second and most important function is to assist management in their modification of these prices to arrive at the prices which will be quoted. In this second area a knowledge of the company's and competitors' products, of marketing, of general and industry business conditions, and of customer psychology is invaluable.

Relative quality of products has an effect on the prices which can be realized. When it is known that quality is superior to that of competitors and costs are not higher, it may be possible to secure somewhat higher prices without affecting volume adversely. On the other hand the quality of the products offered for sale should not be significantly better than that of competitors if a higher price is not secured. Unrealistically high quality standards in comparison with those of competitors may be used to compensate for ineffective salesmanship. When it is, the net effect is usually the realization of inadequate profits.

A company may have a superior merchandising program which enables it to secure higher prices or a greater share of the market. The managerial accountant must appraise this added cost of merchandising in relation to the added profit dollars which it brings into the company.

In a period of high activity the beneficial effects of volume on profit are used all too often to cover at least a part of coincident cost-level increases. The result is an unrealistic price structure which is too low when volume declines, and there is no commensurate reduction in cost levels. The managerial accountant must segregate the added costs due to cost-level increases, such as higher wage rates and raw-material costs, from those which are necessary to produce the peak volume, such as overtime premium and the use of nonpreferred equipment. The benefit of volume should not be used to offset increases in cost levels. On the other hand it would not be an indication of bad practice if prices were not increased to cover overtime premium and other similar costs which will disappear when volume declines. If competitive conditions permit the costs which are added because of the high volume to be recovered in higher prices, this should be done because more profit dollars will be realized and because prices can then be decreased when volume drops to normal levels; thus reduced customer demand tends to be counteracted with lower prices.

Competition is not limited to like products. It extends to other products which serve the same purpose and even to unlike products which compete for the customers' available dollars. This latter is particularly true in the consumer-goods field. A manufacturer of fiberboard acoustical material is not only competing with other manufacturers of this product but also with manufacturers who make acoustical treatment products from other raw materials such as glass fiber or mineral wool. A manufacturer of television sets is competing with the manufacturer of air conditioners for the customers' available dollars. There are also mental price ceilings which are set by customers. No amount of merchandising could create any wide market for a product that is priced above this psychological ceiling; the money will be spent for something else. In these competitive considerations the managerial accountants and the market research staff must work hand in hand in guiding pricing policy.

Marginal Business

The fact that some costs do not vary in direct ratio to changes in volume has been recognized by accountants for a long time. The interpretation of this behavior pattern to management has had both good and bad effects on pricing decisions. Recognition of the fact that a price which is higher than the directly variable or out-of-pocket cost of production will give some contribution to fixed expense, and profit has resulted in price cutting to secure sales which otherwise would have been lost. It has also lead to the deterioration of entire price structures with long continued adverse effects on individual companies and industries. The true value of marginal business taken at "contribution" prices can be appraised only in the light of the long-range effects on other prices. As in all pricing decisions management must decide what shall be done, but the managerial accountant should put a price tag on each alternative.

REVIEW QUESTIONS

1. Why must pricing responsibility and profit responsibility rest with the same person?
2. Where standard costs are used, do they provide a satisfactory cost basis for pricing? Why?
3. "Frequently a company appears to have a competitive-pricing problem when it actually has a cost-reduction problem." Discuss.
4. With a known cost of raw materials, under what conditions would a higher cost be used in determining product costs for pricing purposes?
5. To what extent should deviations from standard direct labor costs be included in costs used as bases for sales prices?
6. What factors determine the volume selected for unitizing fixed expense for pricing purposes?
7. Should nonpreferred equipment be considered in selecting the volume at which fixed expense rates are determined for pricing purposes?
8. How do factory expense budgets aid in determining the amount of expense to be reflected in costs for pricing?
9. If expense includes depreciation calculated on other than the straight-line method, what effects may this have on competitive pricing?
10. To what extent should the budgeted distribution and administrative expenses be adjusted when used for developing costs for pricing?
11. Discuss the relative merits of applying markup on conversion cost, direct cost, and total cost.
12. How is a sales price calculated which will yield a desired return on capital employed?

13. What is the objective in providing for discounts in setting gross sales prices?

14. To what extent is it desirable to use the benefit of volume in a period of high activity to offset cost increases and thus avoid or minimize a price increase?

15. When should prices be quoted which will provide only a contribution to fixed expense and profit?

PROBLEM

The standard unit material cost of a product is $2.80. This includes $0.40 for one raw material on which a cost increase of 10% is expected within 30 days. Formula, usage, and yield standards are being attained.

The standard unit direct labor cost is $1.40. Experience shows that labor standards have never been met and the best performance was a deviation of 5%. This was achieved a number of times.

Direct or variable expense standards are $0.30 per unit. Period or fixed factory expenses are budgeted at $1,267,000 and include no unusual items. Distribution expenses are budgeted at $717,000; this includes $15,000 for a salesmen's conference, which is held every 3 years. Administrative expenses are budgeted at $364,000 and include no unusual items. Experience shows that deviations from budgeted expenses are very minor.

There are no scrap losses in process.

Productive capacity is 1 million units. For the past 5 years annual sales have been 600,000 units, 700,000 units, 700,000 units, 800,000 units, and 700,000 units. The budget for next year is 750,000.

Fixed capital employed is $575,400 and variable capital employed is 40% of net sales income.

Cash discount terms are 3% 15 days. All customers do not take the discount, and actual cash discounts average 2% of the gross sales price. Terms are f.o.b. shipper's plant.

Calculate a sales price to yield 20% return on capital employed, before taxes on income.

CHAPTER 30

Setting Intracompany Trading Prices

Intracompany trading prices are those prices charged to one unit of an enterprise for products produced in another unit of the same enterprise. The enterprise may be a single proprietorship, a partnership, or a corporation; but it is an entity for which financial statements are prepared and income tax returns are filed. When a corporation has wholly owned subsidiaries, they may sell to each other, and the parent may buy from, and sell to, its subsidiaries. The prices applied to these transactions are intercompany prices. Since tax considerations require "arm's-length" dealings between corporations, the prices for intercompany sales are usually the same as those charged outside customers. However, there may be products traded between such corporations which are not sold to outside customers. Where this is true, the problems of price determination are the same as for intracompany trading, except that cost is not acceptable as an intercompany trading price.

The purpose of intracompany trading prices is to measure the contribution to profit of units of an enterprise (a company) and to permit the separation of company units in the internal accounts. In a single-plant company the unit and total factory cost of different products is determined by bringing together, either by job-order or process cost systems, the costs incurred in the production of each product. Here intracompany prices are not required for accounting purposes. However, management policy may call for the measurement of the profitability of departments within the plant, which would require intracompany prices for departments. In multiunit companies where goods are produced in one unit and will be either further processed or sold by another unit, intracompany prices are required for accounting purposes and usually are required by management policy to measure profits of each unit.

Since the profit of one unit of a company is affected by the price which it pays to another company unit, family disagreements on intracompany prices are frequent. They are usually referred to the managerial accountant with the request that he determine an equitable basis of pricing with complete impartiality and objectivity.

Considerations of Profit Measurement

It would be entirely satisfactory for accounting purposes to make all intracompany transfers at cost. In fact, this would be the most desirable policy, for it would make it unnecessary to determine intracompany profit and to eliminate it at the company level. However, trading at cost does not provide a measurement of the contribution to profit of each unit of the company. This can be accomplished only when a price other than cost is established for each product which moves from the area of one manager's responsibility to the area of another manager's responsibility before it is sold to outside customers.

Where profit responsibility is placed below the level of the chief executive, intracompany prices at other than cost are required for preparing performance reports for each area of profit responsibility. A division manager's profit and loss report will be a true measure of his performance only if products of his division are sold to other divisions at prices which result in either profit or loss to his division, depending upon his managerial abilities. For example, let it be assumed that the industrial-specialties division of the fiberboard company does not have a board-forming unit in their Harrisburg plant. They buy the large blanks from the building-products division's Atlanta and Mobile plants and fabricate the specialties in their plant. The transfer of the board at cost would provide no measure of the profit performance of either unit. Production inefficiencies or efficiencies in the building-products-division plants would be passed on to the industrial-specialties division. The profits of the latter would be determined in part by the performance in plants which are under another division manager.

Intracompany pricing at other than cost may also be used in the preparation of information reports. These can be prepared with the intracompany transfers made at cost, but not with the degree of preciseness sometimes demanded by management. Continuing the example of the fiberboard company, let it be assumed that periodic information reports are requested on the profitability of the Atlanta and Mobile plants of the building-products division. These could be prepared by segregating sales income according to the plants which produced the products and then deducting from this the factory cost of the respective plant and its applicable shares of distribution and administrative expenses. In practice, information reports on plant profitability prepared in this manner often generate internal bickering, especially if profits are unsatisfactory. The bases of allocation of distribution and administrative expenses are subjected to continuous attack, and questions are raised as to the relative efficiency of the production and distribution functions. Also, if products move to district warehouses, there is a time lag between shipment from the plant and sale to the customer. Extra accounting effort is required to eliminate the effect of this. It is multiplied if two or more plants produce the same product, necessitating the segregation of warehouse stocks and shipments by producing plants. These problems in preparing information reports by plants are also encountered when management requests information reports on profits of departments within a plant. They would not arise if a plant or department "sold" its products at an intracompany price with its reported profit being the difference between these prices and its cost.

Objective of Intracompany Pricing at Other than Cost

The objective of intracompany pricing at other than cost is to permit each unit of a company to earn a profit commensurate with the functions it performs. It is not the intent that any unit should be guaranteed a profit. Under sound intracompany prices the possibility of incurring a loss will exist just as it does on sales to outside customers.

The return on capital employed provides the best basis for measuring profits of a unit of a company. It gives recognition to the effectiveness of the utilization of assets as well as to the interrelationship of income and costs. Different functions within a company require different amounts of capital. A production unit will have a lower turnover of capital than will a selling unit. Therefore, to earn the same return on its capital employed it will require a higher per cent profit on its sales. In contrast, the selling unit will have more rapid turnover and will require a lower profit on sales. The profit opportunity which is commensurate with the function performed can be measured by the return on capital employed, and where total profit must be divided between units of a company, the capital employed provides a basis for the division.

Total Profit on a Product Line

The determination of profit and return on capital employed by units of a company makes it impossible to tell from the periodic reports how much total profit a company realizes on a product line on which there are intracompany transactions. For example, in the fiberboard company the company profit on a line of industrial specialties fabricated by that division would in part be in that division and in part in the building-products division which produces the board used by the industrial-specialties division. Thus the objective of intracompany pricing at other than cost runs counter to the objective of reflecting total operating results for a product line. Where the latter are needed for management decisions and products are transferred at other than cost, they are developed through special studies. The preparation of two sets of periodic operating reports, one showing total company profit for each product line and the other profit by areas of responsibility, would be cumbersome, costly, and confusing.

List Prices

When the same product is sold to outside customers and to other units of the company, it is customary to use the same prices for trade and intracompany sales. These prices are based on published price lists and give consideration to the volume purchased. Where special tooling or machine setups are required, the intracompany prices are usually the same as would be charged to an outside customer for the same quantity on an order. However, company policy may call for all intracompany prices to be based on the lowest price quoted to outside customers to offset the reduced sales effort required. Where stock items are sold, the lowest list price may be used regardless of the size of individual intracompany orders, both because of less sales effort and of the probability of annual volume exceeding the quantity at which a customer pays the lowest list price.

The use of published list prices is the most defensible basis of intracompany pricing. The buyer is paying prices which are just as low as those charged to the most favored customers. The seller is receiving the same income, his costs considered, that he would receive if he sold the same products to outside customers. Also, the buyer will be paying prices which are the same as, or lower than, he would pay if he bought the products from competitors. Disagreements on intracompany prices are eliminated or reduced to a very few which can be readily resolved.

Negotiated Prices

Frequently products manufactured by one unit of a company for another unit, which will either use them as raw materials or component parts or sell them, are not also sold to outside customers. Thus, there are no list prices which can be used for intracompany trading. The prices must then be set in negotiation between the managers of the buying and selling units or by the application of an established formula. The former may result in differences of opinion which must be resolved by the chief executive. The latter requires that the formula be stated as company policy, or there will be constant pressure for the modification of the formula or some of its factors.

In the absence of published list prices negotiation results in the most

equitable intracompany prices. They are prices which the seller is willing
to accept and the buyer is willing to pay. Each will base his decision on
the effect which the price will have on his profit and return on capital
employed. It is, in effect, arm's-length pricing.

The desirability of having the intracompany prices negotiated must be
appraised in the light of the amount of management time which will be
consumed in the negotiations and the probability of frequent inability to
agree on a price, with resultant demands on the time of top management
in resolving the differences of opinion or in setting the price. The latter
has the effect of removing profit responsibility from the buyer and seller
and placing it with the chief executive.

Discounts from List Prices

When list prices or negotiated prices are not used for intracompany
trading, certain formulas may be established as company policy for determining intracompany prices. If one unit sells a product to trade and
also to other units of the company, who sell it in other markets, a discount from the list prices may be allowed to the buying unit. Such discounts would give recognition to the costs and capital employed of each
unit. For example, if the fiberboard company had an export division
which purchased its products from the other divisions, the intracompany
prices to the export division could be based on the list prices of the domestic divisions less a discount determined by a formula established as
company policy.

Since such discounts give recognition to costs and capital of each unit,
some period must be selected for determination of these items. They may
be based on several prior years, on the budget for the year for which the
discounts are to apply, or an average of prior years and the budget. In
calculating the discounts the following factors would be considered:

1. The average cash discounts and freight allowed to outside customers
   of the company unit selling to another company unit.
2. Distribution expenses of the producing unit.
3. Gross margin applicable to the distribution function. This may be
   calculated as follows:
   a. Determine gross margin (net sales less direct cost) as a per cent
      of gross sales for the particular product.
   b. Determine selling expense as a per cent of gross sales to trade for
      the particular product.
   c. Determine the per cent of the capital employed in distribution
      functions to total capital employed. This percentage may be de-
      veloped by products or for the unit. The share of capital employed
      in distribution functions would consist of cash relative to distribu-

tion expense, accounts receivable, and property and equipment employed for the distribution functions.

d. Determine the per cent to be included in the pricing discount by:

(1) Subtracting the per cent determined under step *b* from the per cent determined under step *a*.

(2) Multiply this result by the per cent determined under step *c*.

The ratio of items 1 and 2 to the sales to customers at list prices by the producing unit plus the rate calculated under item 3 would be the discount granted to the buying unit. This formula permits each unit to earn a return on the capital employed in its distribution functions and permits the producing unit also to earn a return on the capital employed in its manufacturing functions.

Budgeted Cost Plus Profit

Products of a company unit which are not sold to outside customers would be sold to another unit for resale without further fabrication, or for use by the second unit in the production of a product which it sells. In either case the producing unit would not have customer list prices from which a discount could be developed by the application of a formula. For these products which are sold to outside customers by the buying unit of the company, without further fabrication, the discount formula could be applied to the buying unit's customer price list. However this would be a satisfactory method only if the customer prices were not set by the buying unit. Otherwise they would be determining what they will pay the producing unit when they set their sales prices.

One method used to set intracompany prices for products which the producing unit does not sell to outside customers is to use the budgeted cost plus a specified return on the capital employed.

The budgeted cost includes the factory cost and any administrative expense related directly to the production function, such as cost accounting, production planning, industrial engineering, and research and development. Direct-material, -labor, and -expense costs are based on the standard rates approved for the budget period. Factory period or fixed expenses and administrative expenses are unitized at either forecast or normal volume. The latter is preferable in that it tends to level the intracompany prices over a period of years. However, where the production volume is determined primarily by the demands of the unit of the company which is buying the product, there is justification for using the volume budgeted for the period. This places the effect of volume on the unit costs and profits in the buying unit whose business determines the level at which the producing unit operates.

Profit is determined as a percentage return on the capital which is budgeted to be employed at the budgeted or the normal volume used for unitizing period expenses. The percentage is set by company policy. It may be the average return budgeted for the company, for the producing unit, or for the buying unit. Or, it may be a constant rate established by policy to be used for all intracompany trading. Table 30-1 shows the calculation of an intracompany price by this method.

The objection to this method is that the producing unit is guaranteed a profit at normal volume if it meets its unit standard costs and holds its

TABLE 30-1

Unit standard cost—material	$1.00
labor	0.60
direct expense	0.40
	$2.00

Factory period expense	$12,000
Administrative expense	4,000
	$16,000

Normal volume 10,000 units, per unit	$1.60
Total unit cost	3.60

Capital employed—cash	$ 3,000
inventories	7,000
property, plant, and equipment	15,000
	$25,000

Desired return on capital employed—8%	$2,000
Profit per unit to yield desired return at normal volume of 10,000	$0.20

Intracompany price = cost $3.60 plus profit $0.20, or $3.80

period expenses to budgeted amounts. It will incur gains or losses as volume exceeds or falls below normal. If budgeted volume were used, the producer could also have gains or losses as volume varied from the budgeted level, if policy did not provide for those to be passed on to the buying unit. This method does provide an incentive to the producing unit to meet or beat its standards and budgets, so that it will equal or exceed the return on capital employed on the product which is established by the intracompany trading policy. At the same time profits of the buying unit will not be affected by efficiencies or inefficiencies of the producing unit. To the extent that achieved efficiency is reflected in the standards for the next budget period, it will be passed on to the buying unit in that and future periods.

Where the budgeted cost plus profit method is used for setting intracompany prices, there is usually a provision for adjustment for changes in raw-material prices and wage and salary rates. The effect of these is passed on to the buying unit, which must then decide if its prices to customers should be changed accordingly.

Base-period Cost plus Profit

Another method of setting intracompany prices is to base them on the costs and capital employed at a given time, thus permitting the producing unit to retain the benefits of any cost reduction which it achieves over a long period of time. Under this method, changes in prices of raw material and supplies and wage and salary rates are reflected in adjustments to the intracompany prices. This can be accomplished by segregating these costs from the total unit cost, and applying adjusting factors to

TABLE 30-2

Unit standard direct cost...	$1.80
Factory period expense—increased for cost added by new machine........	$13,000
Administrative expense..	4,000
	$17,000
Normal volume 10,000 units, per unit...................................	$1.70
Total unit cost..	3.50
Capital employed before machine was acquired..........................	$25,000
New machine...	10,000
Total capital employed..	$35,000
Profit on 10,000 units at intracompany price of $3.80..................	$3,000

Return on capital employed = $3,000 ÷ $35,000, or 8.57%

them. Raw materials and supply items may be adjusted specifically by item or in total by the use of a suitable price index. The wage and salary component may be adjusted in total by applying experienced percentage changes in wage and salary rates.

This method does not necessarily guarantee a profit to the producing unit after the first period for which the prices are set. After that it can gain or lose as it changes its production methods and efficiencies. It can make capital expenditures for cost reduction with the knowledge that the savings can be retained beyond the current budget period. In the preceding illustration $3.80 was set as the intracompany price. If this were a base-period-cost-plus-profit price, the producer could improve his return on capital by adding equipment to reduce cost. Assume that an investment in a $10,000 machine would reduce direct labor cost $0.20 per unit. Other conditions remaining the same, the producer would then realize profit and return on capital employed as calculated in Table 30-2.

There are two problems created by the use of the base-cost-plus-profit method. The first is the acceptance of the base cost and capital. The base cost should reflect the best efficiency attainable at the time the cost is set, and the capital should be only the amount actually required to service the selected production volume. Any "loading" of costs or capital will provide a cushion for the producer and place the buyer in a disadvantageous competitive position. The second problem is determining when the base costs and capital are no longer satisfactory for setting intracompany prices. If the producing unit reduces its costs, it will want to reflect the benefits in its return on capital indefinitely. At the same time competitors probably also achieved cost reduction and may have reflected it in their sales prices. If they have, the intracompany buying unit is in an unfavorable competitive position unless it reduces its prices, and if it does, it will lower its return on its capital. The buyer will request a new intracompany price set on a new base period, and if the producer does not grant it, the all-too-frequent disagreement on intracompany prices arises again.

Factory Cost

Some intracompany price must be used for accounting purposes when products are transferred from one unit of a company to another, as from plant to plant, plant to district warehouse, or division to division. It is necessary to relieve the Inventory of one unit and charge the Inventory or Cost of Sales of the other. Where there is no requirement for performance or information reports on the profit by company units, the transfer is made at cost. When standard costs are used, the transfers are made at standard cost and the variances from standard rest in the unit from which the product was transferred. Products for which standard costs are not developed are transferred at actual costs.

Many companies which do prepare internal reports of profits by company units use cost as the intracompany price for transfers between company units. When standard costs are used, the variances from standard may follow the products or be reflected in the unit in which they occurred. If the return on capital employed is also determined for company units, the capital must be moved with the cost. With transfer at cost, the profit reported for a unit and the return on capital employed will be limited to that earned on the products which it sold to trade, plus or minus its variances from standard on intracompany products, if they do not follow the products. These profit reports are of value only for information; they do not provide a measure of performance of any unit which does not sell all the products which it produces.

The use of cost as the intracompany trading price does not eliminate all the problems which arise through intracompany pricing. A unit which has an unsatisfactory profit will attack the costs at which products of other units are transferred to it just as vigorously as it will prices determined by a formula, for its profit will be affected by costs over which it has no control. If capital employed is also transferred to it, the problems are multiplied. For these reasons companies which measure profits of units by the return on capital employed are usually forced into a policy of intracompany trading on some basis other than cost.

Opportunity to Purchase Outside

The intracompany pricing problems which have been stated arise in large part because the buying units are captive customers of the selling units. It is unlikely that a seller will give as much price consideration to a customer that he cannot lose as he will to one who can take his business elsewhere. For this reason many companies which have a policy of selling between units and of measuring profits of units couple it with a statement that the buying unit is permitted to purchase the products outside the company if intracompany prices are unsatisfactory to it.

The opportunity to purchase outside the company places the buying unit on an equal footing with the selling unit in negotiating prices. The seller must meet competitive outside prices or lose the business. He does not have a captive customer. The policy of permitting purchases from outside firms cannot be a tongue-in-cheek policy if it is to be effective. Top management must encourage the practice with praise for the buyer who secured lower prices and censure for the company unit which lost the business.

In this practice the interest of a company unit may run counter to the over-all company interest. The unit buying on the outside would have lower costs than if it bought within the company, but the difference may not be enough to offset the adverse effect on profits of the lower volume of the unit which lost the business. It is questionable if top management will permit company profits to suffer in order that a unit may improve its profits, or to avoid disagreements on intracompany prices. At the same time, if each manager gives first consideration to company profits and second consideration to profits of his unit, each will be willing to compromise in the interest of the company.

A policy of permitting products to be purchased from outside firms, when another company unit cannot or will not meet the price, tends to reduce the number of problems related to intracompany pricing; it does not eliminate them.

Product Specification

Specifications defining the nature and quality of semifinished products involved in intracompany trading are usually set by the buying unit.

Where finished products involved in intracompany trading are sold outside the company primarily by the producing unit, the producing unit establishes the quality specifications. In the case of finished products sold primarily by the buying unit, the buying unit sets the specifications. However, for all products processing formulations and methods are usually wholly within the responsibility of the producing unit.

Claims and Allowances

Claims from a buying unit for allowances for defective materials, improper shipments, etc., are usually permitted. These claims should receive the same type of consideration and treatment as given an outside customer. If there is a difference of opinion as to the responsibility for a claim, it must be resolved by the units involved or by top management.

Accounting for Intracompany Trading

Any profit or loss realized by a unit of a company on sales to another unit of the company must be eliminated at the company level, for these are not realized profits or losses of the company. This problem of elimination may exist when trading is at cost and will always exist when trading is at other than cost.

When units trade at cost and the product is valued in the inventory of the receiving unit at the value which was credited to the inventory of the selling unit, there is no intracompany profit. Where companies use standard costs, the standard of the receiving unit may be different from that of the selling unit because the standards were built at different times or because one unit made an interim adjustment to its standards. The difference between the two standards results in an intracompany profit or loss. This is usually segregated in computing the purchase variance of the receiving unit and debited or credited to a balance sheet suspense account, thus removing it from company profit or loss. Records must then be maintained of inventories and sales to customers of the intracompany product. When sales are made to outside customers, an applicable amount is taken from the suspense account and reflected in profit or loss at the company levels.

When products are traded at other than cost, in order to provide measurements of profits of the respective company units, it is necessary to show the amounts received as sales of the selling unit rather than as credits to its inventories. This is accomplished by using a separate account for Intracompany Sales. The sales income of the unit doing intracompany selling would be the total of its trade sales and intracompany sales. Cost of sales would also be recorded in separate accounts for Cost of Sales—Trade and Cost of Sales—Intracompany. At the company level the difference between the Intracompany Sales and Cost of Sales would be eliminated and transferred to a suspense account. Records of inventories and shipments to customers of these intracompany items would be maintained, and applicable amounts removed from the suspense account and reflected in profit or loss at the company level when the products were sold to customers.

REVIEW QUESTIONS

1. What are the advantages and disadvantages of using actual production cost as the price for intracompany transfers?
2. How can the return on capital employed be used as a factor in intracompany-trading-price determination?
3. Why is the use of published list prices the most defensible basis for intracompany pricing?
4. What is the major disadvantage in establishing intracompany prices by negotiation between the seller and buyer?
5. Describe three methods of determining intracompany prices by formulas.
6. What are the advantages of using base-period costs rather than budgeted costs in formulating intracompany prices?
7. What are the advantages and disadvantages of a policy which permits a company unit to purchase products from outside sources when they are produced by other company units?
8. Who should set the product specifications for products in intracompany trading?
9. What accounting problems are created by intracompany trading at other than actual cost?
10. How can disagreements on intracompany prices be eliminated?

PROBLEMS

1. A product manufactured and sold to trade by a unit of a company is also sold to other company units for resale. It is company policy to establish intracompany prices by setting discounts from list prices which will allow the manufacturing unit to earn the same percentage return on its capital employed in manufacturing for intracompany sales as it earns on its sales to trade. Ten per cent of the capital employed is related to the distribution function.

The list price of the product is $10, cash discount and freight allowances are 8% of list price, and selling expense is 9% of list price. Direct factory costs are $5.06 per unit.

Calculate the intracompany trading price.

2. A company has two divisions, the domestic division, which manufactures the products and sells them in the United States, and the foreign division, which purchases all its products from the domestic division and sells them in foreign markets. The foreign division buys from the domestic division at prices determined by applying discounts to the domestic division's list prices.

For the month intracompany sales of the domestic division were $100,000, and the related cost of goods sold was $80,000. The foreign division had no inventory on the first of the month and $10,000 of inventory at the close of the month.

Condensed operating statements of the divisions are shown in Table P30-2. Assume the ratio of cost of sales to intracompany sales prices is the same on all products.

TABLE P30-2

	Domestic division	Foreign division
Net sales..	$600,000	$120,000
Cost of goods sold.................................	455,000	90,000
Distribution and administrative expense..............	55,000	15,000
Profit before income tax............................	$ 90,000	$ 15,000

What were the sales and profit before taxes on income for the company, consolidated for the month?

Summary Problem

The Felt Company

This problem covers the development of standard costs and operating budgets, the standard cost closing, the preparation of reports and analysis of operations of The Felt Company. The company has two divisions: the Industrial and the Flooring. Each has a general manager with profit responsibility. The general offices are located at the Hartford plant. For the most part, the problems are based on the Industrial Division and its Owego plant.

Do not carry any rates beyond the nearest cent, except where it is necessary to secure an average standard direct cost of the two gaskets for which standards will be built. Carry extensions only to the nearest dollar in the application of standards and the preparation of reports.

Industrial Division

The Industrial Division has a sales manager who reports to the general manager. Its products are manufactured in the Oswego, New York, plant and the manager of this plant reports to the general manager of the division.

Products of the division which are sold to trade are flooring felt, lining felt, gasket felt, and gaskets. The Oswego plant also makes the felt used by the Flooring Division, and this is sold to the Hartford plant of this division by the Industrial Division.

Oswego Plant

This is principally a felt-manufacturing plant with one paper machine and auxiliary equipment. The plant also has die-cutting equipment for cutting gasket felt into gaskets.

The raw materials used in making felt are rags, scrap felt, wood, and saturant, the latter used only in gasket felt. Costs of unloading and storing raw materials are charged to General Plant Expense. Rags are shredded and beaten into fiber in the pulp-preparation operation. Wood is chipped, cooked, and fibrated in the wood-preparation operation. Rag fiber and wood fiber are held suspended in water in separate storage chests after fiber preparation. Stock from the two chests is blended and further refined in the paper-machine beaters, where scrap felt and saturant are added if they are used in the product being made.

The paper-machine operation includes the beaters from which the stock is pumped to the machine and formed into felt. After being formed the felt passes through the drying unit of the machine, after which it is inspected as it is rolled into large rolls.

Production operations are pulp preparation, wood preparation, paper machine, die cutting, packing, and shipping.

Flooring Division

The Flooring Division produces and sells printed felt-base floor covering, piece goods and rugs. The plant manager of the Hartford plant reports to the general manager of the Flooring Division.

Management Accounting

The company has a complete system of budgetary planning and control. Process standard costs are used in the plants, and all internal reports are on a direct-cost basis. The system of internal reports is integrated to provide performance and information reports to each level of management.

1. Develop the unit standard material and labor cost for flooring felt, lining felt, gasket felt, and gaskets no. 10683 and no. 21717. Allow space on the form to add standard direct expense. Standard data are given in Tables SP-1*a* and SP-1*b*. Additional data are:

Flooring felt is not wrapped or packed. Rolls are sealed with tape, at the paper machine, but the cost of tape per ton of felt is so low that it is included as supplies expense of the paper-machine operation. There is no standard allowance for scrap on this product.

Gasket felt has a standard scrap allowance of 2% after the paper-machine operation. The rolls of this felt to be sold to trade are wrapped in kraft paper by the paper-machine crew after the felt is inspected at the paper machine. Gasket felt to be cut into gaskets is not wrapped.

Lining felt is slit into 200-square-yard rolls and wrapped in the packing operation. There is a scrap loss of 5% at this operation. Slitting and wrapping material and labor standards are per roll of lining felt after scrap loss. (Reference: Chapters 8 and 11)

2. Develop factory expense budget allowances for the paper-machine operation from the data listed in Table SP-2. Show period expense allowances as dollars and variable or direct expense allowances as rates per machine-hour. (Reference: Chapter 15)

3. Complete the standard direct cost of flooring felt, lining felt, gasket felt, and gaskets no. 10683 and no. 21717. The expense for the paper machine will be determined from the budget allowances for this operation. Additional data

TABLE SP-1a
MATERIAL STANDARDS

Fiber Yield

Pounds

Rags................ 1,800 per ton
Wood............... 1,800 per cord
Scrap felt........... 1,950 per ton

Standard Formula

	Flooring felt, lb	Gasket felt, lb	Lining felt, lb
Rag fiber.............	1,200	1,800	1,000
Scrap-felt fiber........	200	———	200
Wood fiber............	600	———	800
Saturant..............	———	200	
Total..............	2,000	2,000	2,000

Felt Weights per Square Yard

Pound

Flooring felt........... 1
Gasket felt........... 0.5
Lining felt........... 0.4

Gaskets

Per Square Yard

No. 10683.................... 4
No. 21717.................... 5

Packing Materials

Gasket felt................ 20 lb kraft paper per ton
Lining felt................ 2 lb kraft paper per roll
Gaskets.................. 1 carton per 100 gaskets

Standard Purchase Prices

Rags.................... $45.00 per ton
Wood.................. 18.00 per cord
Scrap felt.............. 39.00 per ton
Saturant............... 0.30 per lb
Kraft paper............ 10.00 per cwt
Cartons................ 0.30 each

Note: Because of saturant in the formula gasket-felt scrap cannot be reused.

Wood Preparation

0.432 Labor hours per cord
Average rate $2.50 per hour

Pulp Preparation

1.5 Labor hours per ton of rags
Average rate $2.40 per hour
Note: There is no preparation cost for scrap felt.

Paper Machine

	Tons per machine-hour
Flooring felt	5
Gasket felt	4
Lining felt	10

Crew	*Per hour*
Machine operator	$ 2.75
Beater operator	2.50
Helper	2.25
Helper	2.00
Inspector	2.50
Total	$12.00

Die Cutting

Gasket no. 10683	100 per labor hour
Gasket no. 21717	200 per labor hour
Average rate	$2.00 per hour

Packing

Gasket no. 10683	500 per labor hour
Gasket no. 21717	800 per labor hour
Slit and wrap lining felt	10 rolls per hour
Average rate	$2.00 per hour

Shipping

Flooring felt	$0.45 per ton
Gasket felt	0.60 per ton
Gaskets	0.15 per catron
Lining felt	0.10 per roll

TABLE SP-2
DATA FOR PAPER MACHINE EXPENSE BUDGET

Salary Schedule per Month

One shift, 5 days:
General foreman	$ 600
Time clerk	300
Production clerk	300
Total	$1,200

Add for each additional 5-day shift:
Shift foreman	$ 500
Extra clerk	250

Add for sixth day operation............... 30% of 5-day allowance

	Machine-hours per month		
	400	500	600
Indirect labor	$1,100	$1,300	$1,500
Maintenance	1,900	2,000	2,100
Supplies	500	600	700
Other sources	200	225	250

Property tax, insurance, depreciation......................... $3,000 per month

Employer wage taxes and employee benefits................... 10% of labor

TABLE SP-3
DATA FOR EXPENSE STANDARDS

	Fixed, per month	Variable rate
Paper-machine share of service operations....	$2,000	$1.15 per machine-hour
Total operation expense, including shares of service operations:		
Wood preparation	4,000	100% of direct labor
Pulp preparation	6,000	110% of direct labor
Die cutting	2,000	50% of direct labor
Packing	800	20% of direct labor
Shipping	1,500	20% of direct labor

for this and the other operations are given in Table SP-3. (Reference: Chapters 8, 10, 11, and 15)

4. The sales budget of The Felt Company is shown in Table SP-4. Assume that the average cost of gaskets no. 10683 and no. 21717 is representative of the entire line of gaskets.

Opening inventories are flooring felt, 1,000 tons; lining felt, unslit, 500 tions; lining felt, finished, 4,875 rolls; and gasket felt, unwrapped, 332 tons.

TABLE SP-4
ANNUAL SALES BUDGET

| | | Gross sales | |
| Industrial Division | | | |
	Units	Price	Dollars
Trade sales:			
Flooring felt...............	6,000 tons	$ 90.00	$ 540,000
Lining felt................	112,500 rolls	4.00	450,000
Gasket felt................	7,500 tons	195.00	1,462,500
Gaskets...................	10,000,000 units	———	787,500
Total..................	———	———	$ 3,240,000
Intracompany sales:			
Flooring felt...............	14,000 tons	76.50	1,071,000
Total...................	———		$ 4,311,000

Flooring Division			
⅜ piece goods...............	10,000,000 sq yd	0.39	$ 3,900,000
1⅛ piece goods..............	5,000,000 sq yd	0.40	2,000,000
6 by 9 rugs.................	300,000 rugs	4.00	1,200,000
9 by 12 rugs...............	400,000 rugs	9.00	3,600,000
12 by 15 rugs..............	200,000 rugs	15.00	3,000,000
Total.....................	———	———	$13,700,000

Sales Deductions

Cash discounts:
  Flooring, lining, and gasket felt..................... 2% to trade
  Gaskets... None
  Floor division products........................... 3%
Allowances:
  1% of trade sales of both divisions
Freight:
  Allowed on flooring felt trade.............. average $1.00 per ton
  Allowed on gasket felt.................... average $2.00 per ton
  Lining felt and gaskets.................... f.o.b. Oswego
  Piece goods and rugs..................... f.o.b. Hartford

There are no gaskets in process or finished. Closing inventories are shown in Table SP-5.

Develop the budgeted activity by operations for the Oswego plant. (Reference: Chapter 22)

5. Estimated opening inventories and planned closing inventories of raw materials of the Oswego plant are listed in Table SP-5.

a. Develop the raw material usage budget.

b. Develop the purchase budget. (Reference: Chapters 22 and 23)

TABLE SP-5

	Unit	Estimated opening inventory	Estimated closing inventory
Rags......................	Tons	3,300	4,000
Wood.....................	Cords	2,200	2,000
Scrap felt.................	Tons	300	400
Saturant..................	Pounds	140,000	150,000
Wrapping paper............	Pounds	25,000	30,000
Cartons...................	Units	8,000	10,000
Flooring felt..............	———	———	2,200
Lining felt, unslit...........	———	———	300
Lining felt, finished..........	———	———	4,000
Gasket felt, unwrapped.......	———	———	600

TABLE SP-6

OSWEGO PLANT

PERIOD EXPENSE AT BUDGETED PRODUCTION VOLUME

Per year

Wood preparation.................................		$ 48,000
Pulp preparation.................................		72,000
Paper machine—6,815 hours:		
Salaries:		
3 shifts, 5 days........................	$32,400	
6th day, 8 months.....................	6,480	
Indirect labor............................	3,600	
Maintenance............................	18,000	
Supplies.................................	1,200	
Other sources............................	1,200	
Tax, insurance, depreciation...............	36,000	
Wage tax and employees benefits...........	4,248	
Service operations.......................	24,000	127,128
Die cutting.......................................		24,000
Packing..		9,600
Shipping...		18,000
Total.......................................		$298,728

6. Improved production methods, not reflected in the standards will reduce the labor time and cost of gasket cutting 5%.

Since the material purchase price standards were set, the price of wood has gone up $0.20 per cord, and the price of saturant has gone up $0.01 per pound.

Period expense is shown in Table SP-6.

Develop the budgeted factory cost of sales of the Oswego plant. (Reference: Chapters 22 and 23)

7. The budgeted factory cost of sales of the Hartford plant is given in Table SP-7*a*. The budgeted distribution, administrative, and miscellaneous expenses and capital employed are shown in Table SP-7*b*. The income tax rate is 50%.

TABLE SP-7*a*

HARTFORD PLANT

BUDGETED COST OF SALES

Standard direct cost of sales.................	$7,933,300
Budgeted variances—production.............	(18,500)
—purchasing.............	(23,600)
Period expense............................	906,480
	$8,797,680

Note: There are no planned changes in Hartford inventories during the year. Parentheses denote gains.

TABLE SP-7*b*

THE FELT COMPANY

	Industrial division	Flooring division	Total
Distribution expense............	$486,000	$1,500,000	$1,986,000
Administrative expense..........	364,000	750,000	1,114,000
Miscellaneous expense..........	14,720	———	14,720
Capital employed..............	$2,399,600	$8,768,000	$11,167,600

Prepare budgeted profit and loss statements for the Industrial Division, the Flooring Division, and The Felt Company, calculating per cent profit on sales, turnover, and return on capital employed. (Reference: Chapters 23 and 24)

8. Actual data for the month of January are given in Tables SP-8*a* and SP-8*b*. With these, and the standards already built, the January standard cost closing data can be prepared and the entries made.

a. Prepare a summary of purchasing variances from standard cost.

b. Prepare a summary of material usage.

c. Prepare an in-process production summary.

d. Prepare a finished production summary, including the actual scrap and the standard allowance for scrap.

e. Prepare the journal entries for the January standard cost closing based on the preceding summaries, and for the standard direct cost of sales.

f. Prepare a material utilization and direct labor efficiency variance report by operations. (Reference: Chapters 11, 12, 13, and 14)

9. Table Sp-9*a* presents the budgeted operating statement for the Industrial Division for the month of January. Additional data for January are shown in Table SP-9*b*.

From these and data provided in preceding tables or other problems, prepare a comparison of actual and budgeted profit and loss and return on capital employed of the Industrial Division for the month of January. Analyze the

TABLE SP-8a
OSWEGO PLANT
January Actual

	Sales	Production
Flooring felt—trade..............	600 tons	1,800 tons
Flooring felt—intracompany.......	1,200 tons	1,800 tons
Lining felt......................	10,000 rolls	10,000 rolls
Gasket felt.....................	600 tons	600 tons for sale
		100 tons for gaskets
Gasket no. 10683................	400,000 units	400,000 units
Gasket no. 21717................	500,000 units	500,000 units

Production by Operations

	Flooring felt	Lining felt	Gasket felt	Gaskets
Shipping...........	1,800 tons	10,000 rolls	600 tons*	900,000
Packing...........	———	10,000 rolls	———	900,000
Die cutting........	———	———	———	900,000
Paper machine......	1,800 tons	425 tons†	715 tons	
	360 hr	43 hr	180 hr	

* Wrapped at the paper machine.
† Slit in the packing operation.

Raw Material

	Unit	Receipts	Usage
Rags......................	Tons	2,200 @ $46.00	2,100
Scrap felt..................	Tons	300 @ 39.00	230
Wood.....................	Cords	825 @ 18.00	850
Saturant...................	Pounds	140,000 @ 0.31	142,000
Kraft paper................	Pounds	30,000 @ 0.10	32,000*
Cartons....................	Units	10,000 @ 0.30	9,000
Gasket-felt, cut..............	Tons		52

* 13,000 tons of this total used for wrapping gasket felt at the paper machine.

Actual Scrap

Lining felt	25 tons at slitting
Gasket felt...................................	15 tons at the paper machine

424   *Management Accounting for Profit Control*

TABLE SP-8*b*
JANUARY ACTUAL

	Direct labor	Direct expense
Pulp preparation...........	$ 7,780	$ 8,613
Wood preparation..........	865	1,011
Paper machine.............	6,810	3,810
Die cutting................	12,400	6,600
Packing...................	4,910	960
Shipping..................	3,490	792
Total....................	$36,255	$21,786

TABLE SP-9*a*
INDUSTRIAL DIVISION, JANUARY BUDGET

	Units	Price	Amount
Gross sales trade:			
Flooring felt............................	650 tons	$ 90.00	$ 58,500
Lining felt..............................	9,000 rolls	4.00	36,000
Gasket felt.............................	600 tons	195.00	127,000
Gaskets................................	1,000,000 units	———	78,750
Total................................			$300,250
Intracompany...........................	1,200 tons	76.50	91,800
Total................................			$392,050
Sales deductions:			
Cash discount.........................			4,430
Allowances...........................			3,000
Freight...............................			1,850
Total................................		$	9,280
Net sales................................		$	382,770
Standard direct cost of sales...............			225,748
Variances—production			———
—purchasing...........................			1,400
Total................................		$	227,148
Gross margin............................			155,622
Factory period expense....................			22,600
Distribution expense......................			40,500
Administrative expense....................			30,300
Miscellaneous expense.....................			222
Profit before income tax...................		$	62,000
Capital employed.........................			$2,400,000

TABLE SP-9*b*

INDUSTRIAL DIVISION, JANUARY ACTUALS

	Units	Price	Amount
Gross sales trade:			
Flooring felt...............................	600 tons	$ 90.00	$ 54,000
Lining felt.................................	10,000 rolls	4.00	40,000
Gasket felt.................................	600 tons	195.00	117,000
Gasket no. 10683.........................	400,000	97.00	38,800
Gasket no. 21717.........................	500,000	59.00	29,500
Total.......			$279,300
Intracompany sales:			
Flooring felt...............................	1,200 tons	76.50	$ 91,800
Sales deductions:			
Cash discount...........................		$	4,420
Allowances.............................			2,800
Freight.................................			1,800
Oswego plant period expense........................			25,800
Distribution expense—equalized.....................			40,500
Administrative expense—equalized....................			30,300
Miscellaneous expense............................			358
Capital employed..			$2,400,000

Budgeted sales prices were realized.

deviation from budgeted profit before tax as to areas of management responsibility, as in Exhibit 26-3.

Assume that production volume was as budgeted. To simplify the calculation of the variances due to sales volume and mixture, calculate them from the relationship of gross sales to standard direct cost, and show a separate variance for sales deductions. (Reference: Chapters 23 and 26)

10. Calculate the break-even point and the margin of safety for the Industrial Division based on (*a*) the budget for the year and (*b*) the January actual results. Explain the reasons for the differences between these for the two periods. (Reference: Chapter 28)

Index

427